Pragmatism, Critique, Judgment

Essays for Richard J. Bernstein

Edited by Seyla Benhabib and Nancy Fraser

The MIT Press
Cambridge, Massachusetts
London, England

MIT Press books may be purchased at special quantity discounts for business or sales promotional use. For information, please email special_sales@mitpress.mit.edu or write to Special Sales Department, The MIT Press, 5 Cambridge Center, Cambridge, MA 02142.

This book was set in New Baskerville on 3B2 by Asco Typesetters, Hong Kong, and was printed and bound in the United States of America.

Library of Congress Cataloging-in-Publication Data

Pragmatism, critique, judgment: essays for Richard J. Bernstein / edited by Seyla Benhabib and Nancy Fraser.
  p. cm.
Includes bibliographical references and index.
ISBN 0-262-02567-1 (hc.: alk. paper) — ISBN 0-262-52427-9 (pbk.: alk. paper)
1. Philosophy. I. Bernstein, Richard J. II. Benhabib, Seyla. III. Fraser, Nancy.
B29.P666   2004
100—dc22   2003069088

10 9 8 7 6 5 4 3 2 1

Contents

Acknowledgments

The editors would like to thank the contributors to this volume for their patient collaboration over a period of several years. We owe special thanks to Carol Bernstein, who knew about this project at its inception, and who collaborated with us in keeping it a secret from Richard J. Bernstein until its unofficial presentation on his seventieth birthday in 2002 in New York City.

Finally, a word of gratitude to David Leslie, who encountered this project in *medias res*, and whose diligent and painstaking stylistic and copyediting efforts enabled us to bring this book to a completion. We also thank Adrienne Stafford and Raluca Eddon for their assistance in the early stages of this volume.

Introduction

Seyla Benhabib and Nancy Fraser

I

When Richard J. Bernstein began his career in the early 1960s, analytic philosophy reigned supreme. In the United States, at least, the governing ethos of the discipline was scientistic. The most admired philosophers honed their wits on metaphysical and epistemological puzzles. Philosophical creativity was equated with technical ingenuity, as the best and the brightest competed to devise the cleverest counterexamples and the most precise arguments. The favored genre of publication was the technical journal article, preferably brief and replete with formal notation, accessible to specialists only. Books in contrast were *déclassé*, betokening a woolly-headed incapacity for succinct expression, if not a pathetic craving for popularity. Science, finally, had nothing to do with the arts or the affects; efforts to blur categorial distinctions between them were simply confused.

To launch a career in this context by publishing a book on John Dewey was effectively to refuse the dominant understanding of philosophy. Defying the scientistic ethos of the analytic mainstream, Bernstein's *John Dewey* (1960) offered a countermodel of philosophy for a democratic society. In this model, the philosopher abandons the distanced, aristocratic posture of the Cartesian spectator for the engaged stance of the public intellectual. Rejecting sharp

Seyla Benhabib and Nancy Fraser

a priori distinctions between the cognitive and the aesthetic, she draws on the full fund of human experience to reflect in solidarity with her fellow citizens on the bases of their common concerns. Refined in his 1966 edition on *Dewey* for the Great American Thinker Series, and extended in his 1965 edited volume on Charles Sanders Peirce, Bernstein's model of philosophy refused the fetishism of technique. Substituting the spirit of inclusive dialogue for the sectarian scientism of the mainstream, he found in American pragmatism the core of a democratic ethos that has pervaded his philosophizing ever since.

For forty-some years Bernstein has embodied the Deweyan ethos he first articulated as a young philosopher. Thanks in part to this posture, he has played a key role in broadening the scope of U.S. philosophy. As editor of the *Review of Metaphysics,* he pursued an inclusive policy, and as a founding editor of *Praxis International* (precursor of *Constellations*), he promoted dialogue with Eastern European philosophers. As a founding Director of the course on "Philosophy and Social Science" held annually at Dubrovnik (and later at Prague), he helped to secure the continuing development of critical theory. As a close observer of developments in the social sciences, he fostered philosophical reflection on the cultural turn. As President of the Eastern Division of the American Philosophical Association, he promoted pluralism in the discipline, helping to ensure a place for "continental" and feminist philosophy. Finally, as Chair of the Philosophy Department at the New School's Graduate Faculty and eventually as that Faculty's Dean, he fostered philosophical dialogue with psychoanalysis, the U.S. reception of Jürgen Habermas, the legacy of Hannah Arendt, and the philosophical (as opposed to literary) reception of Jacques Derrida in the United States.

The Deweyan view of philosophy as the self-reflection of democratic society has infused Bernstein's work through all of its later permutations. Bernstein, however, not only stood within the pragmatist tradition; he changed it. Whereas James and Dewey developed a specifically American school of philosophy, and rarely engaged with the European philosophers of their day, Bernstein opened pragmatism to international intellectual currents, including phenomenology, deconstruction, and critical theory. The result was a more cosmopolitan pragmatism, one less centered on the United States and more appropriate to a globalizing world.

As a consequence of these efforts, Bernstein has long been at the center of a remarkable international network of distinguished philosophers, many of whom have contributed to the present volume. Although these colleagues hail from a number of different countries and were formed in a number of different intellectual traditions, they nevertheless share at least one core pragmatist aspiration: the desire to relax overly sharp canonical distinctions between the cognitive, the aesthetic, and the moral. Their exchanges with Bernstein and with one another amount to a rich dialogic reflection on the state of philosophy.

It is fitting, therefore, that this festschrift opens with a group of essays that examine the place of philosophy in a democratic society. Richard Rorty continues a longstanding conversation with Bernstein about the legacy of American pragmatism. In fact, these two philosophers have been battling for Dewey's soul ever since they were students together at the University of Chicago in the 1950s. Both of them stress the pragmatist critique of epistemologically centered philosophy, to be sure. For Bernstein, however, Dewey appears, like Habermas, as a proponent of social critique, aiming to demystify the ideologies and expose the power concentrations that impede democratic communication. For Rorty, in contrast, Dewey is closer to Nietzsche and Heidegger: a champion of the aesthetic imagination, who sees literature rather than science as the model for a desirable culture. In his contribution to the present volume, Rorty continues the dialogue. Construing philosophy as a transitional genre between the religion that dominated previous epochs and the literature destined to dominate the future, he looks forward to philosophy's disappearance. In his view, social and political philosophy contributes nothing essential to democratic society. Literary culture, in contrast, constitutes the latter's very soul.

Like Rorty, Jürgen Habermas has sustained a longstanding dialogue with Bernstein about the place of philosophy in a postmetaphysical age. Unlike Rorty, however, Habermas contends that philosophy retains an important role, as it "rationally reconstructs" the normative presuppositions of communication in order to ground a standpoint for social critique. Throughout much of his career, however, Habermas has sharply distinguished questions of justice from questions of the good life. Assuming the traditional dualism of *Moralität* versus *Sittlichkeit*, he has limited philosophy's task to clarifying the former, while denying it any role vis-à-vis the latter.

In his contribution to this volume, Habermas engages in a surprising conversation with John Dewey and with Søren Kierkegaard, reaffirming once more, and in the face of Bernstein's persistent skepticism, that practical philosophy, while not renouncing normative concerns, must restrict itself to questions of justice. Dewey challenges democratic proceduralism in the name of a democratic ethos without forfeiting it; Kierkegaard shows that all philosophical ethics, and not only those that prioritize the right over the good, cannot answer the question of which way of life the individual should choose. This is a decision that he or she alone can answer from within the history of a *unique* form of life. Habermas argues that neither Dewey nor Kierkegaard subvert the distinction between the right and the good; they reveal its limits. In Bernstein's book on *Radical Evil*, Habermas finds an unexpected convergence around these matters.

Geoffrey Hartman's essay exemplifies yet another approach to the ethical problem of authenticity. Sketching a genealogy of the rhetoric of first-person affirmations of identity, Hartman exposes the tensions inherent in efforts to write oneself into self-identity. Equally important, he reads philosophers' strategies of ethical self-constitution, especially those of Ludwig Wittgenstein, together with those of poets, especially Gerard Manley Hopkins. The effect is to reveal the inextricable entwinement of philosophy with literature. In this way, by situating philosophical treatments of identity in relation to literary rhetorics of authenticity, Hartman validates the pragmatist project of recovering connections between ethics and aesthetics, work and play. Along the way, he supplies a rich context for reflecting on the contemporary academic fashion of "positional" self-situation, in which the writer identifies herself as, for example, white homosexual North American woman.

Pragmatism's softening of canonical boundaries is also central to Charles Taylor's contribution. Claiming to engage in an exercise of "catch-up," Taylor considers for the first time whether or not he can join Richard Bernstein and other friends in claiming the mantle of pragmatism. The answer depends, of course, on what exactly "pragmatism" means. Taylor canvases two possibilities, both of which blur the boundary between the cognitive and the affective. A "broad church" view endorses an account of the human agent as dialogically enculturated, as well as the primacy of practical reason over theoretical reason; but it does not abandon the quest for truth. A "radical" view, in contrast, renounces the aspiration to "get things right." Arguing that the radical view is bound to fail, Taylor maintains that he is not a pragmatist in that sense. But neither, in his view, was William James, whose account of religious belief continued to invoke the idea of "unreducible truth," even as it also assumed that some truths may be undiscoverable in the absence of desire. By reading James in this way, Taylor effectively supplies a brief for a version of pragmatism that does not displace the center of gravity away from truth-seeking toward "what works."

As Richard Bernstein has often insisted, pragmatism emerged from, and still bears the traces of, Hegelian philosophy. Yirmiyahu Yovel implicitly reveals the connections in his masterful interpretation of Hegel's famous aphorisms about "the true." Unraveling the complex layers of meaning behind the dictum that the true is subject as well as substance, Yovel reveals a fundamental tension at the heart of the *Phenomenology of Spirit*: that work tries to preserve an absolute God (albeit one translated into immanent, this-worldly terms) at the basis of the modern world's self-understanding. As a result, Hegel fails to do justice to the full implications of human finitude. But Yovel also finds much to endorse: the rejection of abstract a priori normativity; the insistence on the link between knowledge and action; the view of rationality as involving life and feeling; the sense of philosophy's historical situatedness and of the need to contextualize ideas in order to understand them; the view of subjectivity as non-self-identical and self-transcending. If these orientations resemble those of Bernstein's Dewey, it is thanks to pragmatism's historical encounter with Hegel's philosophy.

Seyla Benhabib and Nancy Fraser

II

In the 1970s and '80s, Richard Bernstein turned his energies to the philosophy of social sciences. With the publication of three major books on this subject, he elaborated a distinctive position: a post-positivist conception of social inquiry that could support a reconstructed understanding of "critique." Along the way, he helped to transform the sterile polemics of the old "positivist dispute" into a broad and lively conversation about the character and purposes of social knowledge. To appreciate Bernstein's contribution, one need only recall the exchange between Theodor Adorno and Karl Popper in the 1960s.[1] Echoing earlier Frankfurt School criticisms of positivist sociology, Adorno had argued that to reduce social inquiry to a "science of social facts" was to reify social conditions, making them appear independent of human activity, when in fact they were consequences of it. The effect was to obscure, and thereby to diminish, the freedom to alter oppressive conditions. For Popper, in contrast, the threat to freedom came not from positivism but from Frankfurt School Critical Theory. Viewing the latter as a variant of the historicism he had criticized in *The Open Society and Its Enemies,* he (mis)attributed to Adorno the aspiration to decipher the logic of history all the better to subordinate humanity to it. More a dialogue of the deaf than a real engagement, this exchange reflected a deep political disagreement about the purposes of social knowledge: whereas Adorno sought to reveal potentials for social transformation, Popper warned against radical social experiments. The overall effect, at the height of the Cold War, was to cast doubt on the legitimacy of critique.

It was with the aim of dispelling that doubt that Bernstein undertook to reconstruct the idea of social inquiry. Eschewing the sterile polemics of earlier exchanges, he expanded the discussion to include a far broader range of perspectives. In *Praxis and Action* (1971), he interrogated the respective understandings of action in Western Marxism, existentialism, pragmatism, and analytic philosophy. The effect was to disclose the shared revolt against Cartesianism that underlay those seemingly unrelated projects. Similarly, in *The Restructuring of Social and Political Theory* (1976), he unearthed hidden correspondences among apparently disparate challenges to mainstream U.S. social science, including the analytic philosophy of Peter Winch, the phenomenology of Alfred Schutz, and the critical theory of Jürgen Habermas. Rejecting received dichotomies between fact and value, description and evaluation, understanding and explanation, Bernstein argued for a mode of social inquiry that was at once normative, empirical, and interpretive. Finally, in *Beyond Objectivism and Relativism* (1983), he disclosed common concerns about rationality in seemingly unrelated debates over paradigm incommensurability in science, the scope and sufficiency of hermeneutics, and the nature of practical judgment. The conclusion here was that rationality was dialogical, and that this had political consequences: to care about reason meant to foster dialogical communities—and the solidarity and mutual recognition on which these depend. In all three books, Bernstein exemplified in practice what he also defended in theory: the legitimacy of critique and the dialogical character of social inquiry.

The essays in part II owe much to Bernstein's understanding of critique. Benefiting from the opening his interventions created, and drawing on his postpositivist view of social science, they embody modes of inquiry that are at once normative, empirical, and interpretive. In addition, they continue the pragmatist tradition by training philosophical reflection on the problems of the age.

Nancy Fraser examines the new grammar of political conflict in the postsocialist era. Citing Bernstein's penchant for seeing beyond false antitheses, she proposes to reconcile two paradigms of social contestation, often decoupled from each other and assumed to be mutually incompatible: the politics of redistribution, aimed at promoting social equality, and the politics of recognition, aimed at promoting acceptance of difference. Rejecting either/or analyses that would force us to choose between these paradigms, Fraser undertakes to integrate the best features of each in a larger understanding of social justice. In her contribution to this volume, she considers two questions: what sorts of institutional arrangements can redress maldistribution and misrecognition simultaneously, while minimizing the mutual interferences that can arise when we try to combat both aspects of injustice at once? And what sorts of political strategies can help us move closer to such institutional arrangements under current conditions in which a reified identity politics accompanies increasing economic inequality?

The next chapter honors Bernstein's work on Hannah Arendt. Linking Arendt's reflections on statelessness with Kant's writings on cosmopolitanism, Seyla Benhabib surveys the dilemmas of a territorially centered and state-centric view of citizenship in an increasingly globalized world. Famously, Kant restricted cosmopolitan right to the duty we owe to the stranger of temporary leave to stay on our land and in our midst, when not doing so would lead to their demise. This obligation was strictly limited in that the republican sovereign had no moral duty to offer the other permanent sojourn and eventual membership in the political community. The breach opened by Kant between the right of temporary sojourn and the privilege of permanent residence is reflected still, Benhabib argues, in contemporary international law and practice. Whereas the obligation to grant refuge and asylum is binding on those states that are signatories to the Geneva Convention on the status of refugees and its various protocols, there is no obligation to grant citizenship rights to nonmembers. Proceeding from Arendt's reflections on "the right to have rights," which recapitulate Kant's dichotomies, Benhabib argues that these principles still lack an adequate institutional expression a world in which territorially bounded political sovereignty is under siege.

Drawing on Bernstein's view of critical theory, Thomas McCarthy interrogates the failure of liberal political philosophy to theorize racial subordination. He notes that, although liberal theorists overwhelmingly oppose racism, most have neglected to reflect systematically on "race" as a major ordering principle of modern society. Seeking to understand why that should be so, McCarthy examines John Rawls's influential distinction between "ideal theory" and "nonideal theory." Noting that this distinction assumes a sharp separation of abstract normative concepts from the messy particularities of empirical history, McCarthy contends that it encourages the illusion that normative theory can be "freestanding." Lacking any mediation between the ideal and the real, this approach proves unable to bridge the gap between "a color-blind ideal theory and a color-coded political reality." The upshot, according to McCarthy is that Rawlsian theory is an "unsuitable vehicle for theorizing racial injustice." Only an approach that is at once normative, empirical, and interpretative can be adequate to this task.

Modern philosophy is implicated not only in the history of racism, but also in that of the death penalty. In his contribution to this volume, Jacques Derrida reminds us that Enlightenment thinkers like Rousseau, Kant, and Hegel justified the death penalty as a form of "auto-imposed justice," a punishment willed by the criminal himself, through his transgressive exercise of freedom. Drawing on the Catholic political theologian Donoso Cortes and the Nazi legal theorist Carl Schmitt, Derrida unravels the paradoxes of this institution. *Qua* secular punishment, the death penalty is supposed to differ sharply from the mythico-religious practice of human sacrifice. Yet its justification has always relied on a doctrine of sovereignty that has an ineliminable mythico-religious dimension. Moreover, limiting the sovereignty of the sovereign is a particularly vexing issue for liberal democracies like the United States, in which capital punishment continues to be legally practiced. Derrida remarks, too, on the company in which the U.S. finds itself on this point: leading the list of death penalty practitioners are one-party dictatorships like China and Iraq and theocracies like Iran and Saudi Arabia. Derrida's participation in this volume constitutes further evidence of Bernstein's dialogic approach to philosophy.

Sensitive to the ethical implications of Derrida's thought, Bernstein has long sought to promote communication between critical theorists and deconstructionists. In a series of essays collected in *The New Constellation: The Ethical-Political Horizons of Modernity/Postmodernity* (1991), he proposed to circumvent the unnecessarily sharp polarization of the two camps. Writing in the aftermath of Habermas's *The Philosophical Discourse of Modernity,* and aiming to disclose heretofore obscured common ground, Bernstein spoke simultaneously to both sides. On the one hand, he urged deconstructionists to reckon more seriously with the political consequences of their work; on the other, he advised critical theorists that questioning binary oppositions could have emancipatory effects, by broadening the range of conceptual and normative options.

III

The 1990s brought new themes to the fore for Richard Bernstein. With the publication of *Hannah Arendt and the Jewish Question* (1996), *Freud and the Legacy of Moses* (1998), and *Radical Evil: A Philosophical Interrogation* (2002), he turned his attention to trauma and memory, tradition and identity, evil and judgment, all considered in the shadow of the Holocaust. Less metaphilosophically and methodologically oriented than his previous writings, Bernstein's works of this period exhibit a nuanced combination of cultural-historical analysis and philosophical reflection.

The conversation with Hannah Arendt has been a strong and influential strain in Bernstein's philosophical work since the early 1980s. Nevertheless, it was only with *Hannah Arendt and the Jewish Question* that he undertook an analysis of her thought as a whole. Placing her reflections on the cultural, ethical, and political dimensions of modern Jewish identity at its center, Bernstein offered a nuanced reading of Arendt that integrated the philosophical with the political, the essayistic with the systematic aspects of her writing.

Arendt once remarked that if one was attacked as a Jew, one had to defend oneself as a Jew—however one felt about Jewish identity. That notion meets its litmus test in "Moses and Monotheism," the subject of Bernstein's *Freud and the Legacy of Moses*. One of Freud's most puzzling and disturbing writings, this work argues both that Moses was an Egyptian and that he was murdered by the Israelites. Written in 1939 on the eve of the Holocaust, it seems not only scandalous and historically baseless, but also morally and politically callous. Bernstein, however, insists on refusing the easy conclusions. Pleading rather for a careful reading, and then proceeding to offer one himself, he maintains that Freud's essay is about the hope and the promise of Jewish survival.

In *Radical Evil*, in contrast, Bernstein grapples more with the perpetrators than the victims. This magisterial dialogue weaves together reflections on evil in the philosophies of Kant, Hegel, and Schelling with the observations of Nietzsche and Freud and the ethics of Emmanuel Levinas, Hans Jonas, and Hannah Arendt.

Introduction

Noting the enormous gulf between the frequent references to "evil" in our daily moral and political vocabulary and the poverty of our intellectual resources for coming to grips with it, Bernstein draws a quintessentially Kantian conclusion: the ultimate subjective ground of moral conduct is inscrutable. Social scientific analysis and philosophical reflection can never bridge the "black hole" in our accounts of why some individuals make the choices they do. But far from leading to despair, this inscrutability of the grounds of our actions is also the basis of human freedom and dignity, of what it means to be a free and responsible person. Inspired by Bernstein's late work, the essays in part III deal with themes of memory, judgment, and evil. Agnes Heller surveys the debates about *Moses and Monotheism* that inspired Bernstein's book about Freud. Noting that psychoanalysis had claimed to solve the mystery of religion, the historian of Judaism, Hayim Yerushalmi appealed instead to religious history to solve the mystery of psychoanalysis; thus, where Freud traced religion's force to a repressed patricidal act, Yerushalmi reversed the causal relation: the real agent of patricide was Freud, who repressed his own Jewish heritage. That conclusion, however, was disputed by Jacques Derrida, who argued in *Archive Fever* that, far from rejecting his Jewish identity, Freud had complicated it as a means of preserving it. Bernstein's intervention followed in turn. Recalling that Freud himself had posed the question in 1930—in what sense was he, an atheist who lacked any sense of national loyalty, nevertheless still a Jew—the American philosopher read *Moses and Monotheism* as Freud's attempt to answer his question. In her contribution, finally, Heller synthesizes the best insights from all these perspectives, while adding a further twist: henceforth we must read *Moses and Monotheism* as the testament of "ein gottloser Jude" (a godless Jew) who admits that he has murdered the Jewish God.

Psychoanalysis is also at the center of Joel Whitebook's contribution, but his principal focus is Hannah Arendt. Noting that Arendt explicitly rejected Freudianism as a mode of intellectual inquiry, Whitebook undertakes to look beyond her surface hostility. It is true, he grants, that she saw in psychoanalysis the continuing obsession with intimacy in the twentieth century; thus, Freudianism was for her a symptom of modern "worldlessness." Nevertheless,

Seyla Benhabib and Nancy Fraser

claims Whitebook, to reduce her attitude to simple rejection is to miss the deeper resonances. Returning to a central focus of Bernstein's book on Arendt, Whitebook shows that what she meant by radical evil can be interpreted in psychoanalytic terms. In his reading, the project of "rendering human beings as such superfluous" expresses the wish for omnipotence and dedifferentiation. Behind the drive to rearrange the world according to one's own will, analysis discerns the wish to obliterate the other's alterity.

The search for modes of representation that could do justice to the horrors of the twentieth century is central to Jerome Kohn's contribution. Rereading Arendt's posthumously published reflections on Kant's theory of judgment, Kohn picks up the challenge posed by Bernstein: "what then was Arendt really about in her own reflections on Kant's notion of reflective aesthetic judgment?" That she never really established the connections between judging, thinking, and moral evil is widely believed. Yet, argues Kohn, "Arendt's concern with Kantian reflective aesthetic judgment, with common sense and the *exemplary* validity of particular judgments, was about both the possibility and difficulty of establishing a common world today." Far from aestheticizing the political, she was trying to politicize aesthetic judgment—not in the sense of subjecting it to doctrinal constraints but by probing its capacity to reestablish a common world of appearances. Testing this thesis in relation to pictorial representation in painting, Kohn offers Arendt-inspired interpretations of Georges de la Tour's *Prisonnier,* Pierro della Francesca's *Resurrezione,* and Goya's *Perro.*

The theme of radical evil also runs through Carol Bernstein's reading of Jorge Semprun's novel, *Literature or Life.* For Semprun, who was sent to Buchenwald for joining the French Resistance while a student of philosophy in France, the concentration camp became "the primal scene of evil and its accomplice death." For him, however, radical evil is not the horror of the camps but "the experience of having lived through death as a collective." The writer is less a survivor than a ghost, a "revenant" who revisits his own death again and again.

How to narrate and communicate these experiences after Auschwitz? In Shoshana Yovel's contribution, excerpted from her novel

The Seventh Demon, the narrator, Amos, meditates on absolute evil. "Absolute evil arbitrarily denigrates the basic universal solidarity by denigrating the other's humanity. That's the nucleus of it all. From where the venom spreads. When suddenly the 'you' must justify his right to exist, which only the 'I' can then approve.... But what kind of 'I' can there be without a 'you'? When the 'I' obliterates the 'you,' he erases himself...."

IV

A Festschrift should celebrate its subject's life as well as his work. Fittingly, therefore, this volume ends with a biographical essay by Judith Friedlander, "The Philosopher from New York." Based in part on a series of conversations with Bernstein (who was then unaware that a festschrift in his honor was under way), this piece brings to light some little-known details and episodes of his life and career. A list of Bernstein's publications follows.

Note

1. Theodor Adorno, et al., *The Positivist Dispute in German Sociology*, trans. by Glyn Adey and David Frisby (New York: Harper Torch Books, 1976).

I

Philosophy's Scope and Limits

1

Philosophy as a Transitional Genre

Richard Rorty

1 Introduction

Richard Bernstein and I are almost exact contemporaries, were educated in mostly the same places by mostly the same people, have been exalted by many of the same hopes, and have been talking to one another about how to fulfill those hopes for more than fifty years. We share not only many enthusiasms, but the vast majority of our convictions, both philosophical and political.

Though Bernstein has been much more politically active than I, I doubt that we have ever seriously disagreed about what measures to support, whom to vote for, or in what direction we want history to go. So what disagreements remain might be called "merely philosophical." This essay is one more attempt to restate my philosophical views in a form that may be a bit less vulnerable to Bernstein's objections.

This attempt is made easier because Bernstein's are among the most careful, detailed, and searching criticisms of my writings. He always understands my motives and intentions perfectly, never distorts or mocks what I say, yet often concludes that the view I am offering is largely wrong. I have been grateful for Bernstein's willingness to spend time reading my stuff ever since he gave me some invaluable advice about how to revise my *Philosophy and the Mirror of Nature*. That book owes a great deal to his comments, as does much that I have written since.

Bernstein has remarked, accurately, that the "aesthetic strain in [my] writings has become more and more pronounced over the years."[1] He has also pointed out that I spend a lot of time reiterating "a version of the narrative of the history of philosophy that has its origin in Nietzsche, has been refined and perpetuated by Heidegger and Derrida, and has been disseminated by many of those who identify themselves as poststructuralist, postmodern or deconstructionist writers" (NC, p. 251). In this essay I rehearse this narrative yet again, and argue that its outcome should indeed be seen as the triumph, if not exactly the aesthetic (a Kantian notion for which I have little use), of what I call the "literary." Once again, I am telling the old Nietzschean story about how "Truth" took the place of "God" in a secular culture, and why we should get rid of this God-surrogate in order to become more self-reliant. I am a hedgehog who, despite showering my reader with allusions and dropping lots of names, has really only one idea: the need to get beyond representationalism, and thus into an intellectual world in which human beings are responsible only to each other.

Bernstein is right to suspect that Dewey would have been unwilling to tell this story, and might have emphatically refused to endorse it. He has always had doubts about my attempts to fabricate a Nietzscheanized James, a Wittgensteinian Derrida, and a Heideggerianized Dewey. But what he calls my "ruthless and violent" readings of these authors are not eliminable extravangances. A way of getting Nietzsche, James, Wittgenstein, Derrida, Heidegger, and Dewey under the same antirepresentationalist tent, and a focus on the overlap between their views rather than on their disagreements, is pretty much all I have to offer. I want us to see all six of them as heralds of a new dawn—not just a new stage in the history of philosophy, but a new self-image for humanity. I think of them all as assisting in the takeover by what I call a "literary culture," a culture unlike anything that has existed in the past. Help in spelling out how they (and various other philosophers, such as Sellars, Davidson, and Brandom) do this is the only contribution I have to make.

Bernstein thinks that we need to move away from such visions of a new intellectual world and get back to the rough ground: to continue discussing the questions that Dewey took seriously and that I do not—questions, for example, about how "the structural dynamics of bourgeois society systematically undermine and belie liberal ideals" (*NC*, p. 245). He believes philosophers can serve good political causes by studying topics that I find relatively fruitless. He wants theoretical arguments for political stances, whereas I think such stances can be justified only by pointing to the results of actual or imagined social experiments. I doubt that he and I will ever break this deadlock, since our disagreement is not about the truth of propositions but about the fruitfulness of topics. All of us, by neglecting some issues and focusing on others, place our bets on what will and what will not seem worth discussing to future generations. Bernstein and I have made slightly different wagers.

I see discussing the structural dynamics of bourgeois society as a distraction from questions about how to use the tools of political reform available in the actually existing constitutional democracies to keep the rich from controlling the government. The gap between the level at which political theorists operate and the political alternatives we presently face seems to me just too great. Although I admire the skill with which Dewey and Habermas weave abstractions together in their writings on political theory, I cannot connect these abstractions with the political decisions we need to make. That is why I greatly prefer *geistesgeschichtlich* books like *Reconstruction in Philosophy* and *The Philosophical Discourse of Modernity* to such books as *The Public and Its Problems* and *Between Facts and Norms*.[2]

Although the bulk of this essay is, as I have said, just one more retelling of my tediously familiar up-from-representationalism story, its last two sections were written in an attempt to deal with the sorts of doubts that Bernstein has expressed about my philosophical project. In these pages, Bernstein is the reader over my shoulder. I hope they may persuade him to see my use of the private-public distinction in a somewhat more favorable light. But whether they do or not, I am glad to have this occasion to express my gratitude for the stimulation that his criticisms have provided.

2 The Existence of Truth

Questions such as "Does truth exist?" or "Do you believe in truth?" seem fatuous and pointless. Everybody knows that the difference between true and false beliefs is as important as that between nourishing and poisonous foods. Moreover, one of the principal achievements of recent analytic philosophy is to have shown that the ability to wield the concept of "true belief" is a necessary condition for being a user of language, and thus for being a rational agent.

Nevertheless, the question "Do you believe in truth or are you one of those frivolous postmodernists?" is often the first one that journalists ask intellectuals whom they are assigned to interview. That question now plays the role once played by the question "Do you believe in God, or are you one of those dangerous atheists?" Literary types are frequently told that they do not love truth sufficiently. Such admonitions are delivered in the same tones in which their predecessors were reminded that the fear of the Lord is the beginning of wisdom.

Obviously, the sense of the word "truth" invoked by that question is not the everyday one. Nobody is worried about a mere nominalization of the adjective "true." The question "Do you believe that truth exists?" is shorthand for something like "Do you think that there is a natural terminus to inquiry, a way things really are, and that understanding what that way is will tell us what to do with ourselves?"

Those who, like myself, find themselves accused of postmodernist frivolity do not think that there is such a terminus. We think that inquiry is just another name for problem solving, and we cannot imagine inquiry into how human beings should live, into what we should make of ourselves, coming to an end. For solutions to old problems will produce fresh problems, and so on forever. As with the individual, so with both the society and the species: each stage of maturation will overcome previous dilemmas only by creating new ones.

Problems about what to do with ourselves, what purposes to serve, differ, in this respect, from scientific problems. A complete and final unified science, a harmoniously orchestrated assemblage of scientific theories none of which will ever need to be revised, is, perhaps, an intelligible goal. Maybe scientific inquiry could terminate, simply because anomalies stopped turning up. So if a unified account of the causal relations between all spatiotemporal events were all that were meant by "truth," even the farthest-out post-modernists would have no reason to doubt truth's existence. The existence of truth only becomes an issue when another sort of truth is in question.

I shall use the term "redemptive truth" for a set of beliefs that would end, once and for all, the process of reflection on what to do with ourselves. Redemptive truth would not consist in theories about how things interact causally, but instead would fulfill the need that religion and philosophy have attempted to satisfy. This is the need to fit everything—every thing, person, event, idea, and poem—into a single context, a context that will somehow reveal itself as natural, destined, and unique. It would be the only context that would matter for purposes of shaping our lives, because it would be the only one in which those lives appear as they truly are. To believe in redemptive truth is to believe that there is something that stands to human life as elementary physical particles stand to the four elements—something that is the reality behind the appearance, the one true description of what is going on, the final secret.

Hope that such a context can be found is one species of a larger genus. The larger genus is what Heidegger called the hope for authenticity—the hope to become one's own person rather than merely the creation of one's education or one's environment. As Heidegger emphasized, to achieve authenticity in this sense is not necessarily to *reject* one's past. It may instead be a matter of reinterpreting that past so as to make it more suitable for one's own purposes. What matters is to have seen one or more alternatives to the purposes that most people take for granted, and to have chosen among these alternatives—thereby, in some measure, creating yourself. As Harold Bloom has recently reminded us, the point of reading a great many books is to become aware of a great number of alternative purposes, and the point of *that* is to become an autonomous self.[3] Autonomy, in this un-Kantian and distinctively Bloomian sense, is pretty much the same thing as Heideggerian authenticity.

I shall define an intellectual as someone who yearns for Bloomian autonomy, and is lucky enough to have the money and leisure to do something about it: to visit different churches or gurus, go to different theatres or museums, and, above all, to read a lot of different books. Most human beings, even those who have the requisite money and leisure, are not intellectuals. If they read books it is not because they seek redemption but either because they wish to be entertained or distracted, or because they want to become better able to carry out some antecedent purpose. They do not read books to find out what purposes to have. The intellectuals do.

3   From Religion through Philosophy to Literature

Given these definitions of the terms "redemptive truth" and "intellectual," I can now state my thesis. It is that the intellectuals of the West have, since the Renaissance, progressed through three stages: they have hoped for redemption first from God, then from philosophy, and now from literature. Monotheistic religion offers hope for redemption through entering into a new relation to a supremely powerful nonhuman person. Belief in the articles of a creed may be only incidental to such a relationship. For philosophy, however, beliefs are of the essence. Redemption by philosophy is through the acquisition of a set of beliefs that represent things in the one way they really are. Literature, finally, offers redemption through making the acquaintance of as great a variety of human beings as possible. Here again, as in religion, true belief may be of little importance.

From within a literary culture, religion and philosophy appear as literary genres. As such, they are optional. Just as an intellectual may opt to read many poems but few novels, or many novels but few poems, so he or she may read much philosophy, or much religious writing, but relatively few poems or novels. The difference between the literary intellectuals' readings of *all* these books and other readings of them is that the inhabitant of a literary culture treats books as human attempts to meet human needs, rather than as acknowledgements of the power of a being that is what it is apart from any such needs. God and Truth are, respectively, the religious and the philosophical names for that sort of being.

The transition from religion to philosophy began with the revival of Platonism in the Renaissance, the period in which humanists began asking the same questions about Christian monotheism that Socrates had asked about Hesiod's pantheon. Socrates had suggested to Euthyphro that the real question was not whether one's actions were pleasing to the gods, but rather which gods held the correct views about what actions ought to be done. When that latter question was once again taken seriously, the road lay open to Kant's conclusion that even the Holy One of the Gospels must be judged in the light of one's own conscience.

The transition from a philosophical to a literary culture began shortly after Kant, about the time that Hegel warned us that philosophy paints its gray on gray only when a form of life has grown old. That remark helped the generation of Kierkegaard and Marx realize that philosophy was never going to fill the redemptive role that Hegel himself had claimed for it. Hegel's supremely ambitious claims for philosophy almost instantly flip-flopped into their dialectical opposite. His system was no sooner published than it began to be treated as a self-consuming artifact, the *reductio ad absurdum* of a form of intellectual life that suddenly seemed to be on its last legs.

Since Hegel's time, the intellectuals have been losing faith in philosophy. This amounts to losing faith in the idea that redemption can come in the form of true beliefs. In the literary culture that has been emerging during the last two hundred years, the question "Is it true?" has yielded to the question "What's new?" Heidegger thought that that change was a decline, a shift from serious thinking to mere gossipy curiosity.[4] Many fans of natural science, people who otherwise have no use for Heidegger, would agree with him on this point. On the account I am offering, however, this change is an advance. It represents a desirable replacement of bad questions like "What is Being?" "What is really real?" and "What is man?" with the sensible question "Does anybody have any new ideas about what we human beings might manage to make of ourselves?"

In its pure form, undiluted by philosophy, religion is a relation to a nonhuman person. This relation may be one of adoring obedience, or ecstatic communion, or quiet confidence, or some combination of these. But it is only when religion has become mingled with philosophy that this noncognitive, redemptive relation to a person begins to be mediated by a creed. Only when the God of the philosophers has begun to replace the God of Abraham, Isaac, and Jacob is correct belief thought to be essential to salvation.

For religion in its uncontaminated form, argument is no more in point than is belief. To become a New Being in Christ is, Kierkegaard insisted, not the same sort of thing as being forced to grant the truth of a proposition in the course of Socratic reflection, or as the outcome of Hegelian dialectic. Insofar as religion requires belief in a proposition, it is, as Locke said, belief based on the credit of the proposer rather than belief backed by argument. But beliefs are irrelevant to the special devotion of the illiterate believer to Demeter, or to the Virgin of Guadelupe, or to the little fat god on the third altar from the left at the temple down the street. It is this irrelevance that intellectuals like Saint Paul, Kierkegaard, and Karl Barth—spiritual athletes who relish the thought that their faith is a folly to the Greeks—hope to recapture.

To take seriously the idea that redemption can come in the form of true beliefs, one must believe both that the life that cannot be successfully argued for is not worth living, and that persistent argument will lead all inquirers to the same set of beliefs. Religion and literature, insofar as they are uncontaminated by philosophy, share neither of these convictions. Uncontaminated religion may be monotheistic in the sense that a community may think it essential to worship only one particular god. But the idea that there can *be* only one god, that polytheism is contrary to reason, is one that can take hold only after philosophy has convinced us that every human being's reflections must lead to the same outcome.

As I am using the terms "literature" and "literary culture," a culture that has substituted literature for both religion and philosophy finds redemption neither in a noncognitive relation to a nonhuman person nor in a cognitive relation to propositions, but in noncognitive relations to other human beings, relations mediated by human artifacts such as books and buildings, paintings and songs. These artifacts provide a sense of alternative ways of being human.

This sort of culture drops a presupposition common to religion and philosophy—that redemption must come from one's relation to something that is not just one more human creation.

Kierkegaard rightly said that philosophy began to set itself up as a rival to religion when Socrates suggested that our self-knowledge was a knowledge of God—that we had no need of help from a nonhuman person, because the truth was already within us. But literature began to set itself up as a rival to philosophy when people like Cervantes and Shakespeare began to suspect that human beings were, and ought to be, so diverse that there is no point in pretending that they all carry a single truth deep in their bosoms. Santayana pointed to this seismic cultural shift in his essay "The Absence of Religion in Shakespeare."[5] That essay might equally well have been called "The Absence of Either Religion or Philosophy in Shakespeare" or simply "The Absence of Truth in Shakespeare."

I suggested earlier that "Do you believe in truth?" can be given both sense and urgency if it is reformulated as "Do you think that there is a single set of beliefs that can serve a redemptive role in the lives of all human beings, that can be rationally justified to all human beings under optimal communicative conditions, and that will thus form the natural terminus of inquiry?" To answer "yes" to this reformulated question is to take philosophy as the guide of life. It is to agree with Socrates that there is a set of beliefs that is both susceptible of rational justification and such as to take rightful precedence over every other consideration in determining what to do with one's life. The premise of philosophy is that there is a way things really are—a way humanity and the rest of the universe are and always will be, independent of any merely contingent human needs and interests. Knowledge of this way is redemptive. It can therefore replace religion. The striving for Truth can take place of the search for God.

It is not clear that Homer, or even Sophocles, could have made sense of this suggestion. Before Plato dreamt them up, the constellation of ideas necessary to make sense of it were not available. Cervantes and Shakespeare understood Plato's suggestion, but they distrusted his motives. Their distrust led them to play up diversity and downplay commonality—to underline the differences between human beings rather than looking for a common human nature. This change of emphasis weakens the grip of the Platonic assumption that all these different sorts of people should be arranged in a hierarchy, judged on the basis of their relative success at attaining a single goal. Initiatives like Cervantes's and Shakespeare's helped create a new sort of intellectual—one who does not take the availability of redemptive truth for granted, and is not much interested in whether either God or Truth exist.

This change helped create today's high culture, one to which religion and philosophy have become marginal. To be sure, there are still numerous religious intellectuals, and even more philosophical ones. But bookish youngsters in search of redemption nowadays look first to novels, plays, and poems. The sort of books which the eighteenth century thought of as marginal have become central. The authors of *Rasselas* and of *Candide* helped bring about, but could hardly have foreseen, a culture in which the most revered writers neither write nor read either sermons or treatises on the nature of man and the universe.

For members of the literary culture, redemption is to be achieved by getting in touch with the present limits of the human imagination. That is why a literary culture is always in search of novelty, always hoping to spot what Shelley called "the gigantic shadows which futurity casts upon the present,"[6] rather than trying to escape from the temporal to the eternal. It is a premise of this culture that though the imagination has present limits, these limits are capable of being extended forever. The imagination endlessly consumes its own artifacts. It is an ever-living, ever-expanding, fire. It is as subject to time and chance as are the flies and the worms, but although it endures and preserves the memory of its past, it will continue to transcend its previous limits. Though the fear of belatedness is ever present within the literary culture, this very fear makes for a more intense blaze.

The sort of person I am calling a "literary intellectual" thinks that a life that is not lived close to the present limits of the human imagination is not worth living. For the Socratic idea of self-examination and self-knowledge, the literary intellectual substitutes the idea of enlarging the self by becoming acquainted with still more ways of being human. For the religious idea that a certain book or tradition might connect you up with a supremely powerful or supremely lovable nonhuman person, the literary intellectual substitutes the Bloomian thought that the more books you read, the more ways of being human you have considered, the more human you become—the less tempted by dreams of an escape from time and chance, the more convinced that we humans have nothing to rely on save one another. The great virtue of the literary culture that is gradually coming into being is that it tells young intellectuals that the only source of redemption is the human imagination, and that this fact should occasion pride rather than despair.

From the point of view of this culture, philosophy was a transitional stage in a process of gradually increasing self-reliance. Philosophy's attempt to replace God with Truth requires the conviction that a set of beliefs that can be justified to all human beings will also fill all the needs of all human beings. But that idea was an inherently unstable compromise between the masochistic urge to submit to the nonhuman and the need to take proper pride in our humanity. Redemptive truth is an attempt to find something that is not made by human beings but to which human beings have a special, privileged relation not shared by the animals. The intrinsic nature of things is like a god in its independence of us, and yet— so Socrates and Hegel tell us—self-knowledge will suffice to get us in touch with it. One way to see the quest for knowledge of such a quasi-divinity is as Sartre saw it: it is a futile passion, a foredoomed attempt to become a for-itself-in-itself. But it would be better to see philosophy as one our greatest imaginative achievements, on a par with the invention of the gods.

Philosophers have often described religion as a primitive and insufficiently reflective attempt to philosophize. But, as I said earlier, a fully self-conscious literary culture would think of both religion and philosophy as relatively primitive, yet glorious, literary genres. They are genres in which it is now becoming increasingly difficult to write, but the genres that are replacing them might never have emerged had they not been read as swerves away from religion, and later as swerves away from philosophy. Religion and philosophy are not merely, from this point of view, ladders to be thrown away. Rather, they are stages in a process of maturation, a process that we should continually look back to, and recapitulate, in the hope of attaining still greater self-reliance.

4 The Culmination of Philosophy: Idealist and Materialist Metaphysics

In the hope of making this account of philosophy as a transitional genre more plausible, I shall say something about the two great movements in which philosophy culminated. Philosophy began to come into its own when the thinkers of the Enlightenment no longer had to hide themselves behind the sort of masks worn by Descartes, Hobbes, and Spinoza, and were able to be openly atheistic. These masks could be dropped after the French Revolution. That event, by making it plausible that human beings might build a new heaven and a new earth, made God seem far less necessary than before.

That newfound self-reliance produced two great metaphysical systems. First came the metaphysics of German idealism, and second, the reaction against idealism which was materialist metaphysics, the apotheosis of the results of natural science. The first movement belongs to the past. Materialist metaphysics, however, is still with us. It is, in fact, pretty much the only version of redemptive truth presently on offer. It is philosophy's last hurrah, its last attempt to provide redemptive truth and thereby avoid being demoted to the status of a literary genre.

This is not the place to recapitulate the rise and fall of German idealism, nor to eulogize what Heidegger called "the greatness, breadth, and originality of that spiritual world." It suffices for my present purposes to say that Hegel, the most original of the idealists, believed himself to have been given the first satisfactory proof of the existence of God, and the first satisfactory solution to the traditional theological problem of evil. He was, in his own eyes, the first fully successful natural theologian—the first to reconcile Socrates with Christ by showing that the Incarnation was not an act of grace on God's part but rather a necessity. "God," Hegel said, "had to have a Son" because eternity is nothing without time, God nothing without man, Truth nothing without its historical emergence.

In Hegel's eyes, the Platonic hope of escape from the temporal to the eternal was a primitive, albeit necessary, stage of philosophical thinking—a stage that the Christian doctrine of Incarnation has helped us outgrow. Now that Kant has opened the way to seeing mind and world as interdependent, Hegel believed, we are in a position to see that philosophy can bridge the Kantian distinction between the phenomenal and the noumenal, just as Christ's stay on earth overcame the distinction between God and man.

Idealist metaphysics seemed both true and demonstrable to some of the best minds of the nineteenth century. Josiah Royce, for example, wrote book after book arguing that Hegel was right: simple armchair reflection on the presuppositions of common sense, exactly the sort of philosophizing that Socrates practiced and commended, will lead you to recognize the truth of pantheism as surely as reflection on geometrical diagrams will lead you to the Pythagorean theorem. But the verdict of the literary culture on this metaphysics was nicely formulated by Kierkegaard when he said that if Hegel had written at the end of his books that "this was all just a thought experiment" he would have been the greatest thinker who ever lived, but that, as it was, he was merely a buffoon.[7]

I would rephrase Kierkegaard's point as follows: if Hegel had been able to stop thinking that he had given us redemptive truth, and claimed instead to have given us something *better* than redemptive truth—namely, a way of holding all the previous products of the human imagination together in a single vision—he would have been the first philosopher to admit that a better cultural product than philosophy had come on the market. He would have been the first philosopher to self-consciously replace philosophy with literature, just as Socrates and Plato were the first self-consciously to replace religion with philosophy. But instead Hegel presented himself (at least part of the time) as having discovered Absolute Truth, and men like Royce took him with a seriousness that now strikes us as both endearing and ludicrous. So it was left to Nietzsche, in *The Birth of Tragedy*, to tell us that the premise common to Socrates and Hegel should be rejected, and that the invention of the idea of self-knowledge was a great imaginative achievement that has outlived its usefulness.

Between Hegel's time and Nietzsche's, however, there arose the second of the great philosophical movements. It bore the same relation to Democritus and Lucretius that German idealism had borne to Parmenides and Plotinus. This was the attempt to put natural science in the place of both religion and Socratic reflection, to see empirical inquiry as providing exactly what Socrates thought it could never give us—redemptive truth.

By the middle of the nineteenth century, it had become clear that mathematics and empirical science were going to be the only areas of culture in which one might conceivably hope to get unanimous, rational agreement—the only disciplines able to provide beliefs that would not be overturned as history rolls along. They were the only sources of cumulative results—of propositions that were plausible candidates for the status of insight into the way things are in themselves. Unified natural science still seems to many intellectuals to be the answer to Socrates' prayers.

On the other hand, pretty much everybody in the nineteenth century had come to agree with Hume that Plato's model of cognitive success—mathematics—was never going to offer us anything redemptive. Only a few flaky neo-Pythagoreans still saw mathematics as having more than practical and aesthetic interest. So nineteenth century positivists drew the moral that the only other source of rational agreement and unshakable truth, empirical science, just *had* to have a redemptive function. Since philosophy had always taught that an account that bound everything together into a coherent whole would have redemptive value, and since the collapse of idealist metaphysics had left materialism as the only possible candidate for such an account, the positivists concluded that natural science was all the philosophy we would ever need.

This project of giving redemptive status to empirical science still appeals to two sorts of present-day intellectuals. The first is the kind of philosopher who insists that natural science attains objective truth in a way that no other portion of culture does. These philosophers usually go on to claim that the natural scientist is the paradigmatic possessor of intellectual virtues, notably the love of truth, that are rarely sought among literary critics. The second sort of intellectual who continues along the lines laid down by the nineteenth century positivists is the kind of scientist who announces that the latest work is in his discipline has deep philosophical implications: that advances in evolutionary biology or cognitive science, for example, do more than tell us how things work and what they are made of. They also tell us, these scientists say, something about how to live, about human nature, about what we really are. They provide, if not redemption, at least wisdom—not merely instructions on how to produce more effective tools for getting what we want but wise counsel about what we should want.

I shall take up these two groups of people separately. The problem about the attempt by philosophers to treat the empirical scientist as a paradigm of intellectual virtue is that the astrophysicist's love of truth seems no different from that of the classical philologist or the archive-oriented historian. All these people are trying hard to get something right. So, when it comes to that, are the master carpenter, the skilled accountant, and the careful surgeon. The need to get it right is central to all these people's sense of who they are, of what makes their lives worthwhile.

It is certainly the case that without people whose lives are centered around this need we should never have had much in the way of civilization. The free play of the imagination is possible only because of the substructure literal-minded people have built. No artisans, no poets. No theoretical scientists to provide the technology of an industrialized world, few people with sufficient money to send their children off to be initiated into a literary culture. But there is no reason to take the contributions of the natural scientist to this substructure as having a moral or philosophical significance that is lacking in those of the carpenter, the accountant, and the surgeon.

John Dewey thought that the fact that the mathematical physicist enjoys greater prestige than the skilled artisan is an unfortunate legacy of the Platonic–Aristotelian distinction between eternal truths and empirical truth, the elevation of leisured contemplation above sweaty practicality. His point might be restated by saying that the prestige of the scientific theorist is an unfortunate legacy of the Socratic idea that what we might all agree to be true is, as a result of rational debate, a reflection of something more than the fact of agreement—the idea that intersubjective agreement under ideal communicative conditions is a token of correspondence to the way things really are.

The current debate among analytic philosophers about whether truth is a matter of correspondence to reality, and the parallel debate over Kuhn's denial that science is asymptotically approaching the really real, are disputes between those who see empirical science as fulfilling at least some of Plato's hopes and those who think that those hopes should be abandoned. The former philosophers take it as a matter of unquestionable common sense that adding a brick to the edifice of knowledge is a matter of more accurately aligning thought and language with the way things really are. Their philosophical opponents take this so-called common sense to be merely what Dewey thought it: a relic of the religious hope that redemption can come from contact with something non-human and supremely powerful. To abandon the latter idea, the idea that links philosophy with religion, would mean acknowledging both the ability of scientists to add bricks to the edifice of knowledge and the practical utility of scientific theories for prediction while insisting on the irrelevance of both achievements to searches for redemption.

These debates among the analytic philosophers have little to do with the activities of the second sort of people whom I have labeled "materialist metaphysicians." These are the scientists who think that the public at large should take an interest in the latest discoveries about the genome, or cerebral localization, or child development, or quantum mechanics. Such scientists are good at dramatizing the contrast between the old scientific theories and the shiny new ones, but they are bad at explaining why we should care about the difference. They are like critics of art and literature who are good at pointing to the differences between the paintings and poems of a few years ago and those being produced now, but bad at explaining why these changes are important.

There is, however, a difference between such critics and the sort of scientists I am talking about. The former usually have the sense to avoid the mistake Clement Greenberg made—the mistake of claiming that what fills the art galleries this year is what all the ages have been leading up to, and that there is an inner logic to the history of the products of the imagination that has now reached its destined outcome. But the scientists still retain the idea that the latest product of the scientific imagination is not just an improvement on what was previously imagined, but is also closer to the intrinsic nature of things. That is why they found Kuhn's suggestion that they think of themselves as problem solvers so insulting. Their rhetoric remains "We have substituted reality for appearance!" rather than "We have solved some long-standing problems!" or "We have made it new!"

The trouble with this rhetoric is that it puts a glossy metaphysical varnish on a useful scientific product. It suggests that we have not only learned more about how to predict and control our environment and ourselves but have also done something more—something of redemptive significance. But the successive achievements of modern science exhausted their philosophical significance when they made clear that there are no spooks—that a causal account of the relations between spatiotemporal events did not require the operation of nonphysical forces.

Modern science, in short, has helped us see that if you want a metaphysics, then a materialistic metaphysics is the only one to have. But it has not given us any reason to think that we need a metaphysics. The need for metaphysics lasted only as long as the hope for redemptive truth lasted. But by the time that materialism triumphed over idealism, this hope had waned. So the reaction of most contemporary intellectuals to gee-whiz announcements of new scientific discoveries is "So what?" This reaction is not, as C. P. Snow thought, a matter of pretentious and ignorant litterateurs condescending to honest, hardworking empirical inquirers. It is the perfectly sensible reaction of someone who is thinking about ends and is offered information about means.

The literary culture's attitude toward materialist metaphysics is, and should be, something like this: whereas both Plato's and Hegel's attempts to give us something more interesting than physics were laudable attempts to find a redemptive discipline to put in the place of religion, a materialist metaphysics is just physics getting above itself. Modern science is a gloriously imaginative way of describing things, brilliantly successful for the purpose for which it was developed—namely, predicting and controlling phenomena. But it should not pretend to have the sort of redemptive power claimed by its defeated rival, idealist metaphysics.

Questions of the "So what?" sort began to be posed to scientists by intellectuals of the nineteenth century who were gradually learning, as Nietzsche was to put it, to see science through the optic of art, and art through that of life. Nietzsche's master Emerson was one such figure, and Baudelaire another. Although many of the literary intellectuals of this period thought of themselves as having transcended romanticism, they nevertheless could agree with Schiller that the further maturation of mankind will be achieved through what Kant called "the aesthetic" rather than through what he called "the ethical." They could also endorse Shelley's claim that the great task of human emancipation from priests and tyrants could have been accomplished without "Locke, Hume, Gibbon, Voltaire and Rousseau" but that "it exceeds all imagination to conceive what would have been the moral condition of the world if neither Dante, Petrarch, Boccaccio, Chaucer, Shakespeare, Calderon, Lord Bacon nor Milton, had ever existed; if Raphael and Michael Angelo had never been born; if the Hebrew poetry had never been translated, if a revival of the study of Greek literature had never taken place, if no monuments of ancient sculpture had been handed down to us, and if the poetry and the religion of the ancient world had been extinguished together with its belief."[8]

What Shelley said of Locke and Hume he might also have said of Galileo, Newton, and Lavoisier. What each of them said was well argued, useful, and true. But the sort of truth that is the product of successful argument cannot, Shelley thought, improve our moral condition. Of Galileo's and Locke's productions we may reasonably ask "Yes, but is it true?" But there is little point, Shelley rightly thought, in asking this question about Milton. "Objectively true," in the sense of "such as to gain permanent assent from all future members of the relevant expert culture," is not a notion that will ever be useful to literary intellectuals, for the progress of the literary imagination is not a matter of accumulating *results*.

We philosophers who are accused of not having sufficient respect for objective truth—the ones whom the materialist metaphysicians like to call "postmodern relativists"—think of objectivity as inter-subjectivity. So we can happily agree that scientists achieve objective truth in a way that litterateurs do not. But we explain this phenomenon sociologically rather than philosophically—by pointing out that natural scientists are organized into expert cultures in a way that literary intellectuals should not try to organize themselves. You can have an expert culture if you agree on what you want to get, but not if you are wondering what sort of life you ought to desire. We know what purposes scientific theories are supposed to serve. But we are not now, and never will be, in a position to say what purposes novels, poems, and plays are supposed to serve. For such books continually redefine our purposes.

5 The Literary Culture and Democratic Politics

So far I have said nothing about the relation of the literary culture to politics. I shall close by turning to that topic. For the quarrel between those who see the rise of the literary culture as a good thing and those who see it as a bad thing is largely a quarrel about what sort of high culture will do the most to create and sustain the climate of tolerance that flourishes best in democratic societies.

Those who argue that a science-centered culture is best for this purpose, set the love of truth against hatred, passion, prejudice, superstition, and all the other forces of unreason from which Socrates and Plato claimed that philosophy could save us. But those on the other side of the argument are dubious about the Platonic opposition between reason and unreason. They see no need to relate the difference between tolerant conversability and stiff-necked unwillingness to hear the other side to a distinction between a higher part of ourselves that enables us to achieve redemption by getting in touch with nonhuman reality and another part that is merely animal.

The strong point of those who think that a proper respect for objective truth, and thus for science, is important for sustaining a climate of tolerance and good will is that argument is essential to both science and democracy. Both when choosing between alternative scientific theories and when choosing between alternative pieces of legislation, we want people to base their decisions on arguments—arguments that start from premises that can be made plausible to anyone who cares to look into the matter.

The priests rarely provided such arguments, nor do the literary intellectuals. So it is tempting to think of a preference for literature over science as a rejection of argument in favor of oracular pronouncements—a regression to something uncomfortably like the prephilosophical, religious, stage of Western intellectual life. Seen from this perspective, the rise of a literary culture looks like the treason of the clerks.

But those of us who rejoice in the emergence of the literary culture can counter this charge by saying that although argumentation is essential for projects of social cooperation, redemption is an individual, private, matter. Just as the rise of religious toleration depended on making a distinction between the needs of society and the needs of the individual, and on saying that religion was not necessary for the former, so the literary culture asks us to disjoin political deliberation from projects of redemption. This means acknowledging that private hopes for authenticity and autonomy should be left at home when the citizens of a democratic society foregather to deliberate about what is to be done.

Making this move amounts to saying: the only way in which science is relevant to politics is that the natural scientists provide a good example of social cooperation, of an expert culture in which argumentation flourishes. They thereby provide a model for political deliberation—a model of honesty, tolerance, and trust. This ability is a matter of procedure rather than results, which is why gangs of carpenters or teams of engineers can provide as good a model as do departments of astrophysics. The difference between reasoned agreement on how to solve a problem that has arisen in the course of constructing a house or a bridge, and reasoned agreement on what physicists sometimes call "a theory of everything" is, in this context, irrelevant. For whatever the last theory of everything tells us, it will do nothing to provide either political guidance or individual redemption.

The claim I have just made may seem arrogant and dogmatic, for it is certainly the case that some results of empirical inquiry have, in the past, made a difference to our self-image. Galileo and Darwin expelled various varieties of spooks by showing the sufficiency of a materialist account. They thereby made it much easier for us to move from a religious high culture to a secular, merely philosophical one. So my argument on behalf of the literary culture depends on the claim that getting rid of spooks, of causal agency that does not supervene on the behavior of elementary particles, has exhausted the utility of natural science for either redemptive or political purposes.

I do not put this claim forward as a result of philosophical reasoning or insight, but merely as a prediction about what the future holds in store. A similar prediction led the philosophers of the eighteenth century to think that the Christian religion had done about all that it could for the moral condition of humanity, and that it was time to put religion behind us and to put metaphysics, either idealist or materialist, in its place. When literary intellectuals assume that natural science has nothing to offer us except an edifying example of tolerant conversability, they are doing something analogous to what the *philosophes* did when they said that even the best of the priests had nothing to offer us save edifying examples of charity and decency. Reducing science from a possible source of redemptive truth to a model of rational cooperation is the contemporary analogue of the reduction of the Gospels from a recipe for attaining eternal happiness to a compendium of sound moral advice. That was the sort of reduction that Kant and Jefferson recommended, and that liberal Protestants of the last two centuries have gradually achieved.

To put this last point another way: both the Christian religion and materialist metaphysics turned out to be self-consuming artifacts. The need for religious orthodoxy was undermined by Saint Paul's insistence on the primacy of love, and by the gradual realization that a religion of love could not ask everyone to recite the same creed. The need for a metaphysics was undermined by the ability of modern science to see the human mind as an exceptionally complex nervous system and thus to see itself in pragmatic rather than metaphysical terms. Science showed us how to see empirical inquiry as the use of this extra physiological equipment to gain steadily greater mastery over the environment, rather than as a way of replacing appearance with reality. Just as the eighteenth century became able to see Christianity not as a revelation from on high but as continuous with Socratic reflection, so the twentieth century became able to see natural science not as revealing the intrinsic nature of reality but as continuous with the sort of practical problem solving that both beavers and carpenters are good at.

To give up the idea that there is an intrinsic nature of reality to be discovered either by the priests, or the philosophers, or the scientists, is to disjoin the need for redemption from the search for universal agreement. It is to give up the search for an accurate account of human nature, and thus for a recipe for leading the good life for man. Once these searches are given up, expanding the limits of the human imagination steps forward to assume the role that obedience to the divine will played in a religious culture, and the role that the discovery of what is really real played in a philosophical culture. But this substitution is no reason to give up the search for a single utopian form of political life—the good global society.

6 The "Decadence" of a Literary Culture

I have now said all I can to counter the claim that the rise of the literary culture is a relapse into irrationality, and that a proper respect for the ability of science to achieve objective truth is essential to the morale of a democratic society. But a related claim, much vaguer and harder to pin down, has been even more influential. This is that a literary culture is *decadent*—that it lacks the healthy-mindedness and vigor common to proselytizing Christians, science-worshipping positivists, and Marxist revolutionaries. A high culture centered around literature, one that wishes not to get things right but to make things new, will, it is often said, be a culture of languid and self-involved aesthetes.

The best rebuttal to this suggestion is Oscar Wilde's "The Soul of Man Under Socialism." The message of that essay parallels those of Mill's *On Liberty* and of Rawls's *A Theory of Justice*. It is that the only

point of getting rid of the priests and the kings, of setting up democratic governments, of taking from each according to her abilities
and giving to each according to her needs, and of thereby creating
the Good Global Society, is to make it possible for people to lead
the sort of lives they prefer, as long as their doing so does not diminish the opportunities of other humans to do the same thing. As
Wilde put it "Socialism itself will be of value simply because it will
lead to Individualism."[9] Part of Wilde's point is that there can be
no objection to self-involved aesthetes—that is to say, people whose
passion is to explore the present limits of the human imagination—
as long as they do not use more than their fair share of the social
product.

This claim itself, however, strikes many people as decadent. We
were not, they would urge, put on this earth to enjoy ourselves,
but to do the right thing. Socialism, they think, would not stir our
hearts were it no more than a means to individualism, or if the goal
of proletarian revolution were merely to make it possible for everybody to become a bourgeois intellectual. This sense that human
existence has some point other than pleasure is what keeps the
battle between Mill and Kant alive in courses on moral philosophy,
just as the sense that natural science must have some point other
than practical problem solving keeps the struggle between Kuhn
and his opponents alive in courses in philosophy of science. Mill
and Kuhn—and, more generally, utilitarians and pragmatists—are
still suspected of letting down the side, diminishing human dignity,
reducing our noblest aspirations to self-indulgent stimulation of
our favorite clusters of neurons.

The antagonism between those who think, with Schiller and
Wilde, that human beings are at their best when at play, and those
who think that they are at their best when they strive, seems to me
at the bottom of the conflicts that have marked the rise of the literary culture. Once again, I would urge that these conflicts be seen
as recapitulating those that marked the transition from religion to
philosophy. In that earlier transition, the people who thought that
a human life that did not strive for perfect obedience to the divine
will was a relapse into animality faced off against those who thought
that the ideal of such submission was unworthy of beings who could

think for themselves. In the current transition, the people who think that we need to hang onto Kantian ideas like "the moral law" and "things as they are in themselves" are facing off against people who think that these ideas are symptoms of insufficient self-reliance, of a self-deluding attempt to find dignity in the acceptance of bondage and freedom in the recognition of constraint.

The only way to resolve this sort of quarrel, it seems to me, is to say that the kinds of people to whom a utopian society would give the resources and the leisure to do their individualistic thing will include Kantian strivers as well as self-involved aesthetes, people who cannot live without religion and people who despise it, nature's metaphysicians as well as nature's pragmatists. For in this utopia, as Rawls has said, there will be no need for people to agree on the point of human existence, the good life for man, or any other topic of similar generality.

If people who heartily disagree about such issues can agree to cooperate in the functioning of the practices and institutions that have, in Wilde's words, "substituted cooperation for competition,"[10] that will suffice. The Kant versus Mill issue, like the issue between metaphysicians and pragmatists, will seem as little worth quarreling about as will the issue between the believers and the atheists. For we humans need not agree about the nature or the end of man in order to help facilitate our neighbor's ability to act on her own convictions on these matters, just so long as those actions do not interfere with our freedom to act on our own convictions.

In short, just as we have, in the past few centuries, learned that the difference of opinion between the believer and the atheist does not have to be settled before the two can cooperate on communal projects, so we may learn to set aside all the differences between all the various searches for redemption when we cooperate to build Wilde's utopia. In that utopia, the literary culture will not be the only, or even the dominant, form of high culture.

That is because there will be *no* dominant form. High culture will no longer be thought of as the place where the aim of the society as a whole is debated and decided, and where it is a matter of social concern which sort of intellectual is ruling the roost. Nor will there be much concern about the gap that yawns between popular culture, the culture of people who have never felt the need for redemption, and the high culture of the intellectuals—the people who are always wanting to be something more or different than they presently are. In utopia, the religious or philosophical need to live up to the nonhuman, and the need of the literary intellectuals to explore the present limits of the human imagination will be viewed as matters of taste. They will be viewed by nonintellectuals in the same relaxed, tolerant, and uncomprehending way that we presently regard our neighbor's obsession with bird watching, or collecting hubcaps, or discovering the secrets of the great pyramids.

To get along in utopia, however, the literary intellectuals will have to tone down their rhetoric. Certain passages in Wilde will not bear repeating, as when he speaks of "the poets, the philosophers, the men of science, the men of culture—in a word, the real men, the men who have realized themselves, and in whom all humanity gains a partial realization."[11] The idea that some men are more really men than others contradicts Wilde's own better wisdom, as when he says "There is no one type for man. There are as many perfections as there are imperfect men."[12] The same words might have been written by Nietzsche, but to take them seriously we must actively forget Zarathustra's contempt for the "last men," the men who feel no need for redemption. In utopia, the literary culture will have learned not to give itself airs. It will no longer feel the temptation to make invidious and quasi-metaphysical distinctions between real and less real men.

To sum up, I am suggesting that we see the literary culture as itself a self-consuming artifact, and perhaps the last of its kind. For in utopia the intellectuals will have given up the idea that there is a standard against which the products of the human imagination can be measured other than their social utility, as this utility is judged by a maximally free, leisured, and tolerant global community. They will have stopped thinking that the human imagination is getting somewhere, that there is one far off cultural event toward which all cultural creation moves. They will have given up the identification of redemption with the attainment of perfection. They will have taken fully to heart the maxim that it is the journey that matters.

Notes

1. Richard Bernstein, *The New Constellation: The Ethical-Political Horizons of Modernity/Postmodernity* (Cambridge: Polity Press, 1991), pp. 233–234. Page references to this edition in the text are preceded by *NC.*

2. John Dewey, *Reconstruction in Philosophy* (Boston, Mass.: Beacon Press, 1948), and *The Public and Its Problems* (Chicago, Ill.: Gateway Books, 1946); Jürgen Habermas, *Philosophical Discourse of Modernity: Twelve Lectures*, trans. Frederick Lawrence (Cambridge, Mass.: The MIT Press, 1987), and *Between Facts and Norms*, trans. William Rehg (Cambridge, Mass.: The MIT Press, 1996).

3. Harold Bloom, *How to Read and Why* (New York: Scribner, 2000).

4. Martin Heidegger, *Sein und Zeit* (Tübingen: Max Niemeyer Verlag, 1967), pp. 167–173. See the discussions of *das Gerede* and *die Neugier* in sections 35–36.

5. George Santayana, "The Absence of Religion in Shakespeare" (1900) in *Interpretations of Poetry and Religion*, ed. William G. Holzberger and Herman J. Saatkamp Jr. (Cambridge, Mass.: The MIT Press, 1990), pp. 91–101.

6. Percy Bysshe Shelley, "A Defense of Poetry" (1821) in *The Major Works*, ed. Zachary Leader and Michael O'Neill (Oxford: Oxford University Press, 2003), p. 701.

7. Søren Kierkegaard, *Papers and Journals: A Selection*, trans. Alastair Hannay (London: Penguin, 1996), p. 182.

8. Shelley, *Major Works*, p. 695.

9. Oscar Wilde, "The Soul of Man Under Socialism" (1891) in *The Complete Works of Oscar Wilde* (London: Collins, 1966), p. 1080.

10. Ibid.

11. Ibid.

12. Ibid., p. 1087.

2

The Moral and the Ethical: A Reconsideration of the Issue of the Priority of the Right over the Good

Jürgen Habermas

The context of a "festschrift," dedicated to a personal and philosophical friend, provides the author with a license for starting with a fond recollection. In 1972, during a stay at the Center for Humanities in Middletown, I received a telephone call with a surprising invitation that brought me to Haverford to meet Dick for the first time. On the other end of the line, the warm, spontaneous, and suggestive voice of a colleague, who had read *Knowledge and Human Interests*, assured me that the two of us would share essential philosophical concerns. That unexpected visit did, indeed, lead to my first encounter with the exemplary incarnation of a spirit that I had no longer expected to be alive in the United States.

Only a few years before I had visited American philosophy departments that were still under the spell of either Carnap and his followers or the British followers of Wittgenstein. At those places K.-O. Apel's and my American hero, Charles Sanders Peirce, was remembered as "odd" at best, while Dewey was perceived as a "fuzzy thinker."[1] At Haverford, however, I now met—even before glancing at his recently published book, *Praxis and Action*[2]—a living example of pragmatism. Not just of the kind of naturalized *Kantian* pragmatism, though, that I had in mind at the time. Dick Bernstein immediately started teaching me the right kind of detranscendentalized *Hegelian* pragmatism, with an Aristotelian touch of his own. And he continued that pedagogical treatment more or less successfully when I returned to Haverford for a term several years later: He admonished me not to stick to fixed distinctions and pushed me to exercise what then came to be known as the deconstruction of conceptual oppositions.

Dick is a great teacher, even if I haven't learned all of his lessons. From a historical point of view, he is the one who comes closest to the original spirit of pragmatism, closer than my two other pragmatist friends who I fortunately became acquainted with a bit later. Among these two friends, by Dewey's standards at least, Larry Kohlberg retained too much and Richard Rorty too little of the cognitivist heritage of German idealism, of which Dick Bernstein has always remained aware. In spite of his deep American roots, Dick's open and receptive attitude toward European philosophy, more specifically his steady interest in the works of Hannah Arendt and Hans-Georg Gadamer, and his engagement with the Marxian tradition of critical social theory, have shaped the distinctive intellectual physiognomy of an interpreter who is famous for his hermeneutic skills and his unfailing sense of fairness.

Though I have always felt a strong convergence of the ideas both he and I pursue, Dick Bernstein has never hesitated to pinpoint and discuss our differences. The controversy always circles around the issue of how to use differences that make a difference—and how to deflate clear cut conceptual distinctions, in the first place Kantian distinctions between form and content, the right and the good, justification and application, procedure and substance: "Rather than serving to clarify relevant issues, some of these hard and fast distinctions actually obscure more than they illuminate. It is the reification of distinctions that are, and ought to be, fluid, open, and flexible that troubles me."[3]

Let me use this occasion for continuing our discussion. I will first repeat (one version of) the thesis of the priority of the Right over the Good and then cast a second look on one of Bernstein's objections.[4] Kierkegaard will then serve as a guide to the kinds of ethics, both political and existential, that are compatible with a postmetaphysical mode of thought. Bernstein's reflection on "radical evil" will finally provide a cue for a reconsideration of the supposedly formal nature of our postmetaphysical ethical self-understanding.

I Justice and the Good Life: The Modern View

As long as philosophers still had faith in their ability to discuss
the whole of nature and history, they still assumed authority for
telling some sort of grand narratives into which the human life of
individuals and communities had to fit. The order of the cosmos
and human nature, the stages of secular and sacred history provided normatively laden facts that, so it seemed, could also disclose
the right way to live. Here "right" had the exemplary sense of an
imitation-worthy model for living, both for the life of the individual
and for the political community. Just as the great religions present
their founders' way of life as the path to salvation, so also metaphysics offered its models of life—for the select few, of course,
who did not follow the crowd. The doctrines of the good life and
of a just society—ethics and politics—made up a harmonious
whole. But with the acceleration of social change, the life spans of
these models of the good life have become increasingly shorter—
whether they were aimed at the Greek polis, the estates of the
medieval *societas civilis*, the well-rounded individual of the urban
Renaissance or, as with Hegel, at the system of family, civil society,
and constitutional monarchy.

Rawls's political liberalism marks the endpoint of this development, precisely as a response to the pluralism of worldviews and to
the spreading individualization of lifestyles. Surveying the rubble of
philosophical attempts to designate *particular* ways of life as exemplary or universally obligatory, Rawls draws the proper conclusion:
that the "just society" ought to leave it to individuals to choose how
to live. It guarantees to each an equal freedom to develop an ethical
self-understanding, so as to realize a personal conception of the
"good life" according to one's own abilities and choices.

It is certainly true that individual life-projects do not emerge
independently of intersubjectively shared life-contexts. However, in
complex societies one culture can assert itself against other cultures
only by convincing its succeeding generations—who can also say
no—of the advantages of its world-disclosing semantic and action-
orienting power. "Nature reserves" for cultures are neither possible
nor desirable. In a constitutional democracy the majority may also

not prescribe for minorities aspects of its own cultural form of life (beyond the common political culture of the country) by claiming for its culture an authoritative guiding function (as *Leitkultur*).

As the foregoing remarks indicate, practical philosophy by no means renounces all of its normative concerns. At the same time, it does restrict itself, by and large, to questions of justice. In particular, its aim is to clarify the moral point of view from which we judge norms and actions whenever we must determine what lies in the equal interest of everyone and what is equally good for all. At first glance, moral theory and ethics appear to be oriented to the same question: What ought I, or what ought we, to do? But the "ought" has a different sense once we are no longer asking about rights and duties that everyone ascribes to one another from an inclusive "we" perspective, but instead are concerned with our own life from the first-person perspective and ask what is best "for me" or "for us" in the long run and all things considered. Such ethical questions regarding our own weal and woe arise in the context of a *particular* life history or a *unique* form of life. They are wedded to questions of identity: how we should understand ourselves, who we are and want to be. Obviously there is no answer to such questions that would be independent of the given context and thus would bind all persons in the same way.

Consequently, theories of justice and morality take their own separate path today, at least a path different from that of "ethics," if we understand this in the classical sense of a doctrine of the right way to live. The moral point of view obliges us to abstract from those exemplary pictures of a successful or undamaged life that have been handed on in the grand narratives of metaphysics and religion. Our existential self-understanding can still continue to draw its nourishment from the substance of these traditions just as it always did, but philosophy no longer has the right to intervene in this struggle of gods and demons. Precisely with regard to the questions that have the greatest relevance for us, philosophy retires to a metalevel and investigates only the formal properties of processes of self-understanding, without taking a position on the contents themselves. That may be unsatisfying, but who can object to such a well-justified reluctance?

To be sure, moral theory pays a high price for its division of labor with an ethics that specializes in the forms of existential self-understanding: it thereby dissolves the context that first linked moral judgments with the motivation toward right actions. Moral insights effectively bind the will only when they are embedded in an ethical self-understanding that joins the concern about one's own well-being with the interest in justice. Deontological theories after Kant may be very good at explaining how to ground and apply moral norms; but they still are unable to answer the question of why we should be moral *at all*. Political theories are likewise unable to answer the question of why the citizens of a democratic polity, when they disagree about the principles of their living together, should orient themselves toward the common good—and not rather satisfy themselves with a strategically negotiated modus vivendi. Theories of political justice that have been uncoupled from a thick ethical context can only *hope* that processes of socialization and political forms of life meet them halfway.

At this point Bernstein raises his objection against the rigid distinction between thin principles of a "political conception of justice" on one side, and the thick value contexts of the political community's shared "ethical life" on the other side. He critically compares the *proceduralist* notion of a democratic process—presented as the sole source of political legitimation—with Dewey's *substantive* conception, and arrives at the conclusion that a discourse theory of law and democracy (as developed in my *Between Facts and Norms*)[5] must tacitly presuppose a substantial notion of a democratic form of ethical life:

Dewey ... is most concerned with "the means by which a majority comes to be a majority," that is, with the public debate, discussion, and persuasion that precedes and influences this voting practice. We can, of course, call this complex process "procedural" ... because, even after the most responsible and enlightened discussion, it is still an open question as to which substantive decisions will be made by majority rule. It is here that the crucial ambiguity arises, for this is a very different sense of procedure. Such a procedure involves substantial-ethical commitments. When Dewey speaks about "debate, discussion and persuasion," he is not simply referring to formal rules of communication, rather his major concern is with the ethos of such a debate. For democratic debate, ideally, requires a *will-*

ingness to listen to and evaluate the opinions of one's opponents, *respecting* the views of minorities, advancing arguments *in good faith* to support one's convictions with new evidence or better arguments. There is an ethos involved in the practice of democratic debate.[6]

On a weak interpretation, this means that the *stability* of any democratic process depends on the context of a liberal political culture and on the value orientations of a population that is already accustomed to the use of political freedoms. Such a reading of the democratic ethos would not challenge the priority of the Right over the Good. *In the order of justification*, it is still the other way around: The political ethos of a democratic community is designed for complementing the legal implementation of constitutional principles with a shared cultural form of life that meets certain cognitive and motivational requirements: "We might even say that the practice of debate in a democratic polity requires the democratic transformation and appropriation of classic virtues: practical wisdom, justice, courage, and moderation."[7]

Democratic theory thus provides a posttraditional conception for the political ethos in a similar way as existentialism did for an ethical life of the individual person. Both conceptions are analogues with regard to the premises of postmetaphysical thought they fit.

II A Theological Approach to Modern Ethics

Kierkegaard was the first philosopher who answered the basic ethical question regarding the success or failure of one's own life with a postmetaphysical concept of "being-able-to-be-oneself." In his engagement with Hegel's speculative thought, Kierkegaard answered the question of the right way to live with an answer that was indeed *postmetaphysical*, and at the same time *theological.* Kierkegaard's philosophical descendents—Heidegger, Jaspers, and Sartre—found a radical Protestant's obsession with a merciful God a bit much. But these existentialist philosophers who were committed to one or the other kind of methodological atheism recognized Kierkegaard as a thinker who revived the ethical question in the most innovative manner and provided an answer that was sufficiently formal—that is, sufficiently formal in view of a legitimate pluralism of worldviews that prohibits any form of paternalism in the area of genuinely ethical advice. The Kierkegaard of *Either/Or*, with his concept of the "ethical stage" of existence, offered the natural point of connection.

In contrast to the romantic picture of an egocentrically playful form of life that is lazily carried along by the present moment and dominated by reflected pleasure, Kierkegaard opposes an ethically resolute conduct of life. The latter demands that I *gather* myself and detach myself from the dependencies of an overwhelming environment, jolting myself to the awareness of my individuality and freedom. Once I am emancipated from a self-induced objectification, I also gain distance from myself as an individual. I pull myself out from the anonymous, scattered life that is breathlessly disintegrating into fragments and give my life continuity and transparency. In the social dimension, such a person can assume responsibility for his or her own actions and can enter into binding commitments with others. In the temporal dimension, concern for oneself makes one conscious of the historicity of an existence that is realized in the simultaneously interpenetrating horizons of future and past.

Kierkegaard assumes that, as a self-consciously existing individual, one continuously gives an account of one's life in light of moral standards. He does not waste many words on standards that found secular expression in Kant's egalitarian universalism. Rather, all his attention is on the structure of the ability to be oneself, that is, on the form of an ethical self-reflection and self-choice that is determined by the infinite interest in the success of one's own life project. With a view toward future possibilities of action, the individual self-critically appropriates the past of his factually given, concretely re-presented life history. Only then does he make himself into a person who speaks for himself, an irreplaceable individual.

Such an individual regrets the reproachable aspects of his past life and resolves to continue only in those ways of acting in which he can recognize himself without shame. In this way, he articulates the self-understanding of the person he would like others to know and acknowledge. Through a morally scrupulous evaluation and critically probing appropriation of his factually given life history, he constitutes himself as the person he both is and would like to be:

"Everything that is posited in his freedom belongs to him essentially, however accidental it may seem to be.... This distinction is not a product of his arbitrariness so that he might seem to have absolute power to make himself into what it pleased him to be.... To be sure, the ethical individual dares to employ the expression that he is his own editor, but he is also fully aware that he is responsible, responsible for himself personally,... responsible to the order of things in which he lives, responsible to God."[8]

Kierkegaard is convinced that the ethical form of existence produced by one's own efforts can be stabilized only in the relation of the believer to God. As long as we ground morality as the standard for self-scrutiny in human knowledge (as in the Socratic or Kantian approaches), the motivation for converting moral judgments into practice is lacking. Kierkegaard objects not so much to the cognitive meaning of morality as to its intellectualistic misunderstanding. If morality could move the will of the knowing subject *solely* through good reasons, then we could not explain that desolate condition against which Kierkegaard as critic of the contemporary age directed his barbs again and again—the condition of an enlightened and morally self-righteous, but deeply corrupt Christian society: "It is tragic-comic to see that all this knowledge and understanding exercises no power at all over men's lives."[9]

The cynical acceptance of an unjust world, the normality of repression for so many people, is evidence not of a deficit in *knowledge* but of a corruption of the *will*. The human beings who could know better do not *want* to understand. For this reason, Kierkegaard does not speak of guilt, but of sin. However, as soon as we interpret guilt as sin, we know that we have need of forgiveness and that we must set our hope on an absolute power that can intervene retroactively in the course of history and can *restore* the wounded order as well as the integrity of the victims. The promise of salvation forms the motivating connection between an unconditionally demanding morality and care for oneself. A postconventional morality of conscience can become the seed around which a conscious life conduct thus can crystallize only if it is embedded in a religious self-understanding. Kierkegaard develops the problem of motivation over and against Socrates and Kant in order to go beyond both of them and arrive at Christ.

To be sure, Climacus—Kierkegaard's pseudonymous author of *Philosophical Fragments*—is not at all sure that the Christian message of redemption, which he considers hypothetically as a "project" for thought, is "more true" than the immanent thinking that moves within the postmetaphysical boundaries of neutrality toward worldviews.[10] Thus, Kierkegaard presents Anticlimacus as one who does not try to compel his secular counterpart with argument but aims rather to induce him with the help of a psychological phenomenology "to go beyond Socrates."

Drawing on symptomatic forms of life, Kierkegaard describes the visible forms of a healing "sickness unto death"—the patterns of a despair that is initially repressed, then creeps into awareness, and finally forces conversion on an ego-centered consciousness. These forms of despair are so many manifestations of the lack of a fundamental relationship that alone could make an authentic being-oneself possible. Kierkegaard depicts the unsettling condition of a person who is indeed aware of her destiny, that she must be a self, but thereupon flees into the alternatives: "in despair not to will to be oneself. Or even lower: in despair not to will to be a self. Or lowest of all: in despair to will to be someone else."[11] The one who finally realizes that the despair has its source not in circumstances but in one's own flight responses will make the defiant, but equally unsuccessful attempt "to will to be oneself." The hopeless failure of this last act of will—the stubborn wanting to be oneself entirely on the basis of one's own resources—pushes finite spirit to transcend itself and recognize its dependence on an Other as the ground of its own freedom.

This conversion marks the turning point in the movement of overcoming the secularized self-understanding of modern reason. Kierkegaard describes this rebirth with the help of a formulation that recalls the opening paragraphs of Fichte's *Wissenschaftslehre,* yet at the same time inverts the autonomous sense of the deed [*Tathandlung*] into its opposite: "In relating itself to itself and in willing to be itself, the self rests transparently in the power that established it."[12] The fundamental relation that makes being oneself possible as the form of right living thereby becomes visible. Although the literal reference to a "power" as the ground of being-able-to-be-oneself *need not* be understood in a religious sense,

Kierkegaard insists that the human spirit can arrive at a right understanding of its finite existence only through the awareness of sin: the self exists authentically only in the presence of God. The self survives the stages of hopeless despair only in the form of a believer, who by relating herself to herself relates to an absolutely Other to whom she owes everything.[13]

Kierkegaard emphasizes that we cannot form any consistent concept of God—neither *via eminentiae* nor *via negationis*. Each idealization remains captive to the basic predicates from which the operation of intensification takes its point of departure. And the attempt of the understanding to characterize the absolutely Other by negating all finite determinations fails for the same reason: "The understanding cannot even think the absolutely different; it cannot absolutely negate itself but uses itself for that purpose and consequently thinks the difference in itself."[14] The chasm between knowing and believing cannot be bridged by thought.

III Moral Self-Understanding as Responsible Persons—A "Freestanding" Conception?

Kierkegaard's philosophical followers naturally find this point annoying. To be sure, even "Socratic" thinkers who cannot invoke revealed truths can follow the suggestive phenomenology of the "sickness unto death" and can agree that finite spirit depends on enabling conditions beyond its control. The ethically conscious conduct of life should not be understood as narrow-minded self-empowerment. They could also agree with Kierkegaard that we should not understand this dependence on a power beyond our control in naturalistic terms, but above all as an interpersonal relation. For the defiance of a rebellious person who finally "in despair wills to be herself" is directed—as defiance—against a second person. Under the premises of postmetaphysical thinking, however, that "power beyond us"—on which we subjects, capable of speech and action, depend in our concern not to fail to lead worthwhile lives—cannot be identified with "the God in time."

The linguistic turn toward a deflationary interpretation of the "wholly Other" shows a way out of this impasse. As historical and social beings we find ourselves always already in a linguistically structured life-world. In the forms of communication through which we reach an understanding with one another about something in the world and about ourselves, we encounter a transcending power. Language is not a kind of private property: no one possesses exclusive rights over the common medium of those communicative practices we share intersubjectively. No single participant can control the structure, or even the course, of processes of reaching understanding and self-understanding. How speakers and hearers make use of their communicative freedom to take yes or no positions is not a matter of their discretion. For they are free only in virtue of the binding force of the justifiable claims they raise toward one another. The *logos* of language embodies the power of the intersubjective, which precedes and grounds the subjectivity of speakers.

This weak proceduralist reading of the "Other" preserves the fallibilist as well as the antiskeptical meaning of the "unconditioned." The *logos* of language escapes our control, and yet we, the subjects capable of speech and action, are the ones who reach an understanding with one another through this medium: language remains "our" language. The unconditional meaning of truth and freedom is a necessary presupposition of our linguistic practices, but beyond the constituents of "our" form of life they lack any ontological guarantee. Similarly, the "right" ethical self-understanding is neither revealed nor "given" in some other way. It can only be achieved or renewed in a common endeavor. From this perspective, what makes our being-ourselves possible appears more as a transsubjective power than an absolute one.

Even if we allow for such a postreligious perspective, Kierkegaard's postmetaphysical ethics still permits us to evaluate a misspent as distinguished from not unsuccessful life. His general statements about the modes of being-able-to-be-oneself are formal —that is, they are not *thick* descriptions—and yet contain normative content. Because this ethics judges the existential *mode*, not the particular value orientations, of individual life-projects and specific forms of life, it satisfies the condition of a pluralism of worldviews. The same is true for the kind of equally formal democratic ethos that offers itself as the political counterpart to an existentialist ethos of the individual person. Since an intersubjectively shared ethos of the political community must equally meet the fact of pluralism, Bernstein insists on the "thin" character of the "dispositions and virtues required for engaging in democratic procedural practices."[15]

The argument for a postconventional kind of ethics in both, the existential and the political dimension, does not yet challenge, in the order of justification, the priority of the Right over the Good. It does not, therefore, quite explain Bernstein's Hegelian furor against the reification of distinctions "that ought to be fluid, open, and flexible." In other words, the argument developed so far does not exhaust the reasons for crossing the boundaries between form and content, procedure and substance. There must be more than just considerations of motivation and stability behind the claim that political justice and morality need roots in a democratic ethos or in a self-conscious mode of being-oneself. The postmetaphysical abstention from grounding universalist moral claims in ethical contexts runs up against its limits only when questions of a "species ethics" [*Gattungsethik*] arise. As soon as the modern moral *cum* ethical self-understanding is at stake *in its entirety*, philosophy can no longer avoid taking a more substantive position.

I have pursued this idea in view of some possible consequences of a scientistic, naturalist self-conception of *Homo sapiens*. Such an alternative self-understanding of us as members of the human species would lift moral constraints on a kind of enhancing genetic engineering that might become available in the future. Spreading practices of genetic modification could induce the habit of "co-authoring future lives" and thereby inconspicuously shift the self-understanding of persons and political communities as responsible authors of their own lives or their shared forms of life. For as soon as adults treat the desirable genetic traits of their descendents as a product they can design according to their own preferences, they are exercising a kind of control over their offspring that intervenes in the naturally fixed ranges of opportunities and scopes for possible decision within which the future person will one day use her freedom to give her own life its ethical shape.[16]

This thought experiment is meant to reveal possible alternatives in the self-understanding of us as human beings that are no longer consistent with what I take to constitute the "modern" self-understanding of persons (and citizens) who live in the awareness of an expectation of ethical self-determination and moral responsibility. The fact that there are such alternatives in no way proves that the *validity* of our conception of morality (and political justice)—of what we "ought to" do and "owe" to one another—depends on a species-specific ethical image of "us as humans." Universalist and egalitarian concepts of moral autonomy and human dignity (the core of human rights and democracy) are "freestanding" in view of their justification. Those alternative "identities" make us, instead, aware of the fact that the embedding in an appropriate environment of species-ethical beliefs *helps to stabilize* our modern self-understanding as moral persons (and democratic citizens), once they are seriously challenged—not by fundamentalist but by modern, and yet categorically different, self-images.

What interests me in the present context is the fact that, in view of competing species-ethical beliefs that contradict our entire moral cum ethical self-understanding, the question of stabilization assumes a cognitive ring: against a hard-boiled scientistic naturalism that aims to replace our normative vocabulary as a whole, some of us start to *argue* for an image of us as rule-following and reason-giving creatures—creatures who are dependent on sociality, and committed to discursive practices, and who are sensitive to the violation of normative expectations and care for the "yes" or "no" of others. However, these arguments are of an "ethical" kind—evaluations rather than straight normative arguments. We look for reasons *why we should prefer* to live rather in a universe of legitimately ordered interpersonal relationships than in a moral vacuum.

Reading Bernstein's ingenious interpretation of Kant's conception of radical evil,[17] it came to my mind that a similar move can be motivated even from within the moral point of view. The profound reflection on a *malignant reason* and the diabolical mind who freely adopts a lasting disposition, a *Gesinnung*, to repudiate the moral law consistently leads Bernstein to the conclusion that the ultimate ground for the choice between good and evil is inscrutable: "We want to know why it is that some individuals choose evil and others resist it. ... But it never adds up to a complete explanation of why individuals make the choices they do. There is always a gap, a 'black hole,' in our accounts."[18] Kant's reinterpretation of Original Sin is only the shadow of the abyss of freedom.

There is no denying this deep insight. However, as soon as we turn away from an individual person's choice and ask why we human beings cannot *want* the devilish person's maxim of "doing evil for its own sake" to spread, or, more to the point, why it is not *desirable* for us to live in a universe of moral indifference—where, pace Kant, nobody would care anymore for the very distinction between good and bad—we do have answers. And again, these arguments for a form of life, not devoid of any moral and even cynical expectations, would not be moral arguments themselves, but ethical ones. On Kantian premises, such a final reversal of the priority of the Right over the Good can only come under consideration once we, unlike Kant, envisage the possibility of a challenge that questions, in future generations, the survival of the *entire* moral *cum* ethical self-understanding, as we know it.

Translated in part by William Rehg

Notes

1. Cf. my interview with M. Aboulafia, in *Habermas and Pragmatism*, ed. M. Aboulafia, M. Bookman, and C. Kemp (London: Routledge, 2002), pp. 225ff.

2. R. J. Bernstein, *Praxis and Action* (Philadelphia, Penn.: University of Pennsylvania Press, 1971).

3. R. J. Bernstein, "The Retrieval of the Democratic Ethos," in *Cardozo Law Review*, vol. 17, March 1996, 4, pp. 1127–1146, here p. 1128.

4. Cf. J. Habermas, Reply, *Cardozo Law Review*, vol. 17, March 1996, 5, pp. 1480–1485.

5. J. Habermas, *Between Facts and Norms* (Cambridge, Mass.: The MIT Press, 1996).

6. Bernstein, "The Retrieval of the Democratic Ethos," p. 1131.

7. Ibid.

8. Søren Kierkegaard, *Either/Or*, part 2, ed. and trans. H. V. Hong and E. H. Hong, in *Kierkegaard's Writings*, vol. 4 (Princeton, N.J.: Princeton University Press, 1987), p. 260.

9. Søren Kierkegaard, *The Sickness unto Death*, ed. and trans. H. V. Hong and E. H. Hong, in *Writings*, vol. 19 (Princeton, N.J.: Princeton University Press, 1980), p. 90.

10. Søren Kierkegaard, *Philosophical Fragments*, ed. and trans. H. V. Hong and E. H. Hong, in *Writings*, vol. 7 (Princeton, N.J.: Princeton University Press, 1985), p. 111.

11. Kierkegaard, *Sickness unto Death*, pp. 52–53.

12. Ibid., p. 14.

13. M. Theunissen, *Das Selbst auf dem Grund der Verzweiflung* (Frankfurt am Main: Athenäum, 1991).

14. Kierkegaard, *Philosophical Fragments*, p. 45.

15. Bernstein, "The Retrieval of the Democratic Ethos," p. 1136, note 20: "By 'thin' I mean those virtues and substantial-ethical convictions required for engaging in democratic debate, discussion, and persuasion. Exercising such virtues does not by itself determine the substantial ethical content of one's everyday life."

16. J. Habermas, *The Future of Human Nature*, (Cambridge: Polity Press, 2003).

17. R. J. Bernstein, *Radical Evil: A Philosophical Interrogation* (Cambridge: Polity Press, 2002), pp. 9–45.

18. Ibid., p. 235.

3

"... *Ergo sum*"—Between Poetry and Philosophy

Geoffrey Hartman

[P]hilosophy should only be written in the way poetry is.... [W]ith that statement I acknowledged that I was one who cannot quite do what he would like to be able to do.
—*Ludwig Wittgenstein*[1]

The World is not Conclusion.
—*Emily Dickinson*[2]

Political and psychological theories have often questioned unity of mind or introduced a more complex stratification of any such unity. An unconscious is posited, or a process of socialization that reveals a mediated self. We—the work of our hands, emotions, brains—do not belong entirely to ourselves. I—do not belong entirely to myself. At the same time, the pressure of the developmental ideal of personal autonomy has increased.

A tension therefore dominates political discourse when it comes to the relation of individual and collective. In a great deal of public speech at the academic level a rhetoric of positionality has taken hold, which tells us where the speaker is coming from. "I am a white, neo-Marxist, feminist student of popular literature," and so on. Hardly a topos of modesty, yet not quite an old-fashioned vaunt, it is difficult to know how to take such pronouncements. They wish to establish a sort of authenticity, in the sense of a self that coincides with itself: "This is what I am, at least this is what I presently recognize myself to be." The problem with such validation is to know whether the self, having defined itself to include, in a jumbled if imperative manner, collective determinants or markers, remains free to make a variety of similar claims. What would a change of mind mean, what kind of self-discovery or uncovering? A histrionic element, in any case, cannot be ruled out, even when it is not acknowledged, because of the presenter's wish to project strength of character in terms of a clearly asserted identity. Or has the concept of identity become little more than a sales ploy and trademark?[3]

Of course, if one learns by listening, observing, reading, speaking, in all due patience—the kind of patience literary criticism as well as philosophy, indeed all study, strives for—then the search for certainty in this area, or at least consistency, begins to appear as an infinite task. All positional assertions by "elaborately-/vested Angels of naked truth" (to adapt Geoffrey Hill's ironic words) would be open to qualification despite the hope for closure, and so excursive not just declarative.[4]

Even the most patient mind, however, might sympathize with Wittgenstein's identity statement when he resorts to a down-to-earth metaphor: "If I have exhausted the justifications I have reached bedrock, and my spade is turned. Then I am inclined to say: 'This is simply what I do'" (*Philosophical Investigations*, no. 217). The "pitch" of this saying, to borrow Stanley Cavell's musical and sporty metaphor,[5] seems quite different from the self-pronouncement with which I began. It is more iffy, less assertive, and with a tinge of resignation. "This is simply what I do" hovers between a philosophical minimalism (and we know how much installation space, paradoxically, minimalist artifacts demand), and a pragmatic acknowledgment that doing—whether it refers to one's professional activity generally, such as philosophizing, or, what may be the same for Wittgenstein, the dissolution of theories about what can be meaningfully said in searching for their ground (even a "cure of the ground")—is also a kind of being. Doing, in this sense, or thinking as an inquiry concerned with the use, or *praxis* rather than truth claim, of words,[6] leads Wittgenstein in two directions: toward an appreciation of nonphilosophic language as a "form of life" and toward seeing philosophy itself as a potential source of language abuse. It also encourages what Keats called "negative capability": the ability to refrain from "irritably reaching after fact and reason." Yet Keats admired an instinctual purposiveness. "I go among the Fields and catch a glimpse of a stoat or a fieldmouse peeping out of the withered grass—the creature has a purpose and its eyes are bright with it."[7] Is Wittgenstein's statement a philosophic shrug, when silence rather than speech seems appropriate, or is it something stronger: a form of witnessing, comparable to what Gerard Manley Hopkins describes in the poem that begins "As kingfishers catch fire, dragon flies draw flame"? Each mortal thing, Hopkins continues,

Deals out that being indoors each one dwells;
Selves—goes itself; *myself* it speaks and
                spells,
Crying *What I do is me: for that I came.*[8]

There is, of course, a difference close to incongruity between Wittgenstein's investigations and Hopkins's rendering of the creature's I am, I am. The double self-reference in *"What I do is me: for that I came"*[9] has an emphasis on "pitch" of self in clear contrast to the philosopher's disclaimer of a destined personal mission. But there is also a convergence between poet and philosopher, as the pressure to make a "bedrock" statement mounts from within speech and the nimbus (*Dunstkreis*) of words. The temptation of assertiveness, the "fieldmouse" force of everyday language in relation to philosophic or poetic diction, the coincidence or noncoincidence of saying and meaning, the difficulty of controlling inferences or associations, the possibility of symbolic action and questions about who is speaking and by what authority—these aspects of language use are with us daily, and not just in literature. That Wittgenstein's searches remain secular does not in the least affect the propriety of juxtaposing him with a poet of a similar, if religiously based and less curtained intensity, directed toward the ecphrastic as well as pragmatic functioning of words.[10]

Hopkins, in the sestet of "As Kingfishers catch fire," moves within and yet beyond the realm of the creatures. "Í say more: the just man justices...." What does that "more" imply? In the sestet doing is still related to being[11] but now passes from a strong redundance (an eloquent stutter, always felt in Hopkins's verse, as in its divine prototype "I am that I am") to action. The concordance between subject and predicate ("just ... justices") results in a further tautology linked to an assumption based on *human* witnessing, its higher-pitched, intimate relation to God.

The just person, Hopkins continues, "Acts in God's eye what in God's eye he is—/ Chríst...." This maintains—and escalates—a proposition about the creature's selved identity: again no distinction is made between doing and being. Human performance, here, either acts out or brings about the "is." The startling identification, moreover, of man with Christ (that word is placed in a most emphatic position, as if an imploration had become an assertion) reenforces a leap to a transcendent identity that transforms personality without cancelling it and implies an individuating principle beyond mortal existence. The common enough pun of "eye" and "I" is put to climactic use: from the perspective of both justice and grace God's I is enacted, humanly honored.

The clearest distinction between Wittgenstein and Hopkins suggested by these verses lies in the relation of being to being just, and also, by implication, justified. "Having exhausted the justifications" has no obvious religious connotation in Wittgenstein. The philosopher has done his best with the analytic equipment at his command. It is a tool; he has used it as well as he can, so that "my spade is turned."[12] Digging will get him no deeper. Perhaps there is an allusion to the famous concluding propositions of the *Tractatus* that set a limit to what can be said, though not to "showing." Moreover, if we associate showing with the making or *poiesis* of art, at least of art in the sense of a craft, as if its inwrought working were a more durable, more imaginative type of labor, and verse a rule-bound yet surprising use of words whose reason remains to be found, then both philosopher and poet would be moving toward a larger though still modest concept of *praxis*—in religious terms, justified work: "shéer plód makes plough down sillion/ Shine...."[13]

Thinking about the way words are used is a dialogue of one in Wittgenstein, close to an examination of conscience. He rarely cites interlocutors by name, although his prose incorporates their positions or objections. The received truths he struggles with are dissolved in the forge of his meditative aphorisms as well as elaborately dissected. Apodictic pronouncement mingles with provocative if controlled simile. Despite his adaptation, perhaps via Kierkegaard, of Boethius's *si tacuisset, philosophus mansisset*,[14] Wittgenstein does not give up being a witness to what is the case. Yet it is impossible (for this reader) to determine whether Wittgenstein's bedrock statement signals an impasse, or (to adopt his own, habitual metaphor) part of a propaedeutic clearing of the ground. If the latter, to what end is he creating a new blueprint or foundation plan? What can he build with his "I say less" whose implication is "I mean more, or more than I can say"? How different this stripped-down pragmatism is from that of a high-flyer like Emerson, who ends his essay, "Experience," with: "There is victory yet for all justice; and the truest romance which the world exists to realize will be the transformation of genius into practical power."

The accent, in any case, does not fall on the "I" as a word needing particular emphasis or scrutiny: egotisms may even get in the way of thoughts that wish to be other than confessional, so that the "I" remains a grammatical and abstract entity. Wittgenstein generally avoids psychologism, like many philosophers of his time on the European continent. When Hopkins, however, announces "Í say more," after his vivid account of the way creatures make themselves—their selves—known, the extra (metrical) stress on the first person intimates an explicit awareness. The poem selves the poet. His "nature," beyond that of the natures he has been describing, is linked to a *specifically generic* self—the figure of the poet—whose identity it is to "say more."

More than what? To reply "more than nature does" is a correct yet easy way out. For the poet's word is not incremental merely in the sense that humans are speaking animals. Poets fashion a qualitatively different sort of speech. The cry or effulgent "shine" of the phenomena that reach human consciousness does not account for the stress on what Paul Ricoeur might have called Hopkins's "mandated self"[15] unless that has an orphic duty or its equivalent to perform; nor does it entirely encompass, even as "widowed

insight," "The roll, the rise, the carol, the creation."[16] In answer to
"more speech than what?" the poem itself must enter as proof-text.
"I say more," then, while affirming personal identity as the locus for
an inspiration that leads to *poiesis* (the "fine delight that fathers
thought; the strong/ Spur, live and lancing ..." as well as months
or years of gestation),[17] alludes not only to an articulate, organized
language that nonhumans lack but also to a "father" tongue: a
poetic *and* justified speech, springing from the poet's "justicing."
Hence, at the end of the Kingfisher sonnet, the natural, un-self-
conscious loveliness of the human is consecrated (as if it were a
sweet smelling rather than total sacrifice) to the Father.[18]

"Thou art indeed just, Lord" is the psalmist's cry, which Hopkins
extends in a late, anguished sonnet.[19] But is his poetry just, particularly the inspiration that nourishes it: the physical beauty of man,
woman, and nature as a whole? Can his verse *keep* beauty—preserve
it, lengthen its appeal, store it in a "yonder" beyond the seeing and
singeing of the sun? His poetic efforts to achieve this, do they result
in more than rhythmic, rhyming, stammering keepsakes, one of
which admonishes the maidens of "The Leaden and the Golden
Echo" to "Give beauty back, beauty, beauty, beauty, back to God,
beauty's self and beauty's giver"? If his lament merely gilds a leaden
despair, merely amplifies the pathos of beauty, is that a "saying
more"?

The drama of justification in Hopkins plays itself out on several
levels. The most original and precarious of them is that the work of
poetry should coincide with a justification of incarnate beauty, the
"O-seal-that-so feature."[20] The latter is often, though not exclusively, male beauty, "Churlsgrace ... child of Amansstrength."[21] It
can also be a cosmic sublimity that defies expression: "The shepherd's brow, fronting forked lightning, owns/ The horror and the
havoc and the glory.... But man—."[22] This comes from a taxing
and perhaps unresolved sonnet that presents two contrasts.

First, a contrast between similar aspects of the same human type,
the shepherd facing nature's sublimity (so that, reading this opening, one wonders momentarily whether "shepherd's brow" is not
also the name of a mountain) and, in the sestet, "Man Jack" with

his "hussy mate," both absorbed in the physical demands of their labors and lacking the capacity to express that sublimity. "Angel's fall, they are towers, from heaven—a story/ of just, majestical, and giant groans." Can Man Jack serve as "*our* viol for tragic tones?"

The use of "just" to refer to the groans of the angels, judged and cast out because of their rebellious role in Heaven, stands, moreover, in perplexing contrast to "He! ... Man Jack the man is, just," which seems to affirm the rough, male, unconsciously formed character of this antipastoral shepherd. (Though "just," understood as "barely," could also qualify—even undermine—this meaning, if the line intends that "Man Jack" is "barely just.") The final tercet, then, adverts to a further contrast, between "Man Jack" and the poet himself. Hopkins's attraction to both nature's sublimity and the "Man Jack" kind of life is so strong that it impacts on him, "feed[s] this flame,"—an image that evokes the ambivalence of a desire that wishes desire to be consumed. Yet though it is the poet who "owns"—in the sense of articulate telling and confession— "The horror and the havoc and the glory," he remains confined (this uncovers a contrast within the contrast) to a doubly passive life, that of spying on a mirror: "I ... in smooth spoons spy life's masque mirrored: tame/ My tempests there, my fire and fever fussy." Who, then, is the just man?

Hopkins's sense of waste or exclusion, of failing to participate in a cosmic drama, produces wild turnings more characteristic of a great ode than a unified sonnet. One might still suspect the presence of a method, of Ignatius's technique of meditation, but only as it leads the poet to an empathic going-out, to an imaginary identification, a *participation mystique* (his own term is "ecstasy of interest"), as at the climax of "The Wreck of the Deutschland."[23] The despairing gasp at the center of the "Shepherd's Brow" sonnet ("But man—") is the negative of a compelling, participatory turn always potentially present.

In "The Windhover" this turn comes fully upon the poet as a usurping montage. A typological figure is born and fulfilled in a flash that superimposes a sacred on a secular image. The sonnet's dedication, "To Christ our Lord," is key to why its masterful picture of the high-riding windhover implodes to become "a billion/ Times told lovelier, more dangerous, O my Chevalier!" "Told" (and tolled) fuse, like "owns" does, possession and manifestation. The heart-in-hiding has come out of hiding and entered into a romance ("O my Chevalier") more sublime than the sheer plod of everyday, priestly duties that the last tercet of the sonnet, with its sacrificial, but still naturalistic, imagery redeems:

> shéer plód makes plow down sillion
>> Shine, and blue-bleak embers, ah my dear,
>>> Fall, gall themselves, and gash gold-vermilion.

The very idea of self-sacrifice draws flame; and poetry, if those embers imply it also, catches fire. As a speech-manifestation, an "Í say more," the poem comes close to matching—imaginatively—what nature "owns."

Hopkins's quest for justified poetic speech goes beyond illustrating doctrines about the role of nature (or natural law) in man's spiritual economy. Yet doctrine is always there as both framework and fuel. The submission to doctrine—which does not exclude its tacit revision—is the closest Hopkins comes to accepting a collective identity, and that is always involved with envisioning the human form and cosmic presence of Christ.[24] Christ embodies the very principle of individuation and founds the specific difference of the human in the chain of beings: a capacity for heightened witness. The poet, in turn, by energetic illustration, adds a tongue exceeding nature's tongue that "fling[s] out broad its name" ("Kingfisher," lines 2–3). What Hopkins represents in that poem's octave as a natural sounding-off is only a phenomenal overflow, a charged, inarticulate appeal; and speaking, spelling, crying, are analogical (tending to anagogical) metaphors characterizing that telling/tolling, peal/appeal.

But the sestet picks up and revises Saint Paul's context of justification. Hopkins now invokes an identity based on a visionary understanding. I have already motioned toward his lines on the just man who "Keeps gráce; thát keeps all his goings graces...." The double accent on "gráce: thát" is semantic as well as rhythmic: in his search for just poetic speech the poet goes further than the mother, so often associated with nature, as in mystical sentiments expressed by Jakob Boehme's *De Signatura Rerum* (chapter 1): "Each thing has its mouth for revelation. And this is the language of nature in which each thing speaks out of its own property, and always reveals and manifests itself.... For each thing reveals its mother, who therefore gives the essence and the will to form."

In a famous scene from Augustine's *Confessions* (book 10) the beauty of things are a mute equivalent of speech, as the creatures point to their creator: "He made us." Augustine remembers *Romans* 1:20 in this passage. But nature's "*for that I came,*" in Hopkins, is not a message to inculpate unbelievers who might question the justness of a God who had not manifested Himself before the coming of Christ. "For the invisible things of Him," Paul asserts in *Romans* 1:20, "are clearly seen from the creation of the world, understood by the things that are made: His eternal power and Godhead, so that they [who claim ignorance] are without excuse."

The traditional interpretation of these words is that they are directed against paganism and exempt a nonhuman nature "subjected in hope" (*Romans* 8:19–20) from God's wrath. "Thou canst but be," the poet writes of a landscape in his "Ribblesdale" sonnet,[25] which quotes that second proof-text from *Romans* 8 on the "earnest expectation of the creature." Hopkins, as we have seen, understands mere being positively: nature's selving, which it has in common with mankind, is not a claustral matter. "Each mortal thing ... Deals out that being indoors each one dwells, / Selves— goes itself."

Nature, Goethe said, extending the renaissance topos of the Book of Nature, is an open mystery. Hopkins too "deals out" that mystery by capturing in his poetry "inscapes" with their "instress" on the observer. The beauty he responds to, human or natural, or (as in lines 12–14) Christ's, is insistently earthy, and has a material, even bodily thisness or thusness (Don Scotus's *haecceitas*)[26] as its signature. Although the sorrow inherent in beauty's evanescence is often rendered, so is the pressure of, even despair at, beauty's dangerous presence. "To what serves Mortal Beauty?"[27] The conventional theological argument from design is jettisoned: Hopkins's

emphatic and redundant phrasing, "Earth, sweet Earth, sweet landscape" ("Ribblesdale"), honors a communication without tongue
or heart ("heaven that [thou] dost appeal/ To, with no tongue to
plead, no heart to feel").

But in this atmosphere of demand there is a partial disconnect
between the human and the natural when the poet trumps nature
with "Í say more." The "I" of the selved creature in the natural
realm has no hidden life or agenda. "[Thou] canst but only be, but
dost that long." Duration, at the same time, is not an insignificant
matter. The creature's self-revelation, coinciding with its phenomenality, implies an argument for the lastingness of the created
world, God being a supreme artificer whose work, as distinguished
from labor, is exemplary for *homo faber*.[28] In that sense the relation
between man and the natural world is a theological stage on which
the fate of creation plays itself out, as the nonhuman creatures look
in hope to the "sons of God" (*Romans* 8:19–21).

It is also a theopolitical stage, should the question be raised of
the relation between mere being or "bare life," affirmed in the
"Kingfisher" sonnet's sestet, and political justice. Can one link the
sequel, "Í say more: the just man justices," to Aristotle in the *Politics*,
who passes from the "voice" (*phonē*) of all living beings to the
"language" (*logos*) exclusive to mankind, and states explicitly that
"language is for manifesting the fitting and the unfitting and the
just and the unjust," an action that leads to the *polis*?[29] In Hopkins's
Christocentric perspective, nature's bare and bared self has its own
justification: it stands against the apocalyptic turn of the Book of
Revelations. Made explicit, the poet's argument runs: Christ justifies
mankind (potentially, as mediator, but also once and for all by having assumed individuated human form),[30] so mankind, through
contemplating Christ's exemplary assumption of human and physical being, could imitate him and justify nature, removing in that
way the latter's subjection.

The strongest scriptural proof, of course, for the durability of the
world—a world without end—is the creation story itself, the "And
God saw that it was good." As Hopkins reiterates, in a verse I have
quoted in part: "Thou canst but be, but that thou well dost; strong/
Thy plea with him. . . ." Nature's appeal, plea, pleading, conveyed

here in stumbling yet emphatic monosyllables, averts the danger of apocalypse, of the total loss of created, colorful being,[31] but raises at the same time the issue of human responsibility, of the "I" that says more than I and inherits nature even when uncaring: "Ah, the heir/ To his own selfbent so bound." The I that says more than I is not just a speaking (if still stuttering) creature: mankind's "*for that I came*"—came into being—leads, in and through poetry, to so physical a response to natural phenomena that a double fulfillment is suggested. There is an identity-movement toward the Christ whom Hopkins envisions as embodying highest pitch of self, all the more since he freely put off divine privilege and accepted human status. Then there is a parallel condescension on the part of mankind, in response to "sweet Earth" soliciting a mystical marriage. "And what is Earth's eye, tongue, or heart else, where/ Else, but in dear and dogged man?"

Two distinct burdens, then, weigh on the poet. One is Wordsworthian: not to turn away from nature's beauty, brute or sweet. Hopkins meets that beauty, struggles with its appeal. The poet, not God alone, must sustain nature's being, "not chose not to be."[32] His poems are less a mirror-projection of the spiritual combat between priest and poet than a struggle for justification, and thus for lastingness or even eternal being. It is a burden the poet, as shepherd of being, accepts from nature. The second responsibility, though in harmony with this task, involves Hopkins's own theological insight, or *cosmopoiesis*. He writes, trying to reconcile self, self-sacrifice, and creation (the creation of the world, even the creation of a poem): "It is as if the blissful agony or stress of selving in God had forced out drops of sweat or blood, which drops were the world."[33]

Poetry as blissful agony. Could one not claim, however, that poetry seeks to be justified play rather than justified work? And that, radically considered, all work, in the severe light of justification, is play? Already in the realm of art and pragmatic thought the line between play and work is often hard to draw. Intellectual "action," as it uncovers potentialities, has a fuzzy boundary and tolerates uncertainty. Yet, however playful it is, at some point it comes up against "action" in the public or political sphere, and exhibits the limit of what was deemed possible. Pragmatism respects such interaction and interdetermination. How desperate, therefore, would a thinker have to be to absolutize categories, as Kierkegaard does, with an either/or severing apostle from genius and ethicist from aestheticist! How can play become morally serious, moreover, without respecting a freedom that, as Kant remarked, must be present for an act to be called ethical, even when that freedom limits itself by submitting to universally valid moral maxims? As Kierkegaard's trouble with authority (in the sense of authoritative self-pronouncement) shows, he continues a kind of "play"—as does Wittgenstein with his language games. And poetry may have one advantage over philosophy in terms of the difference between play and reality: it remains, in permanence, what Winnicott named a transitional object.

Kierkegaard fails to pass from one category to another *in allo genere*—from irony, indirect communication, pseudonyms, and so forth, to a direct identity statement that would achieve, beyond every legitimation crisis, an "I say unto you."[34] Wittgenstein's compartmentalization also decisively rules out such a category shift. When he touches, for example, on the topic of grace he becomes movingly shy and refuses to theorize. "Election by grace: It is only permissible to write like this out of the most frightful suffering—& then it means something quite different. But for this reason it is not permissible for anyone to cite it as truth, unless he himself says it in torment.—It simply isn't theory.—Or as one might also say: if this is truth, it is not the truth it appears at first glance to express. It's less a theory than a sigh, or a cry."[35] In contrast, Hopkins's reflections on how grace may act on free will—without limiting it—by "clothing [the] old self for the moment with a gracious and consenting self," suggest a link between play and truth, as if his thought experiment, his Ignatian exercise, might achieve a transformation: "It is as if a man said: That is Christ playing at me and me playing at Christ, only that is no play but truth; That is Christ *being me* and me being Christ."[36]

Now Christ has a biography, or—to utter an unorthodox thought—God gets himself a life through Christ. Jesus' "I say unto you" preempts, however, when consolidated by Church doctrine, later appropriations of that "I." Nietzsche's proclamational style in *Zarathustra* as well as the identity swirl of much of his other prose seeks to liberate and recover the possibility of prophetic speech. Hopkins's daring is restricted to what he does with poetic form and theological speculation. His spiritual exercises venture a surmise about Christ's manifestation of a selving principle that preceded his appearance on earth,[37] while Hopkins's poetry, though elliptical and orthodox, hints at the "horror and the havoc and the glory" that take place, as it were, in the bosom of God. A foretaste of that turmoil and triumph is attained through the theological virtue of hope, strengthened by the practice of contemplation. Thus a postapocalyptic "comfort of the Resurrection" ("In a flash, at a trumpet crash,/ I am all at once what Christ is ..."),[38] allows the passage from "I am" to "what Christ is."

Hopkins undertakes an *imitatio Christi*, systematically exercising his senses (as prescribed by Ignatius) on the stations of the cross, and indeed on every aspect of Christ's life, even in heaven. The "plays" in "For Christ plays in ten thousand places ..." ("Kingfisher," line 12) could indicate this meditational playing-at, as it blends physical grace with the justified beauty of religious grace. The "grace ... grace" tautology, however, although reinforcing the harmony between physical and spiritual, may seem like a sleight of handsome words that passes too quickly over the seduction of mortal beauty; and when "play" is sanctified by invoking the name of the Father (the loveliness of limbs and eyes played "To the Father through the features of men's faces," lines 13–14) the reader's sense of an unresolved conflict is intensified.

Clearly, the concept of serious play is an inadequate one to value Hopkins's poetry. The question becomes: what *will* bridge the gulf between human unworthiness and a potentially exalted "I"? Ambiguity and pain of individuation remain intact. As Arendt rightly says, Augustine's "What am I then, my God, What is my nature," is a question asked before God and only answerable by the One in whose eyes "I have become a question to myself."[39] Hopkins is caught between the *passio gloriosa* (the cosmic drama) and the *passio humilis* ("sheer plod ..."), most vividly in the extraordinary sonnet "Not, I'll not, carrion comfort, Despair, not feast on thee." The wrestling with God intimated there feels as close and physical as that of Jacob with the angel-man, so that, unable to separate the one from the other, the poet ends with the cry, "O which one? is it each one?"

This perplexity runs parallel to what is found at the end of "Spelt from Sibyl's Leaves," composed in the same year (1885). Its title and tenor may echo the "Dies irae" hymn and indicate a motivating fear of Judgment Day. As evening and "hearse-of-all night" whelm both earth's and the poet's distinctness of self, the imminence of an absolute division into "black, white; right, wrong"—the chiasmatic phrasing expressive of the need for a divine, or the impotence of a human, sorting—leads Hopkins to ablaut "reck" (reckon, although mind here is close to being a wreck) to "rack," upon which "selfwrung, selfstrung, sheathe- and shelterless, thoughts against thoughts in groans grind."

We seem to have left behind the lecturer with an attitude. Such speakers, of course, especially in an academic setting, may actually deliver nuanced and complex words, for this sort of initial confession often remains a *captatio benevolentiae* addressing itself to auditors with similar ideological/ethnic features, or aiming to please by disclaiming universality. In another place, Wittgenstein reasons upon his own turn to the first person in exactly the contrary manner, using egotism at the end rather than beginning of a demonstration, when there is—again—nothing further to prove: "*In der conclusio meines Vortrags über Ethik habe ich in der ersten Person gesprochen: Das ist, glaube ich, etwas ganz wichtiges. Hier lässt sich nichts mehr feststellen, ich kann nur als Einzelner hervortreten und in der ersten Person sprechen.*"[40]

Although it is necessary, then, to study separately each verbal turn of this kind, recent and routine usage of the rhetoric of positionality sends a general warning: don't be under any illusion of complete freedom, we are all defined by some ethnic or collective determinants, though you may not share these particular ones. And: I deny that you can pursue knowledge, or produce an authentic narrative, without recognizing this state of affairs.

Wittgenstein notoriously dismisses such pronouncements as nonsense—if you are the phenomenon, then like the world you show what you are. Of course, you can cultivate nonsense, as long as you are not taken in by it. Yet it is hard to figure out exactly what he objects to, since his dislike of ethical declaratives actually serves to emphasize the importance of ethics. Perhaps, then, it is precisely its collectivization that troubles him: as if accountability in this realm were entirely a personal matter, a radical and unremitting labor of the individual conscience. All apology or self-justification, there-fore, is thought to be a failure, possibly even greater than allowing strictly propositional statements to trap us into verbal dilemmas that cloud philosophy and prevent lucid speech.[41]

To rephrase the matter in my own way: at once admonitory and self-licensing, the rhetoric of positionality, with its "determined and distinctive" I,[42] is shadowed by a historical irony. For, by going public so easily, by mimicking the confessional mode, it neglects and even undermines an earlier struggle: to keep matters of con-science in the private realm, subject to neither church nor state, or to use literature as a highly individual way of coming-out, of self-legitimation.

Compare the contemporary facility of self-reference with Emily Dickinson's egotism. Her use of the first person, though habitual and seemingly at ease, remains part of a poet's—and woman's—revolt against established authority. Her equivalents to "I *will* speak" ("Tell all the truth, but tell it slant") imply both hope and will, an insistence on something not yet realized and a determina-tion as strong as the "I will" of the marriage vow.

Or consider Montaigne's essays, where a mobile, flexible con-sciousness of self ("*divers et ondoyant*") openly explores its limits. We might say that, in the light of his self-scrutiny, which accepts the likelihood of error and certainly of *errance*, there is no absolute consistency of self, only a network of self-revising moments that could be termed authentic insofar as his inner freedom does not circumvent accountability. While Coleridge's "dread watch-tower of man's absolute self"[43] never intrudes like a relentless observer or panopticon into the conduct of Montaigne's musings, neither does consciousness become a substitute for conscience. We feel the presence of both, although their convergence is not guaranteed in advance and remains an unpredictable, if desired, coming to-gether. To read Montaigne we are obliged to absorb his writerly rhythm, to allow him his *momentum*. We follow Montaigne as we follow nature, we enjoy the segue.

In Wittgenstein's essayings there is a heightened problem, because the segue is often so close to a nonsequitur. Startled, unable to follow, we suspect we have missed a transition whose path must be found. The result, as in Dickinson too, is that authenticity moves closer to inimitability. Though the shared, rule-bound nature of intelligible speech is maintained, Wittgenstein's conceptual analysis,[44] like Kant's critique of the inadequacy of concepts to aesthetic experience, or of the impossibility of deriving ethical imperatives solely from experience, opens a virtual space in which genius, whether attributed to individual, or species-self, or to language as such, formulates a universal law or reveals *in actu* a previously undiscovered potentiality. Wittgenstein asks us to rotate statements in verbal rather than visual space in order to discover their properties—their reason or unreason.

While the relation of imagination, in its histrionic zest, to authenticity of character or self-pronouncement does not yield readily to historical analysis,[45] certain things in that regard stand out. Let us suppose that Montaigne's essayistic and Shakespeare's theatrical temper are related, perhaps because both writers lived in an era of great social mobility. Even so, the "I" representative, the right to represent oneself (to speak in one's person for oneself, let alone for others, or the state, or a distinct political faction, or as the leader of a military venture or a religious or reformist mission, etc.)—this "I," apparently self-fashioned, had to be accompanied by ritual process and protected or justified by temporal power. Legitimacy and succession remain guiding principles.

This is made clear not only by Shakespeare's historical dramas but also by *Hamlet*. While young Harry in *Henry IV* deliberately delays his appearance as a power player, Hamlet's hesitation is of a different kind. Many theories have been offered for it; what is sure is that, unlike the Harry of Henry IV, he is deprived of his coming-out. Mallarmé calls Hamlet "*le Seigneur latent qui ne peut devenir.*" Unable to renounce the office and occupation that are rightfully his, he cannot emerge into a different role. Yet there must be, we feel, a maturity beyond inherited power wisely used, a sort of passive dignity akin to persistent thought and contemplation, as in philosophy, or what is suggested by an urbane pastoral literature in praise of retirement, such poems as Vergil's *Eclogues* or Marvel's "The Garden" and "Upon Appelton House."

Though Shakespeare hints at that other maturity, *Hamlet* does not allow a different and perhaps truer vocation to emerge. There is no such role breakthrough as some attribute to Queen Elizabeth, who is said to have renounced taking a husband in order to secure the state's safety as well as her own, marrying instead the English people, becoming (with sacred overtones) the Virgin Queen. Hamlet, in any case, cannot withdraw into the pale of thought. As in all of Shakespeare's exceptional moments, the astounding metaphorical whirl characterizing Hamlet's soliloquies reflects the fact that he is placed among confronting circumstances that pressure and defeat his intervention. They seem to run by another clock, so that he cannot right the time. The mimetic arts generally play that dilemma back, condensing the world into a stage. A microcosmic theater is particularly effective as public vehicle. In the tragedies, Shakespearean rhetoric is almost completely on the side of persuasion, quarreling, goading, action; but in the romantic comedies, although there is always something to be gained or lost, a liberal magic takes over and saves the enchanted or self-enchanted, deluding or self-deluded, characters from their own stratagems. The importance for culture of such vicarious, jousting-jesting elements is the subject of Huizinga's magisterial *Homo Ludens*. Yet acting out repressed feelings or positions in fictional, and especially dramatic form, is an extraordinarily direct kind of slanted telling that can endanger the artist politically. There is often a backlash to theatricality and cathartic extroversion. Jonas Barish traces outbursts of "antitheatrical prejudice" during and after the religious turmoil of early modernity.[46]

In addition, for those who wish to lead an exemplary life (even if their ambition is to gain worldly influence), the very "character" of God is of importance. How is *imitatio dei* possible (as a way to transcendence through histrionic self-persuasion), given a deity who is infinitely mysterious, or absent to the point of seeming to be *absconditus,* and who may even have permitted a pseudo-God, a demiurge, to interpose as the god of the world, and the only (deceiving) god we can get to know?

The question appears to lead to an abyss, a nonexit of introspection; yet both Milton and Pascal seek to justify the ways of God to mankind. The impression conveyed by their effort is often that of serious jesting (*serio ludere*), since nothing can justify the justifier from the perspective of orthodox doctrine. Luther and Calvin deplore even the very attempt at justification as a reprehensible vanity, a covert exaltation of human reason. Indeed, the bafflement, the darkness of this vain endeavor, when expressed in a public medium, projects a heightened form of self-consciousness: so a Milton Agonistes appears who wrestles with the flawed or fallen human condition: "Can God demand day-labor, light denied?" This exculpatory sentence concerning the author's blindness suggests how much he might do were light vouchsafed—a light that is surely also an inner light, though this too is not guaranteed, however empty and kenotic his eyes have become.

It is not necessary to rehearse sectarian quarrels about justification to suggest that these uncertain spiritual labors intensify the emotions surrounding self-consciousness. All the more so since Protestantism, by denying the ultimate efficacy of all mediators except Christ, opens a void between God and the individual soul that is at once a terrifying and a hopeful space of virtual encounter—a theater with very few props, where individuals continually scrutinize their actions and conscience. In that field of conscience the individual soul is like Dickinson's "bewildered gymnast" whose adversary, as in the primal religious scene of Jacob's wrestling match with the angel, turns out to be God. I suspect the birth pangs of a still prevalent concept of authenticity are here, in a preter-journalistic activity, a record keeping whose secular aspect has been linked to the beginnings of capitalism. Though the question of whether there is such a thing as an authentic *injustice* of God (as the doctrine of predestination seems to imply) cannot be resolved by the individual, at least an account of the soul's internal labors becomes available. God may not need this accounting but it becomes a moral legacy for those who live after.

Identity statements, as complex as poems or novels, as dialectical or pseudonymous as in Kierkegaard,[47] as pithy as Descartes's cogito,[48] come in all shapes and sizes and are not always linked overtly to creed or ideological message. Something, however, puts individuals under pressure to attempt an assertion of identity, both personal and corporate. In an explicitly religious thinker like Coleridge, whose effort it was to justify, in philosophical language, the faculty of imagination, and to specifically relate its presence in poets to the *logos* as the power of naming or self-naming, this type of assertion allows him to move from the priority of attributive statements (prayerful Thou-saying) to a primordial identity statement (I-saying):

The *Imagination*, then, I consider either as primary or secondary. The primary imagination I hold to be the living power and prime agent of all human perception, and as a repetition in the finite mind of the eternal act of creation in the infinite I AM. The secondary I consider as an echo of the former.... (*Biographia Literaria*, end of chapter 14)

Yet to insist that identity statements balance attributive statements —and so rescue or maintain personal autonomy through reference to a divine prototype of self-naming—may not be saying much. In the first place, it is hard to think of any verbal tender that is not (sometimes perversely) affirmative even when it is negative:[49] it seems impossible to utter a statement in the first person without making a promise, or entering a communitarian and dialogic field of force.[50] That is true even of confessions, insofar as they enter public space. The "I have sinned, I am unworthy, I have done this or that, I have betrayed the party ..." may be cathartic or purifying in a confessional space that remains private or fictional, but it has disastrous consequences in show trials when implicating an entire group. In the second place, the "I am" or "... therefore I am" (the sum of those decisive, arrogant, logical ergos, as if ego and ergo were morphs of each other) suggests a prior uncertainty about the "I" that is impelled to make the statement. This ergo factor in the "... *ergo sum*" points to the quest for logical certainty that has dominated philosophical thinking and is not absent from political thinking. Yet it is precisely this kind of dogmatizing Wittgenstein

wished to keep out of the ethical or religious sphere, where
certainty does not come through logic or some other, broader
grammar of norms ("a more comprehensive syntax") but is an
emotional striving for "security" in the midst of the individual's existential (as if inevitable) insecurity.

An example of a negative identity statement would be Bartleby
the Scrivener's "I prefer not to," in Melville's story. Since we have
the gift of speech, to refuse it remains an act. An emphasis on
withholding speech is all the more puzzling in philosophy, which, it
has been said, may talk about anything as long as it also talks about
itself. Wittgenstein's reticence concerning ethics and his rejection
of the possibility of meaningful propositions in that area (most in-
tractably expressed in *Tractatus* 6.42ff.) is a silence act. Ethical and
mystical converge,[51] and what he avoids are assertive propositions
that have the appearance of dogma (of authoritative ergos). His
elective silence is very different, then, from either a consecrated or
a pathological silence. "Elected silence, sing to me" Hopkins writes
in "The Habit of Perfection," "and beat upon my whorléd ear."

Hopkins's "invitation" structures his conversion lyric by means of
positive negations. Written in 1866, the year he is received into the
Roman Catholic Church, it reviews the sensory world he is tempted
by. As each stanza redirects rather than renounces one of the six
senses (speech is included), the poet sustains his opening paradox suggestive of a higher, if still sensuous, form of attraction. Even
the title's connotation of "habit" as dress returns at the end, not
only skillfully continuing a metaphor but also, by dint of this figural
constancy, anticipating ample reward ("And ... And ... And") for
his poetic as well as ascetic labor of the negative. No wonder Saint
Francis's marriage is evoked:

And, Poverty, be thou the bride
And now the marriage feast begun,
And lily-colored clothes provide
Your spouse not laboured-at nor spun.[52]

Could one talk of Wittgenstein's habit?[53] "This is what I do." His
near mythic status in intellectual circles comes from a perseverance
aiming to speak only of what can be spoken about, a quality as ob-

servant in its decorum at the discursive level as the demeanor of orthodox religious persons at the level of conduct. But, though convinced that there were rules concerning the construction of sense that his language games would bring to light, he is still in the process of discovering rather than codifying them. Although he does not assert, then, in his post-*Tractatus* writings, the existence of a nomothetic code rather than a grammar, he does display a "habit of perfection" that refuses to be satisfied with justifications previously offered.

There are many questions one is left with. Wittgenstein's cultural pessimism is well known through his letters and obiter dicta, though it does not often enter formally into his writings. He belongs to the era of Spengler, whose *Decline of the West* elaborated in genial detail the birth and death of cultures as organisms, and the usurping rise of science and technology in the West. Despite Wittgenstein's early attraction to the mathematical logic of Russell and Whitehead, he would not have agreed to consider science and its methodology a "culture"—as Charles Snow insisted it was, in his famous pamphlet on *The Two Cultures*.

Spengler may have reinforced in Wittgenstein a fatalistic melancholy. More positively, Wittgenstein carried forward, like Spengler, Goethe's countermechanistic idea of science as a morphology, a "form-language" based on the living organism (whether plant or language) and allowing us to intuit, by synoptic visualization, its developmental structure. The book on which he collaborated with Waismann talks of imaginatively transforming verbal configurations "so as to gain a view of the whole of space in which the structure of our language has its being."[54]

He may also have been impressed by Spengler's deterministic view that cultures, because they were self-enclosed entities with their own laws of development, could not really understand one another. (Multiculturalism as an impossibility.) His privacy argument has a family resemblance to Spengler's view of this incommunicability. What I take from Wittgenstein's flirtation with cultural theory is that he was after two things. Absolute clarity, on the one hand, as the intellectual equivalent of *visibilia*. There would be no shadows, no obscurity to hide in, so that "justification" becomes unnecessary. On the other hand, his cultural pessimism (and so his refusal to value the collective factor in identity-formation)[55] may have led him to believe that, outside the individual's religious quest, outside that zone of privacy, a culture or particular society with its apparently ineradicable injustices could not be justified. Or even remedied, in the philosophical sense of a remediation of its intellectual life, the dismantling of metaphysical preconceptions or other "mind-forged manacles" (William Blake).

Wittgenstein offers a variant type of philosophic astonishment: "Not *how* the world is, is the mystical, but *that* it is" (*Tractatus* 6.44).[56] Why was he not as explicitly astonished by that emotion's adult and disenchanted version: that there is nothing rather than something?[57] He knows that only the writing hand—of a philosopher or poet—in its very plodding ("*Practice* gives the words their sense")[58] makes verbal plough "down sillion shine." Only this creative light, emanating from labors of intellect and imagination, alleviates our anguish at the void within the world's mocking plenitude, a void depicted by Hopkins in another poem of his conversion year:

> Like a lighted empty hall
> Where stands no host at door or hearth
> Vacant creation's lamps appal.[59]

Wittgenstein tolerates a darkness his intelligence lights up, here and there, like stars the silence of those infinite, appalling spaces.

Appendix

"As Kingfishers Catch Fire" by Gerard Manley Hopkins

> As kingfishers catch fire, dragonflies draw flame;
> As tumbled over rim in roundy wells
> Stones ring; like each tucked string tells, each hung bell's
> Bow swung finds tongue to fling out broad its name;
> Each mortal thing does one thing and the same:
> Deals out that being indoors each one dwells;
> Selves—goes its self; *myself* it speaks and spells,
> Crying *What I do is me: for that I came.*

Between Poetry and Philosophy

Í say more: the just man justices;
  Keeps gráce: thát keeps all his goings graces;
Acts in God's eye what in God's eye he is—
  Chríst. For Christ plays in ten thousand places,
Lovely in limbs, and lovely in eyes not his
  To the father through the features of men's faces.

Notes

1. *Culture and Value: A Selection from the Posthumous Remains*, ed. G. H. von Wright, revised text by Alois Pichler (Cambridge, Mass.: Blackwell, 1997), p. 28e, translation slightly modified.

2. *Complete Poems*, ed. Thomas H. Johnson (Boston, Mass.: Little, Brown, 1960), no. 501, p. 243.

3. For a lively and comprehensive analysis of the modern concept of collective identity, see Luz Niethammer, *Kollektive Identität: Heimliche Quellen einer unheimlichen Konjunktur* (Hamburg: Rohwohlt Taschenburg Enzyklopädie, 2000).

4. A problematic exception could be made for the prophet or apostle, whose discovery of a mission is not seemingly dependent on a purely immanent scrutiny of the self but on a transcending or absolute source. On the distinction, see Soren Kierkegaard, *The Book on Adler*, ed. and trans. H. V. Hong and E. H. Hong (Princeton, N.J.: Princeton University Press, 1998), appendix 3.

5. *A Pitch of Philosophy: Autobiographical Exercises* (Cambridge, Mass.: Harvard University Press, 1994), p. 14. In *The Claim of Reason: Wittgenstein, Skepticism, Morality, and Tragedy* (New York: Oxford University Press, 1979), pp. 18–19, Cavell discusses this statement among others and its qualified dogmatic or authoritative claim.

6. *Praxis* here does not refer exclusively to a philosophy or ideology of political action but does point to the link between speech and action that Hannah Arendt eloquently exposits in chapter 5 on "Action" in *The Human Condition* (Chicago, Ill.: University of Chicago Press, 1958), sections 24 and 25. On the development of the concept of praxis, especially its linguistic turn, see Richard Bernstein, "The Concept of Action: Analytic Philosophy," *Praxis and Action: Contemporary Philosophies of Human Activity* (Philadelphia, Penn.: University of Pennsylvania Press, 1971), and Richard Rorty, *The Linguistic Turn* (Chicago, Ill.: University of Chicago Press, 1967).

7. Letter to the George Keatses, March 19, 1819.

8. *Poems of Gerard Manley Hopkins*, ed. W. H. Gardner and N. H. Mackenzie, Fourth Edition (New York: Oxford University Press, 1967), no. 57, p. 90. The entire poem is appended to the end of this essay.

9. On Hopkins's use of "pitch" as that essential ("determined and distinctive") aspect of each being that precedes even its existence, see Christopher Devlin, ed. *The Sermons and Devotional Writings of Gerard Manley Hopkins* (London: Oxford University Press, 1959), pp. 122–123, 150–152, 342–343, and notes.

10. By ecphrastic is meant the distinctly referential, energetically descriptive, or amplifying, power of language. It is a pictorial or picturing capacity (picturing in Wittgenstein's sense of "A picture held us captive"). Yet the way out, probably, the way of delivering the mind from the captivating picture, is to replace it with another or to recognize what is pictured as no more than a simile.

11. Hopkins's reflections on doing-being take a vernacular turn when he remarks in his "Spiritual Writings" that "pitch" as "simple positiveness" is "with precision expressed by the English *do* (the simple auxiliary)," as well as "the copula in logic and the Welsh *a*." He goes on: "So that this pitch, might be expressed, if it were good English, *the doing* be . . . ," *Sermons and Devotional Writings*, p. 151.

12. Wittgenstein is not staking out a personal identity position but rather indicating a limit to giving reasons for a rule that might justify our following it. The German words for "justification" in this paragraph are "rechtfertigung" and "begründung." That this kind of statement, however, may have a controversial ethical component, if "following a rule" is convertible into "obedience to law and order," can be seen from Judith Shklar's opening sentence in *Legalism: Law, Morals, and Political Trials* (Cambridge, Mass.: Harvard University Press, 1964): "What is legalism? It is the ethical attitude that holds moral conduct to be a matter of rule following, and moral relationships to consist of duties and rights determined by rules."

13. Maria R. Lichtman, "The Windhover," in *The Contemplative Poetry of Gerard Manley Hopkins* (New York: Oxford University Press, 1989), an excellent study of the centrality of Ignatius's method of contemplation in Hopkins, defines "praxis" somewhat obscurely as "in effect the reader response, of the poem" (p. 130). She seems to conflate the poem as Hopkins's response to contemplation and the reader's parallel response to his poem.

14. Kierkegaard, *The Book on Adler*, p. 8. Ray Monk's *Ludwig Wittgenstein: The Duty of Genius* (New York: Free Press, 1990) leaves no doubt of the importance of Kierkegaard to Wittgenstein's thinking, although Monk's subtitle is deceptive, because the biographer does not go into Kierkegaard's problematic distinction between genius and apostle in *The Book on Adler* (or the more common, postromantic distinction between genius and talent that Wittgenstein often struggles with).

15. See Paul Ricoeur, *Oneself as Another*, trans. Kathleen Barney (Chicago, Ill.: Chicago University Press, 1992), especially the references given on pp. 23–25. Ricoeur in general differentiates the (religious) response to a call and the (argumentative) answering of a question. His book analyzes analytic philosophy's concept of action as an essential "detour" to the issue of the "I am," a detour that, like Continental philosophy, seeks what he calls "attestation," or the "*assurance of being oneself acting and suffering.*"

16. "To R. B." (Robert Bridges), *Poems*, no. 76, p. 108.

17. Ibid.

18. In his *Journals* Hopkins talks of "our Lord to and in whom all that beauty [of stars emerging at night] comes home."—The gender issue may also enter because Hopkins seeks to invigorate the "mother" tongue through an infusion of the Anglo-Saxon vernacular. He is, metaphorically at least, both father and mother to the poem.

19. "Thou art indeed just, Lord, if I contend," *Poems*, no. 74, p. 106.

20. "To what serves Mortal Beauty?" *Poems*, no. 62, p. 98.

21. "Harry Ploughman," *Poems*, no. 71, p. 104.

22. "As kingfishers catch fire," *Poems*, no. 57, p. 10. The entire poem is quoted in the appendix.

23. "The Wreck of the Deutschland," *Poems*, no. 28, stanzas 24–28, pp. 59–60.

24. Consider also his quite daring (baroque) conceit and analogy: "The Blessed Virgin compared to the Air we Breathe," *Poems*, no. 60, pp. 93–94.

25. *Poems*, no. 58, p. 90.

26. Hopkins spells it "ecceitas" as if thisness created an "ecce," the "behold" of manifestation. See Christopher Devlin, ed. *Sermons and Devotional Writings*, p. 151, and pp. 293–294, note 3.

27. *Poems*, no. 62, p. 98.

28. Cf. Arendt, *The Human Condition*, chapter 4, "Work."

29. I am indebted for this thought to Giorgio Agamben, *Homo Sacer: Sovereign Power and Bare Life*, trans. Daniel Heller–Roazen (Stanford, Calif.: Stanford University Press, 1998). The passage from *Politics* 1253a, pp. 10–18, is quoted on pp. 7–8.

30. For Hopkins's theological reflections on Christ's incarnation as both a becoming flesh (*ensarkosis*) and becoming human (*enanthropesis*), see his "Spiritual Writings" and the editor's introduction to them in *Sermons and Devotional Writings* (especially p. 114).

31. For renditions of this loss, see "Spelt from Sybil's Leaves," and "That Nature is a Heraclitean Fire and of the Comfort of the Resurrection," in *Poems*, no. 61, no. 72, pp. 97, 105.

32. *Poems*, no. 64, p. 99.

33. *Sermons and Devotional Writings*, p. 111.

34. Kierkegaard cannot pass from one to the other mode, but he can choose the direct mode, as in his later writings. It may be symptomatic that, in his *Journals*, when he does imagine passing from a fictive and impersonal to a nonfictive and *in propria persona* mode of discourse, he thinks of the following situation: "A man wishes to write a novel in which one of the characters goes mad; while working on it he himself goes mad by degrees, and finishes it in the first person." See the entry for July 9, 1837 in Søren Kierkegaard, *Journals and Papers*, vol. 5, Howard V. Hong and Edna H. Hong, eds. (Bloomington, Ind.: Indiana University Press, 1978), p. 105.

35. *Culture and Value*, pp. 34e–35e. As in Kierkegaard, moreover, this cry or sigh cannot be alleviated by a collective ideology. Christianity itself, although a refuge for the sufferer, recognizes an intractable individual suffering. "A cry of distress

cannot be greater than that of *one* human being." "The Christian religion is only for the one who needs infinite help, that is, only for the one who suffers infinite distress." "The whole Earth cannot be in greater distress than *one* soul." *Culture and Value*, p. 52e.

36. *Sermons and Devotional Writings*, p. 154.

37. Ibid., pp. 122, passim. Not that everything in these mysterious matters becomes clear. Much turns on a discussion of free will, the nature of sin, grace and the justness of God (pp. 149ff.). Pitch, writes Hopkins, is prior to self which is, as personality, prior to nature, but, empirically experienced, is "a definite self ... identified with moral pitch, determination of right and wrong" (p. 148). One occasionally feels, reading Hopkins's spiritual notes, that he was a frustrated epic poet, close to Milton in wishing to give theology a new, imaginative presence. Or, alternatively, that, like Ricoeur, he would have appreciated analytic (ordinary language) philosophy as a "detour" (i.e., an examination of the indirectness and indirection of the question of selfhood) to a religious hermeneutics.

38. "That Nature is a Heraclitean Fire and of the comfort of the Resurrection," *Poems*, no. 72, p. 105.

39. *The Human Condition*, chapter 1, section 1. Augustine's question is again from *Confessions*, book 10.

40. Brian McGuiness, ed., *Friederich Waismann, Wittgenstein und der Wiener Kreis* (Oxford: Blackwell, 1967), p. 117.

41. Kierkegaard, reacting to Hegel, solved (but really intensified) the dilemma of subjectivity by rejecting "mediation" and insisting on "paradox." The latter cannot be digested by mere (sheer) reflectiveness. And it guarantees the category of the individual in an increasingly mass society. It is fascinating that the "new criticism," without being overtly religious or Kierkegaardian, made paradox (also irony, which Kierkegaard validated only in part) the distinguishing feature of literary language's singularity.

42. It is possible, I think, to pass from academic identity statements to the issue of political rhetoric more generally. I recall that at convention time for the presidential elections, with great hoopla and audience enthusiasm the shameless "I am" of the candidates bolsters itself by reference to genealogy, locality, family, and other "roots." Their independence and leadership must be pugnaciously asserted as they throw doubt on these same qualities in the candidate of the opposing party.

43. See his "To William Wordsworth: Composed on the night after his recitation of a Poem on the Growth of an Individual Mind" (1806).

44. The phrase used in P. F. Strawson's development of Wittgenstein's investigative method. See Bernstein, "The Concept of Action: Analytic Philosophy," in *Praxis and Action*, especially pp. 252–258.

45. See, however, Lionel Trilling's exemplary attempt, covering intellectual history from the Renaissance to postmodernism, in *Sincerity and Authenticity* (Cambridge, Mass.: Harvard University Press, 1972).

46. *The Antitheatrical Prejudice* (Berkeley, Calif.: University of California Press, 1981). In "late" modernity too: so Emmanuel Lévinas, while attacking Christian figural typology as flattening and petrifying the ethical dimension of Hebrew Scripture, writes in *Difficult Freedom*, trans. Seán Hand (Baltimore, Md.: Johns Hopkins University Press, 1990), p. 121: "Are we on stage or are we in the world? Is to obey God to receive from him a role or a command?"

47. With the single exception of the pamphlets of his last years and the *Journals*.

48. Self-affirmation can also inhere in a covert—e.g., anagrammatic—self-naming. Descartes's name, as Sanford Budick points out, is projected as he suggests the nondependence of his cogito on the presence or absence of worldliness: "In the crowded throng of a great and active nation ... I can live as solitary and retired as in deserts the most remote [*les déserts les plus écartés*]." See Sanford Budick, *The Western Theory of Tradition: Terms and Paradigms of the Cultural Sublime* (New Haven, Conn.: Yale University Press, 2000), p. 5.

49. That also holds for "it" statements, though their neutral or neuter (ne/uter) implication has led to considerable philosophical brooding in Heidegger, Levinas, and Blanchot.

50. I am not qualified to judge Kant's categorical imperative in this respect; but although it presupposes, and insists on, human freedom, it cannot but assume both individual agency and an addressee. Even if the addressee implies a metaempirical, universal "Thou," as in scriptural commandments, he/she must feel addressed (summoned, mandated) by the imperative before it can take effect, so that what I have suggested above remains relevant. Bakhtin, it is well known, said that in Dostoievski's novels every statement is a "rejoinder in an unfinished dialogue," a thought applied by Maurice Blanchot to literature generally through his notion of an "entretien infini." Bakhtin may himself have been influenced by Martin Buber's famous book on the primordial words "I" and "Thou." The question of how the "it" or "it-is" can be physically perceived or addressed, i.e., the (invisible) "being" behind phenomena who does not enter sense perception directly, opens another issue. Paul's statement in *Romans* 1:19 concerning the invisible presence of the creator perceived through the *visibilia* seems to adapt a dictum of the pre-Socratic thinker Anaxagoras: "*Opsis ton adelon ta phainomena.*"

51. For an illuminating discussion, to which I am indebted, of what the ethical means for Wittgenstein, see Arnulf Zweig, "Wittgensteins Schweigen," in Gertrud Koch, ed. *Bruchlinien: Tendenzen der Holocaust Forschung* (Cologne: Böhlau, 1999), pp. 163–167.

52. The rhyme in this last stanza, however, must be called labored. It produces a curious inversion, giving the impression that the *spouse* is not labored at. Surely the poet intends us to understand "And lily-coloured clothes, not laboured-at nor spun, provide ...". But in that case is it the bride, Poverty, who provides for the poet-novice-spouse? The paradox might have pleased Kierkegaard.

53. He did wear a kind of uniform, of course, always dressing up (rather, dressing down) in a hiking or similar outfit.

54. In my exposition of Spengler's influence, particularly the emphasis on what Wittgenstein called "synoptic presentation" and later "perspicuous representation,"

Geoffrey Hartman

I follow Ray Monk's *Ludwig Wittgenstein,* pp. 302ff., and Wittgenstein's own fragmentary remarks in *Culture and Value.*

55. He does recognize, of course, collective resemblances, and he often makes ambivalent remarks about Jewish traits. But does he value, in the sense of appreciate, their relevance to moral issues?

56. Cf. his inclination "to use such phrases as 'how extraordinary that anything should exist'" to express what he calls his "experience *par excellence*": "when I have it *I wonder at the existence of the world.*" *Philosophical Occasions: 1912–1951,* ed. James C. Klagge and Alfred Nordmann (Indianapolis, Ind.: Hackett, 1993), p. 41.

57. Of course, to an extent, he does express such astonishment, but at the fact that what exists dies into the light of common day. He therefore startles normal or stabilized perception by inventive similes that provoke imaginative yet orderly extensions.

58. Quoted by Monk, *Wittgenstein,* p. 573, from *Culture and Value.*

59. "Nondum," *Poems,* no. 23.

4

What Is Pragmatism?

Charles Taylor

This essay is an exercise in catch-up. Many philosophers whom I esteem see part of the sources of their own thought in American pragmatism. Richard Bernstein is prominent among these. Moreover, these thinkers seem to associate their interest in, or even identification with pragmatism with the attempts to deconstruct the dominant epistemology that comes down to us in modern times from Descartes and Locke. Once again, Richard Bernstein is a paradigm figure in making this link. He has made a singularly important contribution to this "deconstruction," with such works as *The Restructuring of Social and Political Theory*, and *Beyond Objectivism and Relativism*. These are works from which I have learned much in my attempts to elaborate a critique of epistemology. So perhaps I too, am some kind of pragmatist? What exactly is pragmatism anyway? I have some catching up to do, trying to find the meaning of this key philosophical descriptor, with which my friends are familiar, and I am not.

One way of understanding pragmatism might be to define it by the negation of certain key features of this mistaken epistemological tradition. Let me try to characterize schematically what I take to be the structure of thinking in modern epistemology; by this I mean more than a set of theories that have gained widespread acceptance, but rather, the underlying picture that is only semiconsciously entertained, yet controls the way people think, argue, infer, make sense of things in this area. I am speaking of a "picture" here in the sense that Wittgenstein used the word when he said "A picture held us captive."

At its most blatant this structure operates with a picture of individuals as knowing agents, who build up their understanding of the world through combining and relating, in more and more comprehensive theories, the information that they take in and that is couched in inner representations, be these conceived as mental pictures (in the earlier variants), or as sentences to be held true in the more contemporary versions.

Characteristic of this picture are a series of priority relations. (1) Knowledge of the self and its states comes before the knowledge of external reality and of others. (2) Knowledge of reality as a neutral fact comes before our attributing to it various values and relevances. And, (3) knowledge of the things of "this world," of the natural order, precedes any theoretical invocation of forces and realities transcendent to it.

On one reading, then, pragmatism would refer to views that reverse some of these priority relations. In particular, the target would be (2). Instead of understanding our knowledge of the world as being, in the first place, a grasping of neutral facts, and only later taking certain evaluative attitudes to them, we adopt some version of the primacy of practical reason. We are from the very beginning at grips with the world, aiming at certain goals, purposes, seeking things desired, trying to fend off things feared. Our entire understanding of things comes to be framed only within this committed and active perspective. Things appear for us from the very beginning with their relevances, as "pragmata," to use the Greek term that Heidegger invokes. "Pragmatism" would then be the view that we primordially, and in a sense always, are dealing with pragmata, and not just neutral objects. This might be the core meaning.

But by a series of arguments that are not hard to understand, the denial of (2) would quickly extend to a denial of (1). Once we begin to see the human agent as actively engaged with the world from the very beginning of his or her development as a conscious being, then it is obvious that this activity is from the beginning that of agent and other together: agent and primary caregiver, agent and playmates, agent and teacher, and so on. The games we learn to play are social games. And so it is not surprising that the pragmatist tradition early on begins to challenge the primacy of the monological agent in the epistemological tradition. A crucial figure here is, of course, George Herbert Mead. As to (3), I want to leave it aside here for the moment. It is by no means the case that most "pragmatists" have wanted to reverse this priority relation. But I invoke it here, because I want to return later to a passage of the work of one who did. I mean William James.

Anyway, it looks as though we potentially have a "broad church" definition of the family of pragmatists. In this sense, it would include, say, Heidegger, Merleau-Ponty, Wittgenstein, as well as the great American figures of the last turn of the century who embraced the designation. But there is also a narrower sense of the term. Here the theory would negate something that epistemology assumes, but that is also more widely held. This can perhaps be told the following way. In our enquiries we seek truth, and getting to the truth means characterizing things according to the way they are: this is sometimes articulated in terms of the notion of "correspondence"—descriptions "correspond" to reality. Often, this is a perfectly adequate way of speaking. The statement that there are ten chairs in this room is true if there are just ten chairs in this room. Davidsonian T-theorems capture this way of grasping the relation. But there are some true sayings that don't fit this model. For instance, when I come to rearticulate what I am about, I also bring about a change in myself. "Now it's clear to me that I don't really want that job," "now I see that I was always in love with her," and the like. Truth here has to be articulated not so much in terms of correspondence to an already existing reality (like the 10 chairs), but in terms of something like the idea that I am now leading my life, articulating my existence, in a less distorted or a more illusion-free way. Correspondence is not the key category, but the dimension of getting it right is still there via such key antonyms as "distortion," or "illusion."

The narrower, or perhaps one might say, more radical sense of pragmatism defines it by a denial of this assumption. What we call "truth" doesn't depend on getting it right, either in the sense of correspondence, or in any sense in which "illusion" would be the antonym. What we call the truth is what works for us, in the sense of what lets our crucial activities go forward in the most successful and unimpeded way. Obviously, a lot reposes on the term "crucial" in the above sentence. Since we are engaged in all sorts of activities, of unequal importance, and very often aimed at ends that conflict, the kind of "working" that constitutes what ordinary people call "truth" can only be of the most important, or fundamental, or perhaps comprehensive kind. There are lots of ways of defining this, about which pragmatists in this radical sense may disagree. But there is a fundamental idea here, that sense can be made of our ordinary concept of truth by radically shifting the center of gravity of what was thought to be its point. Not faithfulness to reality, but rather some kind of working, or working for us, is its justificatory point.

Obviously, if this kind of shift is going to come off, the account of "working" can't itself refer us back to getting it right. We wouldn't really have displaced the center of gravity of truth if we had said something like: "true in science is what works for scientists," if it turned out to be the case that we couldn't account for what scientists are after without reintroducing something like truth as correspondence.

I myself believe that this kind of displacement of the center of gravity is always going to fail. This might appear less obvious in a case like the one above, where I rearticulate what I'm about or what's important to me: "now I see that I don't really want that job." Here we might be tempted to say that "getting it right" is just things going better for me. That I am happier, or more serene, or less divided and conflicted, or anguished and distressed, now that I have made the decision to refuse that (at first tempting) offer. But in order to consider this as a real displacement of the center of gravity, we would have to discredit altogether insights about illusion and distortion. (Here the understanding implicit in "distortion" is that there is a way of being that is mine, and that is being twisted, not allowed to be its proper shape. The rearticulation is right because it allows this to be undistorted. There is a crucial reference here to the way I properly am.) This attempt to excise illusion, I believe, doesn't really do justice to our situation (it gets it wrong: it's untrue to our condition), and thus the radical shift doesn't come off.

I won't be able to defend this position fully here (or perhaps anywhere). But it does clarify my interest in this question of pragmatism. I certainly am not a pragmatist in this radical sense. But maybe the paradigm figures in pragmatism weren't either.

I'd like to look at this question through a particular case: William James's discussion of the varieties of religious experience.[1] This is a work of extraordinary power, which, in spite of having been written some 100 years ago, reads in some ways like a contemporary work. Its stress on religious *experience* is in some ways more pertinent in the beginning of the twenty-first century than it was back in 1902, when the lectures were delivered in Edinburgh. But what is even more remarkable is the Jamesian description and discussion of the "twice-born," those who had come to some kind of religious belief or conversion through a powerful experience of fear and/or loathing. The fear is of a meaninglessness that engenders a debilitating melancholy, but also of evil and personal sin.

The first might be called "religious melancholy." "The world now looks remote, strange, sinister, uncanny." Things seem unreal, distant, as though seen through a cloud (*V*, pp. 151–152). Another way of putting this would be to speak of a loss of meaning. In describing Tolstoy's experience, James says of him that "the sense that life had any meaning whatever was for a time wholly withdrawn" (*V*, p. 151).

The second, which James also calls "melancholy," is characterized by fear. This is incidentally the form of melancholy that was experienced by James's "Frenchman" (*V*, pp. 160–161). The intentional object here is not so much the world as meaningless, but rather as evil. And as we get to the more severe forms, what threatens is "desperation absolute and complete, the whole universe coagulating about the sufferer into a material of overwhelming horror, surrounding him without opening or end. Not the conception or intellectual perception of evil, but the grisly blood-freezing heart-palsying sensation of it close upon one.... Here is the real core of the religious problem: Help! Help!" (*V*, p. 162).

The third form of the abyss is the acute sense of personal sin. Here he is talking about, for example, people reacting to standard Protestant revival preaching and feeling a terrible sense of their own sinfulness, even being paralyzed by it—to be later perhaps swept up into the sense of being saved.

James speaks again here of the superiority of the "morbid-minded" view. The normal process of life contains many things to which melancholy (of the second kind, the fear of evil) is the appropriate response: the slaughterhouse, death;

Crocodiles and rattlesnakes and pythons are at this moment vessels of life as we are; their loathsome existence fills every minute of every day that drags its length along; and whenever they or other wild beasts clutch their living prey, the deadly horror which an agitated melancholiac feels is literally the right reaction to the situation. (*V*, pp. 163–164)

The completest religions would therefore seem to be those in which the pessimistic elements are best developed. Buddhism, of course, and Christianity are the best known to us. They are essentially religions of deliverance: the man must die to an unreal life before he can be born into the real life. (*V*, p. 165)

Those who have been through this kind of thing and come out on the other side are the "twice-born." Just as genuine religious experience is the more authentic reality of religion, so this experience is the deeper and more truly religious one. It is thus at the heart of religion properly understood. It is an experience of deliverance; it yields a "state of assurance," of salvation, or the meaningfulness of things, or the ultimate triumph of goodness. Its fruits are a "loss of all worry, the sense that all is ultimately well with one, the peace, the harmony, the *willingness to be*, even though the outer conditions should remain the same" (*V*, p. 248, italics in original). The world appears beautiful and more real, in contrast to the "dreadful unreality and strangeness" felt in melancholy. We are also empowered; the inhibitions and divisions that formerly held us back melt away in the condition James calls "saintliness" (*V*, p. 271). It gives us a sense of being connected to a wider life and a greater power, a sense of elation and freedom, "as the outlines of confining selfhood melt down," a "shifting of the emotional centre towards loving and harmonious affections" (*V*, pp. 272–273).

This is at the heart of religion for James, because this experience meets our most dire spiritual needs, which are defined by the three great negative experiences of melancholy, evil, and the sense of personal sin. Some of the perennial interest in James's book comes from his identifying these three zones of spiritual anguish that continue to haunt our world today.

What did James's take on religion do for James? Or put more impersonally, what was the wider agenda of which it was part? I believe it was a crucial part of James's argument, with himself and his contemporaries, about the admissibility of belief. It was an important part of his *apologia pro fide sua*.

Like any sensitive intellectual of his time and place, James had to argue against the voices, within and without, who held that religion was a thing of the past, that one could no longer in good conscience believe this kind of thing in an age of science. Already a passage in *Varieties* gives a sense of what is at stake in this inner debate. James is speaking of those who are for one reason or another incapable of religious conversion. He refers to some whose "inaptitude" is intellectual in origin:

Their religious faculties may be checked in their natural tendency to expand, by beliefs about the world that are inhibitive, the pessimistic and materialistic beliefs, for example, within which so many good souls, who in former times would have freely indulged their religious propensities, find themselves nowadays, as it were, frozen; or the agnostic vetoes upon faith as something weak and shameful, under which so many of us to-day lie cowering, afraid to use our instincts. (*V*, p. 204)

But a fuller discussion of these "agnostic vetoes," and the answer to them, occurs in "The Will to Believe."[2] Here it is plain that the main source of the vetoes is a kind of "ethics of belief" (and William Clifford's work is explicitly cited, e.g., *WB*, pp. 17–18).[3] This starts from a view of what proper scientific procedure is: never turn your hypotheses into accepted theories until the evidence is adequate. It then promotes this into a moral precept for life in general. The underlying picture of our condition is that we find certain hypotheses more pleasing, more flattering, more comforting, and are thus tempted to believe them. It is the path of manliness, courage, and integrity to turn our backs on these facile comforts and face the universe as it really is. But so strong are the temptations to deviate from this path that we must make it an unbreakable precept never to give our assent unless the evidence compels it.

With his unrivalled gift for striking rhetoric, mixed with irony and gentle, over-the-top parody, James evokes this view:

> When one turns to the magnificent edifice of the physical sciences, and sees how it was reared; what thousands of disinterested moral lives of men lie buried in its mere foundations; what patience and postponement, what choking down of preferences, what submission to the icy laws of outer fact are wrought into its very stones and mortar; how absolutely impersonal it stands in its vast augustness—then how besotted and contemptible seems every little sentimentalist who comes blowing his voluntary smoke-wreaths, and pretending to decide things from out of his private dream! (*WB*, p. 17)

On the same page, James quotes Clifford: "Belief is desecrated when given to unproved and unquestioned statements, for the solace and private pleasure of the believer.... Whoso would deserve well of his fellows in this matter will guard the purity of his belief with a very fanaticism of jealous care, lest at any time it should rest on an unworthy object, and catch a stain which can never be wiped away."[4] The pleasure of illicit belief is a stolen one, asserts Clifford. "It is sinful, because it is stolen in defiance of our duty to mankind. That duty is to guard ourselves from such beliefs as from a pestilence, which may shortly master our own body and then spread to the rest of the town.... It is wrong always, and everywhere, and for anyone, to believe anything upon insufficient evidence" (*WB*, pp. 17–18: One wonders who is more over the top?).[5]

We can see behind Clifford's strictures a stance that draws a good part of its power from the force of the epistemological picture, with its three priority relations mentioned above: (1) self-knowledge before that of others; (2) neutral knowledge before relevances and meanings; (3) knowledge of the natural order before anything beyond. Clifford is drawing on the third priority. But we can see how the plausibility of this third builds on that of the first two. The priority relations tell us not only what is learnt before what, but also what can be inferred on the basis of what. These are foundational relations. I know the world through my representations. I must grasp the world as fact before I can posit values. I must accede to the transcendent, if at all, by inference from the natural. On this understanding, it is obvious that the inference to the transcendent is at the extreme and most fragile end of a series of inferences; it is the most epistemically questionable. And indeed, granted the lack of consensus surrounding this move, as against earlier steps in the chain (e.g., to "other minds"), it is obviously highly problematic.

But once one overturns the first two priorities, the issue of the transcendent begins to appear in a different light. If there is no self-knowledge except through the other, the issue can arise whether this must exclusively be the human other. The work of Lévinas, for instance, poses this question. And if we see meaning, relevance, as primordial in experience, the issue of what kinds of meaning are inescapable arises, and to what extent these might point to the transcendent. These are both mere questions; they don't yield their own answers. But they are plainly James's questions; and they are off the radar screen for Clifford, immersed as he is in the traditional picture.

In any case, James opposes to Clifford's strictures his own counterprinciple:

The thesis I defend is, briefly stated this: Our passional nature not only lawfully may, but must, decide an option between propositions, whenever it is a genuine option that cannot by its nature be decided on intellectual grounds; for to say, under such circumstances, "Do not decide, but leave the question open," is itself a passional decision—just like deciding yes or no—and is attended with the same risk of losing the truth. (WB, p. 20)

Backing this principle is his own view of the human predicament. Clifford assumes that there is only one road to truth: we put the hypotheses that appeal to us under severe tests, and those that survive are worthy of adoption—the kind of procedure whose spirit was recaptured in our time by Popper's method of conjectures and refutation. To put it dramatically, we can only win the right to believe a hypothesis by first treating it with maximum suspicion and hostility.

James holds, on the contrary, that there are some domains in which truths will be hidden from us unless we go at least halfway towards them. Do you like me or not? If I am determined to test this by adopting a stance of maximum distance and suspicion, the chances are that I will forfeit the chance of a positive answer. An analogous phenomenon on the scale of society as a whole is social trust; doubt it root and branch, and you will destroy it.

Here are, then, cases, where a fact cannot come at all unless a preliminary faith exists in its coming. *And where faith in a fact can help create the fact*, that would be an insane logic that should say that faith running ahead of scientific evidence is the "lowest kind of immorality" into which a thinking being can fall (*WB*, pp. 28–29).

But can the same kind of logic apply to religion, that is, to a belief in something that by hypothesis is way beyond our power to create? James thinks it can. What is created is not God or the eternal,[6] but there is a certain grasp of these, and a certain succor from these that can never be ours unless we open ourselves to them in faith. James is, in a sense, building on the Augustinian insight that in certain domains love and self-opening enable us to understand what we would never grasp otherwise, rather than just following on understanding as its normal consequence.[7]

What does that tell us about what the path of rationality consists in for someone who stands on the threshold, deciding whether he should permit himself to believe in God? On one side, there is the fear of believing something false if he follows his instincts here. But on the other, there is the hope of opening out what are now inaccessible truths through the prior step of faith. Faced with this double possibility it is no longer so clear that Clifford's ethic is the appropriate one; because it was only taking account of the first possibility. The two possibilities define an option, and indeed, a forced one, in that there is no third way: to suspend judgement is just as surely to forgo the hope of new truth as to judge negatively.

So Clifford's principle has to be rephrased as a choice: "*Better risk loss of truth than chance of error*—that is your faith-vetoer's exact position" (*WB*, p. 30). But in what does this demonstrate superior rationality to the contrary option?

To preach skepticism to us as a duty until "sufficient evidence" for religion be found, is tantamount therefore to telling us, when in the presence of the religious hypothesis, that to yield to our fear of its being error is wiser and better than to yield to our hope that it may be true. It is not intellect against all passions, then; it is only one passion laying down its law. And by what, forsooth, is the supreme wisdom of this passion warranted? Dupery for dupery, what proof is there that dupery through hope is so much worse than dupery through fear? I, for one, can see no proof; and I simply refuse obedience to the scientist's command to imitate his kind of option, in a case where my own stake is important enough to give me the right to choose my own form of risk. (*WB*, pp. 30–31)

I, therefore, cannot see my way to accepting the agnostic rules for truth-seeking, or wilfully agree to keep my willing nature out of the game. I cannot do so for the plain reason, that *a rule of thinking which would absolutely prevent me from acknowledging certain kinds of truth if those kinds of truth were really there, would be an irrational rule.* (*WB*, pp. 31–32)

The minimal form of James's argument is then, that the supposed superior rationality of the "agnostic veto" on belief—don't believe in God until you have overwhelming evidence—disappears once you see that there is an option between two risks of loss of truth. Everybody should be free to choose their own kind of risk. But this minimal form easily flips into a stronger variant, which is captured by the italicized clause I have just quoted. Taking the agnostic stance could here be taxed as the less rational one.

This is for grounds similar to those laid out in Pascal's famous wager. James has already evoked this above (*WB*, pp. 16–17), and treated it rather caustically. But on reflection, this may be because the Pascalian form is specifically directed to converting the interlocutor to Catholicism, to "masses and holy water." But if one takes the general form of Pascal's argument here, that you should weight two risks not only by their probabilities but also by their prospective "pay-offs," then James himself seems to entertain something of the sort. Religion is not only a "forced option," that is, one in which there is no third way, no way of avoiding choice, but it is also a "*momentous* option. We are supposed to gain, even now, by our belief, and to lose by our non-belief, a certain vital good" (*WB*, p. 30).

The likeness increases when one reflects that Pascal never thought of his wager argument as standing alone, appealing as it were purely to the betting side of our nature, to the instincts that take over when we enter the casinos at Las Vegas. He too, holds the Augustinian view that in matters divine we need to love before we know:

Et de là vient qu'au lieu qu'en parlant de choses humaines on dit qu'il faut les connaître avant de les aimer; ce qui a passé en proverbe, les saints au contraire disent en parlant de choses divines qu'il faut les aimer pour les connaître, et qu'on n'entre dans la verité que par la charité, dont ils ont fait une de leurs plus utiles sentences.[8]

But the issue could be put in other terms again. The single-risk view of the agnostics seems more plausible than James's double-risk thesis, because they take for granted that our desires can only be an obstacle to our finding the truth. The crucial issue is thus the place of "our volitional nature" in the theoretical realm. The very idea that things will go better in the search for truth if you keep passion, desire, and willing out of the picture seems utterly implausible to James. Not just for the reason he thinks he has demonstrated that certain truths only open to us as a result of our commitment, but also because it seems so clear to him that we never operate this way.

So one way he frames the issue is that the agnostic vetoers are asking that he "wilfully agree to keep my willing nature out of the game." But from another standpoint, neither side is really doing this. Agnosticism "is not intellect against all passions, then; it is only intellect with one passion laying down its law" (*WB*, pp. 30–31). To put it in the harsh language of a later politics, those who claim to be keeping passion out are suffering from false consciousness. This is not the way the mind works at all.

This is the point he makes in a subsequent article in *The Will to Believe*, called by the arresting title of "Reflex Action and Theism" (*WB*, pp. 90–113, esp. pp. 99–102). But we can return to *Varieties* and see the claim laid out there. Rationalism gives an account of only a part of our mental life, and one that is "relatively superficial."

It is the part which has the *prestige* undoubtedly, for it has the loquacity, it can challenge you for proofs, and chop logic, and put you down with words. But it will fail to convince or convert you all the same, if your dumb intuitions are opposed to its conclusions. If you have intuitions at all, they come from a deeper level of your nature than the loquacious level which rationalism inhabits. Your whole subconscious life, your impulses, your faiths, your needs, your divinations, have prepared the premises, of which your consciousness now feels the weight of the result; and something in you absolutely *knows* that that result must be truer than any logic-chopping rationalistic talk, however clever, that may contradict it. (*V*, p. 73)

James has in a sense opened up to view an important part of the struggle between belief and unbelief in modern culture. We can see it, after a fashion, from both sides of the fence: even though James has himself come down on one side, we can still feel the force of the other side. Of course, the objections to belief are not only on epistemological grounds. There are also those who feel that the God of theism has utterly failed the challenge of theodicy, how we can believe in a good and omnipotent God, given the state of the world. James addresses this question too, in another essay in *The Will to Believe* ("Is Life Worth Living," *WB*, pp. 34–56).

But if we keep to the epistemological-moral issue of the ethics of belief, James clarifies why it always seems to end in a stand-off. (a) Each side is drawing on very different sources, and (b) our culture as a whole cannot seem to get to a point where one of these no longer speaks to us. And yet (c) we cannot seem to function at all unless we relate to one or the other.

(a) The reason the argument is so difficult, and so hard to join, is that each side stands within its own view of the human moral predicament. The various facets of each stance support each other, so that there seems nowhere you can justifiably stand outside. The agnostic view propounds some picture (or range of pictures) of the universe and human nature, partly constituted by the epistemological picture. This has going for it that it can claim to result from "science" with all the prestige that this carries with it. It can even look from the inside as though this was all you needed to say. But from the outside it isn't at all clear that what everyone agrees are the undoubted findings of modern natural science quite add up to a proof of, say, materialism, or whatever the religion-excluding view is.

From the inside the "proof" seems solid, because certain interpretations are ruled out on the grounds that they seem "speculative" or "metaphysical." From the outside, this looks like a classical *petitio principii*. But from the inside the move seems unavoidable, because it is powered by certain ethical views. These are the ones that James laid bare: it is wrong, uncourageous, unmanly, a kind of self-indulgent cheating, to have recourse to this kind of interpretation, which we know appeals to something in us, offers comfort, or meaning, and which we therefore should fend off, unless absolutely driven to them by the evidence, and this is manifestly not the case. The position holds firm because it locks together a scientific-epistemological view and a moral one.

From the other side, the same basic phenomena show up, but in an entirely different shape. One of the crucial features that justifies aversion to certain interpretations from the agnostic standpoint, namely that they in some way *attract* us, shows up from the believer's standpoint as what justifies our interest. And that very much for the reasons that James explores, namely that this attraction is the hint that there is something important here that we need to explore further, that this exploration can lead us to something of vital significance that would otherwise remain closed to us. Epistemology and ethics (in the sense of intutions about what is of crucial importance) combine here.

From this standpoint, the agnostic's closure is self-inflicted, the claim that there is nothing here that ought to interest us a kind of self-fulfilling prophecy. A similar accusation of circularity is hurled in the other direction. The believer is thought to have invented the delusion that beguiles him.

Each stance creates in a way a total environment, in the sense that whatever considerations occur in one appear transformed in the other. They can't be appealed to in order to decide the issue, because as they pass from one stance to the other they bear a changed meaning that robs them of their force in the new environment. As we have seen, the attraction of certain feelings and intuitions has a totally different significance in the two stances. This totality forces a choice; one cannot accord the two rival meanings to these crucial features at the same time. You can't really sit on the fence, because you need some reading of these features to get on with life. The attraction of theism can be lived as a temptation, or as a promise, but not easily as both at once (unless, of course, you change the meaning of "temptation" or "promise"). The option is forced in James's terms.

(b) And yet both these stances remain possible to many people in our world. Secularists once hoped that with the advance of science and enlightenment, and the articulation of a new, humanist ethic, the illusory nature of religion would be more and more apparent, and its attractions would fade, indeed, give way to repulsion.

Their assumption is often what I have called "the view from Dover Beach": the transition to modernity comes about through the loss of traditional beliefs and allegiances. This may be seen as coming about as a result of institutional changes: for example, mobility and urbanization erode the beliefs and reference points of static rural society. Or the loss may be supposed to arise from the increasing operation of modern scientific reason. The change may be valued positively—or it may be judged a disaster by those for whom the traditional reference points were valuable, and scientific reason too narrow. But all these theories concur in describing the process: old views and loyalties are eroded. Old horizons are washed away, in Nietzsche's image. The sea of faith recedes, following Matthew Arnold. This stanza from his *Dover Beach* captures this perspective:

The Sea of Faith
Was once, too, at the full, and round earth's shore
Lay like the folds of a bright girdle furled.
But now I only hear
Its melancholy, long, withdrawing roar,
Retreating, to the breath
Of the night-wind, down the vast edges drear
And naked shingles of the world.[9]

The tone here is one of regret and nostalgia. But the underlying image of eroded faith could serve just as well for an upbeat story of the progress of triumphant scientific reason. From one point of view, humanity has shed a lot of false and harmful myths. From another, it has lost touch with crucial spiritual realities. But in either case, the change is seen as a loss of belief.

What emerges comes about through this loss. The upbeat story cherishes the dominance of an empirical-scientific approach to knowledge claims, of individualism, negative freedom, instrumental rationality. But these come to the fore because they are what we humans "normally" value, once we are no longer impeded or blinded by false or superstitious beliefs and the stultifying modes of life that accompany them. Once myth and error are dissipated, these are the only games in town. The empirical approach is the only valid way of acquiring knowledge, and this becomes evident as soon as we free ourselves from the thralldom of a false metaphysics.

Increasing recourse to instrumental rationality allows us to get more and more of what we want, and we were only ever deterred from this by unfounded injunctions to limit ourselves. Individualism is the normal fruit of human self-regard absent the illusory claims of God, the Chain of Being, or the sacred order of society. It is clear how this understanding of things gives comfort to the priority relations that define the epistemological picture.

In other words, we moderns behave as we do because we have "come to see" that certain claims were false—or on the negative reading, because we have lost from view certain perennial truths. What this view reads out of the picture is the possibility that Western modernity might be powered by its own positive visions of the good, that is, by one constellation of such visions among available others, rather than by the only viable set left after the old myths and legends have been exploded. It screens out whatever there might be of a specific moral direction to Western modernity, beyond what is dictated by the general form of human life itself, once old error is shown up (or old truth forgotten). For example, people behave as individuals, because that's what they do "naturally" when no longer held in by the old religions, metaphysics, and customs, though this may be seen as a glorious liberation, or a purblind enmeshment in egoism, depending on our perspective. What it cannot be seen as is a novel form of moral self-understanding, not definable simply by the negation of what preceded it.

We might say that all these accounts "naturalize" the features of the modern, liberal identity. They cannot see it as one, historically constructed understanding of human agency among others.

The subtraction story, inadequate though it is, is deeply embedded in modern humanist consciousness. It is by no means propounded only by the more simplistic theorists. Even such a penetrating and sophisticated thinker as Paul Bénichou subscribed to a version of it in his *Morales du grand siècle*: "*L'humanité s'estime dès qu'elle se voit capable de reculer sa misère; elle tend à oublier, en même temps que sa détresse, l'humiliante morale par laquelle, faisant de nécessité vertu, elle condamnait la vie.*"[10] Modern humanism arises, in other words, because humans become capable of sloughing off the older, other-worldly ethics of asceticism.

Moreover, this story is grounded in a certain view of human motivation in general, and of the wellsprings of religious belief in particular. This latter is seen as the fruit of misery and the accompanying self-renunciation is "making a virtue of necessity." Belief is a product of deprivation, humiliation, and a lack of hope. It is the obverse of the human desire for flourishing; where we are driven by our despair at the frustration of this desire.

Thus human flourishing is taken as our perennial goal, even though under eclipse in periods of misery and humiliation, and its content is taken as fairly unproblematic, once one begins to affirm it.

Against this narrative of the inevitable shrinkage of the transcendent, many believers—some of whom also subscribed to their own version of the subtraction story—thought that unbelief was so clearly a willed blindness that people would one day wake up and see through it once and for all. But this is not how it has worked out, not even perhaps how it could work out. People go on feeling a sense of unease at the world of unbelief: some sense that something big, something important has been left out, some level of profound desire has been ignored, some greater reality outside of us has been closed off. The articulations given to this unease are very varied, but they persist and recur in ever more ramified forms. But at the same time, the senses of dignity, control, adulthood, autonomy, connected to unbelief go on attracting people, and seem set to do so into an indefinite future.

What is more, a close attention to the debate seems to indicate that most people feel both pulls. They have to go one way, but they never fully shake off the call of the other. So the faith of believers is made fragile, not just by the fact that other people, equally intelligent, often equally good and dedicated, disagree with them, but also by the fact that they can still see themselves as reflected in the other perspective, that is, as drawn by a too indulgent view of things. For what believer doesn't have the sense that her view of God is too simple, too anthropocentric, too indulgent? We all lie to some extent "cowering" under "the agnostic vetoes upon faith as something weak and shameful" (*V*, p. 204).

On the other side, the call to faith is still there as an understood temptation. Even if we think that it no longer applies to us, we see it as drawing others. Otherwise the ethics of belief would be incomprehensible.

Part of the great continuing interest of James's century-old work is that it lays out the dynamics of this battle so well and clearly. He is on one side, but he helps you imagine what it's like to be on either. In one way, one might interpret him as having wanted to show that you ought to come down on one side, the stronger thesis I offered above; but the weaker reading is that he wanted simply to rebut the idea that reason forces you to the agnostic choice. As Edward Madden puts it in the introduction to *The Will to Believe,* James might be seen as arguing really for a "right to believe" (*WB,* pp. xiii–xxiv); the right to follow one's own gut instinct in this domain, free of an intimidation grounded on invalid arguments.

So what kind of a pragmatist is James? It seems clear to me that he is the "broad" kind, rather than a "radical." There is a continuing invocation of unreduced truth in his argument. The "pragmatist" insight is the one that reverses the priorities of the traditional picture. In particular, he argues convincingly that so far from being able to establish facts quite independent of our desires and loves, in certain domains, truth is undiscoverable without desire. Here he is taking the same line as Pascal. But what you discover is how things really are.

We might object that for James, part of the confirmation of his belief in the validity of certain modes of twice-born experience is precisely the transformation that it wreaks in the convert, as I invoked a few pages back. We have an experience of deliverance, of assurance of the meaningfulness of things, of the triumph of goodness; the world appears beautiful and more real, in contrast to the "dreadful unreality and strangeness" felt in melancholy. We are empowered.

It is clear from these descriptions that things go much better for the one who has come through this crisis twice-born. But it cannot really be sustained that we have here a sense of things "working" that really displaces the center of gravity away from truth as usually understood. It is not just that there are references here in the description of this superior condition to a recovered contact with reality. It is also that the entire superiority of this state is bound up with its being seen to be in more profound contact with reality. The conversion yields a "state of assurance," James says, that things have meaning, that good will triumph. This is the source of the empowerment, and cannot be separated from this empowerment as a merely contingent cause, as I might get high on some drug. Should I come to see it like this, a mere subjective feeling that nevertheless makes me feel better, I would be back in the crisis. The whole account of the twice-born refers us to and grounds on an unreduced understanding of truth.

If this is pragmatism, then count me in. But is it? Have I got James (and pragmatists in general) right? Perhaps I still have lots of catching up to do.

Notes

1. William James, *The Varieties of Religious Experience* (Harmondsworth: Penguin, 1982). Page references to this edition in the text are preceded by *V*.

2. William James, *The Will to Believe and Other Essays in Popular Philosophy* (Cambridge, Mass.: Harvard University Press, 1979). Page references to this edition in the text are preceded by *WB*.

3. William Kingdon Clifford, "The Ethics of Belief" (1877) in volume 1 of his *Lectures and Essays*, ed. Leslie Stephen and Sir Frederick Pollock (New York: Macmillan, 1901), 2 vols., pp. 163–205. [W. K. Clifford (1845–1879) was Professor of Applied Mathematics and Mechanics at University College, London. A legendary polymath, Clifford wrote on topics as diverse as the foundations of pure mathematics, psychology, morality and the decline of religious belief, and "the scientific grounding of right and wrong." Bertrand Russell claimed that, in his theory of the relation of geometry and physics, Clifford had anticipated Einstein's theory of relativity, making him a thinker "ahead of almost all the best thinking of his time." In the year following Clifford's premature death at the age of thirty-three, James wrote a review of his posthumously published *Lectures and Essays* and *Seeing and Thinking* that responded to Clifford's emphatically positivistic notion of the ethics of religion and belief. See William James, "Clifford's 'Lectures and Essays'" (1879) in *Collected Essays and Reviews* (New York: Longmans, 1920), pp. 137–146.—Ed.]

4. Clifford, "Ethics of Belief," pp. 170–171.

5. Ibid., p. 175.

6. But even this stronger claim might have some truth to it: "I confess that I do not see why the very existence of the invisible world may not depend on the personal response which any one of us may make to the religious appeal. God himself, in short, may draw vital strength and increase of very being from our fidelity" (*WB*, p. 55).

Charles Taylor

7. *"Non intratur in veritatem, nisi per charitatem"*; Augustine, *Contra Faustum*, lib. 32, cap. 18.

8. Pascal, quoted in Martin Heidegger, *Sein und Zeit* (Tübingen: Max Niemeyer Verlag, 1967), p. 139, n. 1. ["Instead of speaking about human matters that they have to be known before they can be loved, which has become a proverb, the saints, speaking of divine matters, say that you have to love them in order to know them, and that you enter into truth only by charity, which they have made into one of their most useful pronouncements." Translated in *Pensées and Other Writings*, trans. Honor Levi, ed. Anthony Levi (Oxford: Oxford University Press, 1999), p. 193.—Ed.]

9. Matthew Arnold, "Dover Beach" (1867) in *The Poems of Matthew Arnold*, ed. Kenneth Allott (New York: Barnes and Noble, 1965), pp. 239–243.

10. Paul Bénichou, *Morales du grand siècle* (Paris: Gallimard, 1948), p. 376. ["Humanity comes to esteem itself as soon as it realizes that it is capable of conquering its own wretchedness. It tends to forget, along with its distress, the humiliating morality by which, making a virtue of necessity, it condemned life."—Ed.]

5

Hegel's Aphorisms about "The True"

Yirmiyahu Yovel

Among the diverse topics in which Richard Bernstein excels, Hegel's philosophy—of which he is an outstanding teacher, interpreter, and critical user—occupies a notable place. Hegel's thought is a major source that energizes and gives substance to many of Bernstein's other interests in European philosophy. Since I have recently worked on a commentary on the preface to Hegel's *Phenomenology of Spirit*,[1] I affectionately offer Dick this essay (drawn from the introduction to that commentary), which revolves on the famous dicta, or aphorisms, contained in that classic text: the true [or "absolute"] is subject; the absolute is a result; the true is the whole.

It is ironic that Hegel should use aphorisms to explain his ideas, he who, in the same text—indeed, in those very aphorisms—denies the possibility of saying anything significant about philosophy in a single generalized statement. Such a statement, in addition to lacking truth, fails to contain the meaning that it claims to convey. Truth and meaning require an evolving context; hence, they can arise only at the end, as the result of the full explication and self-transformation of the idea that the general statement purports to enounce, but inevitably misses. Nevertheless, Hegel happily uses those inadequate means of philosophical communication as introductory devices, in prefacing both the *Phenomenology* and the *Philosophy of Right* ("what is rational is actual and what is actual is rational"). Hegel seems to believe that the initiation to a "speculative" (i.e., dialectical) mode of thinking requires a surprising shock, a sense of paradox or enigma that puzzles ordinary rationality (*Verstand*) and calls for the *Aufhebung* of its customary ways of thinking, by which alone the paradox can be resolved. Neither an argument nor a "deduction," this shock treatment is an auxiliary device—call it "Socratic"—serving the process of philosophical *Bildung*.

No less important, Hegel, here as elsewhere, is caught in the grip of what I have called "the antinomy of language." On the one hand he has a strong systematic reason for denying the propriety in philosophical discourse of using the predicative proposition (which is built as a unilateral dependence of a predicate on a subject); yet on the other hand, he has an equally valid systematic reason against devising a special, nonnatural language for philosophy. Philosophical discourse, being rooted in society and its history, cannot be severed from the actual historical languages in which philosophy has evolved and that are all predicative in character (and thereby captive of *Verstand*, abstract rationality). Since no theoretical resolution of this antinomy is possible, Hegel's answer is practical. As his actual unit of discourse he uses not the single sentence but the whole paragraph, and even larger portions of a chapter or an oral explication. This technique allows for the back-and-forth movement, the looping, the undermining of what has just been said, so as to progress to a higher viewpoint that Hegel's dialectic requires and for which it is both famous and notorious.

Using blatantly "predicative" aphorisms may be another device of coping with the antinomy of language. These aphorisms are fundamentally self-refuting; what they say contradicts what they are and seem to perform; so they must either explode (when taken at face value), or their indicative appearance must be bypassed, so that, as merely evocative proverbs, they will serve to allude to what officially they must fail to convey. Either way, these aphorisms are meant to do a preparatory *rhetorical* work, in helping clear the way for the dialectical mode of thinking.

This will have occurred if the newly initiated learner proceeds to a detailed systematic explication of these ironic dicta that despite their dialectical sterility and illusory form, nevertheless point out to an important objective that the learner will have conquered when he or she overcomes the temptation and false promise of learning *from* those dicta.

As given, then, these ironic dicta have a real, important reference and a delusive, vacuous meaning. They bear from the outset a false and a true promise at the same time, which clash at first, creating puzzlement, yet can and must be separated for actual knowledge to proceed.

The view above creates a problem for an interpreter who wishes to explicate the historical Hegel as faithfully as possible, yet does not accept his organistic view of philosophical discourse. Inevitably, I shall use the good old "predicative" language, knowing that an orthodox Hegelian (if any is left) will call my text a mere *conversation about* Hegel rather than expressing the *Sache selbst.*

History, Ontology, and Religion

I also owe a few words about my approach. In my reading, Hegel as social and historical thinker cannot be understood in separation from the specifically Hegelian ontology, according to which being is not given at the outset as finished and actual, but *evolves* toward actuality (more later). In addition, Hegel's account of being discloses several quasi-theological interests. Although Hegel views religion as inferior to philosophy, a kind of metaphoric expression of it—this is true of their form or medium only. With respect to their content, religion and philosophy share the same subject matter and have the same object. This is a rare position in modern philosophy that has, since Descartes and Locke, taken great care to distinguish religion from philosophy, assigning a different and usually more modest role to philosophy. In Hegel, the religious substrate of philosophy is essential and formative, though not in itself, but as *aufgehoben,* and this in two main senses.

First, philosophy stands on a higher level than religion because it is capable of conceptualizing religion's spiritual content: reason is superior to image and metaphor. True, that superiority is not accorded to the abstract rationalism of Descartes and the Enlightenment, which is relegated to lifeless unreason; the Hegelian *Begriff* is rational only insofar as it also contains the essence of the experiences of imagining, feeling, and being, and links them to a historical tradition. This constitutes a different kind of rationality (*Vernunft*) that is distinguished from formal and analytic reason; yet in the final analysis, within the synthesis that all the elements of *Vernunft* are supposed to constitute, it is the rational-conceptual medium that reinstates itself as supreme. In this way the Enlightenment is essentially preserved in Hegel's philosophy, but only after it has reappropriated and encompassed its opponents rather than excluding them.

Second, Hegel takes a heterodox position even *within* the world of religious imagery. Absolute being, God Himself, does not exist as absolute from the outset, but evolves in stages, mediated by the becoming of spirit and human history. This is Hegel's heterodox-dialectical version of Christianity: God does not only become man, He also *becomes God* through the mediation of His becoming man. Human history is the phenomenal manifestation of spirit's process of becoming, and consequently of God's own becoming. These are indeed metaphors, not concepts, but religious metaphor carries philosophical weight for Hegel, since it expresses absolute truth in images.

In a word, Hegel's important social theory is dependent on his view of history, which must be understood against the background of his ontology and with reference to religion. Religion, as a system of images, endows philosophy with experiential and historical depth. Yet Hegel transcends religion to the higher, philosophical concept; and interprets the religious imagery itself in a strongly heterodox way.

Hegel's philosophy thus gives priority to universal thought—the *logos*—though in a dialectical manner that incorporates history, life, social relations, the imagination, and existential experiences within the rational concept itself. Hegel is not a mystic, quite the contrary, but the life experience he calls "absolute knowing" is supposed to offer the individual, in a *rational* manner, that which mystics have always sought in vain to offer through irrational means like enthusiasm, concentration, indeterminate feeling, and so on— namely, a dialectical union with the absolute that encompasses one's whole existential experience and is not confined to one's intellectual mind only. This distinguishes Hegel from other rationalist philosophers—Plato, Aristotle, or Spinoza—for whom such union can only occur through the intellect, and by a separate, extraordinary mental act. The Hegelian "absolute knowing" is supposed to evolve and take shape within the ordinary, secular life-world—through work, family, social concerns, practical engagements, participation in the polity, and so forth—and also through ordinary religious practice: only thus can it attain to pure, conceptual expression.

As I read it then, Hegel's "absolute knowing" is not merely an intellectual event but a living experience and a mode of life. As such it arises from concrete life forms located in some definite historical time and in a social and geographical place. This is how we are anchored in the universe, immersed in a social life and a cultural milieu, and tied to our ordinary, earthly existence. In Hegel's philosophy, the highest spiritual state needs to be realized in and through worldly life. It is not an ascetic ideal aspiring to purity and dependent on mere intellectual concentration.

This was an innovative idea, though Hegel conceived it in a manner partially outdated *even for his time*. Although he wrote when modern capitalism was already on the rise, for him spirit's worldly dimension did not manifest itself primarily in economics, as in Calvinism, but in more solid forms of social life such as the family and the polity, leading to citizenship and the state. Economics *per se* is for Hegel the domain of particular interests fighting a war of all against all—anticipating the jungle capitalism of late nineteenth century and its recurrence in today's globalist era—and therefore lacks spirit. Nevertheless, a social-democratic reading of Hegel might argue that since the state is based on civil society (as its sublation), and Hegelian civil society presupposes the interplay of economic interests, therefore the state's universality must permeate economic life and gives it, too, a universal significance beyond itself.

In a word, Hegel's thought assigns importance and weight to worldly (social and personal) secular life, while viewing it as embodying a meaning that extends beyond itself, a rational meaning in Hegel's sense that translates (or *aufhebt*) a religious meaning. Spirit is realized in the secular world, but the secular world is not merely a contingent, inferior being; it is precisely the embodiment of spirit and the sole terrain in which it evolves. Even absolute knowing, the top intellectual and existential state, is not severed from the rest of this worldly life, but is realized through it.

With these background remarks in mind, we can turn to the two main aphorisms in the preface.

The Absolute as Subject

According to my way of seeing ... everything depends on
    comprehending and expressing the true not as *substance*,
    but equally also as *subject*.

This famous dictum has several meanings and implications, historical and systematic.

The Historical Meaning: A Synthesis of Spinoza and Kant

Historically, this dictum calls for a synthesis between Spinoza's concept of substance and Kant's (and Fichte's) concept of subject. Each of these poles is to be liberated from its one-sidedness, so that the road to "absolute knowing" can be opened. Hegel declared this synthesis to be the final goal of his philosophy, and a task defining philosophical modernity in general. In fact, at least in Germany, this project stood at the center of philosophical, cultural, and even political interests for almost a century following Kant's *Critique*. The divergent attempts to establish a union between Kant and Spinoza is visible in Fichte, the early Schelling, Hegel himself, Schopenhauer, and some of the left Hegelians, including (in a less obvious way) Marx.

Being as a Process of Self-Actualization

From an *ontological* standpoint, asserting that "the absolute is subject" means, in the first place, that *being itself exists as a process of becoming*; it is not given in its perfect state from the outset, but has to be actualized. For this reason, absolute being (as another famous dictum says in this text) is a *result*—of its own movement and self-becoming. It is therefore equally a purposive process that has itself—in its actualized essence—as the immanent goal of its movement. This also implies that the movement of mediation—philosophical knowledge—is not external to being but is being's own movement. Being-as-subject knows itself, and this knowledge actualizes being according to its true essence.

The process to which this difficult and profound idea refers is not only the movement of something *in* being, but the movement of being itself—its evolution toward higher levels of actuality. In its lower stages, being's subjective character, that is, its self-actualizing movement, is manifest in the organic domain: the phenomenon of life. In its higher stages it is a historical movement—the movement of culture, practical life, social forms and institutions, and of the consciousness they enable and embody. And at still a further stage this is the movement of *self*-consciousness, pure contemplative cognition, and absolute spirit.

An Aristotelian idea is hiding in this Hegelian view: there are several stages of being, and reality evolves (in Hegel: dialectically, and in spirals) from one to the other until it attains *energeia*, actuality, or "entelechy." The Aristotelian God, however, as the unity of the knower and the known, exists outside humans and outside the world itself (at least on its limits), and is perfect from the outset; whereas in Hegel's strictly immanent and historical approach, God, or the absolute, can make sense only in so far as he exists in time and within the world, and attains his perfect state through human culture and its evolution.

Knowledge and Culture as States of Being

The "subjectivity" of being thus indicates (a) the self-*actualizing* movement of being, and (b) the self-*knowledge* of being. The two senses are complementary, and the second is the climax of the first, its "entelechy" of sorts. Both senses are united at the top stage, where being is supposed to be fully actualized in knowing itself through human philosophy, religion, and art. Thus the idea of the "absolute as a result" follows from the idea of absolute-as-subject. It also follows that human culture, with its necessary social and historical frame, is not some external, contingent relation into which being happens to enter, but is a state of being's own development.

Truth as an Ontic State

This also affects Hegel's philosophical concept of truth, as distinguished from the truth of a formal or an empirical statement. In philosophy, truth is not the concept's adequacy with external reality but, first of all, the adequacy of reality with its own inner concept, or end. Truth is therefore an ontic state and not a state of consciousness (or a property of sentences) only. It is linked to the process of the actualization of being and its several degrees. This is why Hegel refers to a higher stage as the "truth" of the one preceding it: the higher stage does not only *disclose* what the lower one implicitly contains, but thereby also *actualizes* it.

Another important way of viewing the absolute as subject concerns the structure of the movement by which being is actualized, and the role that negation fulfills within it. And this has direct relevance to the logic and method of philosophy.

The Subject and Self-Negation

To be a subject is to exist according to a certain ontological structure (or "logic") that differs from that of a substance or mere thing. The most crucial difference lies in the subject's characteristic activity, which is to negate, or generate negation. This negation is first directed at the subject itself, and at any content or definite state with which the subject seems initially to be identified. The subject therefore exists as distinguished from itself, it transcends its own particular states and negates any immediacy that exists within it, or is attributed to it. Of course, in the last analysis, the subject has also a positive activity in which it recognizes certain stable contents as "its own," identifies with them, and reconstitutes its identity through them. Yet even this positive activity is performed and mediated by negation. It presupposes a series of negations that do not return the process to its point of departure; rather, each negation constitutes a new state of affairs, and of consciousness. As a result, the subject attributes to herself a diversity of states and contents that are seen in retrospect as expressing her selfhood, and even as the subject's own particularization. Yet this is a selfhood *in process*, a becoming-selfhood, which will not actually exist until it reaches the end of the road. In other words, as long as the process is still ongoing, *there is no actual subject.*

Self-Identity as a Result

This implies a crucial distinction between the identity of a substance and the identity Hegel attributes to a subject. A substance or mere thing is directly identical with itself: its self-identity is conceived as a simple primary datum, A=A. A subject, however, does not have a simple identity of the same form (I=I). Its self-identity must be understood as an activity of *self-identification* that takes place through the mediation of otherness and is attained only at the end of the process. Therefore, as mentioned above, the subject is not immediately self-identical, but acquires and constitutes its identity both through the complete process and as its *result.*

This idea is pertinent to today's debates concerning the subject: does the subject have identity and ontological status in itself? Hegel's negative answer to the question above has its origin in the "transcendental deduction" of the *Critique of Pure Reason*, where Kant explicates the structure of the "I think" while tacitly polemicizing against Descartes. Today, many uninformed writers simply equate Descartes's *cogito*, or immediate self, with Kant's and Hegel's concept of the subject; yet the latter is fundamentally anti-Cartesian, because it lacks self-identity until it enters a reciprocal relation with the world. Descartes presented the "I think" (a) as a simple, primary datum; (b) as substance; and (c) as a *thinking* thing (*res cogitans*). Opposing Descartes, Kant argued that "I think" is neither a substance nor a simple datum, but a complex structure whose self-identity presupposes a series of *preconditions*. Put succinctly: the identity of the "I" is made possible because the "I" refers to a plurality of sensible data, unites it according to patterns of connectivity (the "categories") established by the intellect—which follow from the implicit structure of the "I" itself—and attributes those connections to the unity of an objective world and to a temporal sequence that is separate from the "I" and faces it. Only through this complex process can the "I" eventually *return* to itself as identical, say "I think" to itself, and thus constitute, or actualize, the self-identity that was lacking at the outset.

From this it follows—already in *Kant's* philosophy—that: (a) the subject's self-identity occurs as the result of a set of relationships—or of a process—and is not primordially given; (b) it is an activity of self-identification, not an inert fact; (c) the pure subject is identified with itself through the mediation of its opposites—the sense impressions opposing the understanding, and the outer world opposing the "I."

"The Absolute Is a Result"

Hegel adopts this Kantian model and extends its application from the finite "I" also to infinite, comprehensive reality. Absolute being itself has the structure of a subject. It, too, is not from the outset that which it will ultimately become, but *proceeds toward itself* through multiplicity and otherness, namely, through its opposites. Yet in addition, multiplicity and otherness are now considered to be the subject's *own* particularization. Thereby, Hegel breaks away from the boundaries of the Kantian critique of reason—which requires the subject to have an external source for all its particular contents—and gives the subject a daring metaphysical (and also theological) interpretation. The subject discussed in Hegel's theory is not only the "I" of a finite individual—of this or that man or woman—but also of the overall subject, God as immanent in nature and history, or the Spinozistic substance become subject-object. Thus, Hegel uses the Kantian model of the subject—with a crucial change—in order to explicate not only the ontology of finite, conditioned beings, as Kant did, but also the ontology of the infinite, absolute being. Hence again the dictum that "the absolute is a result."

The Subject's "Self-Particularization"

Hegel's readers are often puzzled by an apparently mysterious problem. Against Kant, Hegel demands that the multifold of particulars that the subject ascribes to itself be seen not as utterly external but, in a certain sense, as the subject's own particularization. This is hard to grasp, and still harder to accept, when considering the individual mind in separation from spirit's broader context; in other words, when trying to understand the issue ahistorically, in pure epistemological terms. Who in his or her right mind would agree that, for instance, the particular contents of our sensation, or the contingent facts that face us and lie beyond our control, have their "material" source in our own consciousness? (That Kant had spoken problematically, and Schelling in an affirming mode, of some supersensible "common origin" of all our mental functions and activities is, if not mysticism, at least an unprovable transcendent wish.) Many interpreters struggling with this problem have felt forced to attribute a mystical position to Hegel, according to which the mind spontaneously particularizes itself into the rich, manifold system of the world. I think however that Hegel's doctrine is better understood by realizing that it is not primarily concerned with epistemology and the individual mind, but with the ontology (indeed, the historicized ontology) of the comprehensive "I," or spirit. From this perspective it follows that:

(a) The particularization in question does not concern contingent empirical particulars, like facts or sense perceptions (not Professor Krug's pen), but primarily the ontological categories: Being, Being-there, Quantity, Essence, and so forth. Only *these* are said to derive from the absolute subject, and in *The Science of Logic* they follow indeed a structured dialectical development, rather than forming a mere assemblage, which Hegel says both Aristotle and Kant have done.

(b) All the other contents that eventually appear in the system of philosophy, concepts like "matter," "family," "passion," "Stoicism," "civil society," or "magnetism," and so forth—are first borrowed from historical experience. But since the historical experience has been philosophically shaped as the unfolding of the spirit, these contents, too, can be seen as spirit's own particularization in the process in which spirit is realized; and from this viewpoint they are neither contingent nor external. To be sure, the *particular* individual person will always see such contents as contingent and external to herself; but here the process of philosophy comes in, whereby the individual sets out to understand herself, her history, the formation of her consciousness, and thereby reaches the point where she views these ingredients as belonging to her own identity and not as contingent and imposed by accident. For this to happen, the individual must (1) attain a self-consciousness that grasps her connection to world spirit as a whole; and (2) she must be living in an era that is not completely alienated, and within circumstances that allow the individual, in great measure, to rationally identify with the basic ingredients of her social, political, and cultural environment.

In such a case Hegel would say that the particular contents of the individual's world are not external and contingent even for that individual person. They are rather the spiritual, historically shaped particulars that participate, at least partially, in constituting the individual's own self—in so far as the self can link and identify with the universal spirit as embodied in that individual's culture, time, and place. In a word, the question of "particularization" must not be dealt with in epistemological terms mainly, but in social and historical ones.

A crucial role is assigned here to the concept of *memory*. Memory (as substantive memory) is the inventory of past experiences and cultural forms that human spirit has accumulated, and that it must bring to self-consciousness in the proper systematic form. (In Hegelian parlance, the interiorized and memorized *in-itself* must become *for-itself*.) *Erinnerung*, in its dual meaning as interiorization and recollection, creates a mental inventory of images, language, experiences, items of knowledge, aspirations, conflicts, norms, and so forth, which serve as the material substrate of spirit's evolution, and from which its components can pop up and be recollected as the need arises. This *erinnert* substrate enables the philosophical system to particularize itself into specific topics and categories. The thought contents of the past, having fulfilled their role in the life of the spirit, are thereby interwoven into spirit's own texture, even though they have not attained self-consciousness. Whenever the dialectic reaches a point in which the former state has become incoherent in a specific way, defining a *specific* lack, and calling for something new whose contours are marked by that specific lack (although its actual content remains unknown), the sought after element is supposed to emerge from the *erinnert* substrate of spirit's evolution—from its substantive memory, so to speak—and, recalled and articulated, be integrated into the further progress of the dialectic. The particulars of the system are thereby both derived and novel; their genesis depends on what has gone on before, but performs new, nonanalytic leaps mediated by recollection, and therefore are seen as spirit's own. This, again, is why Hegel considers his system's particularization into specific concepts to be self-particularization; for when spirit derives these concepts from its recollection of its own past, it can be said to be deriving them from itself.

Philosophical knowledge in Hegel is thus, as in Plato, basically recollection. Indeed, specifically, I take the theory of *Er-innerung* to be Hegel's chief version of Plato's theory of recollection, and to be as central, for the following reasons:

(1) It stands at the background of the concept of *Bildung* (cultural education);

(2) it explains why the system's plurality of concepts is considered in Hegel as self-particularization;

(3) it enables the dialectic itself, because only on the basis of a spiritual (or mental) process that is capable of memory can a double negation create a new state rather than return to the point of departure. Moreover, without the capacity of *Erinnerung*, no subject-like characteristics can conceivably pertain to being, or to any subsystem of it, and no process of self-actualization can take place: there can be only self-identical, inert "facts," "data," numbers, "simple propositions," and so on, governed by an all-embracing law of simple identity and noncontradiction; in other words, there can be only *Verstand*.

The Absolute as a Totality-in-Becoming

However, in being construed as subject, "the true" (being) is neither inert nor immediately identical with itself; it constitutes its self-identity by becoming other than itself, and by rediscovering itself in its otherness, and as the result of its own development. This also implies that the latent rational essence of all there is externalizes itself in the empirical world, and exists in a variety of shapes and degrees in nature and history. Those shapes diverge from the rational essence in ways that cause them to oppose it, and that often alienate the essence to itself. Yet although the essence seems to have been lost in its contradictions, it in fact remains present and active in them, and continues through them to structure the movement of the evolving reality. That process is supposed to continue until the stage at which the rational essence is capable of rediscovering itself in and through the empirical world, and to adequately actualize itself.

The self-actualization of spirit is equally conceived as a process of *liberation*. Freedom has both an ontological sense and a sociopolitical sense in Hegel, which mediate one another. It entails freedom from political oppression as well as the autonomy of self-realization—the subject's becoming a true individual through both political rights and standing, and through personal awareness—an awareness that is no less practical and experiential than intellectual, that her natural, social, and political environment is not an alien (or even alienating) "substance" but the active expression—and a buttressing externalization—of her own rational self: this view of freedom is a central aspect of the idea of substance becoming a subject.

To say that the process ends in freedom is a human perspective; from the standpoint of being it ends with its actualization as the absolute, when the immanent totality of all there is reaches self-understanding through human culture and philosophy. This development fully actualizes the subjective character of substance and makes it into a subject-object. Thus, according to Hegel, the emergence of "absolute knowing"—and of human freedom—is a crucial event not only in the history of the human race, *but also in the history of being itself.*

Society and Politics as Conditions for Knowledge

A well-known feature of Hegel's philosophy is that the ontological process (the actualization of being), and the process of knowledge that serves it, are carried and mediated by social and historical evolution. Opposing a common belief maintained from Plato to analytic philosophers today, this genuinely Hegelian idea—perhaps his most innovative—maintains that philosophical knowledge does not occur within a separate logical space of its own, but is the conceptualization of diverse forms of social, political, mental, religious life, as they have already been realized in the world. Knowledge depends on its own history, and also on the history of other, practical forms of culture embodied in the objective world that philosophical knowledge explicates.

Hence the crucial importance of human *practice* in the history of being's realization. In this context, the subjectivity of the absolute indicates that social and cultural life, with its multifeatured forms of private and public consciousness, are genuine modes in which *being itself* exists and develops.

This further implication of the subject-like character of being is equally expressed in Hegel's familiar concept of "objective spirit," its externalization in social and political institutions, through which—by its *Aufhebung*—spirit can be actualized and know itself also in its inner dimensions, including philosophy, art, and religion. The latter, which Hegel dignifies as "absolute spirit," presupposes the evolution of the normative and institutional world, created by the rational human will (rather than by theoretical reason) as it embodies itself in public norms and customs, contractual relations, the family, law, the state, civil service, and the patterns in which these formal and informal institutions are shaped and operate. Even the mind's relation to nature is mediated by its relation to other minds and institutions, since in knowing nature and in using nature (as technology, property, etc.) it is engaged in socially mediated activities. Since Hegel, not satisfied with pronouncing this thesis in the abstract, spells it out in detail in such works as the *Phenomenology* and *The Philosophy of Right*, it may seem that the social dimension of the absolute-as-spirit is its most important; however, philosophical knowledge, although dependent on that process, stands higher. Like Plato, Aristotle, and Spinoza, Hegel maintains in the final analysis the primacy of knowledge.

"Absolute Knowing" as Hegel's Secular "Love of God"

If overall being attains self-knowledge through human knowledge, it is because it contains human knowledge as one of its integral constituents. Hegel insists that this is internal knowledge, that is, knowledge that contemplates its object because it belongs to its very constitution. As such, philosophical contemplation is not only knowledge *about* reality, it is, in a major sense, reality's contemplation of itself. Hence, from the individual philosopher's viewpoint, the act of philosophical knowledge involves her dialectical unification with the whole of being. This is Hegel's own, rational and nonmystical version of the goal or stage that mysticism misleads its followers to expect, but (because it strays into indefinite meaninglessness) cannot deliver. When a person is engaged in the philosophical act of knowing and in the social and political activity that makes that act possible, he or she, the finite human being, is contemplating actualized being from within, and is an inner moment of it. This person is thereby not only united with absolute being but, in a minor way, even helps constitute it. Philosophy is not a detached, analytical contemplation through the intellect only, but a mode of being, a living experience of the person who contemplates being from within. At the same time, this is not a vague and isolated romantic event, because it occurs through the medium of conceptual thinking, and because the thinker is equally engaged in practical life, which enables philosophical knowing to be actualized. This sociopractical involvement "secularizes" the act and deromanticizes the experience.

Thus again, the phase known as "absolute knowing" involves an *Aufhebung* of religion and mysticism that preserves their underlying interests. It radically differs from mysticism yet pursues similar goals. The difference lies, first, in the rational character of the Hegelian method that translates everything to the medium and level of the concept. And second, the experiential element that Hegel's absolute knowing preserves is largely nourished by practical concerns—the individual's immersion in worldly affairs, in social relations and political activity and participation. It is not a privileged mental event confined to a person's interior world, nor a form of contemplation that takes us beyond this world to a transcendent domain. Even at the highest stage, the individual continues living an ordinary life in the external world, in society, in her daily work and occupation, as an active member of the polity, in the privacy of the family, and the public arena of politics, without retiring into a closed inner world, or being carried away by romantic enthusiasm. This, I take it, is Hegel's version of Spinoza's "intellectual love of God." More broadly, it is Hegel's this-worldly substitute for the mystical notion that knowing God is union with him.

Implications for the Method and System of Philosophy

The subjective nature of the absolute has far-reaching effects also on the method and system of philosophy. Since reality itself has a subject-like structure, Hegel concludes that philosophical logic, which has to express that structure, must likewise have a subject-like character. From a methodological point of view, to say that "the absolute is subject" amounts to saying that actuality is shaped by dialectical logic rather than by ordinary, formal logic.

Subject and substance each obey a different ontic logic. The logic of substance is the logic of entities that are directly and tautologically self-identical (A=A), and therefore obey the law of non-contradiction. Within this domain, the negation of negation is a tautology that simply reverts to the point of departure ($\sim\sim p = p$). However, such items are not actual beings in Hegel's judgment, but abstractions. True actuality is governed by another kind of *logos*, the *logos* of evolving, subject-like systems that are not self-identical at the outset, and in which double negation produces something new.

Another consequence of viewing the absolute as subject is that philosophical logic must derive from the structure of the subject matter that it is investigating, rather than being imposed on ("applied to") it externally. Hegel derives "logic" from *logos*, the principle the Greeks understood as structuring reality; and partly also from Kant's concept of "transcendental logic." As in Kant, philosophical logic is not an abstract calculus but a "logic of objects," the constitutive element of real beings; but unlike Kant, it is not an *a priori* set of norms preceding its subject matter and "applied" to it externally. Hegel's dialectical, subject-like logic cannot be formalized, not even by Fichte's famous formula "thesis-antithesis-synthesis." All we can learn in advance from this logic are a few general characteristics: for example, that every domain of actual being will have a subject-like shape; that it will thereby have an evolving, organic nature that must be actualized through otherness; and that, as such, it can be expected to return to itself as the result of a three-stage process. Beyond those generalities, one cannot produce a set of formal, mandatory a priori rules that must be followed in all particular cases. One must rather depend on some intellectual intuition—or "phenomenological insight" in the modern sense—which immerses itself in the philosophical subject matter and follows its movement "from within."

Formal logic is valid and binding in mathematics, the natural sciences, and daily discourse and argumentation, areas that Hegel sees as abstract because they peel off a single, one-sided aspect of being and grasp it as if it were the whole. The elements in these domains are allegedly simple, self-identical units of discourse (simple data, numbers, symbols, facts, self-identical arguments, inert systems, and objects built as aggregates of such entities), whose identity is modeled on that of a substance, not a subject, and which therefore must obey the law of noncontradiction. Hence formal logic is the supreme canon of *Verstand*, but not *Vernunft*; and the entities under its legislation are, in Hegel's ontology, abstract, imaginary beings—not complete nothingness, to be sure, but impoverished reflections of being, similar to Plato's "appearances."

It is ironic that both Hegel and the positivists make the same criticisms of each other. The positivist believes the concrete world to be constructed from allegedly "simple" units (sensible and logical), and sees a dogmatic metaphysician in any philosopher who, like Hegel, regards the empirical particulars as expressing an inner conceptual "essence." For Hegel, however, the dogmatic metaphysician is the positivist, because he/she takes such abstractions and imaginary entities ("the simple") to be actual beings.

Subject-like logic is appropriate to all areas that express the movement of self-actualizing systems: the philosophy of mind, of being (ontology), of society, culture, and history. Above all, it is the way philosophy *itself* is to construe and relate to its objects. Philosophy, too, is a mode of being's movement and actualization; therefore, dialectical logic, with its subject-like shape, must come to bear on the structure of philosophy and the way its specific areas are organized.

The chief methodological demand implied here is that philosophical truth be shaped as an organic totality that maintains itself through its own negations. If true philosophy must express the structure of reality from within, and if that structure is subject-like, then philosophy must share the same structure. Hence the second famous dictum of our preface, "the true is the whole."

The True Is the Whole

This famous dictum is usually understood as a principle of method only. It is said that Hegel holds a coherence theory of truth, and therefore requires that all the system's ingredients be given in order to be reciprocally verified. This reading is only partially adequate. It ignores the ontological basis of Hegel's view, and also the developmental character of truth in his system.

When Hegel asserts that the true is the whole, he immediately adds his *own* explanation: "The true is the whole. Yet the whole is but the essence which brings itself to fulfillment through its development. Of the absolute it must be said that it is essentially a result, that only at the end is the absolute what it is in truth; and herein consists its nature—to be actual, subject, or becoming-its-own-self" (*Phenomenology of Spirit*, preface [my translation]).

This passage links the three dicta: The true is subject, the absolute is a result, the true is the whole—which are disclosed here as ingredients of a single idea. Therefore the claim that the true is the whole says more than the ordinary coherence theory. First, Hegel is speaking of an organic, or dialectical coherence, not of external links of inference connecting static, self-identical items. Second, the "whole" in question includes its own generation as one of its elements. The philosopher cannot therefore sever the result from its genesis and view the process of development as a scaffold only, to be discarded when the goal is reached, as can be done in mathematical demonstrations and analytical arguments. This applies to both the history of philosophy and the resulting system of philosophy. In the finished system of philosophy, every member is supposed to point to all the others in a process of negation and negation-of-negation, so that thought cannot rest until it runs the whole course of the system; even then, it cannot hold on to it as something fixed and finished, but rather as a self-repeating conceptual movement.

In this sense the history of philosophy is preserved (as *aufgehoben*) in the pure system of philosophy. The diachronic process that has generated the system is negated, but preserved in new form, within the synchronic movement of the resulting system of philosophy that emerges from it. If we forego that movement and make do with a simple list of concepts and principles that constitute the final system, like Kant's list of the categories, we shall lose the dynamic structure of their mutual inter-negation, and thereby their truth. And if we offer some general proposition or formula as a concluding summary, again we shall have an abstract and unrealized universal, which cannot, as such, be true; rather, in so far as it is abstract and only part of the story, it is false.

An ironic illustration of this is given by our own dictum—"the true is the whole." Because it stands in the preface as an abstract generality severed from its systematic context—given in the remainder of the book—the dictum fails to convey its own purported meaning and is, dialectically speaking, false.

Third, the true is the whole not only in the sense that its diverse elements form a unified system of discourse, but also in that knowledge is therein unified with its object. The system of philosophy does not reflect the world from the outside; it expresses in the subject's domain the same structure that has successfully realized itself in the objective world. Hence the ontic character of truth, by virtue of which it *is* truth. "Truth" does not denote the property of a sentence or a statement, but a certain mode of being, which is revealed to itself in philosophical knowledge. It is therefore the ontic nature of truth from which its methodological conditions are also derived, including the principle of coherence.

Truth has been traditionally—and notoriously—defined as *adequatio rei et intellectus*. This definition views the thing and the concept as two foreign elements sharing nothing in common: there is a world of things and a world of thoughts, and the latter must conform to the former. Hegel, like Kant, has no problem accepting the nominal definition (because it is so broad it says practically nothing), but rejects the dualism inherent in it. If the concept agrees with reality, it is because reality has evolved until it agreed with its concept (which includes its self-knowledge through philosophy). Or, putting it conversely, the two agree because the concept is latent in reality as its essential principle that drives reality to develop and agree with it (and thus, in the final analysis, to agree with *itself*, with its own essence). Rather than being radically foreign, heterogeneous elements, reality and the concept are complementary moments within a single dialectical process. This is expressed in yet another Hegelian aphorism, which many readers take to be social or political, but which *is primarily ontological*: "What is rational is actual, and what is actual is rational." Hegel does not intend to confer the adjective "rational" (or, for that matter, "actual") on *any* contingent existence, but only on that existence (or existent) that has been actualized and reached its rational telos. The rational and the actual are united only at the final stage of being's evolution. (This peculiar speculative view can be called "an ontic theory of truth.")

Hegel rejects (a) the representational view of truth, for which the concept corresponds to reality because it copies or represents the real as it is in itself. This view presupposes that being does not change but is forever static, only our concepts about it evolve until they correspond to it. Yet Hegel's objective, evolutional idealism maintains there is a process of self-actualization in being itself, mediated by human thought and action. (b) Hegel rejects the main thesis of Kant's brand of idealism, according to which the concept corresponds to reality because it constitutes it. Kant's flaw consisted in presupposing that concepts are external to reality and injected into it (or imposed on it) by the human mind. This "subjective" idealism, as Hegel calls it, gives priority to the subject over the object, and makes reality a function of knowledge. By contrast, Hegel claims that the concept does not reside in our knowledge alone, but is implicitly at work in the *object* of our knowledge, and as this object—reality, or being—evolves toward its concept, it enables knowledge, too, to develop more clearly and to consciously explicate that implicit concept.

In summary, the true is the whole, but the whole includes the process of its own genesis, as well as the moment of being with which it stands in a dialectical relation. Only in this way does the system of philosophy form an organic, self-grounding whole which, like Spinoza's *causa sui*, bears witness to its own truth.

This leads to several consequences concerning Hegel's theory of discourse (which could also have arisen independently of the speculative background we have just surveyed):

(1) Philosophical statements are said to be true only within their complete dynamic context. It is therefore impossible to sever a proposition from the overall context and still ascribe a truth value to it, as the analytic understanding tends to do. A singular statement, even if it merely summarizes the system's conclusions, must miss those conclusions and function as an "abstract universal" whose form opposes the content it purports to express.

(2) The same applies to the *meaning* of a philosophical statement. Just as singular statements have no autonomous truth value, so they also lack an autonomous meaning. They fail to express adequately what they are said to state. Hegel views meaning as dependent on an implied intentionality (*meinen*), yet every partial statement or sentence is marked by a dialectical opposition between its meaning and what is intended by it: that which the statement says in actuality must fall short of what it says (or "intends saying") implicitly. This opposition explains the need for further development of the statement and serves as the drive for it. As long as the inadequacy persists, it indicates that the explication has not attained its goal and must move on. Only at the end, when the circular totality lacks nothing, is it possible to expound its true meaning—and that of each specific category within the system.

(3) The same must be said of the learner's subjective *process of understanding*. This issue concerns no longer the logical relations between the elements of discourse, but the learner's ability to grasp

the philosophical meanings that they express. And here, again, Hegel argues that philosophical understanding requires the complete system: a person who has carefully gone through the system's detailed stages will grasp a single sentence (a generalization) very differently than someone hearing that sentence for the first time. For the latter person, the sentence is an indeterminate, out-of-context generality, whereas for the person who already knows the system, it compresses and summarizes an entire set of interrelations that are present in his/her memory. Even generalizations like "the true is the whole" or "the absolute is a result" will have a completely different value at the end of the road than at the beginning.

Dialectics as Journey and Dialectics as Science

I should like to conclude by distinguishing two different directions in the Hegelian dialectic, which I label "*dialectic as journey*" and "*dialectic as science*" (using the latter term in Kant's and Hegel's sense of [a philosophical] *Wissenschaft*). These two directions had already existed in Plato's dialectic. Dialectic as journey is basically negative: Socrates puts questions to his interlocutors (for example, Theaetetus) in order to undermine their dogmatic beliefs. As a result, they adopt a new position that resolves, as they believe, the flaws in their previous position. But this is only a tentative resolution. The second position is eventually also undermined and calls for a third to overcome it, and so forth. In this process of negative dialectic, each new stand is nourished by the failure of its predecessor(s), and draws its new positive content from their inadequacy and its negation. For Plato this process is an ascent, a journey toward knowledge and true being, which climbs a preestablished ladder, described in the *Republic* and elsewhere; whereas for Hegel the process traces its own way and builds, as it were, its own ladder. Also, in Plato the road is undergone by a single disciple—a Theaetetus, a Glaucon, and so forth—whereas Hegel historicized Plato's process of education: the pupil or apprentice undergoing the process of dialectics-as-journey *is the entire human race*. Correspondingly, the single individual is limited by his times, and cannot advance beyond the constraints of his or her contemporary culture and the new, if limited, perspective opened up by the *Zeitgeist*. The Platonic trainee, however, is free of such limitations and depends solely on his individual talents and those of his teacher.

Taking a retrospective look, Hegel reviews this process in the *Phenomenology* as it had led to the modern era and made it possible. Human consciousness has experienced all the important positions and standpoints that it might take, and has transcended them because of the one-sided and limited character that undermines each partial position from within, and exposes its immaturity. Dialectic as journey—a journey to truth, or to "science" (*episteme*)— with its successive negations and transcendings, cannot cease before consciousness finally rises to a comprehensive standpoint. At this stage, all the partial perspectives of earlier stages are *aufgehoben* and retained in the higher synthesis, where they do not exclude each other but rather mutually constitute a common result. *At this point, dialectic as journey becomes dialectic as science.* The sequence of negations that links the partial standpoints is interiorized into the system of absolute knowledge in which they function as a positive, constructive factor.

The Platonic philosopher, too, after he has gone through all the stages of dialectic-as-journey, finally arrives at the vision of the ideas (forms). Henceforth he becomes a "dialectician" in a new, positive sense (discussed in the *Republic*, the *Parmenides*, and the *Sophist*)—the one who knowingly moves within the realm of ideas and truth. For Hegel, at least in his middle period, this is the stage at which the *Phenomenology* turns into the *Science of Logic*—the foundation of absolute knowing. The appearance of positive dialectic does not abolish negative dialectics, but reverses its result. Within dialectic-as-science there is also a permanent transcending of each position—or category—but the sum total of these negations and transcendings now upholds the positive system of truth. In a Dionysian image that he takes from the Greek mystics, Hegel draws an analogy with the Bacchanalian dance, where no dancer remains in his or her place; all are whirling in an intoxicated ecstasy (*extasis*—a transcending of oneself), yet their repeated mutual motion creates a stable, transparent, and circular structure. Similarly, dialectic as science is a system of negations and transcendings that have been interiorized and now maintain the system from within.

Dialectic-as-science is thus the "synchronic" movement within which the universe of absolute knowing is achieved, and dialectic-as-journey is the "diachronic" movement toward it. From a textual point of view, we might say that the *Phenomenology* corresponds to dialectic-as-journey and the *Science of Logic* represents dialectic-as-science.

Dialectic as Subjective Education

In its journey mode, the *Phenomenology* has a further, subjective and educational task: to offer the individual a ladder by which he or she can be liberated from the standpoint of naive consciousness, and attain philosophy. This, too, is an aspect of dialectic-as-journey, now seen from the standpoint of the philosophizing individual. The need for a ladder arises from recognition that rational truth cannot be externally imposed on the individual. Consciousness must be able to recognize truth as *its own*—an expression of its selfhood. Yet, philosophical truth at first is alien to the individual and extremely remote from him/her. The *Phenomenology* offers the individual that same ladder that universal human consciousness has been climbing up to his/her time, and helps the individual personally to climb it. It starts from the point where the nonphilosophical individual stands at the present—sense certainty, perception, passion, the familiar world, and so forth—and is supposed to ascend step by step, stage by stage—even if by spiral, roundabout moves—toward absolute knowledge. The evolution of the *Phenomenology* is therefore the development of a personal, subjective mind that experiences the dialectical contradictions arising within it as a *personal* problem and malaise, and is driven beyond them in search of new positions. Within this subjective journey, the *Phenomenology* is supposed to play the role of the Socratic educator, who serves as "midwife" to his pupil and helps draw dialectic-as-science from the pupil's own mind.

Rationality Cannot Be Imposed; Truth and Personal Evidence

Also implied here is the modern principle formulated by Descartes: the individual subject rightfully demands that universal truth not oppose his consciousness, but be *derived* from it. Descartes, however, identified universal truth with subjective certainty ("evidence") and made that identity the starting point of philosophy; whereas Hegel sets a distance between certainty and truth. Each of these two stands at an opposite end of the *Phenomenology*. The process begins with subjective certainty, which, because it is a direct, unmediated personal experience, is not yet truth; truth is attained only at the end, when the individual consciousness has fully overcome its merely particular standpoint and adopted the standpoint of the totality as a development of its (the individual's) *own* self. Needless to say, overcoming particularity does not entail that subjectivity has been abolished. The actual subject—the thinking, feeling, willing, desiring subject—is rather present in all the positions, which he or she attains and adopts, including the most universal standpoint. In this respect, all the standpoints the rational subject undergoes over the course of his mental career are his own, they express his subjective self and identity, and are not imposed on him by external coercion, brainwashing, or manipulation.

This is a crucial point. It preserves the modernity of Hegel's position in stating that *rationality cannot be imposed.* When the individual cannot recognize the universal standpoint as an expression of his or her own self, a fundamental condition of rationality is broken and the position *is not* rational. As with Kant, rationality for Hegel is a union of a subjective recognition and an objective, universal point of view. Both of these ingredients are equally necessary for rationality to exist. Consequently, it is impossible to coerce a person or a society to be free, as Rousseau wanted; one can only help them to evolve of themselves toward freedom and rationality. It is likewise impossible to become rational by mere choice or decision, because rationality, again, must arise from the subject's evolution and self-explication. It is neither an automatic outcome, a position that can be deduced analytically—nor is it an arbitrary existential choice. Rather, rationality must "emerge" from and through the mind's self-evolution, as a kind of novelty, an *Aufhebung* that both depends on what went before and cannot be simply reduced to it. Rationality is attained neither by coercion, nor by choice, but by a self-educational process that draws all its levels and shapes from the philosophizing individual's own mind and, when mature, allows rationality to "emerge" as an outcome, the expression of that mind and of the culture that embodies it.

There is neither an "algorithmic" necessity here, nor an arbitrary occurrence. Hegel sees this rather as a "historical" necessity, meaning that although its outcome can be accounted for by reasons, it can neither be predicted in advance nor recur in precisely the same way. And this also explains the historical *boundaries* that, unlike Plato, limit the individual's capacity to jump ahead and attain full rationality when the rest of the *Zeitgeist* has not yet even reached its threshold.

Hegel thereby addresses a famous existentialist objection raised by Kierkegaard, who complained that Hegel's philosophical "science" may be beautifully constructed, yet he, as a single individual, cannot find himself within it. Though Hegel did not know Kierkegaard, he had fully concurred with his demand. Indeed, the individual must be able to rediscover him or herself within the universal philosophical truth, or else the latter will not be rational. Hegel's original answer is to construct the *Phenomenology* as an educational bridge by which the individual can gradually cross into the absolute standpoint, and thereby be actualized as a genuine individual, rather than existing as an imaginary individual—that is, as a merely particular entity.

One can criticize or reject Hegel's account ("narrative") of this journey, but one cannot say he ignores the demands of the particular consciousness or bans it from his system. True, Hegel does not allow for an absolute or "bare" particularity, the kind that Kierkegaard and other existentialists start from. This is to him as illusory a metaphysical notion as Descartes's disembodied "I," or the "bare simples" on which the positivists build their world. The shape that the historical "universal" (culture, tradition, language, political institutions, rational claims and aspirations, etc.) has taken in the individual's lifetime plays a role in constituting that person's *very individuality*; it is the "spiritual substance" that nourishes each person's "self" and defines the range in which, as individual, he/she is able to move, either identifying with the historical situation, dissenting from it, or seeking to transcend it toward a new shape. In this respect, a "bare" individual, one alleged to be "absolutely particular," is a figment of the imagination, and if *he* demands to find his most particular and personal traits expressed conceptually in thought and in spirit, he can indeed find no satisfaction in philosophy, neither in Hegel's nor in anyone else's.

Thus, parallel to the Socratic midwife who educes dialectics-as-science from his pupil's mind, so the *Phenomenology* presents itself as a historicized kind of midwife; in other terms, it claims to offer the individual the same ladder that the universal human consciousness has been ascending up to his or her time, and helps him to personally ascend it, but also relive its deficiencies as a call to go on.

What can be retained from Hegel's aphorisms and their explication? Construing "the true" as something absolute is, I think, Hegel's greatest defect, alongside the hidden, semisecularized providential structure he attributes to human reason in general, and to human history in particular. These, to use an apt Nietzschean metaphor, are "shadows of the dead God" that *continue to dominate certain rationalist philosophies and linger on in their falsely secular and immanent appearance.* Equally objectionable—and most irrational to me, because reason, finite human reason, is always prone to transcend any of its provisional states and configurations, and therefore cannot find rest in a closed, final system—is the implied Hegelian idea of a realized end—of philosophy, even of history itself—in which human rationality will reach its final actualization. This messianic idea is another shadow of the dead God. If left to merely hover as a wish, a utopian dream which history might one day make true by its own dialectical evolution, this view is not necessarily dangerous per se, and may offer comfort and consolation to certain souls. But if this false consolation becomes a political project, an agenda for action to be consciously driven by the will, then this dream, whether in its theological or falsely secular form, may become a nightmare and unleash a volcano of terror and repression, as Hegel himself was the first to realize, although he restricted the danger to the politics of the abstract *Verstand* only. Yet the problem is no less onerous as implicit in the falsely secularized messianism latent in his own, semitheological *Vernunft.*

I can rephrase my objection by saying that Hegel fails to do justice—hard, realistic, clear-eyed justice—to human *finitude* in all its aspects and implications. In this sense he is a bad Kantian (as Kant himself also was). And this problem, too, arises from the semitheological substrate of his thought—Hegel's belief that the good old absolute God (even in his Christo-Lutheran shape), although being *aufgehoben* and translated into immanent, this-worldly terms, can still be preserved at the basis of the modern world's self-understanding.

On the other hand, Hegel is quite convincing in wanting philosophy to go beyond the abstract intellect without falling into romantic opacity; to avoid abstract a priori normativity (methodological, ontic, moral, political, etc.); to view rationality as internally involving life, feeling, and history; to aspire to deal internally with its subject matter and "evolve with it"; to accept negativity as a positive power, and admit—even require—an element of "memory" as the substrate of the subject matter's evolution; to work in a progressive-regressive mode in which new negations do not revert to the point of departure; to be mindful of the temporal, flesh and blood embodiment of philosophical thinking and its necessary situatedness in its own history, and equally mindful of the need to contextualize and explicate ideas in order to make actual sense of them. Understanding the human subject as never self-identical until "the end" is also most instructive, especially if we deny, against Hegel, that an end is possible, in which case the nonidentity and self-distancing of human subjects will be their ontological situation (or "lot," as the existentialists used to maintain). Indeed, once the absolute, the final end, the overcoming of the merely temporal, and the theology of the becoming-God are renounced, a good deal of what remains of Hegel's view of subjectivity, identity, evolution, and the links between knowledge, action, rights, history, and social evolution—and their respective roles in constituting the never finished human subject—acquires new, relevant light.

Note

1. *Hegel's Preface to the* Phenomenology of Spirit, new translation and running commentary (forthcoming from Princeton University Press, 2005).

II

Reconstructing Social Critique

6

Institutionalizing Democratic Justice: Redistribution, Recognition, and Participation

Nancy Fraser

The philosophical world has long been divided among two kinds of thinkers. On one side stand those we might call "separationists." Tough-minded seekers of truth, their deepest drive is to draw lines, demystifying apparent consensus, clarifying the hard nub of irreconcilable difference, and insisting on the need to choose sides. On the other side stand the "conversationalists." Worldly lovers of dialogic understanding, they prefer to search out avenues of possible agreement beneath surface dissension, ratcheting down polemic, decentering familiar lines of controversy, splitting differences, and promoting communication. Both types have their weaknesses and strengths. Separationists penetrate beneath sentimental obfuscations but are liable to miss the forest for the trees. Conversationalists see past entrenched polarizations but are not always willing to face the hard questions. The ideal, I am convinced, is to incorporate something from each.[1]

My own youthful proclivities tended in the direction of a rather harsh separationism. I was fortunate, therefore, to study philosophy as an undergraduate with Richard Bernstein. The quintessential conversationalist, Bernstein taught me by his example to appreciate the hermeneutical and communicative virtues. As early as *Praxis and Action*, he uncovered unexpectedly shared concerns among the then bitterly polarized schools of Western Marxism, pragmatism, and analytic action theory.[2] Later he sought to defuse some of the more sterile oppositions between modernity and postmodernity, deconstruction and ethical thought.[3] It is only now, with the benefit of hindsight, that I can see how deeply my own work on the relationship between critical theory and poststructuralism, feminism, and postmodernism, is indebted to his example.[4]

Today, in fact, a healthy dose of Bernsteinian conversationalism informs my work on redistribution and recognition. Although these two ways of thinking about justice are often counterposed as mutually antithetical, I am convinced that they can and should be joined together. It is not the case, in other words, that we must face a hard separationist choice between a politics of redistribution, aimed at promoting social and economic equality, on the one hand, and a politics of recognition, aimed at fostering acceptance of cultural differences, on the other. Rather, a conversationalist inquiry reveals hidden possibilities for integrating the best features of each. Thus, whereas separationists posit a sharp either/or choice between class politics and identity politics, multiculturalism and social democracy, I follow the example of Richard Bernstein and diagnose a false antithesis.

It is in Bernstein's spirit, then, that I insist on a general thesis: justice today requires *both* redistribution *and* recognition. Neither alone is sufficient. As soon as one embraces this thesis, however, the question of how to combine them arises. I contend that the emancipatory aspects of the two paradigms need to be integrated in a single, comprehensive framework. In moral philosophy, the task is to devise an overarching conception of justice that can accommodate both defensible claims for social equality and defensible claims for the recognition of difference. In social theory, the task is to understand the complex relations between economy and culture, class and status in contemporary society. In political theory, the task is to envision a set of institutional arrangements that can remedy both maldistribution and misrecognition, while minimizing the mutual interferences likely to arise when the two sorts of redress are sought simultaneously. In practical politics, finally, the task is to foster democratic engagement across current divides in order to build a broad-based programmatic orientation that integrates the best of the politics of redistribution with the best of the politics of recognition.

Elsewhere, I have discussed the moral-philosophical and social-theoretical dimensions of this project.[5] In this essay, I shall examine some of the political-theoretical dimensions. In the conversationalist spirit of Richard Bernstein, I shall seek to answer the following questions: What institutional arrangements can ameliorate injustices of status and class simultaneously? What political reforms can satisfy both defensible claims for redistribution and defensible claims for recognition, yet minimizing the mutual interferences that can arise when the two types of claims are pursued in tandem?

Justice as Participatory Parity; Recognition as Status Equality

Answering these questions requires the right sort of understanding of justice. What is needed is a broad and capacious conception that can accommodate at least two sets of concerns. On the one hand, such a conception must encompass the traditional concerns of theories of distributive justice, especially poverty, exploitation, inequality, and class differentials. At the same time, it must also encompass concerns recently highlighted in philosophies of recognition, especially disrespect, cultural imperialism, and status hierarchy. Rejecting sectarian formulations that cast distribution and recognition as mutually incompatible understandings of justice, such a conception must accommodate both. It must bring the two dimensions together under a common normative measure. This means finding a single normative principle that can encompass both justified claims for redistribution and justified claims for recognition, without reducing either one to the other.[6]

In the framework I have elaborated elsewhere, I have proposed for this purpose the principle of *parity of participation*. According to this principle, justice requires social arrangements that permit all (adult) members of society to interact with one another *as peers*. For participatory parity to be possible, I claim, at least two conditions must be satisfied. First, the distribution of material resources must be such as to ensure participants' mutual independence and "voice." This condition precludes arrangements that institutionalize deprivation, exploitation, and gross disparities in wealth, income, and leisure time, which prevent some people from participating as full partners in social interaction. The second condition requires that institutionalized patterns of cultural value express equal respect for all participants and ensure equal opportunity for achieving social esteem. It precludes institutionalized value patterns that systematically depreciate some categories of people and the qualities associated with them, thus denying them the possibility of participating fully in social life. Both conditions are necessary for participatory parity. Neither alone is sufficient. The first brings into focus concerns traditionally associated with the theory of distributive justice, especially concerns pertaining to the economic structure of society and to economically defined class differentials. The second brings into focus concerns recently highlighted in the philosophy of recognition, especially concerns pertaining to the status order of society and to culturally defined hierarchies of status. When they are joined together, the result is a two-dimensional conception of justice that encompasses *both* redistribution and recognition, without reducing either one to the other.

This understanding of justice has implications for how we understand the politics of recognition. Usually, recognition is viewed through the lens of identity. From this perspective, what requires recognition is group-specific cultural identity. Misrecognition consists in the depreciation of such identity by the dominant culture and the consequent damage to group members' sense of self. Redressing this harm means demanding "recognition." This in turn requires that group members join together to refashion their collective identity by producing a self-affirming culture of their own. Thus, on the identity model of recognition, the politics of recognition means "identity politics."

Without doubt, this identity model contains some genuine insights concerning the psychological effects of racism, sexism, colonization, and cultural imperialism. Yet, as I have argued elsewhere, it is deficient on at least two major counts. First, it tends to reify group identities and to obscure crosscutting axes of subordination. As a result, it often recycles stereotypes about groups, promoting separatism and repressive communitarianism. Second, the identity model treats misrecognition as a freestanding cultural harm. As a result, it obscures the latter's links to maldistribution, thereby impeding efforts to combat both aspects of injustice simultaneously.[7]

For these reasons, I have proposed an alternative conception of recognition. On my account—call it "the status model"—recognition is a question of *social status*. What requires recognition is not group-specific identity but the status of individual group members as full partners in social interaction. Misrecognition, accordingly, does not mean the depreciation and deformation of group identity. Rather, it means social subordination in the sense of being prevented from participating *as a peer* in social life. To redress the injustice requires a politics of recognition, but this does not mean identity politics. On the status model, rather, it means a politics aimed at overcoming subordination by establishing the misrecognized party as a full member of society, capable of participating on a par with other members.

Let me explain. To apply the status model requires examining institutionalized patterns of cultural value for their effects on the relative *standing* of social actors. If and when such patterns constitute actors as *peers*, capable of participating on a par with one another in social life, then we can speak of *reciprocal recognition* and *status equality*. When, in contrast, institutionalized patterns of cultural value constitute some actors as inferior, excluded, wholly other, or simply invisible, hence as less than full partners in social interaction, then we can speak of *misrecognition* and *status subordination*.

On the status model, therefore, misrecognition is a social relation of *subordination* relayed through *institutionalized patterns of cultural value*. It occurs when social institutions regulate interaction according to cultural norms that impede parity of participation. Examples include marriage laws that exclude same-sex partnerships as illegitimate and perverse, social welfare policies that stigmatize single mothers as sexually irresponsible scroungers, and policing practices such as "racial profiling" that associate racialized persons with criminality. In each of these cases, interaction is regulated by an institutionalized pattern of cultural value that constitutes some categories of social actors as normative and others as deficient or inferior: straight is normal, gay is perverse; "male-headed households" are proper, "female-headed households" are not; "whites" are law abiding, "blacks" are dangerous. In each case, the result is to deny some members of society the status of full partners in interaction, capable of participating on a par with the rest.

On the status model, finally, misrecognition constitutes a serious violation of justice. Wherever and however it occurs, a claim for recognition is in order. But note precisely what this means: aimed not at valorizing group identity, but rather at overcoming subordination, claims for recognition seek to establish the subordinated party as a full partner in social life, able to interact with others as a peer. They aim, that is, *to deinstitutionalize patterns of cultural value that impede parity of participation and to replace them with patterns that foster it.*[8]

Redressing Misrecognition: On Gay Marriage and *l'affaire foulard*

To clarify the practical implications, let's consider some contemporary controversies, beginning with same-sex marriage. In this case, as I noted earlier, the institutionalization in marital law of a heterosexist cultural norm denies parity of participation to gays and lesbians. For the status model, therefore, this situation is patently unjust, and a recognition claim is in principle warranted. Such a claim seeks to remedy the injustice by deinstitutionalizing the heteronormative value pattern and replacing it with an alternative that promotes parity. This, however, can be done in more than one way. One way would be to grant the same recognition to homosexual partnerships that heterosexual partnerships currently enjoy by legalizing same-sex marriage. Another would be to deinstitutionalize heterosexual marriage, decoupling entitlements such as health insurance from marital status and assigning them on some other basis, such as citizenship and/or territorial residency. Although there may be good reasons for preferring one of these approaches to the other, in principle either of them would serve to foster participatory parity between gays and straights; hence both are justified in principle.

Now consider another case: the French controversy over the *foulard*. Here the issue is whether policies forbidding Muslim girls to wear headscarves in state schools constitute unjust treatment of a religious minority. This case is more complex because the principle of participatory parity must be applied twice, at two different levels. First, at the *intergroup* level, it supplies the standard for assessing the effects of institutionalized patterns of cultural value on the relative standing of *minorities vis-à-vis majorities.* Second, at the *intragroup* level, it serves to assess the *internal effects of minority practices* for which recognition is claimed. Taken together, these two levels constitute a double requirement. Claimants must show, first, that the institutionalization of majority cultural norms denies them participatory parity and, second, that the practices whose recognition they seek do not themselves deny participatory parity—to some group members as well as to nonmembers.

In the case at issue, accordingly, those claiming recognition for the *foulard* must establish two points. They must show, first, that the ban on the scarf constitutes an unjust majority communitarianism, which denies educational parity to Muslim girls; and second, that an alternative policy permitting the *foulard* would not exacerbate female subordination—in Muslim communities or in society-at-large. The first point, concerning French majority communitarianism, can be established without difficulty, it seems, as no analogous prohibition bars the wearing of Christian crosses in state schools; thus, the current policy denies equal standing to Muslim citizens. The second point, concerning the nonexacerbation of female subordination, has proved controversial, in contrast, as some French republicans have argued that the *foulard* is a marker of women's subordination and must therefore be denied recognition. Disputing this interpretation, however, some multiculturalists have rejoined that the scarf's meaning is highly contested in French Muslim communities today, as are gender relations more generally; thus, instead of construing it as univocally patriarchal, which effectively accords male supremacists sole authority to interpret Islam, the state should treat the *foulard* as a symbol of Muslim identity in transition, one whose meaning is contested, as is French identity itself, as a result of transcultural interactions in a multicultural society. From this perspective, permitting the *foulard* in state schools could be a step toward, not away from, gender parity.

In my view, the multiculturalists have the stronger argument here. (This is *not* the case, incidentally, for those who would recognize what they call "female circumcision"—actually, genital mutilation, which clearly denies parity in sexual pleasure and in health to women and girls.) But that is not the point I wish to stress here. The point, rather, is that the argument is rightly cast in terms of parity of participation. For the status model, this is precisely where the controversy should be joined. Participatory parity is the proper standard for warranting claims.

This standard cannot be applied monologically, however, in the manner of a decision procedure. It must be applied dialogically, rather, through democratic processes of public debate. In such debates, participants argue about whether existing institutionalized patterns of cultural value impede parity of participation and about whether proposed alternatives would foster it.[9] Thus, participatory parity serves as an idiom of public contestation and deliberation about questions of justice. More strongly, it represents *the principal idiom of public reason*, the preferred language for conducting democratic political argumentation on issues of both distribution and recognition.[10]

Affirmation or Transformation? A Separationist Antithesis

Now let's consider the broader political implications. As we saw, justice today requires integrating a politics of redistribution with a politics of recognition. Thus the question arises: What institutional reforms can remedy misrecognition and maldistribution simultaneously, while mitigating the mutual interferences that can arise when those two aims are pursued in tandem?

Consider, again, the remedy for injustice, restated now in its most general form: removal of impediments to participatory parity. At first sight, what this means is clear. To remedy maldistribution one must remove economic impediments via redistribution; what is needed, accordingly, is economic restructuring aimed at ensuring the distributive prerequisites for participatory parity to all. To remedy misrecognition, likewise, one must remove cultural impediments via recognition; what is required here are policies that can supply the status prerequisites—by deinstitutionalizing patterns of cultural value that impede parity of participation and replacing them with patterns that foster it.

The initial appearance of clarity is misleading, however. In both those cases, the general formula of removing obstacles to participatory parity is subject to more than one institutional application. As I just noted, misrecognition can be redressed in more than one way: by universalizing privileges now reserved for advantaged groups or by eliminating those privileges altogether; by deinstitutionalizing preferences for traits associated with dominant actors or by entrenching norms favoring subordinates alongside them; by privatizing differences or by valorizing them or by deconstructing the oppositions that underlie them. Likewise, maldistribution can be redressed in more than one way: by redistributing income and/or wealth; by reorganizing the division of labor; by changing the rules and entitlements of property ownership; or by democratizing the procedures by which decisions are made about how to invest social surpluses. Given this plethora of possible interpretations, the institutional implications are no longer so clear. Which remedies for maldistribution and misrecognition should proponents of justice seek to effect?

To answer this question, we need a way of organizing, and evaluating, the alternatives. I propose to proceed by distinguishing two broad strategies for remedying injustice that cut across the redistribution-recognition divide: *affirmation* and *transformation*.[11] The distinction turns on the contrast between underlying social structures, on the one hand, and the social outcomes they generate, on the other. Affirmative strategies for redressing for injustice aim to correct inequitable outcomes of social arrangements without disturbing the underlying social structures that generate them. Transformative strategies, in contrast, aim to correct unjust outcomes precisely by restructuring the underlying generative framework. Thus, the nub of the contrast is the level at which injustice is addressed: whereas affirmation targets final outcomes, transformation addresses root causes.

The distinction can be applied, first, to the perspective of distributive justice. Here, the paradigmatic example of an affirmative strategy is the liberal welfare state, which aims to redress maldistribution through income transfers.[12] Relying heavily on public assistance, this approach seeks to increase the consumption share of the disadvantaged, while leaving intact the underlying economic structure. In contrast, the classic example of a transformative strategy is socialism. Here the aim is to redress unjust distribution at the root—by transforming the framework that generates it.

Today, of course, economic transformation is out of fashion, as much of the institutional content of socialism has proven problematic.[13] But it is a mistake to conclude that we should drop the idea of deep economic restructuring *tout court*. That idea is still meaningfully contrasted with affirmative redistribution, which leaves the root causes of maldistribution in place. In today's neoliberal climate especially, it is important to retain the general idea of economic transformation, even if we are currently uncertain of its precise institutional content.

The contrast between affirmation and transformation is intuitively familiar in the perspective of distribution. What may be more surprising, however, is that it can also be applied to remedies for misrecognition. An example of an affirmative strategy in the latter perspective is what I shall call "mainstream multiculturalism."[14] This approach proposes to redress disrespect by revaluing unjustly devalued group identities, while leaving intact both the contents of those identities and the group differentiations that underlie them. It can be contrasted with a transformative strategy that I shall call "deconstruction."[15] This second approach would redress status subordination by deconstructing the symbolic oppositions that underlie currently institutionalized patterns of cultural value. Far from simply raising the self-esteem of the misrecognized, it would destabilize existing status differentiations, changing *everyone's* self-identity.

The idea of deconstructive recognition may sound to some like an oxymoron. Nevertheless, it has a precise and useful sense in contemporary politics. To illustrate that sense, consider two alternative strategies for remedying heterosexism: gay identity politics, which aims to revalue gay and lesbian sexuality, and "queer politics," which proposes to deconstruct the binary opposition between homosexuality and heterosexuality. Whereas the first—affirmative—approach seeks to enhance the standing of an existing sexual orientation, the second—transformative—one would destabilize the current grid of mutually exclusive sexual statuses. Deconstructive strategies can also be found in feminist and antiracist movements, where they aim to substitute a shifting field of multiple differences for rigid male/female and black/white oppositions.

In general, then, the distinction between affirmation and transformation applies equally to distribution and recognition. It can be used in both perspectives to sort the plethora of possible remedies for injustice. Of course, the ultimate aim of the sorting is to draw some conclusions concerning what is to be done. To do that, however, one needs to assess the relative merits of affirmation and transformation. Which of those approaches is better able to redress maldistribution and misrecognition simultaneously?

Considered abstractly, independent of context, affirmative strategies have at least two major drawbacks. First, when applied to misrecognition, they tend to reify collective identities. Valorizing group identity along a single axis, they drastically simplify people's self-understandings—denying the complexity of their lives, the multiplicity of their identifications, and the cross-pulls of their various affiliations. At their worst, moreover, such approaches tend to pressure individuals to conform to a group type, discouraging dissidence and experimentation, which are effectively equated with disloyalty. Suppressing exploration of intragroup divisions, they mask the power of dominant fractions and reinforce crosscutting axes of subordination. Far from promoting interaction across differences, affirmative strategies for redressing misrecognition lend themselves all too easily to separatism and repressive communitarianism.[16] Meanwhile, affirmative remedies also prove problematic for a second reason: when applied to maldistribution, they often provoke a backlash of misrecognition. In the liberal welfare state, for example, public assistance programs channel aid to the poor, while leaving intact the deep structures that generate poverty; thus, they must make surface reallocations again and again. The result is to mark the disadvantaged as inherently deficient and insatiable, as always needing more and more. In such cases, affirmative approaches not only fail to redress maldistribution; they also intensify misrecognition.

In contrast, transformative strategies largely escape these difficulties. Applied to misrecognition, deconstructive remedies are in principle dereifying. Acknowledging the complexity and multiplicity of identifications, they seek to replace overweening master dichotomies, such as black/white or gay/straight, with a decentered congeries of lower-case differences. Thus, they tend to discourage the *en bloc* conformity that often accompanies mainstream multiculturalism. And far from promoting separatism or repressive communitarianism, they foster interaction across differences. Applied to maldistribution, meanwhile, transformative approaches are solidaristic. Focused on expanding the pie and restructuring the general conditions of labor, they tend to cast entitlements in universalistic terms; thus, they reduce inequality without creating stigmatized classes of vulnerable people perceived as beneficiaries of special largesse, and they tend to promote solidarity.

All other things being equal, then, transformative strategies are preferable. But they are not altogether without difficulties. Calls for deconstructing binary oppositions are far removed from the immediate concerns of most subjects of misrecognition, who are more disposed to seek self-respect by affirming a depreciated identity than by espousing the blurring of status distinctions. Similarly, calls for economic transformation are experientially remote for most subjects of maldistribution, who stand to gain more immediate benefit from income transfers than from democratic socialist planning. More generally, transformative strategies are highly vulnerable to collective action problems. In their pure form, at least, they become feasible only under unusual circumstances, when events conspire to wean many people simultaneously from current constructions of their interests and identities.

If transformative strategies are preferable in principle, but more difficult to effect in practice, then something, apparently, must give. Should one sacrifice principle on the altar of realism?

Nonreformist Reform: A Conversationalist *via media*

Fortunately, the dilemma is less intractable than it first appears. In fact, the distinction between affirmation and transformation is not absolute, but contextual.[17] Reforms that appear to be affirmative in the abstract can have transformative effects in some contexts, provided they are radically and consistently pursued. For example, universal unconditional Basic Income grants would guarantee a minimum standard of living to every citizen, regardless of labor force participation, while leaving intact the deep structure of capitalist property right.[18] Thus, in the abstract they appear to be affirmative. That appearance would jibe with reality, moreover, in a neoliberal regime, where the grants would effectively subsidize employers of low-wage, temporary labor and possibly depress wages overall. In a social democracy, however, the effects could be dramatically different. According to proponents, if the level of the grants were set high enough, Basic Income would alter the balance of power between capital and labor, creating a more favorable terrain on which to pursue further change. The long-term result could be to undermine the commodification of labor power.[19] In that case, an apparently affirmative remedy for maldistribution would have transformative effects.

By the same token, Basic Income grants would not, in the abstract, be transformative with respect to gender. To be sure, they would enable primary caregivers, along with others, to withdraw periodically from the labor market. But in and of themselves they would do little to alter a gender division of labor that assigns unpaid caregiving overwhelmingly to women, while leaving male recipients free to surf.[20] In some contexts, in fact, Basic Income would serve to consolidate a "mommy track," a market in flexible, noncontinuous, largely female labor, thereby reinforcing, instead of transforming, the deep structures of gender maldistribution.[21] On the other hand, instituted as one element among others of a social-democratic-cum-feminist regime, Basic Income could be deeply transformative. Combined, for example, with comparable worth and high-quality, abundant public childcare, it could alter the balance of power within heterosexual households, helping to spark changes in the gender division of labor.

Such examples suggest a way of finessing our separationist choice. They point to the possibility of a *via media* between an affirmative strategy that is politically feasible but substantively flawed and a transformative one that is programmatically sound but politically impracticable. The crux of this alternative strategy is the idea of "nonreformist reforms."[22] These would be policies with a double face: on the one hand, they engage people's identities and satisfy some of their needs as interpreted within existing frameworks of recognition and distribution; on the other hand, they set in motion a trajectory of change in which more radical reforms become practicable over time. When successful, nonreformist reforms alter the terrain upon which later struggles will be waged, expanding the set of feasible options for future reform. Over time their cumulative effect could be to transform the underlying structures that generate injustice.

At its best, the strategy of nonreformist reform combines the practicability of affirmation with the radical thrust of transformation, which attacks injustice at the root. In the Fordist period, it informed some understandings of social democracy. From this perspective, social democracy was not seen as a simple compromise between an affirmative liberal welfare state, on the one hand, and a transformative socialist one, on the other. Rather, it was viewed as a dynamic regime whose trajectory would be transformative over time. That view is arguable, to be sure. In the event, it was never fully tested, as neoliberalism effectively put an end to the experiment. The question may now be moot, moreover, as nonreformist economic reform may no longer be possible within a single country, given current conditions of economic globalization. Nevertheless, the general idea of a progressively self-transformative regime is by no means discredited. On the contrary, it is well worth pursuing today—on a transnational scale.

Is such an approach also conceivable for the politics of recognition? Certainly, some proponents of identity politics support affirmative strategies in anticipation of transformative effects further down the road. Cultural feminists, for example, pursue a recognition politics aimed at revaluing traits associated with femininity. Yet not all of them view the affirmation of "women's difference" as an end in itself. Some consider it a transitional strategy that will lead eventually to the destabilization of the male/female dichotomy. One such strategy would celebrate femininity as a way of empowering women to struggle against the gratuitous gendering of social roles; another would valorize women's traditional activities as a way of encouraging men to take them up too. In both cases, proponents of "strategic essentialism" expect an affirmative strategy to have long-term transformative effects.[23] Whether this expectation is plausible, however, depends on contextual factors—on whether, for example, there exist sufficiently powerful forces to counter the reifying tendencies inherent in such a politics.

In any case, there is another way of conceiving nonreformist reform in relation to recognition. Consider, again, *l'affaire foulard*. Here the remedy for misrecognition is not to deconstruct the distinction between Christian and Muslim. As we saw, it is rather to eliminate institutionalized preferences for majority practices by taking affirmative steps to include minorities—without requiring assimilation or exacerbating the subordination of women. In the short term, this approach counts as affirmative, to be sure, as it affirms the right of an existing group to full participation in public education. In the longer term, however, it could have transformative consequences—such as reconstructing French national identity to suit a multicultural society, refashioning Islam for a liberal-pluralist and gender-egalitarian regime, and/or generally decreasing the political salience of religion by rendering such differences routine and mundane. As before, whether or not such transformations occur depends on contextual factors.

The key point, in any case, is this: where status distinctions can be detached from subordination, the strategy of nonreformist reform need not predetermine their ultimate fate. Rather, one can leave it to future generations to decide whether a given distinction is worth preserving. One need only strive now to ensure that that decision can be made freely, unconstrained by institutionalized subordination.

Integrative Postures: Cross-Redressing and Boundary Awareness

In general, then, the strategy of nonreformist reform holds some promise for both dimensions of justice. But it cannot be applied in an additive way. Thus, it will not suffice to develop one such strategy for distribution and another for recognition.[24] That would be to treat the two dimensions as though they were two separate spheres. In fact, however, distribution and recognition are thoroughly imbricated. And neither claims for redistribution nor claims for recognition can be insulated from each other. On the contrary, they impinge on one another in ways that can give rise to unintended— and unwanted—effects.

On the one hand, remedies for maldistribution that are perfectly plausible when considered alone can exacerbate misrecognition— witness the welfare example discussed earlier. Conversely, remedies for misrecognition that are perfectly plausible when considered alone can exacerbate maldistribution—witness no-fault divorce reforms that worsened the economic position of some women, even as they generally enhanced women's status.[25] What is needed to avoid such perverse effects is a bifocal political vision that keeps the two dimensions simultaneously in view. Such a bifocal vision permits one to monitor both the distributive implications of recognition reforms and the recognition implications of distributive reforms.

One way to apply such bifocal vision is through what I shall call *cross-redressing*. This means using measures associated with one dimension of justice to remedy inequities associated with the other— hence, using distributive measures to redress misrecognition and recognition measures to redress maldistribution.[26] Cross-redressing exploits the imbrication of status and class in order to mitigate both forms of subordination simultaneously. To be sure, it cannot be used wholesale, across-the-board. Thus, I reject both the reductive economistic view that one can redress all misrecognition by redistribution and also the vulgar culturalist view that one can remedy all maldistribution by recognition. But cross-redressing is perfectly viable on a more limited scale.

Consider, first, some cases in which redistribution can mitigate misrecognition. Theorists of rational choice contend that increased earnings enhance women's exit options from marriage and improve their bargaining position in households; thus, higher wages strengthen women's capacity to avoid the status harms associated with marriage, such as domestic violence and marital rape.[27] Similarly, some policy analysts claim that the surest way to raise poor women's status in developing countries is to provide them access to paid work.[28] To be sure, such arguments are sometimes overextended to the point of dismissing the need for recognition reforms altogether; and in such forms they are clearly fallacious. But the point is persuasive when stated more modestly: in some cases, redistribution can mitigate status subordination.

That conclusion is also supported by my previous discussion of transformative redistribution. As we saw, that approach favors universal entitlements to social welfare over targeted aid for the poor; thus, instead of stigmatizing the needy, it fosters social solidarity. In fact, transformative remedies for maldistribution have the potential to reduce misrecognition in ways that are especially useful for combating racism. By enlarging the pie, such policies soften the economic insecurity and zero-sum conflicts that typically exacerbate ethnic antagonisms. And by reducing economic differentials, they create a common material form of life, thereby lessening incentives for maintaining racial boundaries.[29] In such cases, redistributive policies can diminish misrecognition—or, rather, those forms of misrecognition that are closely tied to economic conditions.

Consider, too, some cases in which cross-redressing works in the opposite direction. For example, gays and lesbians suffer serious economic disadvantages as a consequence of status subordination. For them, accordingly, measures associated with recognition can mitigate maldistribution. Legalizing gay marriage or domestic partnerships would effectively remove economic penalties currently entrenched in welfare entitlements and in tax and inheritance law; and outlawing heterosexist discrimination in employment and military service would mean higher income and better fringe benefits. The point holds more broadly for misrecognized groups: enhanced respect translates into reduced discrimination—in employment, in housing and access to credit, hence into improved economic position. In such cases, where maldistribution is tied to status subordination, recognition can help to correct it.

In general, then, cross-redressing represents a useful tactic for integrating redistribution and recognition. Deployed judiciously, as part of a larger coordinated strategy of nonreformist reform, it can help circumvent unpalatable trade-offs.

A second posture that facilitates integration I shall call *boundary awareness*. By this I mean awareness of the impact of various reforms on group boundaries. Some efforts to redress injustice serve to sharpen group boundaries, whereas others serve rather to soften them. For example, efforts to redress maldistribution aim to reduce economic differentials; whether affirmative or transformative, they seek to lessen or abolish class divisions—thus to soften or eliminate boundaries. In contrast, affirmative approaches to recognition aim to valorize group specificity; in validating group differentiation, they tend to affirm existing boundaries. Finally, transformative recognition strategies propose to deconstruct dichotomous classifications; effectively blurring sharp status distinctions, they tend to destabilize the boundaries between groups.

Efforts to integrate redistribution and recognition must reckon with these varying aims. Absent awareness of boundary dynamics, one can end up pursuing reforms that work at cross-purposes with one another. For example, affirmative efforts to redress racist misrecognition by revaluing "blackness" tend to consolidate racial differentiation; in contrast, transformative efforts to redress racist maldistribution by abolishing the racial division of labor would undermine racial boundaries. Thus, the two sorts of reforms pull in opposite directions; pursued together, they could interfere with, or work against, each other. What I am calling boundary awareness can anticipate such contradictions; exposing the self-defeating character of certain combinations of reforms, it can identify more productive alternatives.[30]

The need for boundary awareness increases, moreover, given the possibility of unintended effects. After all, reforms of every type may fail to achieve their stated aims. We have seen, for example, that affirmative remedies for maldistribution often generate backlash misrecognition, thereby sharpening the very divisions they sought to reduce; thus, although ostensibly seeking to soften boundaries, they may actually serve to consolidate them. In such cases, too, boundary awareness can anticipate, and help to forestall, perverse effects. Combined with cross-redressing, it facilitates efforts to devise an approach that integrates redistribution and recognition.

By themselves, however, these ideas do not add up to a substantive programmatic strategy for integrating redistribution and recognition. Rather, they represent postures of reflection conducive to devising such a strategy. The question remains as to who precisely should use them to that end.

Communicative Conclusions: Some Guidelines for Deliberation

The task of developing an integrated strategy is not a job for an individual theorist. It is, rather, a project for democratic citizens engaged in deliberation. Instead of proposing a programmatic blueprint, therefore, I shall conclude by suggesting some general guidelines for public deliberations aimed at advancing this political project. Three points in particular follow from the preceding discussion.

The first concerns the role of redistribution in deliberations about how to institutionalize justice. *Contra* fashionable culturalist ideologies, distribution is a fundamental dimension of justice; it cannot be reduced to an epiphenomenon of recognition. *Contra* substantive dualism, moreover, this dimension is not restricted to the official economy, although it is crucially important there; rather, it runs through the entirety of social relations, including those usually considered as cultural. *Contra* reductive economism, finally, maldistribution is not exclusively an injustice of class in the conventional sense; rather, subordinated genders, "races," sexualities, and nationalities are also subject to systematic economic disadvantage. It follows that distributive questions must be central to *all* deliberations about institutionalizing justice. Granted, redistribution alone is not sufficient to redress all modes of subordination; but it remains an indispensable aspect of every defensible program for social change. Movements that ignore or truncate the distributive dimension are likely to exacerbate economic injustice, however otherwise progressive their aims.

A second point concerns the role of recognition in deliberations about institutionalizing justice. Like distribution, recognition is a fundamental and irreducible dimension of justice, whose effects traverse the entire social field. Thus, it too must be central to *all* programmatic discussions. Usually, however, misrecognition is interpreted as depreciated identity, and the politics of recognition means identity politics, aimed at affirming a given group identity. But that interpretation is problematic, as it reifies identities, encourages separatism, and masks intragroup domination. Thus, it should not inform policy deliberations. Instead, misrecognition should be treated as status subordination, in which institutionalized patterns of cultural value impede parity of participation for some. Thus, only reforms that replace those patterns with parity-fostering alternatives should be counted as viable remedies.

A third and final point concerns what I call "the problem of the frame." In all deliberations about institutionalizing justice, participants should ask: who precisely are the relevant subjects of justice? Who are the social actors among whom parity of participation is required? Earlier, before the current acceleration of globalization, the answers to such questions were largely taken for granted. It was assumed, usually without explicit discussion, that spheres of justice were coextensive with states, hence that those entitled to consideration were fellow citizens. Today, however, that answer can no longer go without saying. Given the increased salience of both transnational and subnational processes, the country can no longer serve as the sole unit or container of justice. Rather, notwithstanding its continuing importance, the country is one frame among others in an emerging new multileveled structure. In this situation, deliberations about institutionalizing justice must take care to pose questions at the right level, determining which matters are genuinely national, which local, which regional, and which global. They must delimit various arenas of participation so as to mark out the set of participants rightfully entitled to parity within each. Thus, discussion of the frame should play a central role in deliberations about institutional arrangements.

Together, these three points provide at least some of the guidance democratic citizens need to begin answering what I take to be the key political question of our day: How can we devise a coherent strategy for redressing injustices of both status and class? How can we integrate the best of the politics of redistribution with the best of the politics of recognition so as to challenge injustice on both fronts? This question seems to me to reflect something of the conversationalist spirit of Richard Bernstein. If we fail to ask it, if we cling instead to false antitheses and misleading either/or dichotomies, we will miss the chance to envision social arrangements that can redress maldistribution and misrecognition simultaneously. Only by uniting both efforts in a single effort can we meet the requirements of justice for all.

Notes

1. Portions of this essay are excerpted from Nancy Fraser, "Social Justice in the Age of Identity Politics: Redistribution, Recognition, and Participation," in Nancy Fraser and Axel Honneth, *Redistribution or Recognition? A Political-Philosophical Exchange* (London: Verso, 2004).

2. Richard J. Bernstein, *Praxis and Action* (Philadelphia: University of Pennsylvania Press, 1971).

3. Richard J. Bernstein, *The New Constellation: The Ethical-Political Horizons of Modernity/Postmodernity* (Cambridge: Polity Press, 1991).

4. See, for example, Nancy Fraser and Linda Nicholson, "Social Criticism without Philosophy: An Encounter between Feminism and Postmodernism," in *Feminism/Postmodernism*, ed. Linda Nicholson (New York: Routledge, 1990) pp. 19–38; and the chapters by Nancy Fraser in Seyla Benhabib, Judith Butler, Drucilla Cornell, and Nancy Fraser, *Feminist Contentions: A Philosophical Exchange* (New York: Routledge, 1994).

5. Fraser, "Social Justice in the Age of Identity Politics."

6. For a fuller argument, see Fraser, "Social Justice in the Age of Identity Politics."

7. Nancy Fraser, "Rethinking Recognition: Overcoming Displacement and Reification in Cultural Politics," *New Left Review*, 3 (2000): 107–120.

8. For a fuller argument, see Fraser, "Rethinking Recognition."

9. Actually, there are several different issues potentially in need of deliberative determination: (1) determining whether a claim for the existence of an injustice of misrecognition is justified, i.e., whether institutionalized patterns of cultural value really do entrench status subordination; (2) if so, determining whether a proposed reform would really remedy the injustice by fostering participatory parity; and (3) if

so, determining whether a proposed reform would exacerbate other disparities in participation in a way and to a degree that is unacceptable. I am grateful to Erik Olin Wright (personal communication) for this clarification.

10. For a fuller discussion, see Fraser, "Social Justice in the Age of Identity Politics."

11. Portions of the following discussion are drawn from Nancy Fraser, "From Redistribution to Recognition? Dilemmas of Justice in a 'Postsocialist' Age," *New Left Review* 212 (1995): 68–93; reprinted in Nancy Fraser, *Justice Interruptus: Critical Reflections on the "Postsocialist" Condition* (New York: Routledge, 1997). But some key aspects of the argument have been revised.

12. By "liberal welfare state," I mean the sort of regime established in the United States in the aftermath of the New Deal. It has been usefully distinguished from the social-democratic welfare state and the conservative-corporatist welfare state by Gøsta Esping-Andersen in *The Three Worlds of Welfare Capitalism* (Princeton: Princeton University Press, 1990).

13. Virtually no one, even among radical egalitarians, continues to defend a command economy in which there is little or no place for markets. Nor is there agreement concerning the place and extent of public ownership in a democratic egalitarian society.

14. Not all versions of multiculturalism fit the model described here. The latter is an ideal-typical reconstruction of what I take to be the majority understanding of multiculturalism. It is also mainstream in the sense of being the version that is usually debated in mainstream public spheres. Other versions are discussed in Linda Nicholson, "To Be or Not To Be: Charles Taylor on The Politics of Recognition," *Constellations: An International Journal of Critical and Democratic Theory* 3, no. 1 (1996): 1–16; and Critical Multiculturalism Studies Group, "Critical Multiculturalism," *Critical Inquiry* 18, no. 3 (spring 1992): 530–556.

15. To be sure, my use of the term "deconstruction" is unorthodox, as it denotes a specific type of institutional remedy for misrecognition. Thus, Jacques Derrida might not approve this usage, especially given his recent identification of deconstruction with justice *tout court*. Nevertheless, my usage retains something of the flavor of Derrida's earlier work, as it suggests a utopian cultural ideal of fluid, shifting differences. For Derrida's earlier utopian vision of a deconstructive culture, see Jacques Derrida and Christie V. McDonald, "Choreographies," *Dialectics* 12 (1982): 66–76. For Derrida's later account of deconstruction's relation to justice, see Jacques Derrida, "Force of Law: The 'Mystical Foundation of Authority,'" in *Deconstruction and the Possibility of Justice*, ed. Drucilla Cornell, Michel Rosenfeld, and David Gray Carlson (New York: Routledge, 1992), pp. 3–67.

16. See Fraser, "Rethinking Recognition," for an extended discussion of such difficulties.

17. I owe this point to Erik Olin Wright. I have borrowed several of the formulations in this paragraph from his "Comments on a General Typology of Emancipatory Projects" (unpublished manuscript, February 1997), hereafter cited as "Comments."

18. Philippe Van Parijs, "Why Surfers Should Be Fed: The Liberal Case for an Unconditional Basic Income," *Philosophy and Public Affairs* 20, no. 2 (spring 1991): 101–

131; and *Real Freedom for All: What (If Anything) Can Justify Capitalism?* (Oxford: Clarendon Press, 1995).

19. Philippe Van Parijs, *Real Freedom for All.*

20. In his classic article, "Why Surfers Should Be Fed," Philippe Van Parijs posited the surfer as the litmus test recipient for Basic Income—without remarking on its gender subtext.

21. Nancy Fraser, "After the Family Wage: A Postindustrial Thought Experiment," in Fraser, *Justice Interruptus.*

22. For the idea of nonreformist reform, see André Gorz, *Strategy for Labor: A Radical Proposal*, tr. Martin A. Nicolaus and Victoria Ortiz (Boston: Beacon Press, 1967). Thanks to Erik Olin Wright, "Comments," for suggesting that I incorporate Gorz's idea here.

23. The term "strategic essentialism" was originated by Gayatri Spivak. See Gayatri Spivak with Ellen Rooney, "In a Word: Interview," *differences*, 1–2 (summer 1989): 124–156. The view that an affirmative politics of identity can lead to cultural transformation has been defended by Iris Marion Young in "Unruly Categories: A Critique of Nancy Fraser's Dual Systems Theory," *New Left Review* 222 (March/April 1997): 147–160. For a critique of Young's argument, see Nancy Fraser, "A Rejoinder to Iris Young," *New Left Review* 223 (May/June 1997) pp. 126–129.

24. Some readers of my essay "From Redistribution to Recognition?" inferred that I was proposing such an additive strategy—doubtless because I advocated "socialism in the economy and deconstruction in the culture." Nevertheless, my intention was not to simply to piggyback a politics of recognition on top of a politics of redistribution. Rather, I sought an integrated approach that could obviate mutual interferences and the need for tradeoffs. Here, I hope to forestall this sort of misunderstanding by avoiding formulations that sound additive.

25. See Fraser, "Social Justice in the Age of Identity Politics."

26. The term "cross-redressing" is my own. However, I owe the point to Erik Olin Wright. See his "Comments."

27. Susan Moller Okin, *Justice, Gender, and the Family* (New York: Basic Books, 1989); Nancy Fraser, "After the Family Wage"; and Barbara Hobson, "No Exit, No Voice: Women's Economic Dependency and the Welfare State," *Acta Sociologica 33*, no. 3 (fall 1990): 235–250. See also the general argument about exit and voice in Albert O. Hirschman, *Exit, Voice, and Loyalty: Responses to Decline in Firms, Organizations, and States* (Cambridge, Mass.: Harvard University Press, 1970).

28. Amartya Sen, "Gender and Cooperative Conflicts," in *Persistent Inequalities: Women and World Development*, ed. Irene Tinker (New York: Oxford University Press, 1990).

29. Erik Wright, "Comments."

30. For a detailed comparative assessment of the compatibility of various reform packages with respect to boundary dynamics, see Fraser, "From Redistribution to Recognition?"

7

Political Philosophy and Racial Injustice: From Normative to Critical Theory

Thomas McCarthy

In mainstream political philosophy the history of European racism, with its vast implications for the theory and practice of modern liberalism, has remained largely on the margins.[1] This is nearly as astonishing as the theoretical marginality of gender until quite recently. I say "nearly," because although gender relations have deeply structured every human society, racial relations, in the sense at issue here, have had major structural significance "only" for some five centuries. That is to say, they are contemporaneous with, and deeply implicated with, Western modernity from the first voyages of "discovery" to present-day neocolonialism. If one asked, in Rawlsian terms, which morally arbitrary facts about individuals and groups have had the greatest consequences for their legal and political standing in the modern world, gender and ascribed race would certainly be near the top of the list, along with class, though their comparative significance would vary from context to context. If the context were the global one of European expansionism since the fifteenth century, then racial classification would have a strong claim to being the most significant; for a central ingredient in the process by which more than four-fifths of the globe came to be under European and/or American rule before the start of World War I was the practice and theory of white supremacy.

The linkage of Western modernity and the rise of capitalism to the conquest and exploitation of the nonwestern world is a long-familiar story. Marx had already noted in the first volume of *Capital*,

Thomas McCarthy

"The discovery of gold and silver in America, the extirpation, enslavement and entombment in mines of the aboriginal population, the beginning of the conquest and looting of the East Indies,
the turning of Africa into a warren for the commercial hunting of
black-skins, signalized the rosy dawn of the era of capitalist production."[2] But Marx and Marxism centered on class relations and
generally treated race relations as derivative therefrom. An alternative account, running through W. E. B. Du Bois to the critical race
theory of the present, has, by contrast, viewed racial categorization
not simply as a dependent variable but as an irreducible structuring
principle of social, cultural, and political relations in the modern
world. On this view, the conquest and settlement of the Americas,
the subjugation and extermination of indigenous peoples, and the
massive expansion of the Atlantic slave trade in the early modern
period were integrally bound up with the social construction of
racial differences and racial hierarchies. During the course of this
historical transformation, imperial ideologies of "Christians versus
heathens" gradually gave way to those of "civilized Europeans versus uncivilized savages," which were understood in biologized racial
terms already in the eighteenth century. In the nineteenth century,
the Age of Empire, the rapid expansion of colonialism in Asia, the
Pacific, and Africa, fueled a further development of racial ideologies, particularly in conjunction with the rise of Darwinian biology
and physical anthropology. In short, there was a constant interplay
between colonialism and racism, between the establishment of imperial domination and the formation of racial ideologies.

In the view of this alternative tradition—alternative not only
to Marxism but also to liberalism—these were not ideologies in the
sense of mere epiphenomena of underlying social processes: they
were social constructions that were real social facts with real effects
on the ordering of social relations. This is the view expressed, for
instance, by Omi and Winant in the claim that modernity saw the
rise of "racial formations" at both national and global levels.[3] Systems of racial categorization centered around visible body types
had not only expressive but constitutive significance in modern
society and politics. They not only justified preexisting practices of
racial domination, they entered into and informed them. Stereo-

typical images of racial capacity and incapacity not only reflected institutional reality, they were essential to its very intelligibility and normativity. Similar appeals to "natural" racial differences were just as integral to U.S. immigration policy in the nineteenth and twentieth centuries, to the formation of the American working class and labor movement, to "Jim Crow" and "separate but equal," to eugenics and extermination camps. In short, "race" has functioned as a marker of inclusion and exclusion, equality and inequality, freedom and unfreedom throughout the modern period, locally and globally. And despite the successes of the American Civil Rights movement here and decolonization struggles abroad, there is widespread agreement in this alternative tradition that the legacy of institutionalized racism is still with us, that is, that local and global relations of wealth and power are still structured along racialized lines. In fact, the persistence of "race" as a significant ordering principle of social life, even *after* its political dismantling and theoretical deconstruction, is seen, from an American perspective, to be one of the major problems of the age—"the problem of the color-line."[4]

Since the 1960s, the centrality of race to the modern world in general and to the American experience in particular has finally permeated mainstream scholarship in most areas of the social sciences and the humanities. In mainstream political philosophy, however, the process has only just begun—despite the evident fact that political discourses, practices, and institutions have been suffused with racism throughout the modern period and racial politics persist into the present as the legacy of centuries of oppression.[5] As a result of this continued marginalization, the development of conceptual tools for analyzing the racialized dimensions of modern and contemporary politics has lagged, and the shift from legally institutionalized patterns of racial domination to domination anchored in lifeworld cultures and traditions, norms and values, socialization patterns and identity formations has remained largely untheorized in liberal political theory.

As a number of scholars have recently documented, however, theoretical marginalization is only part of the story. Most of the classical modern theorists were aware of and complicit in the emerging system of white supremacy. Thus Locke famously declared America to be a "vacant land" occupied only by nomadic savages still in the state of nature, and hence a land ripe for European expropriation, as no ownership-conferring labor had yet been mixed with it. Less famously, he was an original shareholder in the Royal African Company, which was chartered in 1672 to monopolize the English slave trade—he increased his investment in 1674 and again in 1675—and a few years before (1669) he had helped author "The Fundamental Constitutions of Carolina," which stated that "[e]very freeman of Carolina shall have absolute power and authority over his negro slaves, of what opinion or religion whatsoever."[6] Thus, the same Locke who declared in the opening line of his *First Treatise* that "Slavery is so vile and miserable an estate of man, and so directly opposite to the generous temper and courage of our nation, that 'tis hardly to be conceived that an Englishman, much less a gentleman, should plead for it,"[7] did in fact support it for the Africans being forcibly shipped to America to serve English gentlemen.

Our inclination might be to see this paradoxical combination as peculiar to him, or in any case untypical. But that is the problem: it is all too typical of Western political thought for the next two centuries and more. Even Kant, who developed what is arguably the philosophically purest version of European humanism, also developed what is arguably the most systematic theory of race and racial hierarchy prior to the nineteenth century.[8] Kant himself was not only abreast of and indeed in some respects ahead of contemporary biological accounts of racial difference, he was also exceptionally well versed in the travel literature of his day. In connection with his lectures on physical geography and anthropology, which he delivered annually from 1756 to 1796, he immersed himself in the reports of explorers, settlers, missionaries, traders, and the like, which constituted a significant part of the "empirical" basis of comparative cultural studies in his day. And though he sometimes ridiculed the reliability of such reports, he nonetheless drew on them in framing his views of non-European peoples. We could say, then, that his views mirrored the scope and nature of European contacts with non-Europeans in the early modern period. And Kant being Kant, that mirror had a power and clarity second to none.

The popular racism attendant upon "New World" conquest and enslavement found there its most highly resolved theoretical reflection prior to the nineteenth century, one that already displayed the chief characteristics of nineteenth-century racial "science": racial differences were represented as biologically inherited determinants of cultural differences, particularly differences in intellectual and moral capacities. In consequence of what he thus took to be biologically grounded differences in talent and temperament, Kant conjectured that non-European peoples were incapable of autochthonously realizing their humanity, and in particular of attaining that perfectly just civil constitution that is the highest task that nature sets to mankind. Hence Europe would "probably legislate eventually for all other continents."[9] This was the plan of nature, and thus God's plan, and thus humanity's best hope. So here we have it already before the close of the eighteenth century: a theoretical rationale for global white supremacy, rooted in biology and featuring hereditary differences in ability and character, and replete with the civilizing mission of the white race favored by nature to be the pacemaker of cultural progress and to give the law to the rest of the world[10]—a rationale that had only to be further developed and adapted to meet the needs of the "floodtide of imperialism" in the nineteenth century.

There are, of course, important variations from context to context and author to author. But there is a also general pattern: non-European peoples are characterized as savage or uncivilized, as not possessed of fully developed rational capacities and incapable of fully rational agency, and thus declared to be in need of tutelage, not only for the good of those who command them but also for their own good, for the full development of their capacities.[11] By the latter part of the eighteenth century, but especially in the nineteenth century, this scheme was filled in with developmental philosophies of history placing European civilization at the apex of social and cultural progress, and with allegedly scientific theories of racial difference and racial hierarchy. More recently, however, especially since World War II, the widespread dismantling of colonial empires and of *de jure* discrimination in regard to citizenship rights has been accompanied by a change in the treatment of race in liberal political theory. There is no longer any attempt theoretically to justify or accommodate racial subordination within a putatively universalistic theory. Rather, the treatment of this persistent feature of the messy political reality we inhabit is consigned to the province of "nonideal theory."

Part of the explanation behind this consignment is the tectonic shift in methodology that Richard Bernstein analyzed in his early study of *The Restructuring of Social and Political Theory*.[12] There he noted the ambivalent attitude toward normative theory of the positivist approach to social and political inquiry that had gained ascendancy in the twentieth century. "On the one hand, there is an insistence on the categorial distinction between empirical and normative theory, but on the other hand, there is a widespread skepticism about the very possibility of normative theory."[13] That skepticism was based on a strict dichotomy between facts and values, the assignment of empirical science to the former domain and of normative theory to the latter, and the view that there could be no rational determination of anything so subjective as "values." Bernstein himself went on in that work to criticize this architectonic and to propose an approach to social and political theory that rejected the empirical/normative dichotomy in favor of a mode of inquiry that was at once empirical, interpretive, and critical—that is, a mode of critical social theory. But just before he offered his diagnosis and proposal in the mid-1970s, a new venture in normative political theory had taken shape, one that by and large accepted the fact/value split, rejected the skepticism concerning rational discourse about values, and proposed another, more cooperative division of labor between empirical science and normative theory: the theory of justice of John Rawls, which has remained the dominant paradigm of normative political theorizing to this day.

In this essay, I want to (I) examine the division of labor between ideal and nonideal theory as it appears in Rawls's thought, (II) identify some of the obstacles this paradigm presents to developing an adequate account of racial injustice, and (III) suggest that to overcome them we have to move in the direction of a critical theory of race.[14]

I

As Susan Moller Okin and others have argued, Rawls effectively screened out gender and the gendered structure of the family from the purview of *A Theory of Justice* by designating the participants in the original position as "heads" or "representatives" of families.[15] Behind the veil of ignorance, not only is one's sex unknown to one, but participants seem to be unaware of the sex-gender systems that have deeply structured every society on record. Accordingly, the massively differential effect of the "morally arbitrary" fact of sexual difference does not become a central theoretical issue for justice as fairness. And although Rawls mentioned gender as a basic problem of our society in the introduction to *Political Liberalism* some 20 years later (*PL*, p. xxviii), it still remained untheorized therein. After a second round of criticism by Okin and other feminist theorists,[16] Rawls briefly addressed the matter in his 1997 *University of Chicago Law Review* piece on "The Idea of Public Reason Revisited" (*CP*, pp. 575–615). There he endorses a principle of equal justice for women that requires that "wives have all the same basic rights, liberties, and opportunities as their husbands" (*CP*, p. 597). He notes that the gendered division of labor in the family has been implicated historically in the denial of such equality, and holds that such a division might persist in a just society only if and when it were "fully voluntary" and arrangements were made to ensure that it did not undermine the equal liberties and opportunities of women (*CP*, p. 600). It seems to follow—and this is my main point—that such arrangements would have to be given full consideration in the original position, and thus that the parties would have to be given access to the knowledge of "social theory and human psychology" (*CP*, p. 601) needed to deal rationally with them. In short, sex-gender would have to be theorized at the same level and in the same detail as other major axes of justice/injustice.

A similar question might be raised concerning cultural and institutional patterns of racial domination. Charles Mills has remarked on the surprising insignificance of racial discrimination as an explicit theme (rather than a tacit subtext) of *A Theory of Justice*, which appeared in a highly charged political atmosphere a few short years after African-Americans had finally won their centuries-long struggle for equal civil and political rights.[17] One might add to this the absence of any sustained discussion of colonialism in a world convulsed with the dying gasps of European-American (formal) global rule. These, it seems, are features of the modern world about which parties in the original position are ignorant and are therefore unconcerned to address explicitly in laying out the basic structures of justice. But though the American Civil Rights movement and the global decolonization struggles of the period did eliminate most forms of *de jure* inequality, many forms of *de facto* inequality remained in place—deeply entrenched in the beliefs and values, symbols and images, practices and institutions, structures and functionings of national and global society. Hence, although certain legalized forms of subordination like slavery and serfdom may now be, as Rawls says in *Political Liberalism,* "off the agenda" (*PL*, p. 151, n. 16), the same cannot be said for racial relations generally, as he acknowledges in the introduction to that same work and as the persistent debates about affirmative action and other proposals for addressing the enduring legacy of legalized racism attest. Why, then, if "race" is admittedly still among "our most basic problems" (*PL*, p. xxviii), is it not theorized therein?

An important part of the answer, I want to suggest, has to do with the nature of "ideal theory." Kantian in conception, ideal theory starts with "rationally autonomous agents" and allows them only so much information as is needed to achieve agreement on basic principles.[18] This point is reached, according to Rawls, when the parties in the original position, represented now as symmetrically situated trustees of free and equal, rational and reasonable citizens, know all and only those "general"—not particular or personal—"facts" about society—that is, laws, theories, and tendencies pertaining to politics, economics, psychology, and social organization—required to design a just *and* feasible basic structure. Or, as Rawls also puts it in his most recent book, ideal theory seeks to construct a "realistic utopia" (*LP*, p. 6). In this respect, it follows Rousseau in taking (a) "men as they are" and (b) "laws as they might be" (*LP*, pp. 7,13).

(a) Rawls understands the former phrase to mean "persons' moral and psychological natures and how that nature works within a framework of political and social institutions" (*LP*, p. 7). To take men as they are in this sense means to "rely on the actual laws of nature and achieve the kind of stability these laws allow" (*LP*, p. 12). Hence parties in the original position must have access to the relevant general knowledge about such laws. This has consistently been Rawls's position. In *TJ*, although the veil of ignorance rules out knowledge of particular personal or social circumstances, the parties do know "the general facts about human society" pertaining to politics, economics, psychology, and social organization. Indeed, "there are no limitations on general information, that is, on general laws and theories, since conceptions of justice must be adapted to the characteristics of the systems of social cooperation which they are to regulate" (*TJ*, pp. 137–138). Some thirty years later, in *The Law of Peoples*, the same idea is expressed in similar terms: ideal theory is "realistic" when it depicts a social world that is "possible," that is, one that is "achievable" in light of what we know about "the laws and tendencies of society" (*LP*, p. 11). But there is added emphasis in the later work on "political culture" as a condition of feasibility. Thus in *The Law of Peoples*, civil society, the religious and moral traditions that support the basic structure of political and social institutions, the industriousness and cooperative talents of members, and their political virtues are all mentioned as "crucial" to the possibility of a society being well ordered (*LP*, p. 108). Accordingly, relevant "general" knowledge—general facts, laws, theories, tendencies—about political culture would have to be added to that concerning economics, politics, social organization, and psychology, if the parties are to design a realistic basic structure, one that is feasible as well as just. At the same time, however, this way of delimiting what is known behind the veil of ignorance entails that the "particular" knowledge required to understand and deal with racial injustice will not be available to parties in the original position—knowledge, for instance, about "the particular circumstances of their own society," or "to which generation they belong" (*TJ*, p. 137), or "the relative good or ill fortune of their generation" (*PL*, p. 273).

(b) Rawls understands Rousseau's phrase "laws as they might be" to mean "laws as they should or ought to be," (*LP*, p. 7) and this too seems to entail that constructions of race have no place in ideal theory—for "race" *should* not be a structuring principle of political and social relations. It is, in short, morally irrelevant. But this then threatens to render normative theory both unrealistic and unfair. To quote Charles Mills: "Failure to pay theoretical attention to this history [of racial subordination] will then just reproduce past domination, since the repercussions of white supremacy for the functioning of the state, the dominant interpretations of the Constitution, the racial distribution of wealth and opportunities, as well as white moral psychology ... are not examined."[19] It is at this point that Rawls's notion of "nonideal theory" comes into play. Taking the principles established by ideal theory as a guide, it approaches the "noncompliance" and "unfavorable conditions" of the real world in a spirit of reform: it asks how political ideals "might be achieved, or worked toward, usually in gradual steps. It looks for policies and courses of action that are morally permissible and politically possible as well as likely to be effective" (*LP*, p. 89). Thus, though "the specific conditions of our world at any time ... do not determine the ideal conception," they "do affect the specific answers to questions of nonideal theory" (*LP*, p. 90). Does this division of labor work?

We can understand this as a question about the relative strengths and weaknesses of alternative theoretical strategies, for political theory has been practiced in a great variety of ways, each with its peculiar advantages and disadvantages. One advantage of Rawls's neo-Kantian strategy is precisely the "purity" of the conception of social justice it constructs: social arrangements are based on equal respect for free and equal moral persons. Morally irrelevant particularities are systematically excluded or, when unavoidable, compensated for, inasmuch as even at this high level of abstraction there are certain "impurities" that cannot be simply excluded from ideal theory if the envisioned "utopia" is to be at all "realistic." Rawls already built some of these into *A Theory of Justice*—for instance, inequalities of birth and natural endowment—and in *Political Liberalism* he in effect added the persistence of deep cultural and ideological differences to the list: ideal theory now has to accommodate, within its theory construction, the "fact of reasonable disagreement" about the meaning and value of human life. And Rawls seems now to concede that feminist arguments for adding sex and gender to the list are irresistible. At the very least, the "general fact" of the biological division of labor in the reproduction of the species has to be acknowledged by the parties in the original position and so accommodated in their design of a basic structure as to ensure women's substantive freedom and equality. Our question now is whether the same may be said of race? For Rawls, I think, the answer has to be "no." If "race," in the sense at issue here, is at bottom a social, cultural, and political formation developed for purposes of subordinating certain groups to others, then it should simply be eliminated as a structuring element in a "well-ordered society."[20] In the ideal society, there would be a total absence of race *in this sense*.[21] So ideal theory cannot be where it is theorized.

In itself, this need not be a problem. Political theorizing has always been carried on at various levels of abstraction. There is, in my view, nothing to be said against even the highest—"Kantian"—levels per se, providing that they are not taken to be exclusively valid for, or inclusively adequate to, their objects. Given that Rawls's political theory is configured as a *multilevel* undertaking, with the intent of addressing relevant problems *at one level or another*, the question for us to consider is how his *overall* strategy, particularly the ideal/nonideal dichotomy, measures up against alternative strategies as a way of theorizing race.[22]

II

To begin with, general "facts" about the social world are, as anyone who has followed the discussions in postpositivist philosophy of social science will be aware, hardly the uncontroversial matter that Rawls represents them to be. Facts are stated in languages, and so long as there is no single general theory on which a consensus has formed within and among the relevant communities of investigators in any of the major domains of social life, the languages, and hence the facts—not to mention the "general laws"—of the social "sciences" are up for debate. Unless Rawls wants to take a firm position on, say, the century-old understanding/explanation debates—and build that position into his "freestanding" political liberalism—he will have to leave open the possibility that social and political inquiry has an ineliminable interpretive dimension and thus that what the general facts about social life are cannot be settled from the standpoint of a neutral observer or a reflective equilibrator.[23] If "realistic" political theory cannot be pursued without incorporating into it knowledge of the general characteristics of the social systems to which it is meant to apply, then political theory will have to get involved in just the sorts of interpretive-historical and social-theoretical disagreements that, in its self-understanding as normative theory, it hopes to avoid. And interpretive approaches to the human world typically place more and different weight on historical modes of inquiry than do positivist or empiricist approaches. Hermeneutic understanding is inherently historical: it aims to comprehend social phenomena as historical phenomena, often in narrative terms. But then Rawls's strict separation of "general" from "particular" knowledge of society become problematic, if, as hermeneutically inclined social theorists maintain, general information about society always comes, even if often only tacitly, with an historical index.

If political theorists do not dispose of interpretation-free "facts" in the way that Rawls intends, neither do they have conflict-free "values" at their disposal. Rawls himself explicitly characterizes the political values that his conception of justice seeks to articulate as belonging to the public political culture of a particular historical society and not to some ideal realm beyond the world. But then it follows that, as such, they do not come with fixed, clear, uncontested meanings; rather, they have to be interpretively worked up from the variable, particular, often conflictual political contexts in which they figure. As a result, the basic terms of his political conception cannot but reflect and project the particular forms of life and situations of conflict from which they are prepared; and they must be understood and assessed in relation to them. Thus his guiding conceptions of "persons" with two "moral powers" as both "free and equal" and "rational and reasonable," of "primary goods" as "specifying citizens needs" in a way that provides a "practicable basis of interpersonal comparison," and of the "stability" of a "well-ordered society" are laden with particular—and contestable—interpretations and evaluations. It makes no sense to suppose that we could insulate their construction from the conflicts of interpretation and evaluation endemic to our public political culture, our constitutional tradition, our legal and political practices and institutions. Working them up theoretically via reflective equilibrium or rational reconstruction cannot remove the traces of their conflictual origins.

In *A Theory of Justice*, Rawls was clear that the method of reflective equilibrium could not simply articulate an already existing consensus on basic political values, for the reason, among others, that such values had always been and continued to be debated in the public political culture. In view of the admittedly deep divisions on many of the matters to which he addressed himself—for example, the meanings and relative weights of liberty and equality—he did not understand his method of reflective equilibrium to be the hermeneutically conservative operation interpreters and critics sometimes mistook it to be. He remarked, for instance, that the kind of wide reflective equilibrium proper to moral philosophy might bring about a "radical shift" in our sense of justice (*TJ*, p. 49). It involved, as he put it a few years later, asking "what principles people would acknowledge and accept the consequences of when they had the opportunity to consider other plausible conceptions and to assess their supporting grounds ... [It] seeks the conception, or plurality of conceptions, that would survive the rational consideration of all feasible conceptions and reasonable arguments for them" ("The Independence of Moral Theory," *CP*, p. 289). But this might well put the theorist in the position of defending a comprehensive moral theory *within* the conflict of interpretations and reconstructions. And that is something that Rawls's recent stress on "overlapping consensus" now explicitly disallows.[24]

In *Political Liberalism* and *The Law of Peoples*, the idea of the "reasonable" undergoes considerable dilution. The overriding concern of both these works is with the "feasibility" of liberal ideals and the "stability" of liberal institutions in the face of cultural and ideological pluralism. The irreducible plurality of basic views on the meaning and value of human life makes it necessary, Rawls now maintains, to construct a purely "political" conception of justice that "stands free" of "comprehensive doctrines" of any sort, including general philosophical views. This "strategy of avoidance" relocates the "reasonable" at some remove from the Kantian notion of reason, with its close connection to the idea of a critique that submits all claims to authority to the free examination of reason. The reasonable pluralism that we might expect to result from "the exercise of human reason under free institutions" (*PL*, pp. 55–58) is, in Rawls's construction of a "political" conception of justice, replaced in effect by the *de facto* pluralism of comprehensive doctrines that satisfy the much weaker requirements set by his revised notion of toleration.[25] As a result, enlightenment and critique can play only a severely restricted role in normative theory of this sort, and that too makes it an unsuitable vehicle for theorizing racial injustice. In my concluding remarks I can do no more than gesture toward an alternative—and in my view more promising—theoretical strategy.[26]

III

In interpreting the languages of political thought, normative theorists too often take abstract formulations at their word, as if what were left out of the saying were left out of the meaning; they neglect to attend to how key terms actually function in the multiplicity of contexts in which authors and their audiences put them to use, or to what in practice are regarded as conditions of satisfaction and acceptability for claims employing them. They tend also to disregard that general norms are always understood and justified with an eye to some range of standard situations and typical cases assumed to be appropriate, and that if that range shifts, then so too do the understandings and justifications of those norms, the conceptual interconnections and warranting reasons considered relevant to them. On the other hand, recognizing that ideals and principles of justice, however abstract their form, always come with contentful preunderstandings that derive from their locations not only in systems of thought but also in forms of life, does not in itself commit us to sheer localism. In the case in point of liberalism's complicity with racial slavery, for instance, many of the ideas implicated in the justifications of slavery were also given more inclusive interpretations in the same cultural contexts as the dominant exclusionary versions highlighted in section I above. That is to say, those contexts also provided resources for arguments against slavery on religious or philosophical grounds, including arguments to the effect that the basic rights possessed by all human beings as such forbade it. One could say, then, that there were competing meanings— networks of inferential connections, ranges of standard situations and typical cases—which partly overlapped and partly diverged, but which were sufficiently interlinked to make disagreements real disagreements and not just incommensurable mutterings. And one might then understand the work of critics—and critical theorists— as an ongoing effort to reweave those connections and redefine those ranges so as to promote more genuinely inclusive versions. In doing so, they adopt the internal perspective of reflective participants and invoke the context-transcending validity claims of putatively universal ideals to argue that they have been betrayed, that existing formulations, though expressed in formally universal terms, are actually exclusionary.[27]

On this view, the search for a genuinely inclusive theory of justice is a never ending, constantly renewed effort to rethink supposedly universal basic norms and reshape their practical and institutional embodiments to include what, in their limited historical forms, they unjustly exclude. What generally drives this effort are struggles for recognition by those whom the norms in their established versions fail to recognize.[28] And the intellectual form it takes is the ongoing contestation of essentially contestable articulations of the universal demands of justice. Judith Butler puts the point this way: "the provisional and parochial versions of universality" encoded in law at any given time never exhaust "the possibilities of what might be meant by the universal."[29] Contestation by subjects excluded under existing definitions and conventions are crucial to "the continuing elaboration of the universal itself," for "they seize the language of [the universal] and set into motion a 'performative contradiction,' claiming to be covered by [it] and thereby exposing the contradictory character" of conventional formulations.[30] Butler here captures the important idea that the possibility of challenging putatively universal representations is inherent in those representations themselves, or more precisely, in their context-transcending claims, and that historically that possibility has been exploited to greatest effect by groups who, though not entitled under existing formulations of the universal, nevertheless appeal to it in formulating more inclusive conceptions of justice.

Viewed in this light, as a part—albeit a reflective part—of historical processes of emancipation, normative theory is clearly not "freestanding" in any fundamental sense. And, as the shock-effects of Foucault's genealogies have made clear, the familiar enlightenment metanarratives of universal principles discovered at the birth of modernity fail to acknowledge the impurity of the demands that have historically been made in the name of pure reason. Accordingly, there is a need for critical "histories of the present," the aim of which is to alter our self-understandings by examining the actual genealogies of accepted ideas and principles of practical reason.[31] This distinguishes critical approaches to moral and political theory from approaches like Rawls's that seek to construct fundamental norms of justice from the "settled convictions" of our "public political culture" by way of "reflective equilibrium." Critical histories make evident that the political values from which political liberalism seeks to construct a political conception of justice have always been and still are deeply contested, often fiercely, and usually in connection with matters of power, desire, and interest. And they make us aware that the quite varied, often conflicting ideas, principles, values, and norms that have been taken to express the demands of justice cannot adequately be comprehended or assessed without understanding this, and how elements of the contexts and situations in which they were propounded entered into them.[32]

It is not only this "context of origins" that contemporary normative theory leaves largely unexamined, but the "context of applications" as well. The distinction that Rawls and others draw between ideal and nonideal theory insulates political theorizing, at least initially, from the messiness of political reality. Subsequent forays into nonideal theory are all too often of limited value because of their loose, *post hoc* connection to empirical work. Specifically, discussions of race following this strategy usually end up as discussions of affirmative action in the broadest sense: since equal citizenship rights are now largely in place, the "unfavorable conditions" at issue are the substantive inequalities that are the enduring legacy of centuries of legalized oppression and discrimination.[33] Of course, one then has to judge any proposed remedial measures, policies, and programs from a pragmatic as well as a moral point of view, for they are put forward as practical means to the desired end of eliminating or reducing those inequities. Hence the case for any concrete compensatory measures has to be made not just "in principle" but "all things considered," that is, it has to take into account empirically likely consequences and side-effects, costs and benefits, comparative advantages and disadvantages vis-à-vis possible alternatives, political viability, long-term efficacy, and so on. Thus nonideal theorizing of this sort turns normative political theory back in the direction of the empirical social reality it began by abstracting and idealizing away from. But—and this is my main point here— there are no theoretical means at hand for bridging the gap between a color-blind ideal theory and a color-coded political reality, for the approach of ideal theory provides no theoretical mediation *between* the ideal and the real—or rather, what mediation it does provide is usually only tacit and always drastically restricted.

On this last score, what Habermas argues in *Between Facts and Norms* to be true of legal theory holds *ceteris paribus* of normative political theory as well—namely, that it always relies on implicit background assumptions drawn from some preunderstanding of contemporary society's structures, dynamics, potentials, and dangers.[34] These implicit "images" or "models" of society tacitly enter into normative-theoretical constructions and often play a covert role in what appear to be purely normative disagreements. Deep differences in normative theory—for instance, those separating classical from social-welfare liberals, or those dividing both from their socialist, radical feminist, or postcolonial critics—often turn on disagreements about the "facts" being assumed, implicitly as well as explicitly, in regard to markets, classes, gender roles, global relations, and so forth. And as we know from the history of theory, significant shifts in thinking often come about as a result of challenges precisely to what have previously been taken for granted as the natural, unalterable facts of social life—class-structured distributions of the social product, gendered divisions of labor, race-based hierarchies of social privilege, ethnocultural definitions of political membership, and the like. These considerations strongly suggest that such understandings, images, or models of society, which are always at work, though usually only tacitly, in normative theorizing, have to become an explicit theme if political theorists hope to avoid exalting intuitive preunderstandings of their social contexts into universal ideals. But political theory would then have somehow to combine intuitive knowledge from the perspective of the "insider" with counterintuitive knowledge from the perspective of the "outsider," in the senses both of the observer and the excluded.[35] It would have to join the constructive and reconstructive aims of normative theory to the interpretive, analytical, and explanatory aims of history and other empirically based human studies, and to the practical aims of social and cultural criticism. Given the existing institutionalization of research and scholarship, it would have to become interdisciplinary to the core.[36] And this means that normative theory would have to become an *interdependent*—not freestanding—*moment of a larger critical enterprise*; that is, it would have to be pursued in a self-consciously interdisciplinary manner and remain theoretically responsive not only to the political struggles of the age but also to contemporary developments in historical, social, and cultural studies. At least it would have to do so if it hoped to have anything of interest to say about racial injustice.

Notes

1. An earlier version of this essay was read at the Central Division Meeting of the American Philosophical Association in April of 2000. I am grateful to Lucius Outlaw for his comments on that occasion. For comments on a first draft, I am indebted to James Bohman, Felmon Davis, Maria Herrera, Richard Kraut, Christopher Zurn, and Robert Gooding-Williams (to whom I also owe many illuminating discussions of issues in race theory).

2. Karl Marx, *Capital* (New York: Random House, 1906), p. 823.

3. Michael Omi and Howard Winant, *Racial Formation in the United States* (New York: Routledge, 1994). They analyze race as a complex of social meanings that shape practices, identities, and institutions. This displaces the idea of race as a biologically fixed nature without reducing it to a mere fiction. Rather, it is a social construction that figures importantly in social, cultural, legal, political, economic, and psychological realities.

4. As famously anticipated by W. E. B. Du Bois in 1903, *The Souls of Black Folk*, edited with an introduction by D. W. Blight and R. Gooding-Williams (Boston, Mass.: Bedford Books, 1997), p. 45.

5. And despite the best efforts of philosophers in the alternative tradition to bring this fact to the attention of mainstream political philosophy. In 1977–1978, for instance, there was a double issue of *The Philosophical Forum* devoted to "Philosophy and the Black Experience." Numerous other publications on political philosophy and race appeared in the 1970s and 1980s, from the hands of Bernard Boxill, Leonard Harris, Bill Lawson, Howard McGary, Lucius Outlaw, Laurence Thomas, and Cornel West, among others. Nonetheless, the agenda of mainstream, liberal, political theory has remained largely unchanged in this regard.

6. Cited in Blackburn, *The Making of New World Slavery* (London: Verso, 1997), p. 275, n. 92.

7. John Locke, *Two Treatises of Government*, Peter Laslett, ed. (Cambridge: Cambridge University Press, 1988), p. 141.

8. See Robert Bernasconi, "Who Invented the Concept of Race? Kant's Role in the Enlightenment Construction of Race," in *Race*, R. Bernasconi, ed. (Oxford: Blackwell Publishers, 2001); and Emmanuel Chuckwudi Eze, "The Color of Reason: the Idea of 'Race' in Kant's Anthropology," in Eze, ed., *Postcolonial African Philosophy* (Oxford: Blackwell Publishers, 1997), pp. 103–140.

9. Immanuel Kant, "Idea for a Universal History with a Cosmopolitan Purpose," in *Kant: Political Writings*, ed., H. Reiss, trans., H. B. Nisbet (Cambridge: Cambridge University Press, 1991), p. 52.

10. However, Kant himself denied that there could be any right to chattel slavery and roundly condemned the European colonialism of his day. For the former, see *The Metaphysics of Morals*, trans., Mary J. Gregor (Cambridge: Cambridge University Press, 1996), p. 66; for the latter, see ibid., pp. 53, 121–122, and "Perpetual Peace," in Kant, *Political Writings*, pp. 106–107.

11. Exceptions to this pattern can be found, for instance, among the *philosophes* of the French Enlightenment. For a brief overview, see David Brion Davis, *The Problem of Slavery in Western Culture* (Oxford: Oxford University Press, 1988), chapter 13, "The Enlightenment as a Source of Antislavery Thought."

12. Philadelphia, Penn.: University of Pennsylvania Press, 1978. See especially the section entitled "The Problems of Normative Theory," pp. 45–51.

13. Ibid., p. 45.

14. A strong case for the inadequacy of mainstream political theory in regard to race and for the consequent need to develop a more historically and socio-culturally informed critical approach is made by Charles W. Mills in *The Racial Contract* (Ithaca, N.Y.: Cornell University Press, 1997) and *Blackness Invisible* (Ithaca, N.Y.: Cornell University Press, 1998). I am indebted to Mills for opening up many of the paths of argument I pursue here, though the conclusions I arrive at sometimes diverge from his. An early call for a critical theory of race in the tradition of Frankfurt school critical social theory was issued by Lucius Outlaw in his contribution to David Theo Goldberg, ed., *Anatomy of Racism* (Minneapolis, Minn.: University of Minnesota Press, 1990), pp. 58–82: "Toward a Critical Theory of 'Race'." The intentionally broad sense in which I use the term "critical theory" in this essay derives from, but is not limited to, that tradition. As the sketch of methodological desiderata in section III should make clear, it is meant to be sufficiently inclusive to accommodate productive strains of critical-historical, social, and cultural studies that answer to different names. It might be worth noting explicitly that a critical theory of race in this sense would not be restricted to the topics or methodologies of the "critical race theory" that has taken shape within the field of critical legal studies. See Kimberlé Crenshaw et al., eds., *Critical Race Theory: The Key Writings That Formed the Movement* (New York: New Press, 1995), and R. Delgado and J. Stefancic, ed., *Critical Race Theory: The Cutting Edge* (Philadelphia, Penn.: Temple University Press, 2000).

15. Susan Moller Okin, *Justice, Gender, and the Family* (New York: Basic Books, 1989). Rawls's works will be cited by abbreviation in the text as follows: TJ, *A Theory of Justice* (Cambridge, Mass.: Harvard University Press, 1971); PL, *Political Liberalism* (New York: Columbia University Press, 1993); CP, *Collected Papers*, Samuel Freeman, ed. (Cambridge, Mass.: Harvard University Press, 1999); and LP, *The Law of Peoples* (Cambridge, Mass.: Harvard University Press, 1999).

16. See, for instance, Susan Moller Okin, "*Political Liberalism*, Justice, and Gender," *Ethics* 105 (1994): pp. 23–43.

17. Mills, *Blackness Visible*, pp. 5, 152. This is not to deny that a deep concern with racial justice may well have been part of the motivation *behind* the argument of *TJ*, but only to point out that it is not systematically discussed *therein*—though there are a few scattered remarks on race and slavery; see, e.g., pp. 99, 158, 248, and 325, and the footnote to Martin Luther King (p. 364n.) in the extended discussion of civil disobedience in chapter 6. A number of theorists interested in questions of racial injustice have remarked and, in various ways, tried to make good on this lack in *A Theory of Justice*, among them Bernard Boxill, *Blacks and Social Justice* (Totowa, N.J.: Rowman & Allanheld, 1984); David Theo Goldberg, *Racist Culture* (Oxford: Blackwell, 1993); and Howard McGary, *Race and Social Justice* (Oxford: Blackwell, 1999). Though some of the themes I pursue in this section and the next are commonplaces of this genre of Rawls critique, my hope is that the particular line of argument I develop will repay revisiting them.

18. Rawls described it this way in "Kantian Constructivism in Moral Theory," (*CP*, p. 336). Despite his shift to a conception of political theory as "freestanding," he continues to acknowledge the Kantian provenance of certain key ideas. Thus the earlier characterization in *TJ* of the veil of ignorance as "implicit, I think, in Kant's ethics" (*TJ*, pp. 140–141) recurs in *PL*, where he characterizes his preference for a "thick" veil of ignorance—in which "the parties are to be understood so far as possible solely as moral persons and in abstraction from contingencies"—as "a

Kantian view" (*PL*, p. 273). A footnote to this passage points us back to the distinction between a thicker and a thinner veil of ignorance that was elaborated in "Kantian Constructivism in Moral Theory" (*CP*, pp. 335–336) and that is credited to Joshua Rabinowitz in both places. There we are told that "a Kantian doctrine aims at the thickest possible veil of ignorance," initially allowing the parties no information at all and then adding "just enough so that they can make a rational agreement," thus ensuring that the first principles of justice are those of "rationally autonomous agents" represented solely as "free and equal moral persons" with no more information than is required for agreement. He contrasts this with a "Humean" approach that would initially allow the parties full information and then rule out just enough "to achieve impartiality in the sense of the elimination of threat advantage." This veil of ignorance is thinner than the Kantian in that the parties still have access to information about the configuration of the society for which they are designing principles of justice. Even if both approaches led to the same principles, Rawls writes, "the thicker veil of ignorance would still be preferable, since these principles are then connected more closely to the conception of free and equal moral persons," whereas the alternative approach "obscure[s] how intimately the principles are tied to the conception of the person."

19. Mills, *Blackness Visible*, p. 108.

20. On the other hand, the evidence seems plain that ethnocentric modes of thought and action have been "general facts" or "general tendencies" of human society throughout recorded history. See Ivan Hannaford, *Race: The History of an Idea in the West* (Baltimore, Md.: Johns Hopkins University Press, 1996), and Davis, *Slavery*. Whether there are any "general laws" at work here is hard to say, particularly as no stable meaning can be given to that notion in political theory, as I shall argue below.

21. As to whether it might be "conserved" in some other sense, see the differing views on Du Bois's "The Conservation of Races" expressed by Anthony Appiah, "Illusions of Race," chapter two of *In My Father's House* (New York: Oxford University Press, 1992); Lucius Outlaw, "'Conserve' Races?," in *W. E. B. Du Bois on Race and Culture*, ed. B. Bell, E. Grosholz, and J. Stewart (New York: Routledge, 1996), pp. 15–37; and Robert Gooding–Williams, "Outlaw, Appiah, and Du Bois's 'The Conservation of Races'," in the same volume, pp. 39–56.

22. Rawls does not use the terminology of "levels" of theory, but of "parts" (ideal and nonideal) and of "stages" (the four-stage sequence). I shall be focusing on the former, but a full treatment of the issues I raise would require examining the latter as well. My conjecture is that similar considerations would apply, as the basic structure of justice is already designed at the first stage, but I cannot argue this here. See Habermas's remarks on the four-stage sequence in "Reconciliation and the Public Use of Reason: Remarks on John Rawls's Political Liberalism," *Journal of Philosophy* 92 (1995): 109–131, pp. 118, 128; and Rawls's "Reply to Habermas," in the same volume, pp. 132–180, here pp. 151–153.

23. For an elaboration and defense of this point, see Richard Bernstein, *Restructuring*, and, in a different but related context, *Between Objectivism and Relativism* (Philadelphia, Penn.: University of Pennsylvania Press, 1983).

24. The resultant strains can, I think, be glimpsed in the tension, in his "Reply to Habermas," between his characterization of discourse in civil society as an

Thomas McCarthy

"omnilogue" in which citizens directly debate the relative merits of competing conceptions of justice (p. 140) and his account a few pages later of public justification as a kind of indirect "overlapping consensus": "Public justification happens when all the reasonable members of political society carry out a justification of the shared political conception by embedding it in their several reasonable comprehensive [doctrines].... [C]itizens do not look into the content of others' doctrines.... Rather, they take into account and give some weight to only the fact—the existence—of the reasonable overlapping consensus itself" (pp. 143–144).

25. For the details of this argument, see my "Kantian Constructivism and Reconstructivism: Rawls and Habermas in Dialogue," *Ethics* 105 (1994): 44–63, and "On the Idea of a Reasonable Law of Peoples," in J. Bohman and M. Lutz-Bachmann, ed., *Perpetual Peace* (Cambridge, Mass.: The MIT Press, 1997), pp. 201–217.

26. I hope to flesh out this alternative in future publications; the discussion here remains at the level of abstract methodological requirements.

27. This is essentially the strategy Charles Mills recommends in *The Racial Contract.*

28. See Axel Honneth, *The Struggle for Recognition,* trans. J. Anderson (Cambridge, Mass.: The MIT Press, 1996).

29. Judith Butler, *Excitable Speech* (New York: Routledge, 1997), p. 89. Her position is interestingly elaborated but not essentially changed in J. Butler, E. Laclau, and S. Zizek, *Contingency, Hegemony, Universality* (London: Verso, 2000).

30. Ibid.

31. See Richard Bernstein, "Philosophy, History, and Critique," in Bernstein, *The New Constellation* (Cambridge, Mass.: The MIT Press, 1992), pp. 15–30.

32. Bernstein makes similar points in regard to Rorty's appropriation of Rawls in *The New Constellation,* pp. 238–249.

33. This is the general approach to racial injustice taken by liberal theorists such as Bernard Boxill, Ronald Dworkin, Gertrude Ezorsky, Thomas Nagel, and Judith Jarvis Thomson, among others. A recent and rich elaboration of it is Amy Gutmann's "Responding to Racial Injustice," in K. Anthony Appiah and Amy Gutmann, *Color Consciousness* (Princeton N.J.: Princeton University Press, 1996), pp. 106–178.

34. J. Habermas, *Between Facts and Norms,* trans. W. Rehg (Cambridge, Mass.: The MIT Press, 1996), chapter 9, "Paradigms of Law."

35. I do not mean to imply here that "counterintuitive" knowledge could not also come from critical "insiders," as is argued by Michael Walzer, for instance, in *The Company of Critics* (New York: Basic Books, 1988).

36. To be sure, critical race theorists from Du Bois onwards have typically worked in interdisciplinary ways. But their work has largely been ignored by mainstream political theory. So this essay could also be construed as an argument for changing the canon.

8

Kantian Questions, Arendtian Answers: Statelessness, Cosmopolitanism, and the Right to Have Rights

Seyla Benhabib

Richard Bernstein, Hannah Arendt, and the Conversation of Philosophy

In 1971 Richard J. Bernstein published *Praxis and Action. Contemporary Philosophies of Human Activity*. This work saliently exhibited the style of philosophizing that was to become the distinguishing feature of Richard Bernstein's contributions to contemporary thought in the next three decades. Arguing that the themes of *praxis* and *action* were fundamental to four philosophical movements, namely Marxism, existentialism, pragmatism, and analytic philosophy, Bernstein observed that, although for many philosophers hardly any commonality could exist between such diverse streams of thought, he intended to show "that there are important common themes and motifs in what appears to be a chaotic babble of voices" (Bernstein 1971, p. 1). The elucidation of common themes, problematics, and concepts across what seem to be mutually exclusive styles of thinking has become the dominant philosophical hermeneutic of Bernstein's work. In works such as *The Restructuring of Social and Political Theory* and *Beyond Objectivism and Relativism*, Bernstein applied this method of reading and analysis to debates in the philosophy of the social sciences and in epistemology, respectively (Bernstein 1978, 1983). What this philosophical hermeneutic reveals is not only the capacious learning, intellect and the generosity of spirit that Bernstein brings to the study of philosophy, but also his conviction that this is the most fruitful method of countering the *inevitable pluralism of philosophy in a postmetaphysical age.*

In many works, Bernstein discusses the temptation, prevalent since Descartes, of countering philosophical pluralism with an exclusive focus on the correct method. If one finds the right method for ordering one's ideas, then one can sift through one's convictions, be it in epistemology or morality, and get rid of those that do not stand up to the test of such rigorous examination. The method itself is defined by a guiding standard such as clear and distinct ideas (Descartes); sense impressions (Locke); elementary propositions and logical connectives (Bertrand Russell and the early Wittgenstein). In *Beyond Objectivism and Relativism,* Bernstein makes an alliance with Hans Georg Gadamer's critique of Cartesian philosophy to show that this fixation on method is an illusion that is itself supported by a number of foundationalist epistemological assumptions, such as the presence of clear and distinct ideas, or sense perceptions, or elementary propositions that express discrete facts, etc. The search for method is a foundationalist quest.[1] When the illusions of foundationalism fail, however, the skeptic is close at hand, to argue that all philosophy is ultimately a ruse. Thus the philosophical pendulum swings from foundationalists to skeptics and back again. Over the years Richard Bernstein has claimed that neither foundationalism nor skepticism are the correct answers. Following an argument developed by John Dewey in *The Quest of Certainty,* he has maintained that when the pretension of philosophy to provide *the only correct answers* to a range of questions is challenged, what remains is not despair and skepticism but a mode of seeing philosophy as the inevitable but fallible human conversation concerning our place in the universe as human beings (Dewey 1929). This conversation can generate insights rather than eternal truths, moral and political judgments about contingent human institutions rather than apodictic certainties; above all, it can reinforce our belief in contingent, but nonetheless, binding procedures of inquiry and conduct. The elucidation of such binding procedures of inquiry and conduct through an examination of common themes and concerns across disparate and often rival philosophical traditions is Bernstein's lasting contribution to the "post-analytic"[2] movement in twentieth-century philosophy.

Hannah Arendt's role as a vital conversation partner in Richard Bernstein's philosophical journey became clear with the publication of *Hannah Arendt and the Jewish Question* (Bernstein 1996). In some ways it is puzzling that her presence was not more pronounced earlier, in *Praxis and Action,* for the very themes of "praxis" (action) and "poiesis" (making) and Arendt's retrieval of the Aristotelian concept of *praxis* as "the doing of just and noble deeds" in the *polis* were cornerstones of her critique of the decline of political life in modern societies. Bernstein acknowledged Arendt's contribution in a footnote to his preface, but a detailed consideration of her work had to await a decade.[3] Furthermore, Arendt's place within the postanalytic conversation in contemporary philosophy is elusive. On the one hand, many themes like action, identity, interpretation, "web of narratives" in human affairs, the role of judgment in moral and political thought, the critique of modernity run not only through Richard Bernstein's work, but are dominant in Jürgen Habermas's, Charles Taylor's, and Alasdair MacIntyre's contributions dating to the early 1970s and 1980s as well.[4] On the other hand, an appreciation of Arendt as a philosopher in contradistinction from a political thinker is rare and infrequent. In this context, Bernstein's retrieval of Arendt's theory of judgment and his valorization of its significance within contemporary debates concerning epistemological foundationalism is unique, and, undoubtedly, has paved the way for a deeper appreciation of her contributions among a future generation of scholars—among whom I would count myself.

The following essay follows a method of reading Arendt's work that has been characterized as "thinking with Arendt against Arendt," and that Richard Bernstein and myself have frequently used in our appreciation of her philosophy.[5] I focus here on the problem of statelessness and the right to have rights in Arendt's work. In Bernstein's reading of Arendt, the condition of rendering human beings as "superfluous" to the social and political order is crucial in paving the way to totalitarian evil. In fact, Bernstein even suggests that radical evil can be identified as that condition that makes human beings superfluous, not only by rendering them bereft of any legal or political rights, but by depriving them of any protection by an organized human body as well and thus, ready to be disposed of as mere bodies in space and time (Bernstein 1996, pp. 71–88, 137ff.). Statelessness, the loss of the right to have rights, and superfluousness are closely linked. Although the first two do not always result in the third, it is inconceivable that a person could be rendered superfluous without first losing the protection of a specific state and juridico-political community. I offer the following considerations on the themes of statelessness, the right to have rights, and cosmopolitanism as a token of appreciation for the deep and lasting guidance set by Richard Bernstein for my own philosophical work.

The Decline of the Nation-State and the "End of the Rights of Man"

More than a quarter of a century after her death in 1975, Hannah Arendt has emerged as the political theorist of the post-totalitarian moment.[6] It is not only her insights about the significance of a vibrant and free public sphere in democratic civil societies, east and west, that earn Arendt the title of "theorist of the post-totalitarian moment." It is Arendt, the theorist of minority rights and statelessness, of refugees and deported peoples, whose words strike the deepest chord in a world shaken by terrorism and ethnic massacres, cultural self-determination movements and weak nation-states. I want to examine Hannah Arendt's reflections on the paradoxes of the state-centric system in the West and its collapse during the interwar period in Europe. Just as Arendt offered us paradoxes —creative and productive ones I want to argue—so too, I will approach the question of borders, boundaries, and crossings in a state-centric world in the spirit of reflection. We may be at a point in history when indeed the state-centric system is waning: global terrorism and the global influx of peoples are part of the same maelstrom. Yet our thinking and acting, laws as well as institutions, practices as well as alliances, are governed by state-centric terms that presuppose the unity of territoriality, the monopoly by the state over the legitimate use of the means of violence, and the attainment of legitimacy through representative institutions. Yet in the treatment of the "others" beyond its borders, the always present tensions within the nation-state system, as between territoriality and legitimacy, reveal themselves. Arendt analyzed this tension through the paradoxical logic of the rights of man. I name this set of philosophical and political puzzles an inquiry into "political geographies."

In *The Origins of Totalitarianism*, Arendt writes:

Something much more fundamental than freedom and justice, which are rights of citizens, is at stake when belonging to a community into which one is born is no longer a matter of course and not belonging no longer a matter of choice, or when one is placed in a situation where, unless he commits a crime, his treatment by others does not depend on what he does or does not do. This extremity, and nothing else, is the situation of people deprived of human rights. They are deprived, not of the right to freedom, but of the right to action; not of the right to think whatever they please, but of the right to opinion.... *We become aware of the existence of a right to have rights (and that means to live in a framework where one is judged by one's actions and opinions) and a right to belong to some kind of organized community, only when millions of people emerge who had lost and could not regain these rights because of the new global political situation.* (Arendt 1968 [1951], p. 177. My emphasis)

The phrase "the right to have rights" and Arendt's resounding plea for the acknowledgment of the right of every human being to "belong to some community," are introduced at the end of part 2 of The *Origins of Totalitarianism*, which is called "Imperialism." To understand Arendt's philosophical intentions it is necessary first to follow the broad historical outlines of this discussion. In the opening sections of "Imperialism" Arendt examines the European "scramble for Africa." Her thesis is that the encounter with Africa allowed the colonizing white nations like the Belgians and the Dutch, the Germans and the French, to transgress moral and civil rules abroad that would normally control the exercise of power at home. In the encounter with Africa, civilized white men, regressed to levels of inhumanity by plundering, looting, burning, and raping the "savages" whom they encountered. Arendt uses Joseph Conrad's famous story, "The Heart of Darkness," as a parable of this encounter. The "heart of darkness" is not in Africa alone; twentieth century totalitarianism brings this center of darkness to the European continent itself. The lessons learned in Africa seem to be practiced in the heart of Europe.

Arendt's attempt to locate in the European scramble for Africa some distant source of European totalitarianism, and in particular of racial extermination policies, is brilliant, although it remains historically as well as philosophically underexplored. Throughout this discussion she examines distinct historical episodes as illustrating the breakdown of the rule of law: the destruction of the ideal of citizens' consent through secret administrative decisions and imperialist manipulations, as in the case of British rule in India and French rule in Egypt; the fragility of principles of human rights to govern interactions among human beings who, in fact, have nothing but their humanity in common, as evidenced by the colonization of Africa; the instrumentalization of the nation-state on behalf of the plundering greed of the bourgeois classes, an experiment in which all major European nations more or less took part. Her discussion of imperialism, which begins with the European "scramble for Africa," concludes with "The Decline of the Nation-State and the End of the Rights of Man."

Through an analysis whose significance for contemporary developments is only too obvious after the civil wars in post-communist succession states, Arendt subsequently turns to the nationalities and minorities question that emerged in the wake of World War I. The dissolution of multinational and multiethnic empires like the Russian, the Ottoman, and the Austro-Hungarian, and the defeat of the Kaiserreich, led to the emergence of nation-states, particularly in the territories of eastern-central Europe, which enjoyed neither religious, nor linguistic, nor cultural homogeneity. The successor states of these empires, like Poland, Austria, Hungary, Czechoslovakia, Yugoslavia, Romania, Bulgaria, Lithuania, Latvia, Estonia, the Greek and the Turkish republics, controlled territories in which large numbers of so-called national minorities resided. On June 28, 1919 the Polish Minority Treaty was concluded between President Woodrow Wilson and the Allied and associated powers, to protect the rights of minorities who made up nearly forty percent of the total population of Poland at that time and who consisted of Jews, Russians, Germans, and Lithuanians among others. Thirteen similar agreements were then drawn up with various successor governments "in which they pledged to their minorities civil and political equality, cultural and economic freedom, and religious toleration" (Fink 1972, p. 331). Not only were there fatal unclarities in how a "national minority" was to be defined, but the fact that the protection of minority rights only applied to the successor states of the defeated powers, whereas Great Britain, France, and Italy refused to consider the generalization of the minority treaties to their own territories, created cynicism about the motivations of the Allied powers in supporting minority rights in the first place (ibid., p. 334).

This situation led to anomalies whereby, for example, the German minority in Czechoslovakia could petition the League of Nations for the protection of its rights but the large German minority in Italy could not. The position of Jews in all successor states was also unsettled: if they were a "national minority," was it in virtue of their race, their religion, or their language that they were to be considered as such, and exactly which rights would this minority status entail? Besides rights to the free exercise of religion and instruction in Hebrew schools, what educational and cultural rights would be granted to populations as diverse as the Austrian Jews on the one hand, Russian Jews on the other, and the Turkish Sephardic community in the former territories of the Ottoman Empire, to name but a few instances?

For Arendt, the gradual discord within, and the resulting political ineptitude of the League of Nations, the emerging conflicts between so-called national minorities themselves, the hypocrisy in the application of the minority treaties, all were harbingers of developments to come in the 1930s. The modern nation-state was being transformed from an organ that would execute the rule of all for all its citizens and residents into an instrument of the nation alone. "The nation has conquered the state, national interest had priority over law long before Hitler could pronounce 'right is what is good for the German people'" (Arendt 1968 [1951], p. 155).

The perversion of the modern state from being an instrument of law into one of lawless discretion in the service of the nation was

Seyla Benhabib

completed when states began to practice massive denaturalizations against unwanted minorities, thus creating millions of refugees, deported aliens, and stateless peoples across borders. Refugees and minorities, stateless and displaced persons are special categories of human beings "created" through the actions of the nation-state. For in a territorially bound nation-state system, that is in a "state-centric" international order, one's legal status is dependent on protection by the highest authority that controls the territory upon which one resides and issues the papers to which one is entitled. One becomes a *refugee* if one is persecuted, expelled, and driven away from one's homeland; one becomes a *minority* if the political majority in the polity declares that certain groups do not belong to the supposedly "homogeneous" people; one is a *stateless* person if the state whose protection one has hitherto enjoyed withdraws such protection, as well as nullifying the papers it has so far granted; one is a *displaced* person if, having been once rendered a refugee, stateless, or a minority, one cannot find another polity to recognize one as its member, and remains in a condition of limbo, caught between territories, none of which desire one to be its resident. It is here that Arendt concludes:

We become aware of the existence of a right to have rights (and that means to live in a framework where one is judged by one's actions and opinions) and a right to belong to some kind of organized community, only when millions of people emerge who had lost and could not regain these rights because of the new global political situation.... The right that corresponds to this loss and that was never even mentioned among the human rights cannot be expressed in the categories of the eighteenth-century because they presume that rights spring immediately from the "nature" of man ... the right to have rights, or the right of every individual to belong to humanity, should be guaranteed by humanity itself. It is by no means certain whether this is possible. (Arendt 1968 [1951], pp. 177–178. My emphasis)

As Frank Michelman has observed in an illuminating essay, "Parsing 'A Right to Have Rights,' "[a]s matters have actually developed ... the having of rights depends on receipt of a special sort of social recognition and acceptance—that is, of one's juridical status within some particular concrete political community. The notion of a right to have rights arises out of the modern-statist conditions and is equivalent to the moral claim of a refugee or other stateless person to citizenship, or at least juridical personhood, within the social confines of some law-dispensing state" (Michelman 1996, p. 203). But what kind of a moral claim is the one advanced by the refugee and the asylum seeker, the guest worker and the immigrant to be "recognized" as a member? What kind of a right is entailed in the "right" to have rights?

The Many Meanings of "The Right to Have Rights"

Let me analyze the phrase "the right to have rights." Is the concept "right" being used in an equivalent fashion in the two halves of the phrase? Is the right to be acknowledged by others as a person who is entitled to rights in general of the same status as the rights to which one would be entitled after such recognition? Clearly not. The first use of the term "right" is addressed to humanity as such and enjoins us to recognize membership in some human group. In this sense the use of the term "right" evokes *a moral imperative*: "Treat all human beings as persons belonging to some human group and entitled to the protection of the same." What is invoked here is a *moral claim to membership* and *a certain form of treatment compatible with the claim to membership.*

The second use of the term "right" in the phrase "the right to have rights" is built upon this prior claim of membership. To have a right, when one is already a member of an organized political and legal community, means that "I have a claim to do or not to do A, and you have an obligation not to hinder me from doing or not doing A." Rights entitle persons to engage in or not to in a course of action, and such entitlements create reciprocal obligations. Rights and obligations are correlated: rights discourse takes place among the consociates of a community. Such rights, which create reciprocal obligations among consociates, that is, among those who are already recognized as members of a legal community, are usually referred to as "civil and political" rights—or as citizens' rights. Let us then name the second use of the term "right" in the phrase "the right to have rights" its *juridico-civil usage*. In this usage,

Seyla Benhabib

"rights" suggests a triangular relationship between the person who is entitled to rights, others on whom this obligation creates a duty, and the protection of the rights claim and their enforcement through some established legal organ, most commonly, the state and its apparatus.

The first use of the term "right" then in the phrase "the right to have rights" does not show the same discursive structure as its second use: in the first mention, the identity of the other(s) to whom the claim to be recognized as a rights-bearing person is addressed is open and indeterminate. Note that for Arendt such recognition is first and foremost a recognition to membership, the recognition that one "belongs" to some organized human community. But who is to give or withhold such recognition? Who are the addressees of the claim that one "should be acknowledged as a member"? Arendt's answer is clear: humanity itself, and yet she adds, "It is not clear that this is possible." The asymmetry between the first and second uses of the term "right" derives from the absence in the first case of a specific juridico-legal community of consociates who stand in a relation of reciprocal duty to one another. And what would this duty be? The duty to recognize one as a "member," as one who is protected by the legal-political authorities and treated as a person entitled to the enjoyment of rights.

Throughout these formulations, which bear more the character of philosophical ruminations than conclusions on Arendt's part, one reads between the lines her preoccupation with Kantian themes. For Kant, the moral law—"Act in such a way that you treat humanity in all your actions as an end, and never as means only"— legitimizes the "right of humanity in one's person," that is, the right to be treated by others in accordance with certain standards of human dignity and worthiness. This right imposes *negative duties* on us, that is, duties that oblige us not to act in such a way as would violate the right of humanity in every person. Such violation would occur first and foremost if and when we were to refuse to enter into civil society with each other, that is, if we were to refuse to become legal consociates. The right of humanity in our person then imposes a reciprocal obligation on us to enter into civil society and to accept that our freedom be limited by civil legislation, such that the freedom of one can be made compatible with the freedom of each under a universal law. The right of humanity leads Kant to justify the social contract of civil government under which we all become legal consociates. In Arendtian language, the right of humanity entitles us to become members of civil society such that we can then be entitled to juridico-civil rights. But who are *these* consociates? Who are the parties to this hypothetical contract? How are the boundaries of the civic community determined? From the principle of duty to recognize the right of humanity in every person in that I ought to enter into a contract of civil society with them, nothing follows about the identity of those who are members of this specific civil society and those others who may not even be parties to the contract. Kant's argument leads to an aspiration toward a global civil society in which the actions of all with respect to one another are to be governed by the right of humanity in our persons. But this global civil community does not permit specification; it is unclear how we can get to individual representative sovereign bodies on the basis of this generalized moral obligation. In effect, if we follow this train of thought, it is unclear how civil and political otherness can be posited at all. Who remains outside the borders of the civil contract of government and why?

The paradox in the very framework of the nation-state derives from two contradictory principles and here the Kantian moral scheme is of little help: first, the nation-states of modern bourgeois revolutions emerge through declaring allegiance to the Universal Declarations of Man and Citizen. "We hold these truths to be self-evident: that all men are created equal, and endowed by their Creator with certain inalienable rights." The concrete nation, "we, the people," bases the legitimacy of its own act of founding on universal truths—"we hold these truths to be self-evident: that all men are created equal." It is the acknowledgment of the commitment to a universality that is then immediately reinscribed within particularity of "we, the people"—that constitutes the paradox at the heart of this formation in Arendt's terms or the "Janus face" of modern nation building in Jürgen Habermas's words (Habermas 1998, p. 115). The sovereign people becomes one by declaring its allegiance to universal principles; but this declaration can only be concretized through the specific legal, political, economic, and cultural framework of a specific human community. This is the root tension between the universal and the particular, the principles of human rights and that of popular sovereignty.

"We, the people," to take just the American case, did not originally include nonwhite people, such as the African slaves, who were granted only three-fifths personhood; nor did the Declaration grant full citizenship and voting rights to women. It made their civil and political status dependent on that of their husbands through a procedure known as "couverture." In many cases, the state constitutions of the thirteen colonies did not grant members of the Jewish faith resident in the colonies full civil and political rights either. I have been discussing the American case but the revolutionary age in Europe from 1789 to 1848 is marked as well by the struggles of various groups contesting these exclusions, and for the extension to them of full citizenship rights. The sovereign "we" of the modern nation did not include the workers, the handymen (*die Arbeitsgesellen*), women and the propertyless. Neither were nonwhite, non-Christian people considered capable of self-government. The history of political modernity is the history of struggles by excluded groups to reinscribe themselves within the circle of addressees of the universal suggested in the phrase "all men are created equal." They obviously are not; it is political struggle throughout history, institution building and learning from past struggles and defeats, cultural transformations and reconfigurations that make this equality a historical principle by transforming the constative of equality into a moral and political performative.

The struggle between the universal and the particular, between the principles of human rights and the sovereignty of a concrete people is one of inclusion and exclusion. The boundaries of the "we" are contested and contestable, but not only within the imagined community of the "we, the sovereign people." For the nation-state system sovereignty always also means control over a *bounded territory*, and this is the second pillar of the state-centric system. The "we" becomes one by defining, controlling, and closing their borders to "others"—strangers, aliens, and refugees. The modern state system is based on the principle of "territorially bounded" citizenship. There are others within as well as without the sovereign people. Without this ability of the modern state to define and defend its territory, the principle of sovereignty becomes irrelevant. Not only is there something paradoxical about reinscribing the universal in the particular; but it is also a paradox to circumscribe membership in such a way that only those within the boundaries of the sovereign territory are protected in their rights claims, whereas the status of those outside remains in a murky zone between morality and the law.

In these particular pages Arendt does not resolve these paradoxes nor does she produce a philosophical argument against foundationalist discourses that would ground human rights on nature or history; instead she produces what we may call a "*zeitgeschichtliche Diagnose*":

Man of the twentieth century has become just as emancipated from nature as eighteenth-century man was form history. History and nature have become equally alien to us, namely, in the sense that the essence of man can no longer be comprehended in terms of either category. On the other hand, humanity, which for the eighteenth century in Kantian terminology, was no more than regulative idea, has today become an inescapable fact. The new situation, in which "humanity" has in effect assumed the role formerly ascribed to nature or history, would mean in this context that the right to have rights or the right of every individual to belong to humanity, should be guaranteed by humanity itself. (Arendt 1968 [1951], p. 178)

It is the political realities of the twentieth century that have rendered the ideals of nature and history hollow as philosophical foundations. The Kantian ideal of humanity, far from being merely regulative, has now become "an inescapable fact" with moral resonance. The addressees as well as claimants of the "right to have rights" are humans themselves, but if it is a specific group of human beings who refuse to recognize others as members, who or which institutions should force a self-determining collectivity to accept others into their midst? How can the international community prevent denaturalizations—loss of citizen status—from occurring—I mean not just at the political level but normatively? How can sovereign states be forced to accept refugees and asylum seekers into their midst? The right to sovereign self-determination involves the right to protect one's territory and to define its boundaries, but how can this right be reconciled with moral obligations that are universal in scope?

I want to recall very briefly Kant's discussion of "cosmopolitan right" in his essay on "Perpetual Peace," for the difficulties of reconciling the moral and the political—the universality of the duty we owe to others with special obligations that derive from our being members of a legal and political consociation—are most vivid here.

"Perpetual Peace" and Cosmopolitical Right

Kant, as is well known, formulates three "definitive articles for perpetual peace among states." These read: "The Civil Constitution of Every State should be Republican"; "The Law of Nations shall be founded on a Federation of Free States"; and "The Law of World Citizenship Shall be Limited to Conditions of Universal Hospitality" (Kant 1914 [1795], pp. 434–443; 1957, pp. 92–103). Much scholarship on this essay has focused on the precise legal and political forms that these articles could or would take, and on whether Kant meant to propose the establishment of a world federation of republics rather than a league of sovereign nation-states (*Voelkerbund*).

What remains obscure and frequently uncommented upon is the third article of perpetual peace, the only one in fact, which Kant himself explicitly designates with the terminology of the "*Weltbuergerrecht.*" The German reads: "*Das Weltbuergerrecht soll auf Bedingungen der allgemeinen Hospitalitaet eingeschraenkt sein*" (Kant 1914 [1795], p. 443). Kant himself notes the oddity of the locution of "hospitality" in this context, and therefore remarks that "it is not a question of philanthropy but of right." In other words, hospitality is not to be understood as a virtue of sociability, as the kindness and generosity one may show toward strangers who come to one's land or who become dependent on one's act of kindness through the circumstances of nature or history; hospitality is a "right" that belongs to all human beings insofar as we view them as potential participants in a world republic. But the "right" of hospitality is odd in that it does not regulate relationships among individuals who are members of a particular civil entity and under whose jurisdiction they stand. The "right" of hospitality is situated at the boundaries of the polity; it delimits civic space by regulating relations among members and strangers.

Hence the "right of hospitality" occupies that space between human rights and civil rights, between the right of humanity in our person and the rights that accrue to us insofar as we are members of specific republics. Kant writes:

Hospitality [*Wirtbarkeit*] means the right of a stranger not to be treated as an enemy when he arrives in the land of another. One may refuse to receive him when this can be done without causing his destruction; but, so long as he peacefully occupies his place, one may not treat him with hostility. It is not the right to be a permanent visitor [*Gastrecht*] that one may demand. A special beneficent agreement [*ein wohltaetiger Vertrag*] would be needed in order to give an outsider a right to become a fellow inhabitant [*Hausgenossen*] for a certain length of time. It is only a right of temporary sojourn [*ein Besuchsrecht*], a right to associate, which all men have. They have it by virtue of their common possession [*das Recht des gemeinschaftlichen Besitzes*] of the surface of the earth, where, as a globe, they cannot infinitely disperse and hence must finally tolerate the presence of each other. (Kant 1914 [1795], p. 443; 1957, p. 103)

Kant distinguishes between the "right to be a permanent visitor," which he calls *Gastrecht,* from the "temporary right of soujourn" (*Besuchsrecht*). The right to be a permanent visitor can only be awarded to one through a freely chosen special agreement that goes beyond the call of moral duty and legal right; Kant names this a "*wohltaetiger Vertrag.*" It is a special privilege that the republican sovereign can award certain foreigners and strangers who abide in their territories, who perform certain functions, who represent their respective political entities, and engage in long-term trade, and so on.

The right of hospitality, by contrast, entails a claim to temporary residency that cannot be refused if such refusal would involve a violation of the rights of humanity in the person of the other. To refuse sojourn to victims of religious wars, to victims of piracy or shipwreck, when such refusal would harm them, is untenable, writes Kant. What is unclear in Kant's discussion is whether such relations among peoples and nations involve acts of supererogation or whether they indeed entail claims concerning "the rights of humanity in the person of the other." We may see here the juridical and moral ambivalence that affects discussions of "the right of asylum" and "the rights of refugees" to this day. Are the rights of asylum and refuge, rights in the sense of being reciprocal moral obligations that, in some sense or another, are grounded on our mutual humanity? Or are these rights claims in the legal sense of enforceable norms of behavior that individuals and groups can hold each other to, and, in particular, force sovereign nation-states to comply with? Kant's construction provides no clear answer. The right of hospitality seems to entail a moral claim with potential legal consequences in that the obligation of the receiving states to grant temporary residency is anchored in a republican cosmopolitical order, which itself requires the voluntary compliance of the member states.

Although Kant's focus fell, for understandable historical reasons, on the right of temporary sojourn, my concern is with the unbridgeable gap he suggests to exist between the right of temporary sojourn and permanent residency. The first is a right, the second is a privilege; granting the first to strangers is an obligation for a republican sovereign, whereas allowing the second is an "act of beneficence." The rights of strangers and foreigners do not extend beyond the peaceful pursuit of their means of livelihood on the territory of another. What about the right to political membership then? Under what conditions, if any, can the guest become a member of the republican sovereign? How are the boundaries of the sovereign defined? Kant envisages a world condition in which all members of the human race become participants in a civil order and enter into a condition of "lawful association" with one another. Yet this civil condition of lawful coexistence is not equivalent to membership in a republican constitution. Kant's cosmopolitan citizens still need their individual republics to be citizens at all. This is why he is so careful to distinguish a "world government" from a "world federation." A "world government," he argues, would be a "soulless despotism," whereas a world federation (*eine foederative Vereinigung*) would still permit the exercise of citizenship within bounded communities (Kant 1914 [1795], p. 453; 1957, p. 112).

Kant and Arendt on the Right to Political Membership

I have recalled at length Kant's argument concerning "the cosmo-political right to temporary soujourn," because this discussion con-tains *in nuce* many of the dilemmas that govern our thinking about the status of foreigners and aliens, immigrants, refugees and asylum seekers. We are still unsure whether the claims of refugees and asylums seekers articulate international obligations, the violation of which should lead to sanctions against sovereign states, or whether vis à vis such claims the prerogative of the political sovereign holds.

We should also note how close Kant and Arendt are on this score. Just as Kant leaves unexplained the philosophical and political step which would lead from the right of temporary sojourn to the right of membership, so too, Arendt could not base "the right to have rights," that is, to be recognized as a member of some organized human community, on some further philosophical principle. For Kant, granting the right to membership remains the prerogative of the republican sovereign and involves an act of "beneficence."

In his commentary on Kant's construction of cosmopolitan right, Jacques Derrida notes the *chasm* that opens up between the moral and ethical imperative of "hospitality"—the receptivity to the other, the responsibility to the other—and the impossibility of ever institutionalizing this imperative in juridico-legal form (Derrida 2001, pp. 11ff., 17ff.). Responsible politics, or a politics of respon-siveness, is situated in the intermediate space created by the obligation to respond to the other and the necessity of creating institutions that circumscribe this obligation to one's legal and po-litical consociates. For Derrida, the inconclusivity in Arendt's as well as Kant's reflections is indicative of their refusal to compromise the ethical and the moral in the name of the political.

For Giorgio Agamben in *Homo Sacer. Sovereign Power and Bare Life*, Arendt's and Kant's inconclusive ruminations on the inability of international law to bend the will of the sovereign simply reveal the true nature of sovereign power (Agamben 1998). Whereas Derrida underscores the necessity as well as the impossibility of ever media-ting the political fully satisfactorily with the ethical, for Agamben the paradoxes of "the right to have rights" reveal the arbitrariness in modern constructions of sovereignty. In a brilliant and obscure synthesis of Carl Schmitt and Michel Foucault, Agamben constructs modern sovereign power as being based on the mythical figure of *homo sacer*—the one who can be killed by the state but not sacrificed by it (Agamben 1998, pp. 126ff.). The modern state can refuse refugees and asylum seekers admittance but cannot sacrifice them even if one's actions could result in their death. The political theology of modern sovereignty cannot be confined to the language of universal rights—"the sovereign is he who decides on the state of exception" (Carl Schmitt) and at no other point is the arbitrariness of sovereign power more evident than when it guards its borders, defines the rights of aliens and foreigners, and refuses admission.

The aporias of the state-centric model of sovereignty are real: the tension between the universality of human rights claims and the principle of sovereign self-determination on the one hand, and the moral and ethical costs of territorially circumscribed citizenship on the other. Where do we go from here?

Conclusion

Since Arendt penned her prophetic analysis of the "Decline of the Nation-State and the End of the Rights of Man," institutional and normative developments in international law have begun to address some of the paradoxes that she as well as Kant were unable to resolve. When Arendt wrote that "the right to have rights" was a fundamental moral claim as well as insoluble political problem she did not mean that aliens, foreigners, and residents did not possess any rights. In certain circumstances, as with Jews in Germany, with Greek and Armenian nationals in the period of the founding of the republic of Turkey (1923), and with German refugees in Vichy France—to name but a few cases—entire groups of people were "denaturalized" or "denationalized," and lost the protection of a sovereign legal body. For Arendt neither the institutional nor the theoretical solutions to this problem were at hand.

Institutionally, several arrangements have emerged since World War II that express the learning process of the nations of this world in dealing with the horrors of this century: the 1951 Geneva Convention relating to the status of refugees and its protocol added in 1967; the creation of the U.N. High Commissioner for Refugees (UNHCR); the formation of the World Court, and most recently, of an International Criminal Court through the Treaty of Rome, are developments intended to protect those whose right to have rights have been denied.

Furthermore, the rise of an international human rights regime, precipitated by the 1948 UN Declaration of Human Rights, has proceeded uninterrupted in the last fifty years. The establishment of the European Union has been accompanied by a European Charter of Human Rights, as well as by a European Court of Human Rights. Following the U.N. Declaration of Human Rights, many other organizations have placed individual rights at the center of their concerns. They include the International Covenants on Civil and Political Rights and on Economic, Social and Cultural Rights, the International Labor Organization, and the Inter-American System for the Protection of Human Rights (Jacobson 1997, p. 75).

To be sure, all these declarations do not amount to agreements that have been signed and ratified; in many cases, they are simply general declarations of intention and not legally binding commitments. In international law, the will of the sovereign state can be bound only by voluntarily self-incurred treaty obligations. There is no sovereign to force the sovereign. Nevertheless, however abstract and necessarily vague these universal principles of human rights may be, they are slowly being transformed from declarations of intent into generalizable norms, capable of enforcement and litigation in the case of specific violations. This transformation of human rights codes into norms that should govern the behavior of sovereign states is one of the most promising aspects of contemporary political globalization processes.

We are witnessing this development in at least three related areas:

Humanitarian Interventions
The practice and theory of humanitarian interventions that the USA and its NATO allies have appealed to in order to justify their

actions in Bosnia and Kosovo suggests that when a sovereign nation-state violates the human rights of a segment of its population on account of their religion, race, ethnicity, language, culture, and so forth, there is a generalized moral obligation to end genocide and ethnic cleansing. In these cases human rights norms can trump state sovereignty claims.[7]

Crimes against Humanity

The concept of crimes against humanity, first articulated by the Allied powers in the Nuremberg trials of Nazi war criminals, signifies that there are certain norms in accordance with which state officials as well as private individuals must treat one another, even, and precisely under, conditions of extreme hostility and war. Genocide, ethnic cleansing, mass executions, rape, and cruel and unusual punishment of the enemy such as dismemberment, can all constitute sufficient grounds for the indictment and prosecution of individuals who are responsible for these actions, even if they are or were state officials, acting under orders. The refrain of the soldier and the bureaucrat, "I was only doing my duty"—is not acceptable for abrogating the rights of humanity in the person of the other—even when, and especially when, the other is an enemy of your state.

Transnational Migration

The third area in which international human rights norms are creating binding guidelines on the will of sovereign nation-states is that of international migration. Humanitarian interventions deal with nation-states' treatment of citizens or residents within the boundaries of their territory, and crimes against humanity concern relations among enemies in national, as well as extraterritorial settings; transnational migrations, by contrast, concern the rights of individuals, when in fact they come into contact with, seek entry into, or want to become members of territorially bounded communities. Whereas civil rights can only be realized by a territorially bounded "people," one does not have to be part of a territorially defined people to enjoy human rights. As international human rights norms are increasingly invoked in immigration, refugee, and asylum disputes, "what we are witnessing today," in the words of Jacobson, "is the transforming of the state and international institutions, of their function and of their very *raison d'être....*" (Jacobson 1997, p. 3). Territorially delimited nations are being challenged not only in their claims to control the borders of their territories but also in their prerogative to define the "boundaries of the national community" (Jacobson 1997, p. 5). Developments in American immigration law over the last twenty years have expanded both the formal and substantive due process rights of immigrants, refugees, and asylum seekers, on the remarkable precedent that "there are no strangers to the Constitution."[8] Furthermore, procedures of constitutional review, which are becoming more prevalent in European political practice through the development of the European Court of Justice, help protect the fundamental civil rights of ethnic, religious, linguistic, sexual, and other minorities against the tyranny of the majority.

We should not forget however that the UN conventions remain nonenforceable humanitarian guidelines, as the tragedy of the war in Kosovo demonstrated very well. To this day, the authority of the World Court in the Hague is contested, and the Bush administration has reversed the United States' participation in the Treaty of Rome, which would lead to the establishment of a standing International Criminal Court of Justice dealing with "crimes against humanity." In this domain, voluntarily self-incurred obligations, international as well as multilateral treaties, pacts, and agreements, remain the norm. We have not yet overcome the "political theology of sovereignty"; the new world order is fragile, as the political always is, but a new consciousness about the significance of human rights is growing. In this respect as well, some of Arendt's considerations proved visionary.

During his exchange with Hannah Arendt on the question of "crimes against humanity," Karl Jaspers argued that these should be thought of as "crimes against humaneness," *Menschlichkeit*, since in the absence of a sovereign with the power of enforcement in the domain of international relations, it made no sense to speak of "crimes against humanity," *Verbrechen gegen die Menschheit*, as if there were a recognized authority who could enforce these rights and punish nations in the event of their violation (Arendt-Jaspers 1992, pp. 413ff.). Arendt insisted that the category made sense even in the absence of a world authority with the power of enforcement. For her the Nuremberg trials and their establishing Charter of 1945 set an unprecedented precedent in declaring the illegitimacy of "crimes against humanity," and by nullifying the defense that they were committed in the name of the state (cf. Benhabib 1996b, pp. 180ff.). We may say that through recognizing crimes against humanity as a justiciable action, mankind created a "new moral fact." There is an equivalent in the international arena to the republican acts of "new beginnings" that Arendt celebrated for individual polities (Arendt 1963, pp. 54ff.). Just as every act of founding a new republican body politic creates an institutional and moral matrix— a *novos ordo saecularum*—which did not exist before in human affairs, so too, such acts of "founding" can take place in the international arena by the concluding of charters, treaties, and conventions to which sovereign nations bind themselves. Although Arendt thought that only the restoration of their national rights could guarantee disempowered minorities their rights of membership,[9] she also believed that an organized humanity itself should act as guarantor of the rights of the dispossessed through the creation of an international normative order, even without executive power. The challenge that we face today is how to preserve the fragile and hopeful gains that have been made toward a more just world order, and which are being threatened by terrorism and war among nations abroad, and the authoritarian abrogation of civil rights at home.

Notes

1. The critique of epistemological foundationalism has its sources in Hegel's discussion of "Consciousness" in the *Phenomenology of Spirit (1807)*. In the first two chapters of this work Hegel dissects the illusions of a mode of consciousness that he describes as "Sense Certainty," and "Perception" respectively. Hegel shows that the first type of consciousness, which is an ideal type characterizing both everyday attitudes and more sophisticated theories of empiricist epistemology, believes in the possibility of identifying the fullness and richness of sensory experience—what Hegel calls "its immediacy"—in the "here and the now," without the use of mediating concepts of language. This attempt to say *what* consciousness is certain of fails. Because communicating what one is certain of involves the use of general terms in language, like "this," "here," and "now," whose attribute is precisely that they are general and not particular, consciousness is continuously frustrated in its attempt

to express the richness of its experience. There are no pure referential functions in language, Hegel is arguing, just as there are no simple descriptions of what we know. *That* we know *what* we know is always mediated through language, which we must share with other knowers. Sense certainty can provide no foundations for knowledge, for to argue that these knowledge claims are valid and not merely what "I" am certain of, involves showing that they are valid for "all," in some communicable medium. The dialectic between the *what* and the *that* of knowledge, or between the certainty of consciousness's experiences, and the claim that what it knows to be the case is also valid for all others, is enacted by Hegel for increasingly more complex knowledge forms. The result of this dialectic in the first three chapters of the *Phenomenology* is the invalidation of the correspondence theory of truth and of foundationalist epistemologies (Descartes, Spinoza, Locke, Berkeley, and Hume). The case of Kant is always more complicated.

Hegel's critique of early modern epistemology has echoes in John Dewey's, Wilfrid Sellars's, and of course Richard Rorty's work. See John Dewey, *The Quest for Certainty* (1929); Wilfrid Sellars, *Empiricism and the Philosophy of Mind* (1956) and *Science and Metaphysics: Variations on Kantian Themes* (1968); Richard Rorty, *Philosophy and the Mirror of Nature* (1979). If there is one dominant epistemic theme running through "postanalytic philosophy," it is this Hegelian critique of epistemic foundationalism. Richard Bernstein has drawn our attention to the deep and subterranean connections between German idealism and American pragmatism; cf. *Praxis and Action* (1971, pp. 165–177).

If I may indulge a personal recollection here: although I never was Richard Bernstein's student, having studied philosophy and history of ideas with Alasdair MacIntyre in Brandeis University from 1970 to 1972, and having entered the Yale Philosophy Department in 1972, the Hegelian roots of American pragmatism as well as the unique mixture of these two traditions in the early work of Jürgen Habermas and Karl-Otto Apel were defining moments in my philosophical education as well. I first met Richard Bernstein when I invited him to give a lecture under the auspices of the Graduate Student Colloquium to the Yale Philosophy Department in 1975; subsequently, Richard Bernstein invited me to attend a conference at the Inter-University Center in Dubrovnik in 1978, which he was at the time codirecting with Jürgen Habermas, Mihailo Markovic, and Albrecht Wellmer.

2. See Cornell West and John Rajchmann, *Post-Analytic Philosophy* (1985).

3. See also Judith Friedlander's essay in this volume. Here she recounts that Arendt had admired Bernstein's early book and had endorsed it to a publisher. In several articles, Bernstein's encounter with aspects of Arendt's thought was announced: "Hannah Arendt: The Ambiguities of Theory and Practice" (Bernstein 1977, pp. 141–158); "Judging—the Actor and the Spectator" and "Rethinking the Social and the Political" in *Philosophical Profiles: Essays in a Pragmatic Mode* (Bernstein 1986, pp. 221–237 and pp. 238–259).

4. See "Self-Interpreting Animals," and "Hegel's Philosophy of Mind" (Taylor 1985, pp. 45–77 and pp. 77–97), and "The Opening Arguments of Hegel's *Phenomenology*" (MacIntyre 1972); see also "Hegel on Faces and Skulls," in this volume, pp. 219–237.

5. See "Hannah Arendt and the Redemptive Power of Narrative" (Benhabib 1990, pp. 167–196); and "The Pariah and her Shadow" (Benhabib 1995, pp. 5–24) and *Hannah Arendt and the Jewish Question* (Bernstein 1996, p. 13).

Seyla Benhabib

6. A short version of this lecture was held at the Hannah Arendt Tage in Hannover, Germany (October 16, 1999), and was published in the *Hannah Arendt Newsletter*, no. 2 (December 1999).

7. One needs to exercise caution here: when, how and for what purposes to intervene in the affairs of organized political communities remains a difficult moral and political question. In reaching such decisions, one has to balance the morality of intervention against concerns of political prudence, without sacrificing one to the other. This is a line that has been difficult to follow historically.

8. See Gerald Neumann, *Strangers to the Constitution: Immigrants, Borders and Fundamental Law* (1996); Peter H. Schuck, *Citizens, Strangers, and in-Betweens. Essays on Immigration and Citizenship* (1998).

9. It is in her writings on Zionism that we find the key to Arendt's critique of nationalism. In an essay published in 1948 and called "To Save the Jewish Homeland: There is Still Time," Arendt criticized all nationalisms, Zionism of Theodor Herzl's type not excluded, for the thesis that "the nation was an eternal organic body, the product of inevitable growth of inherent qualities; it explains peoples, not in terms of political organizations, but in terms of biological superhuman personalities" (Arendt 1978 [1948], p. 156). For Arendt, this kind of thinking was prepolitical in its roots, because it applied metaphors drawn from the domain of prepolitical life, such as organic bodies, family unities, and blood communities, to the sphere of politics. The more nationalist ideologies stress aspects of identity that precede the political, the more they base the equality of the citizens on their presumed commonality and sameness. But equality among consociates in a democratic liberal state should be differentiated from sameness of cultural and ethnic identity. Civic equality is not sameness but entails the respect for difference.

It is important to note that after the Holocaust and the extermination of European Jewry, Arendt's support for a Jewish homeland changed. Although she never accepted Zionism as the dominant cultural and political project of the Jewish people, and chose to live her life in a multinational and multicultural liberal democratic state, the catastrophes of World War II made Arendt more appreciative of the moment of new beginning inherent in all state formations. "The restoration of human rights," she observed, "as the recent example of the State of Israel proves, has been achieved so far only through the restoration or establishment of national rights" (Arendt 1968 [1951], p. 179). Arendt was too knowledgeable and shrewd an observer of politics not to have also noted, however, that the cost of the establishment of the State of Israel was the disenfranchisement of the Arab residents of Palestine, and hostility in the Middle East for the centuries to follow. She hoped throughout the 1950s that a binational Jewish and Palestinian state would become a reality (see Benhabib 1996, pp. 43ff.). Bernstein has a masterful treatment of this issue in *Hannah Arendt and the Jewish Question* (Bernstein 1996, pp. 101–122).

References

Ackerman, Bruce. 1991. *We, the People.* Cambridge, Mass.: Harvard University Press.

Agamben, Giorgio. 1998. *Homo Sacer. Sovereign Power and Bare Life.* Trans. Daniel Heller-Roazen. Stanford, Calif.: Stanford University Press.

Anderson, Benedict. 1991. *Imagined Communities.* Revised edition. London: Verso.

Arendt, Hannah. 1968 (1951). *The Origins of Totalitarianism*. New York: Harcourt Brace Jovanovich.

Arendt, Hannah. 1978 (1948). "To Save the Jewish Homeland. There is Still Time," in *The Jew as Pariah: Jewish Identity and Politics in the Modern Age*. Ron Feldman, ed. and introd. New York: Grove Press.

Arendt, Hannah. 1963. *On Revolution*. New York: Viking Press.

Arendt, Hannah, and Karl Jaspers. 1992. *Hannah Arendt and Karl Jaspers Correspondence: 1926–1969*. Lotte Koehler and Hans Saner, ed. New York: Harcourt Brace Jovanovich.

Benhabib, Seyla. 2002. "Unholy Politics," in *Constellations. A Journal for Critical and Democratic Theory* 9, no. 1 (March): pp. 34–45.

Benhabib, Seyla. ed. 1996a. *Democracy and Difference. Contesting the Boundaries of the Political*. Princeton, N.J.: Princeton University Press.

Benhabib, Seyla. 1996b. *The Reluctant Modernism of Hannah Arendt*. London and New York: Sage. New edition, 2003. Lanham, Md.: Rowman and Littlefield.

Benhabib, Seyla. 1995. "The Pariah and Her Shadow," in *Political Theory* 23, no. 1 (February): pp. 5–24.

Benhabib, Seyla. 1990. "Hannah Arendt and the Redemptive Power of the Narrative," *Social Research* 57, no. 1 (Spring): pp. 167–196.

Bernstein, Richard J. 1996. *Hannah Arendt and the Jewish Question*. London: Polity Press.

Bernstein, Richard J. 1986. *Philosophical Profiles: Essays in a Pragmatic Mode*. Cambridge: Polity Press.

Bernstein, Richard J. 1983. *Beyond Objectivism and Relativism: Science, Hermeneutics and Praxis*. Philadelphia, Penn.: University of Pennsylvania Press.

Bernstein, Richard J. 1978. *The Restructuring of Social and Political Theory*. Philadelphia, Penn.: University of Pennsylvania Press.

Bernstein, Richard J. 1977. "Hannah Arendt: The Ambiguities of Theory and Practice," in *Political Theory and Practice*. Terrence Ball, ed. Minneapolis, Minn.: University of Minnesota Press.

Bernstein, Richard J. 1971. *Praxis and Action. Contemporary Philosophies of Human Activity*. Philadelphia, Penn.: University of Pennsylvania Press.

Derrida, Jacques. 2001. *On Cosmopolitanism and Forgiveness*. Trans. by Mark Dooley and Michael Hughes. New York and London: Routledge.

Dewey, John. 1929. "The Quest for Certainty," in *John Dewey. The Later Works, 1925–1953*, vol. 8. Jo Anne Boylston and Stephen Toulmin, ed. Carbondale, Ill.: Southern Illinois University Press.

Fink, Carole. 1972. "Defender of Minorities: Germany in the League of Nations, 1926–1933." *Central European History*, no. 4: pp. 330ff.

Habermas, Jürgen. 1998. *The Inclusion of the Other. Studies in Political Theory*. Trans. by Ciaran Cronin and Pablo de Greiff. Cambridge, Mass.: The MIT Press.

Hegel, G. F. W. 1977 (1807). *Hegel's Phenomenology of Spirit*. Trans. by A. V. Miller. Oxford: Clarendon Press.

Hegel, G. F. W. 1967 (1821). *The Philosophy of Right*. Trans. by T. M. Knox. Oxford: Oxford University Press.

Jacobson, David. 1997. *Rights across Borders. Immigration and the Decline of Citizenship*. Baltimore, Md. and London: The Johns Hopkins University Press.

Kant, Immanuel. 1914 (1795). "Zum Ewigen Frieden. Ein philosophischer Entwurf," in *Immanuel Kants Werke*. A. Buchenau, E. Cassirer, and B. Kellermann, eds. Berlin: Verlag Bruno Cassirer.

Kant, Immanuel. 1957. "Perpetual Peace," Lewis White Beck, trans. In *On History*. Lewis White Beck, ed. Indianapolis, Ind. and New York: Library of Liberal Arts.

Kant, Immanuel. 1996 (1797). *The Metaphysics of Morals*. Trans. by Mary Gregor. Cambridge: Cambridge University Press.

MacIntyre, Alasdair. 1972. *Hegel. A Collection of Critical Essays*. Garden City, N.Y.: Anchor Books.

Michelman, Frank. 1996. "Parsing 'A Right to Have Rights'," in *Constellations: An International Journal of Critical and Democratic Theory* 3, no. 2 (October): pp. 200–209.

Neumann, Gerald. 1996. *Strangers to the Constitution: Immigrants, Borders and Fundamental Law*. Princeton, N.J.: Princeton University Press.

Rorty, Richard. 1979. *Philosophy and the Mirror of Nature*. Princeton, N.J.: Princeton University Press.

Schuck, Peter H. 1998. *Citizens, Strangers and In-Betweens. Essays in Immigration and Citizenship*. Boulder, Colo.: Westview Press.

Sellars, Wilfrid. 1956. *Empiricism and the Philosophy of Mind*. Cambridge, Mass.: Harvard University Press.

Sellars, Wilfrid. 1968. *Science and Metaphysics: Variations on Kantian Themes*. Boulder, Colo.: Ridgeview.

Taylor, Charles. 1985. "Self-Interpreting Animals" and "Hegel's Philosophy of Mind," in *Human Agency and Language: Philosophical Papers*, vol. 1. Cambridge: Cambridge University Press.

West, Cornell, and John Rajchmann. 1985. *Post-analytic Philosophy*. New York: Columbia University Press.

9

Capital Punishment: Another "Temptation of Theodicy"

Jacques Derrida

It has often been noted that "armed" movements against abortion, so to speak, readily join in the rabid opposition to the abolition of the death penalty, and even to the moratorium that would suspend executions on account of the large number of judicial errors recently discovered. These self-styled unconditional defenders of life are just as often militants of death. It is sometimes a matter of Christian fundamentalists who associate the struggle against abortion with the struggle against the abolition or suspension of the death penalty.

Here, it seems, we have been dealt a *contradictory* hand; at play is an internal tension that works through *almost* all of the history of the death penalty in the West. Up to the twenty-first century, almost without exception, the Catholic Church has been in favor of the death penalty. Sometimes in an active, fervent, militant way. It has always supported state legislation on the death penalty—like the principle of sovereignty, without which the death penalty has no chance. Saint Thomas was not the only eloquent partisan of capital punishment. This has also been the case with "systematic" theoreticians of traditional Catholicism. I am thinking in particular, to illustrate this truth with an exemplary hyperbole, of Donoso Cortès,[1] often cited and praised by Schmitt. Cortès articulated Catholic dogma and the doctrine of capital punishment with a fierce consistency, at once a bit delirious and hyperrational, "rationalizing," as has been known to happen. And in an equally remarkable way, he welded this system (Catholicism + capital punishment) to a general interpretation of blood sacrifice, from Cain and Abel to Christ and beyond.[2] What seems to me interesting, revealing, in fact typical, in this ultrareactionary, excessive, and somewhat mad theorizing is the extreme rigor of the approach.

On the one hand, even if, *stricto sensu,* the death penalty does not appear as a sacrifice and all sacrificial cultures (which is to say *all* cultures) had not produced, in the strict sense here again, a system of criminal law[3] in which a penalty of death had this value of calculating rationality, Cortès is not wrong to include the death penalty within a history of sacrifice. And even of blood sacrifice, even if the blood is tending to disappear, at least *spilled* blood, blood in the immediately visible form of its effusion, whereas the death penalty survives, and undoubtedly will survive for a long time yet, despite its general retreat in the world.

When I name *sacrifice,* I am aware that I designate less a clear and distinct concept than an immense problem to be reelaborated from top to bottom in one of the most obscure, most fundamental, least circumscribable zones of the experience of the living, *all* the living, human or nonhuman.

On the other hand (and a bit like Walter Benjamin will do in "The Critique of Violence"[4] regarding the "great criminals" who horrify but also fascinate inasmuch as they contest the state's monopolization of legitimate violence—*Gewalt*), Cortès thinks, not without profundity, that the distinction between common crime and political crime is always fragile and that the abolition of the death penalty for the latter (in France in 1848, for example, and it is his example, as it is Marx's) would have as its ineluctable consequence a universal abolition of the death penalty—in which he even sees, like Kant in fact, and here is the real place of philosophical discussion, the elimination of all criminal law. There would be no more law—and above all criminal law—without the mechanism of the death penalty, which is thus its condition of possibility, its *transcendental,* if you like (at once *internal,* included: the death penalty is an element of criminal law, one punishment among others, a bit more severe of course, and *external,* excluded: a foundation, a condition of possibility, an origin, a nonserial exemplarity, hyperbolic, more and other than a penalty).

It is this, the death penalty's paradoxical effect of transcendentalization, that a consistent abolitionism must take on. To contribute to this, one would have to attempt a kind of history of blood within a history of the concept of the *exception* (no sovereignty without the right of exception, without the right, Schmitt will say, to suspend the law,[5] for example where there is a right to grant mercy), and a history of *cruelty*, of the scrupulous use and the abuses of the word, of the concept, sometimes of the word without the concept of "cruelty," whether it is visible, theatrical, or not.

All cruelty is not bloody or bloodthirsty, visible and external, to be sure; it can be and undoubtedly is psychological (pleasure taken in suffering or in making suffer merely to make suffer, to see suffering; *grausam*, in German, does not name blood). But *cruor* certainly designates spilled blood, its effusion, and thus a certain exteriority, a visibility of red, its *expression* outside, this color that inundates all Victor Hugo's texts against the death penalty, from the red made to flow by the guillotine, "the blood-swigging old crone,"[6] "the infernal scarlet machine,"[7] up to the posts of red wood that support the blade ("two long joists painted red, a shelf painted red, a basket painted red, a heavy crossbeam painted red in which a thick, enormous blade of triangular shape seemed to be fitted together by one of its sides ... it was civilization that arrived in Algiers in the form of a guillotine").[8]

Let us return to the "Catholic question." Despite all the movements of repentance and forgiveness he has never stopped calling for, despite his discourses on the subject of the Inquisition and the past errors of the Church, despite the statements he made on the cruelty of the death penalty during a recent trip to the United States, and even though the Vatican state abolished the death penalty some twenty years ago, John Paul II, to my knowledge, has never, any more than any of his predecessors, solemnly engaged the Church and the Vatican in the abolitionist struggle. Only a few bishops, notably in France, have publicly taken a stand against the death penalty, at least against its maintenance in France.[9]

How can this be justified? Because this undeniable *fact* (that there has never been any political opposition to the death penalty by the Church) appears to contradict *another* Christianity, another spirit of Christianity, another "theodicy." Take the example of Victor Hugo.

He devoted so many struggles and magnificent texts to the abolitionist cause, to "the abolition pure and simple," which is to say
unconditional, of the death penalty, and always in the name of what
he called, rightly or wrongly, the inviolability of human life.

Now, for reasons that were not only strategic, opportunistic,
or rhetorical, Hugo also claimed to be inspired by the evangelical
message and the passion of Christ. He did so at the very moment
that he sometimes denounced the priests and the "politics" of the
Church (as he condemned the Terror and castigated the guillotine
in the name of the French Revolution, of its "truth," its memory,
and its spirit—of what it *will have to have been*, the death penalty
always remaining "the only tree that revolutions do not uproot"[10]:
"I am not one of those capped in a [revolutionary Phrygian] *red* hat
and heady with the guillotine." I again emphasize *red*).

At the very moment he takes on "the social edifice of the past,"
which rested on "three pillars: the priest, the king, and the executioner," Hugo appeals to the "merciful law of Christ" and to the
day when it "will at last suffuse the Code, which will glow with its
radiance."[11] He thus wishes to "aim his axe into the widening notch
marked sixty-six years ago by Beccaria on the old gibbet that has
towered for so many centuries over Christendom."[12] This is why,
if he is not entirely wrong, Albert Camus simplifies things somewhat, on this point like others, when, in his beautiful and brave
"Reflections on the Guillotine,"[13] he claims that the death penalty
will not be able to survive in a secularized world, or that its abolition
will occur through a humanist and atheist immanentism.[14] Christianity has other resources of internal "division," self-contestation,
and self-deconstruction.[15]

One cannot take up the question of the death penalty in the West
(perhaps this concept of criminal law, *in the strict sense*, is actually
only European, and perhaps the death penalty is not one "penalty"
among others, neither one law among others nor even an element
of criminal law), one cannot recognize its deep bases, without taking
into account the theologico-political discourse, the political theodicy, that underlies it, and which in fact has always founded it. For
the death penalty has always been the effect of an alliance between
a religious message and the sovereignty of a state (if one can even

assume, speaking of an *alliance*, that the concept of the state is not in its essence deeply religious).

Whether or not it has to do with the paradigmatic cases of Socrates, Christ, Joan of Arc, or el-Hallaj, everything is decided, exemplarily, from a religious accusation (profanation or violation of a sacred law), launched or inspired by a religious authority, which is then taken up by that of the state, which decides on the death sentence—and which executes it. In the figure of the monarch, the people, the president or governor, etc., state sovereignty thus defines itself by the power of life and death over subjects. And therefore by the right of exception, by the right to raise itself, so to speak, above the law. This is how Schmitt defines the sovereign: the ability to decide the exception, and the right to suspend the law. In the figure of the president, this right remains; but as it is conferred by an electoral mandate for a limited period, this right to grant mercy may be affected by electoral considerations or public opinion, which is not the case for the absolute monarch of hereditary and divine right.

In any case, one cannot place the death penalty in question in a radical, principled, unconditional way without contesting or limiting the sovereignty of the sovereign. The great Beccaria tried to do so[16] and got caught there in one of his numerous contradictions.

The French Revolution, despite the regicide, reinstituted a sovereignty whose principle had never fundamentally been abandoned, to say the least, after passing to the "people" of "citizens." This took the form (among others) of the Terror, even if, after the conversion of the abolitionist Robespierre to the death penalty, after a series of dilatory rejections of abolition, and despite the eloquent pleas of Condorcet, the Convention was adjourned at the end of 1795 while promising the end of capital punishment the day peace is reestablished ("general peace"!) and publicly declared! "From the day of the announcement of general peace, the death penalty will be abolished in France."

It would take more than two centuries. This is a very long or a very short time in view of the immensity of such an event and the emergence of such a symptom, depending on the scale chosen— here, to put it briefly, the historical scale of European peace, of a postrevolutionary and relatively pacified, secure, reassured Europe, a Europe in which democracy is being laboriously built. For everywhere that the death penalty has been abolished in this European community, which now makes this a condition of membership, some pressure of international origin was necessary. Sovereignty had to be limited—even where, according to proper parliamentary conventions and by all appearances, abolition was a national, internal, spontaneous, sovereign decision, as was in the case of France. I am convinced that the French parliamentarians (including those of the right, like Jacques Chirac, for example) who abolished it in 1981 contrary to public opinion—which favored and perhaps still favors the death penalty—did not only listen to their hearts and obey a principled conviction. They knew that this European and international trend would be irresistible. China and the United States still resist it, along with a certain number of Arab-Muslim countries.

In any case, it is impossible to take up the question of the death penalty without speaking of religion, and of that which, through the mediation of the concept of sovereignty, secures the right to religion. When I speak of a theologico-political or a theologico-juridico-political alliance as the basis or principle of the death penalty, as its being set to work, when I thus invoke a concept of sovereignty (over the life and death of creatures and subjects, including the right to grant mercy), I do not rely on an *already available* theologico-political concept which it would suffice to *apply* to the death penalty as one of its "cases" or examples. No, to the contrary, I would be tempted to say that one can only begin to think the theologico-political, and so the onto-theologico-political, even theodicy in general, from this phenomenon of criminal law that is called the death penalty.

In fact, what is involved here is less a phenomenon or an article of criminal law than, in this tradition, the quasi-transcendental condition of criminal law and of law in general. To put it in a brief and economical way, I will proceed from what has long been for me the most significant and the most stupefying—also the most stupefied—fact about the history of Western philosophy: never, *to my knowledge*, has any philosopher *as such, in his or her own, strictly and systematically philosophical discourse,* never has any philosophy *as such* contested the legitimacy of the death penalty. From Plato to Hegel, from Rousseau to Kant (who was undoubtedly the most rigorous of them all), they expressly, each in his own way, and sometimes not without much hand-wringing (Rousseau), took a stand *for* the death penalty.

This continues in post-Hegelian modernity, *either* in the form of explicit discourses (like Baudelaire, Marx suspects the interest of abolitionists who want to save their own heads, *be it* during the brief episode when the 1848 Revolution abolished the death penalty for political crimes—and Hugo himself expressed this suspicion—*or* in the age of the great abolitionist demonstrations in which the latter took an active and spectacular part),[17] *or* in the troubling form of silence or omission, as if it were not a philosophical problem worthy of the name. Here are the innumerable silences, no doubt different in their implicit axiomatics, of Heidegger (thinker of being-toward-death who, *to my knowledge,* never took up the problem of the death penalty, which he certainly did not think needed to be opposed), Sartre, Foucault, and many others.

To my knowledge, Lévinas devoted only a single sentence to it in 1987, after its abolition in France: "I do not know if you accept this rather complex system which consists in judging *according to the truth* and in treating the one who has been judged *with love* [*dans l'amour*]. The abolition of the death penalty seems to me an essential thing for the coexistence of charity with justice."[18] But, like Kant and Hegel, he tries to shield the biblical and Roman *lex talionis* from its common interpretation—vengeance, revenge, etc., that is, the very one the Gospel of Matthew protested against (v, ll. 38–44)—to see in it, just like Kant, the origin and rational foundation of criminal justice.[19]

Some of them were no doubt, in their hearts, horrified by capital punishment without believing that they had to devote a philosophical argument to it; this, it seems to me, is the case with Lévinas. Others believed, rightly or wrongly, that they saw in it a particular phenomenon or a mere exacerbation of the penal system, even of imprisonment in general, or again a superstructure of juridical formality that would have to be pursued to its infrastructural basis

and to the *interests* of the (socio-economic-political) "last instance."
Those who raised a public discourse against the death penalty never
did so, to my knowledge—and this is my provisional hypothesis—in
a strictly *philosophical* way. They did so either as writers (in France,
Voltaire, Hugo, Camus) or as jurists and men of the law (Beccaria
in the first place, whose influence was considerable and decisive
in the nineteenth century, and of whom I would like to speak again
to complicate things a bit more in a moment; Robert Badinter, of
course; etc.).

If this massive and highly significant "fact" can be proven, we
then have to ask ourselves what *welds*, so to speak, philosophy, and
more precisely ontology, in their essence or, what amounts to the
same thing, in their hegemonic tradition—what *welds* them, then,
to the political theodicy of the death penalty and to the principle of
sovereignty that, across different figures, reigns there supremely
[*souverainement*].

At once powerful and fragile, historical and nonnatural (this is
why this image of a technical *alloy* comes to me here), this *welding*
of ontology to the political theology of the death penalty is also
what has always held together, adjoining or held fast in the same
grasp, the *philosophical* (metaphysics or onto-theology), the *political*
(at least where it is dominated by a thought of the *polis* or the sovereign state), and a certain concept of the "proper to man" [*le pro-
pre de l'homme*, also: man's own]: the proper to man would consist in
his ability to "risk his life" in sacrifice, to elevate himself above life,
to be worth, in his dignity, more and something other than his life,
to pass by death toward a "life" that is worth more than life. This is
Plato's *epimeleia tou thanatou*, the philosophy that enjoins us to exert
ourselves to death; it is the incomparable *dignity* (*Würde*) of the human person, who, as an end in himself and not a means, according
to Kant transcends his condition as a living being and whose *honor* it
is to inscribe the death penalty within his law; it is consciousness's
struggle for recognition, which for Hegel passes through the risk of
its own life; it is the being-toward-death of Dasein that alone can
properly die [die itself and die properly—Trans.], so that according
to Heidegger the animal merely comes to the end and is snuffed
out.

The death penalty would thus be, like death itself, what is "proper to man" in the strict sense. At the risk of once again shocking those who do not want to hear it, I will dare to say that the death penalty has always answered deeply "humanist" pleas. So it has been in European law (and I do not know if, in the strict sense, despite all the phenomena of mass killing, even ritualized mass killing, that our common sense alleges go on outside Europe, there is a "death penalty" that is, I dare say, worthy of the name outside of European law). It is thus to be found at the unique crossroads—which is Europe itself—between, *on the one hand*, the biblical tradition (immediately after the "Thou shalt not kill," in the "judgments," which constitute a true, instituted penal code, God commands that those who transgress this or that commandment be put to death—and we will have to speak again of the *lex talionis* whose interpretation is so controversial), and, *on the other hand*, the onto-theological tradition of which I just spoke.

For a long time I have thus been persuaded that the deconstruction of the speculative scaffolding (not to say the scaffold) that upholds the philosophical discourse on the death penalty is not one necessity among others, a particular point of application. If one could speak here of an architectonic and of building [*édification*], the death penalty would be the keystone or, if you prefer, the cement, the weld, as I just said, of the onto-theologico-political, the prosthetic artifact that keeps it upright, along with the nature-technique distinction and everything that follows from it (*physis/ tekhnè, physis/nomos, physis/thesis*), a nonnatural thing, a historical law, a properly and strictly [*proprement*] human and supposedly rational law.

Kant believes he recognizes a "categorical imperative" and an *a priori* idea of pure reason in criminal law that would not be possible if the death penalty were not inscribed within it, and if it were not commanded by a *jus talionis* to be reinterpreted. When I say "philosophical discourse on the death penalty," and thus a discourse "to be deconstructed," I am thinking not only of the mortiferous [*morticole*] discourse that prevailed in the majority of nation-states that maintained the death penalty until around 1990 (in the last ten years a majority of nation-states have, in one way or another, put an end to the death penalty; the process of "deconstruction" is thus picking up speed in a critical and highly significant way, and this in effect goes for sovereignty, the nation-state, religion, etc.).

I am also thinking, without of course rendering things entirely symmetrical, of the abolitionist discourse, which has my most convinced sympathy. This abolitionist discourse, in its present state, seems to me greatly perfectible, philosophically and politically fragile, also deconstructible, if you prefer. For at least *three reasons*:

(A) First of all, when it is inspired by the logic of Beccaria, as is almost always the case, abolitionist argumentation weakens itself. This can be said even while paying Beccaria, as has often been done since the end of the eighteenth century, the homage owed to this great man and his historic initiative. If one were to apply the list of exceptions Beccaria places on the suspension of capital punishment to the letter, it would be administered almost every day. As soon as the order of a society is threatened, or every time it is not yet secure, it is admissible to put the citizen to death in Beccaria's eyes, even if for him the death penalty is not a "right." Put otherwise, and here we touch on one of the more obscure stakes of the problem, insofar as one has not clearly defined the concept of war, the strict difference between civil war, national war, and partisan war, "terrorism"—whether domestic or not—and so on (so many concepts that have always been and are more than ever, more than ever since September 11, problematic, obscure, dogmatic, manipulable), the abolition of the death penalty within the secure borders of a prosperous and peaceful nation will remain something seriously limited, convenient, provisional, conditional—which is to say not principled. Abolition will be conditioned, as Beccaria himself saw, for that matter—and this gives us much to think about today—by the smooth functioning of the liberal market.[20]

Beccaria, then, concerned with dissuasive exemplarity, judges the death penalty less necessary, more *ineffective* than *unjust*, and hardly cruel enough to dissuade.[21] Perpetual forced labor would be more fearsome, crueler, he thinks, and therefore more effective in the art of dissuasion. It is this utilitarianism or this "exemplarism" that

Kant will criticize very strongly and on both flanks, so to speak, as much among those who believe that the death penalty is a good means in view of an end—security, peace, the well-being of the community or the nation, and so on—as among the abolitionists, who for the most part, and like Beccaria, think the opposite. To this means-end pair that dominates the debate on both sides (for and against the death penalty), Kant opposes an idea of justice and a "categorical imperative" of criminal law that appeals to the human person as an end in himself and his "dignity" (*Würde*).

This dignity requires that the guilty party be punished because he is punishable, without any concern for utility, without sociopolitical interest of any kind. As long as the flaws of such a line of argumentation are not made to appear from the inside, in the rigor of the concept, as long as a discourse of the Kantian or Hegelian type, which claims to justify the death penalty in a principled way, without concern for interest, without reference to the least utility, has not been "deconstructed," so to speak, we will remain within a precarious, limited abolitionist discourse, conditioned by empirical facts and, by its essence, provisional to a context, within a logic of means and ends, short of strict juridical rationality. It is this difficult "deconstruction" that I try to carry out in my seminar on the death penalty. And here is the essence of a programmatic, preliminary, incomplete response I bring to a question asked by Richard Bernstein during the seminars I gave at the New School on the death penalty. In a few words, it would make the following appear untenable from within:

1. The founding distinction of the concept of "punishment" in Kant, that is, the difference between (a) *poena naturalis*, that, entirely interior and private, which the guilty party can inflict on himself, prior to all laws and institutions, and (b) *poena forensis*, punishment strictly speaking, administered from the outside by society through its judicial apparatus and its historical institutions;

2. The distinction between self-punishment and punishment by another [*hétéropunition*]: the guilty party, as a person and a rational subject, should, according to Kant, understand, approve, even demand the punishment—including the supreme penalty; this

transforms all institutional and rational punishment coming from outside (*forensis*) into automatic and autonomous punishment, within or at the indiscernible confines of interior punishment (*peona naturalis*); the guilty party should agree to [*donner raison à*] the sentence, he would have to agree to the juridical reason [*à la raison juridique*] that has the better of him [*a raison de lui*]—and leads him to condemn himself to death. To follow this through to the end, the guilty party would symbolically execute the verdict himself. The execution would be like a *sui-cide*. There would be, for the autonomy of juridical reason, nothing but self-execution. It is "as if the guilty party committed suicide."

But here one can no longer distinguish, in all rigor, the sphere of pure, immune[22] law, intact, not contaminable by everything of which we would want to purify it: interest, passion, vengeance, revenge, the sacrificial drive (moral and juridical reason are as a matter fact in essence expressly sacrificial for Kant), the logic of conscious and unconscious drives, everything that Freud and Reik wrote under the heading "*lex talionis*" in its most archaic and indestructible form.

I did not say that for Kant the execution *is* a suicide. That would be as stupid as saying that capital punishment is murder, pure and simple. All these outlines, hypotheses, aporias, all these paradoxes, do not have as their aim or function to confound obviously different things, to reverse oppositions or replace them with others, but to suspend, to mark or recall the necessity of suspending our naïve confidence, that of common sense or conscious belief, in distinctions or oppositions such as inside/outside, natural and interior/nonnatural and exterior (*peona naturalis/peona forensis*), self- and other-, self-punishment and punishment by another, execution and murder or suicide.

It is the shaking [*tremblement*] of these borders, as well as their permeability, their undecidability, that matter to me here, and not reinstating other reassuring oppositional distinctions that would allow one to say: yes, *there* is suicide, *there* is execution and/or murder. Or, there was execution or murder and not suicide; there, suicide and not the opposite.

3. Kant's reinterpretation of the *lex talionis*, which he powerfully reactivates by displacing the biblical and Roman traditions. An enormous question, an enormous thorny tangle of texts that we cannot reopen here. Kant would be closer to a literally Jewish or Roman tradition than to a certain evangelical spirit (Matthew, I just said, denounced the principle of the *lex talionis*). Kant fails, in my view, on questions that are moreover often sexual, on sex crimes— pederasty, rape, bestiality—to produce a principle of equivalence, and therefore of calculability. This concern with equivalence (not simply literal or quantitative, but spiritual and symbolic: figure of the unfigurable [*figure de l'infigurable*]), in Kant as in Hegel, in fact touches on what we just said about the becoming-self-punishment of punishment by another: regulating the talionic categorical imperative, equality (*Gleichheit*) insists first of all that whatever the harm done to the other, I equally inflict it, a priori, on myself. Kant literally says: "[W]hatever undeserved evil you inflict on another within the people, that you inflict upon yourself;... if you kill him, you kill yourself."[23] Or again, and here I cite from memory: in stealing from the other, you destroy the principle of property and you steal from yourself.

The question of the death penalty is not only that of the political onto-theology of sovereignty; it is also, around this calculation of an impossible equivalence between crime and punishment, their incommensurability, an impossible evaluation of the debt (Nietzsche says some very strong things on this subject), the question of the principle of reason, the interpretation of reason as the "principle of reason," and this as the principle of calculability. This question of "accounting" and of the account to be given, of "giving reasons" (*reddere rationem*), must be debated among others, but first of all, in my view, among the Heideggerian and Kantian interpretations of reason, both of which, although differently, attempt at once to *shield* rationality from and to *submit* it to its calculating vocation.

4. The exception that, in all logic, should allow the sovereign or the legislator (Kant names above all, horrified, Charles I and Louis XVI) to escape all trials and all conventional executions; here is

what would have, along with the Terror, corrupted the French Revolution, which Kant hailed, as you know, as one of the *signs* demonstrating, recalling, announcing the possibility of progress in human history. This sovereign exception, this absolute immunity, is something that many national laws and a certain international law are tending, very laboriously and at the price of many contradictions, again to place in question. There is doubtless nothing fortuitous in the fact that, at the very moment that the immunity of heads of states or armies is, let us say to remain prudent, again placed in question by international criminal authorities, we know that, whatever the crimes they are accused of, the accused will never again be condemned to death.

5. The de facto inapplicability of any death penalty, at the very moment that Kant judges it necessary to inscribe the rational principle in a system of criminal law worthy of the name and worthy of man, worthy of the human person as an end in himself. Kant insists so rigorously on the imperative that commands, out of respect for the person of the condemned, that no "maltreatment" be inflicted on him, no violence that would tend to demean the "person" in his essential, inalienable "innate personality" (that which one can never lose, even if one loses one's "civil personality"); but one could never demonstrate that an execution does not entail any "maltreatment" of this order. No more than one can demonstrate, in all Kantian logic, that the crime was committed freely, in a responsible and not a "pathological" way, in the Kantian and the ordinary sense of this word.

(B) If abolitionist discourse, in its current state, remains perfectible, fragile, or, if one may say so, deconstructible, it is because it limits the respect for life, or prohibits killing, within national law and within a national territory in peacetime. But today nothing seems more uncertain and porous than a border in general or a border between the concepts of war and peace, civil war and international war, war and the so-called humanitarian operations supposedly conducted by nongovernmental authorities. Unauthorized wars of independence like those against the colonial powers, "terrorisms," everything Schmitt calls "partisan war"—here are some of the phenomena that confound the concept of the "public enemy" (Rousseau).

Authorizing supposedly "legitimate defense" and expedited killing without a "death penalty" (without a judgment, without a verdict, without a public execution, etc.), these phenomena recall that this penal question does not play out between life and death, but somewhere else altogether. The question of the death penalty is not a simple question of life or death.

(C) This is why a good number of international declarations since the Second World War have remained, at least in their letter, highly precarious. In a way that was moreover deliberate. They rested on a "right to life" (one of the human rights) whose concept and axiom are more than problematic; they recommended avoiding torture and cruel treatment (a notion that I already called an obscure equivocation); and, avoiding above all any binding resolution, they were always formulated as recommendations that would not have the "force of law," and which, with the best intentions in the world, had to stop at the threshold of the principle of sovereignty and states' right of exception—to which they only *advised* practicing the death penalty only exceptionally and according to legal procedures protecting the rights of the accused. The pressure of the United States (often represented by Mrs. Roosevelt) was not insignificant with regard to this respect for sovereignty. But we will not claim to be able to reconstitute here the rich history of debates that followed World War II, the Nuremberg trials, the creation of the concepts of crimes against humanity, genocide, and so forth. The *Shoah* does not *stricto sensu* fall under the concept of the death penalty. Here there was never any pretense of the least legality, not even of a simulacrum of legality. Here there was neither judgment, nor guilty parties, nor accusation, nor defense. Mass killing (extermination or genocide) requires other categories than that of the death penalty. This explains, without justifying it, why some people feel authorized (incorrectly, in my view) to take debates about the death penalty (always individual and applied to a nameable citizen) as relatively or statistically minor in the light of great crimes against humanity, genocides, war crimes, the denied phenomena of nonassistance to hundreds of millions of people in danger (malnutrition, AIDS, etc.), not to mention the immensity of the phenomenon of imprisonment (where the United States also holds records).

But here it would be necessary to take into account all the "impure" phenomena of executions following expedited, even secret, judgments. In principle, according to European law, the death penalty must be accessible to the public in its procedures of judgment, verdict, and execution. It must be officially announced (prior to the execution). Where this is not the case (in China and Japan, it seems, and no doubt in numerous other places in the world and moments in history), it is not certain that we can, in all rigor, speak of the "death penalty."

As well, the death penalty, in the strict sense, demands respect for the cadaver. The large question of burial [*la sepulture*]. For example, in Greece, in an age when the death penalty was fully justified—with Socrates or Plato—something worse than death was inflicted on the citizen worthy of respect. For certain particularly serious crimes, the corpse of the condemned was thrown over the city walls. He lost his right to a burial. Today in the United States the situation is in a sense the opposite. The pretense is to respect the subject who is put to death, notably in states, like Texas, where the sanction is applied massively. The condemned is allowed to speak before his execution, his last words are recorded and then circulated on the Internet. Indeed, there exists a true corpus of *last statements* [in English]. And they are placed *online* [in English]. The speech of the condemned is respected; the corpse is given to the family and the traces are not hidden. There would be much to say on the question of the visual and audio archive of executions in the United States.

The manifestations of disquiet that are proliferating in the United States point less often to the principle of the death penalty than to the large number of "judicial errors" that, under suspect and monstrously unequal conditions, lead to executions. Perhaps it is necessary to recall a few figures. As of today (June 2001), 73 countries have completely abolished the death penalty, thirteen have abolished it for common-law crimes, for so-called nonpolitical crimes (which awakens our old question: are all crimes not essentially political, like the "great crimes" and "great criminals" that, as Walter Benjamin said, threaten the very foundation of a state law that aims to monopolize violence?—and I think on the other hand of the example of Mumia Abu Jamal, who has always claimed the status of a political prisoner); 22 states have abolished it *in practice*, not in law (the criterion of this distinction: no executions for ten years). In total, a majority of states—108—have abolished, in law or in fact, the death penalty; 87 have kept it.

Since 1979, every year, two or three countries abolish it and expand this majority. In 1999 East Timor, Ukraine, and Turkmenistan abolished it for all crimes, Latvia for common-law crimes. In 1999 more than 1,813 people were executed in 31 countries, and almost 4,000 were condemned to death in 63 countries. *Amnesty International* diffuses these facts, bringing a precision that matters to us more than anything else from a geopolitical perspective (here the quantitative is more than mathematical: it is quantitative in a dynamic way, if I may thus transpose the distinction proposed by Kant on the subject of the "sublime," and the question of the death penalty has some relation to that of the "sublime," even to sublimation):

Eighty-five percent of executions are concentrated in four countries: China, which comes far ahead of all the others in absolute figures (at least 1076). And the figures for the last two years are frightening. Next comes Iran (at least 165), then Saudi Arabia (103), and finally the United States (98). We should also not forget the Democratic Republic of Congo (about 100) and Iraq (hundreds, but sometimes without judgments). At present, aside from a large number of Arab countries, only two "very great" powers maintain the death penalty: China, where it is applied massively, and the United States, where there has nonetheless been a strong abolitionist current since the nineteenth century.

In 1972, as is well known, the Supreme Court decided that the application of the death penalty was incompatible with two constitutional amendments: one concerning discrimination; the other, what falls under *cruel and unusual punishment* [in English]. From this moment, the Supreme Court had found the application of the death penalty to be a "cruel and unusual punishment." It was thus in fact suspended.

Its principle was not thereby abolished, but executions were suspended. It was thus that between 1972 and 1977 no one was executed in the United States. No state could transgress this prohibition by the federal Supreme Court (whose democratic character in this case some in fact contested, since its judges are appointed and not elected. This was argued by a Chicago law professor who claimed that a democratic government could not go against "public opinion," the majority of which favors the death penalty. After having objected that parliamentary democracy does not obey public opinion but the elected majority, and that in France parliament had abolished the death penalty against majority public opinion or the probable result of a referendum, I thought it clever to ask: how then do you explain that the Supreme Court suspended the death penalty in 1972? Is it not a democratic institution? The answer was "no," and it gave me much to think about. In fact, my feeling is that if one day the death penalty is abolished in the United States, it will be by a progressive movement, state by state, moratorium by moratorium, *de facto*, and not by a single federal decision).

After 1977, certain states judged that death administered by lethal injection was neither cruel nor unusual, as against the electric chair, hanging, or the gas chamber. Executions thus resumed, and the Supreme Court was obliged to give in. In certain states like Texas, there were huge numbers of executions, notably during the mandate of Governor George W. Bush. Henceforth the symptoms of a veritable crisis multiplied in American consciousness [*conscience*, also: conscience], notably because of international pressures.

Let us take an example. It was discovered in the state of Illinois that thirteen people who were condemned to die and kept under high security on *death row*, in some cases for decades, were innocent. This was discovered because, accidentally, in a journalism school in Evanston, at Northwestern University, near Chicago, some professors and students had noted the existence of serious irregularities. So the cases were reexamined and the thirteen condemned men were cleared! The governor of Illinois, a very respectable but pro-death penalty Republican, immediately declared a moratorium:

"If there are so many innocents, so many condemned to death who are found to be victims of judicial error, I suspend executions."

Recently, during one of my last stays in the United States, I saw a television program featuring thirteen innocent men who had been condemned to death—twelve black, one white. They told the story of their many years in prison, and then of their liberation. Without compensation! Only one of them had managed, after legal proceedings, to obtain reparations. None of them could find a job; they remained suspect even though their innocence had been established. DNA tests are now allowing a proliferation of evidence of grave judicial errors leading to the death penalty. And it is the whole of the American judicial system that is "under examination" at the moment.

Bush is famous for, among other things, never having granted the least mercy. During the same television program, he was asked: "Do you think that in Texas all the people you refuse to grant mercy are guilty?" And he answered imperturbably: "Yes, in Texas they are all guilty."

Whether it comes to "mental handicaps" or age (but what is an age? a mental age?—an individual can have many ages according to the angle chosen by the experts), the practice is tending to become increasingly harsh in the United States, sometimes in violation of the recommendations of international law. Alleged mental handicaps and the youth of the accused are less and less taken into account.

On the question of "seeing or not seeing killing or cruelty," Foucault speaks of a progressive disappearance of spectacular visibility. This is true, but at the same time, thanks to television and cinematographic production, one sees more and more films that, on the fine pretext of abolitionism, show not only the condemnation to death but the process of execution up to the last moment. Visibility is thus differentiated. The transformation of the media makes it so that one cannot speak only of invisibility, but of the transformation of the field of the visible. Things have never been as "visible" in global space as they are today; this is itself an essential dimension of the problem—and of the struggle. Spectral logic invades everything, especially where the work of mourning and the *tekhnè* of the image cross, which is to say everywhere. (It was this crossing that drew my attention in *Specters of Marx*, and, as far back as I go, the thematic of the phantom or rather of the *revenant*[24] runs under this name through most of my texts; it is not far from merging with that of the trace itself . . .)

Today, attention to a certain spectral logic, almost everywhere, seems to be taking a remarkably insistent form. It is thus of course essentially connected to the question of the technical prosthesis, of technique in general, of the ineluctability of the work of mourning—which is not one work among others but the over-determining mark of all work. It also concerns the impossibility of mourning. Mourning *must* be impossible. Successful mourning is failed mourning. In successful mourning, I incorporate the dead one, I assimilate him to me, I reconcile myself with death, and con-sequently I deny death and the alterity of the dead other [*l'autre-mort*]. I am therefore unfaithful. Where the introjection of mourn-ing succeeds, mourning annuls the other. I take him upon me and consequently I negate or delimit his infinite alterity.

As it happens with the integration of the immigrant, or the as-similation of the foreigner. This "mourning effect" thus does not wait for death. One does not wait for the death of the other to dis-count [*amortir*] his alterity. Faithfulness prescribes to me at once the necessity and the impossibility of mourning. It enjoins me to take the other within me, to make him live in me, to idealize him, to interiorize him, but also to not succeed in the work of mourning: the other must remain the other. He is effectively, actually, undeni-ably dead, but, if I take him in me as a part of me, and if, conse-quently, I "narcissize" this death of the other by a successful work of mourning, I annihilate the other, I reduce or deny his death. Unfaithfulness begins here, even if it does not continue and worsen. The loved object is perpetuated in being betrayed, in being forgotten. The dead one must of course be forgotten, must be for-gotten *well*. As I once said, and it is basically the same transub-stantiation, "of course one must eat/one must eat well [*il faut bien manger*]."[25] Faithfulness is unfaithful.

Translated by James Ingram

Acknowledgments

This essay echoes the discussions Richard Bernstein, his colleagues, and I had at the New School on the death penalty. Its title makes explicit reference to a study Richard Bernstein devoted to Lévinas, "Evil and the Temptation of Theodicy," which has since been published in *The Cambridge Companion to Lévinas*, ed. Robert Bernasconi and Simon Critchley (Cambridge: Cambridge University Press, 2002).

Notes

"Capital Punishment: 'Another Temptation of Theodicy'" from *For What Tomorrow ... A Dialogue* by Jacques Derrida and Elizabeth Rudinesco, translated by Jeff Fort. English translation © Board of Trustees of the Leland Stanford Jr. University. By permission of Stanford University Press. "Deo Quoi Demain" © Librairie Artheme Fayard and Editions Galilee 2001.

1. Juan Donoso Cortès, Marquis de Valdegamas (1809–1853). Spanish jurist and philosopher, author of many political works on the manner of governing peoples. After having been a liberal and an admirer of the French Revolution and the spirit of the Enlightenment, Cortès evolved toward a flamboyant conservatism and a radical adherence to the Catholic religion. In his *Essay on Catholicism, Liberalism, and Socialism*, published in 1851, he maintains that the world is divided into two mutually irreducible civilizations: Catholicism and "philosophism" (where liberalism and socialism are to be found). Cortès chooses Catholicism, scorns liberalism, and respects socialism as a mortal enemy in which he recognizes a diabolical grandeur.

2. Cortès, *Essay on Catholicism, Liberalism, and Socialism Considered in Their Fundamental Principles*, trans. Madeleine Vinton Goddard (Philadelphia, Pa.: J. B. Lippincott, 1862). Cf. especially book 3, chapter 6: "Dogmas correlative with the dogma of solidarity.—Blood sacrifices. Theories of the rationalist schools respecting the death penalty": "We have shown that socialism is an incoherent combination of thesis and antithesis, which contradict and destroy one another. Catholicism, to the contrary, forms a great synthesis which includes all things in its unity, and infuses them in its sovereign harmony. It may be affirmed of Catholic dogmas, that although they are diverse they are one.... Only an absolute negation can be opposed to this wonderful synthesis.... The Catholic word is then invincible and eternal.... Nothing can diminish its sovereign virtue" (pp. 278–279). After having evoked the double dogma of *imputation* and *substitution* (a word and concept one finds, differently, but not without relation, in Massignon as well as in Lévinas), the universal institution of blood sacrifice, from Cain and Abel to Oedipus, Cortès specifies: "The blood of man cannot expiate original sin, which is the sin of the species, the supreme human sin: but it nevertheless may, and does, expiate certain individual crimes, from which follows not only the legitimacy, but also the necessity and propriety of the penalty of death. The universality of this institution testifies to the universality of mankind's belief in the purifying efficacy of blood, when shed under the right circumstances, and in its expiatory virtue when it is thus shed. *Sine*

sanguinis effusione non fit remissio. (Heb. ix. 22) Mankind could never have extinguished the common debt which it contracted in Adam without the blood shed by the Redeemer" (p. 288) (trans. mod.). Cortès likewise violently condemns the abolition of the death penalty for political crimes by the provisional government of the French Republic in 1848, "succeeded by those frightful days of June which, with all their horrors, will live forever in the memories of men" (p. 289).

3. [The French *droit pénal* refers both to penal law and to criminal law more broadly. The broader sense is more common and is used here, but its reference to punishment should be heard throughout.—Trans.]

4. Walter Benjamin, "The Critique of Violence" (1921) in *Reflections: Essays, Aphorisms, Autobiographical Writings*, trans. Edmund Jephcott, ed. and intr. Peter Demetz (New York: Harcourt Brace Jovanovich, 1978). Cf. Jacques Derrida, "The Force of Law," trans. Mary Quaintance, in *Acts of Religion*, ed. and intr. Gil Anidjar (New York and London: Routledge, 2002).

5. [Here as later, Derrida exploits the breadth of the French *droit*: both a particular right and a law or law in general. Thus, the right (*droit*) to suspend the law (*droit*).—Trans.]

6. Victor Hugo, *The Last Day of a Condemned Man*, trans. and intr. Geoff Woollen (Oxford and New York: Oxford University Press, 1992), p. 32.

7. Ibid., preface, p. 17.

8. Victor Hugo, *Choses vues*, 20 October 1842, in *Écrits de Victor Hugo sur la peine de mort*, ed. Raymond Jean (Maussane les Alpilles: Editions Actes/Sud, 1979), p. 53.

9. Robert Badinter correctly recalls this in *L'abolition* (Paris: Fayard, 2000), pp. 163–164. It was in 1978 that the Social Commission of the French Épiscopacy published an official document (*Éléments de réflexion sur la peine de mort*), which, after expressing its regret for the Catholic Church's historic support for the death penalty, unequivocally concludes (while *committing only the signatories, and only within the borders of their country*): "After thorough reflection, the signatories judge that in France the death penalty should be abolished." Even if an analogous position had been taken by *L'Osservatore romano* one year before, this does not yet constitute, it seems to me, a universal and unconditional commitment by the Catholic Church and the Vatican. Nothing comparable, certainly (and the comparison imposes itself once again), to the prescriptions or interdictions concerning sexuality, birth, and abortion.

10. Hugo, *Last Day of a Condemned Man*, preface, p. 15: "the scaffold is the only structure that revolutions do not demolish. For rarely are revolutions innocent of human blood and, since they occur in order to dock, lop, and pollard society, the death penalty is one of the pruning blades they surrender most unwillingly." [trans. mod.].

11. Ibid., p. 33: "But do not believe that law and order will be banished with the executioner.... Civilization is nothing other than a series of successive transformations.... The merciful law of Christ will at last suffuse the Code, which will glow with its radiance. Crime will be considered an illness, with its own doctors to replace your judges, and its hospitals to replace your prisons. Liberty shall be equated with health. Ointments and oil shall be applied to limbs that once were

shackled and branded. Infirmities that once were scourged with anger shall now be bathed in love. The cross in place of the gallows: sublime, and yet so simple" [trans. mod.].

Mutatis mutandis, and to say it again too briefly, I believe that this allusion to a future in which evil would be treated like a disease heralds, among other things, the speculations of a Theodor Reik on the disappearance to come of punishment in general. This will happen when humanity has understood, *like* Freud and *from* Freud, that the feeling of unconscious guilt precedes the crime. A general (psychoanalytic) confession will thus have replaced criminal law. It is at the end of *The Compulsion to Confess: On the Psychoanalysis of Crime and Punishment* (trans. Mrs. E. Jones and Norbert Rie [New York: Grove, 1961]) that Reik, in Freud's name and authorized by him, declares his opposition to the death penalty: "I profess to be an opponent of murder, whether committed by the individual as a crime or by the state in its retaliation" (p. 474). In the seminar that is alluded to, I accord the greatest possible attention to the status and argumentation of these texts by Reik and Freud, as to the question of the relation between psychoanalysis and criminology.

12. Hugo, *The Last Day of a Condemned Man*, preface, p. 15 [trans. mod.].

13. First published in the *Nouvelle Revue française* (June–July 1957), they were taken up again in *Réflexions sur la guillotine*, with Arthur Koestler (Paris: Calmann-Lévy, 1957). One can read the latter today in Albert Camus, *Resistance, Rebellion, and Death*, ed. and trans. Justin O'Brien (New York: Knopf, 1969).

14. "In fact, the supreme punishment has always been, throughout the ages, a religious penalty.... Only religious values, and especially belief in eternal life, can serve as a basis for the supreme punishment because, according to their own logic, they keep it from being definitive and irreparable. Consequently, it is justifiable only insofar as it is not supreme. The Catholic Church, for example, has always accepted the necessity of the death penalty.... But what is the value of such a justification in the society we live in, which in its institutions and customs has lost all contact with the sacred?" (ibid., pp. 222–223, 225).

15. Cf. Jean-Luc Nancy, "Le déconstruction du christianisme," *Les études philosophiques* 4 (1998): 503–519, and Jacques Derrida, *Le toucher. Jean-Luc Nancy* (Paris: Galilée, 1999), pp. 68 passim.

16. Cesare Beccaria, *On Crimes and Punishments and Other Writings*, ed. Richard Bellamy, trans. Richard Davies with Virginia Cox and Richard Bellamy (Cambridge: Cambridge University Press, 1995), p. 66: "By what right can men presume to slaughter their fellows? Certainly not that right which is the foundation of sovereignty and the laws."

17. Charles Baudelaire, "Pauvre Belgique!": "(Abolition of the death penalty. Victor Hugo dominates like Courbet. I hear that in Paris 30,000 petition for the abolition of the death penalty. 30,000 people who deserve it. You tremble, therefore you are already guilty. At least you have an interest in the question. Excessive love of life is a descent toward animality)," *Oeuvres complètes* (Paris: Gallimard, Bibliothèque de la Pléiade, vol. 2, 1976), p. 899. One variant also turns around this word "interested," which bears a good part of the *charge* (and of the accusation, Kantian in its principle or its form, and of the problematic issue around which we have worked systematically in this seminar): "Abolishers of the death penalty—doubtless very interested" (ibid., p. 1494).

Jacques Derrida

With this alliance of perverse cruelty, sometimes frightful and anti-Semitic mean-derings, as I recalled in *Given Time 1, Counterfeit Money,* trans. Peggy Kamuf (Chicago, Ill.: University of Chicago Press, 1992), pp. 130–131 n14, historical clairvoyance, and anti-Christian Christian compulsion, Baudelaire was not deceiving himself, it seems to me, any more than Cortès, about the *sacrificial* essence of the death pen-alty. "The death penalty is the result of a mystical idea, totally misunderstood today. The death penalty does not have as its goal the saving of society, at least materially. For the sacrifice to be perfect, there must be agreement [another Kantian argu-ment!—J. D.] and joy on the victim's part. Giving chloroform to one condemned to die would be an impiety, since it would take away the consciousness of his grandeur as victim and do away with his chance of winning paradise" (ibid., vol. 1, p. 683. I thank Jennifer Bariorek for bringing these two Baudelaire texts to my attention).

18. *Emmanuel Lévinas, Qui êtes-vous?* (Lyon: La Manufacture, 1987), p. 97. To give this proposition its full weight, within a hypothesis that is, *so far as it goes,* mine, to know that there is an essential collusion between philosophy *as such* and the death penalty, let us bring out two features. On the one hand, Lévinas's sentence is not advanced as a *philosophical* demonstration in the space of *justice* or *law,* but in that of *charity,* a Christian notion (see above). Lévinas in fact cites Matthew on the next page. The values of *love* or of *charity* are found at the center of Lévinas's long re-sponse, which names the death penalty in passing. On the other hand, Lévinas's remark rightly belongs to a discourse that tries not to inscribe itself within ontology, but to move beyond philosophy as ontology in the Greek tradition. In the last of the *Quatre leçons talmudiques,* Lévinas notes in passing: "Jewish law does not permit a death sentence on the basis of a majority of only one vote" (*Nine Talmudic Readings,* trans. and intr. Annette Aronowicz [Bloomington, Ind.: Indiana University Press, 1990], p. 74). It is in this direction that I would today be tempted to follow the ex-ploration proposed by Richard Bernstein: "In order to probe the relation of evil and ethics, we must explore how Lévinas characterizes evil" ("Theodicy," ms. 11).

19. Lévinas does not only *justify* the *lex talionis,* he recognizes in it the origin of *jus-tice* itself. The *lex talionis* would deliver a "message of universalism," "one law for all." This would not in the least be "a way of revelling in the vengeance and cruelty in which a virile existence is steeped. Such inspirations were foreign to the Jewish Bible. They come from the pagans [as Matthew himself said of the *lex talionis*: a pa-gan thing—J. D.], or Machiavelli, or Nietzsche.... The principle stated by the Bible here, which appears to be so cruel, seeks only justice.... Rabbis have neither ap-plied nor understood this text to the letter. They have interpreted it in the light of the spirit that pervades the whole of the Bible.... The Bible reminds us of the spirit of gentleness" ("An Eye for an Eye," in *Difficult Liberty: Essays on Judaism,* trans. Seán Hand [Baltimore, Md.: Johns Hopkins University Press, 1990], pp. 146–148 [trans. mod.].

Without being able to undertake the reading required in this connection here, I make do with a reminder: this distinction between the letter and the spirit is not only that of the rabbis but, literally, the essential argument of Kant and of Hegel in their pleading *for* the *lex talionis* and, indissociably, *for* the death penalty.

20. "There are only two grounds on which the death of a citizen might be held to be necessary. First, when it is evident that even if deprived of his freedom, he retains such connections and such power as to endanger the security of the nation, when, that is, his existence may threaten a dangerous revolution in the established form of government. The death of a citizen becomes necessary, therefore, when the nation stands to gain or lose its freedom, or in periods of anarchy, when disor-

der replaces the laws. But when the rule of law calmly prevails, under a form of government behind which the people are united, which is secured from without and from within, both by its strength and, perhaps more efficacious than force itself, by public opinion, in which the control of power is in the hands of the true sovereign, in which wealth buys pleasures and not influence, then I do not see any need to destroy a citizen, unless his death is the true and only brake to prevent others from committing crimes, which is the second ground for thinking the death penalty just and necessary" (Beccaria, *On Crimes and Punishments*, pp. 66–67). Can these lines not be read as one of the most effective pleas in favor of the death penalty?

21. "But if I can go on to prove that such a death is neither necessary nor useful, I will have made the cause of humanity triumph" (ibid., p. 66. This sentence is used as an epigram by Robert Badinter in his book *L'abolition*). Two pages further on, Beccaria applies himself to demonstrating the superiority of perpetual forced labor, crueler than the death penalty and therefore more suitable "to deter even the most resolute soul": "neither fanaticism nor vanity survives in manacles and chains, under the rod and the yoke or in an iron cage; and the ills of the desperate man are not over, but are just beginning" (ibid., p. 68).

22. I allow myself to refer here to this logic of auto-immunity, which I have tried to generalize elsewhere, notably in "Faith and Knowledge," in *Religion*, ed. Jacques Derrida and Gianni Vattimo, trans. Samuel Weber (Stanford, Calif.: Stanford University Press, 1998).

23. Kant, *The Metaphysics of Morals*, trans. and ed. Mary J. Gregor, in *Immanuel Kant: Practical Philosophy*, ed. Allen Wood (Cambridge and New York: Cambridge University Press, 1996), p. 472 (Ak 6:332).

24. I increasingly hold to this distinction between *specter* or *phantom* on the one hand, and *revenant* on the other. Like "phantasm," "specter" and "phantom" carry an etymological reference to visibility, to appearing in the light. In this regard, they seem to suppose a horizon on the basis of which, *seeing* that which comes or comes back, one annihilates, masters, suspends, or discounts (*amortit*) the surprise, the unforeseeability of the event. To the contrary, this latter arises where there is no horizon and where, coming to us vertically, from very high, from behind or below, it allows itself to be dominated neither by a look, nor by a conscious perception in general, nor by a *performative* speech act (which is often credited with producing the event, when it does so only on the condition of "a legitimating convention" and the institutional authority of an "I can," "I am entitled to," etc.). The "*revenant*" comes and returns (singularity *as such* implying repetition) like the "who" [the "*qui*" of "*ce qui arrive*," i.e., it happens—Trans.] of an event without a horizon. Like death itself. Thinking the event and haunting together would thus be thinking the *revenant* rather than the specter or the phantom.

25. "Eating Well, or The Calculus of the Subject," interview with Jean-Luc Nancy, in *Points*, trans. Peggy Kamuf (Stanford, Calif.: Stanford University Press, 1995).

III

Memory, Judgment, Evil

10

Memory Traces, Archive, Historical Truth, and the Return of the Repressed: On the Rediscovery of Freud's Moses

Agnes Heller

The bulk of Freud's writings have never been forgotten, thus they are in no need of being remembered. Both the lovers and sworn enemies of psychoanalysis take care of its continuous influence: the works of Freud persist in the limelight, not in spite of their frequent, sometimes very radical, reinterpretations, but also because of them.

The new debate on Freud's Moses, however, counts as a real rediscovery. The book that had been considered since the death of Freud to be an interesting, yet marginal, attempt at the application of psychoanalysis to culture, religion, and history has recently assumed an eminent significance. The new inspiration comes from outside the psychoanalytical discourse: from the increasing interest taken in memory, especially historical memory; in forgetting; in the relation between memory and identity formation, collective memory and individual memory, conscious and unconscious recollection and/or forgetting; and so on. Historians and philosophers have turned to Freud's odd book once again to rethink the relation between historical truth and scientific truth, or the relevance/irrelevance of the distinction itself.

It is an odd book first and foremost because it was not meant to be a book, yet also because it was meant to be a kind of testimony of an old, dying man. The book, in its final form, was published under the title *The Man Moses and the Monotheistic Religion* and consists of four essays of quite different character written at different times.

The first two essays originally appeared in the journal *Imago*. The first, "Moses, the Egyptian," is a slightly psychologico-historical family romance. As is well known, Freud advances the theory that Moses was not a Jew, but an Egyptian of noble birth. The story unfolds in the second essay ("If Moses Were an Egyptian"). Here we learn how Moses presented the Jews with the monotheistic religion. Fanatically committed to Pharaoh Ekhnaton, he remains true to the cult of Aton, the Sun God. After his own people renounce the true religion, Moses seeks for himself a new people. His choice falls on the Jews, and it was thus that he pressed on them the monotheistic faith and the practice of circumcision. This Moses, however, has never been to Sinai. In Kadesh, the son-in-law of the priest Jethro introduces the cult of Jahve, the Volcano God. The Egyptian Moses is killed by the Jews. Later, as a kind of mythological compromise, memory blends the figure of the Egyptian Moses with the figure of Moses of Kadesh. But the religion of Jahve has in fact occupied for a long time the place of the repressed cult of Aton. Only the Levite priests, the descendants of Moses' retinue, keep the memory of Aton. But long afterward, after many a century, the repressed has returned. The Jewish religion begins to resemble more and more the religion of Aton and assumes a monotheistic character, owing particularly to the work of the prophets. The return of the repressed, that is, the transformation of an unconscious memory trace into an overt and conscious memory, is also the story of an advance in spirituality. Freud's analysis ends with a question: from which source has religion drawn the force that keeps not only individuals but also a whole people under its power? The answer—which will be repeated in this book—was offered earlier by Freud, in *Totem and Taboo*: Religion is a collective neurosis. It can be understood, if not fully explained, by the trauma of the murder of the primordial father and the repression of its memory.

The newly developing discussion, however, does not focus on the issue of the origin and power of religion itself. It is even less interested in the family romance of mythical heroes, or the question of whether Moses was an Egyptian or not. It is not the family romance, but the historical novel that assumes the central point of interest. Freud concentrates on this issue in his third essay, more specifically in both his third and fourth essay, for he wrote two parts, and also wrote them twice, and furnished them with two separate prefaces: the first in March 1938, before the *Anschluss*, while he was still in Vienna, and the second in June 1938, when he was already in England. This book was born in the shadow of the Holocaust; it foreshadows the Holocaust.

The third and fourth parts of the *Moses* book offer a reworked answer to the question raised in the second—What is the root of the force of religions?—and add new answers to new questions: How can one explain or understand the emergence and spiritual power of the monotheistic religions and especially of Judaism?; further on, How can one understand the emergence and the influence of Christianity?, and finally, What are the unconscious motivations of Christian anti-Semitism? In all these "case studies" Freud is interested in a special kind of truth he terms "historical truth." The historical truth of religion is its mythical memory or its memory traces. Freud is looking for this historical truth with the help of another kind of truth: scientific truth. More precisely, scientific method and research are looking for factual (material) truth (what really happened). Freud asks: What can a scholar in his search for scientific truth find in the texts of myths, stories, and memory traces that may guide him as road signs? Myth and religion contain not merely stories, they contain the truth but in a hidden and distorted form, and science teaches us how to decipher and translate that form in terms of scientific truth. Freud says that he can decipher the story of Moses and the story of Jesus also as Christian anti-Semitism from historical truth.

In the language of contemporary debate, Freud makes the well-known distinction (as first defined by Pierre Nora) between *histoire* and *memoire*. Translated into current terminology, what Freud calls historical truth is the truth of *memoire*, and what he calls scientific truth is the truth of *histoire*. Freud (contrary to Nora) gives priority to *histoire* rather than *memoire*, not just because he is a scientist and because science is the modern way of understanding and explanation, but because—so he believes—science can decipher historical truth, understand and translate it, whereas this could not happen the other way around: historical truth cannot understand, even less explain, scientific truth, if it cannot even acknowledge it. Freud speaks as a godless Jew (*gottloser Jude*) for whom the historical truth of Judaism as well as Christianity are the objects of scientific inquiry. But without *mémoire* there is no *histoire*, yet without *histoire* there is still *mémoire* (in Freud's terminology: without scientific truth there is historical truth, without historical truth there is no scientific truth).

Freud's analysis of religion frequently borders that of Nietzsche. Freud also makes the distinction between what religion *is* and what religion *does*. The historical truth of religions is constituted by two heterogeneous factors: essence and function. The content of religions (what they are) must both hide and manifest the unconscious motivation that is responsible for their force (what they do). The two together constitute the historical truth of religions. Thus Freud seeks to understand the nonidentity between the overt content of religions and their motivational force, their drive. The key that unlocks this door is the theory of trauma and repression.

There is an analogy, says Freud, between the psychical life of a single man and the psychical life of collectivities, communities, people. And there is more here than an analogy. Because if we know the one, we are given a key to decipher the secrets of the other. And in fact, he continues, we know much about the traumatic experiences of early childhood in men. We know that they are repressed and that they reappear after a long period of latency in one form or another, especially in the form of neuroses. Similarly, mankind went through a traumatic experience in primordial times, the trauma of the murder of the father. Since this trauma has been repressed, the repressed returns as religious neurosis: the patricidal son will then adore the father as his god.

I will mention only in passing that Freud's analysis of the murder of the primordial father suggests that monotheism as a religion appeared prior to polytheism. This point had already been made by the older Schelling in his Berlin lectures on mythology. Schelling suggests that if we want to know God, we need to follow the history of God, and that the truth of this history is to be found first in the Bible and then in Greek mythology. Prior to the confusion of languages in the Tower of Babel there was only one God for all mankind, and polytheism results from the differentiation of the attributes of the only God, split into many. The Jews, so Schelling also believed, rediscovered monotheism. This happens in Schelling with Abraham, and in Freud with Moses the Egyptian. But, Freud adds, and this is the important issue in his theory of memory and history, that the Jews killed Moses, repeating the murder of the primordial father. The repressed returns in a repetition, yet the new and perhaps greater trauma is also immediately repressed. The story is then repeated for the third time in Christianity, yet in a significantly modified form. The killing of Jesus is transformed by Saint Paul into the story of the return of the repressed. The Christian Jew acknowledges the killing of the father and identifies himself with the son. What does it mean that the son takes upon himself the sin of mankind? Simply, that he acknowledges the murder of the father as a son and that he—as son—takes upon himself the guilt of all the sons of the primordial father. The Jews, contrary to the Christians, however, have never admitted the killing of the father, not even indirectly. Thus this selfsame Jewry will occupy in the psyche of the Christians the place of the older brother. Anti-Semitism is not just hatred, but a manifestation of the traumatic experience.

The thought that Christian anti-Semitism cannot be explained merely by scapegoating and the usual hatred against the stranger is not an idea unique to Freud. Many thinkers shared this thought before him and after him, among others Franz Rosenzweig. What is unique in Freud is the theory of the return of the repressed. To this I will add only one, perhaps minor, perhaps not minor, point. Whereas in the book where Freud has advanced his theory for the first time (*Totem and Taboo*) he puts a great emphasis on sexuality and desire (the son's jealousy and his desire to possess his mother or rather the woman of his father as the motivation for the murder), this motive does not appear in the story of the murder of Moses and the emergence of the monotheistic religion at all. There is here neither sexuality nor mother. Hayim Yerushalmi—as we shall see—wants to rectify this, in adding that the teaching, the Torah itself, is the mother. Freud would certainly not accept this analogy.

After this simplified summary I would like to return to the contemporary discourse and the renewed interest in Freud's book as a historical novel rather than a family romance. The list of motivations for this interest is long, thus I will speak of only a few.

The fact of the Holocaust trauma, of its long latency period and the late discovery of its significance, must be mentioned in the first place. One could reject this suggestion by saying the Holocaust trauma has no connection to the historical novel, as it was the trauma experience of single individuals. Yet the traumas narrated by Freud's "historical novel"—for example, of the killing of Moses— are also individual in the sense that they are first experiences in the psyche of single persons. Still, collective forgetting and remembering are constituted by individual trauma experiences. Freud's philosophical suggestion or "novel" (as he once calls it) is, of course, just one among many. Another example is Halbwachs's theory of collective memory and forgetting, which has also been rediscovered by the participants of the contemporary discourse on memory and history in general, as an alternative way of understanding. At any rate, the attempts at understanding the Holocaust trauma make us rethink the relation between unconscious memory and conscious remembering, of the significance and manifestation of the archive, both overt and covert, of the mythological sedimentation of memory traces, and much else. Sure, the strong presence of the history and memory school in French historiography and its fast dissemination in Germany, the United States, and other places, cannot be linked directly to attempts at deciphering the Holocaust trauma. This tendency has emerged first and foremost due to the growing dissatisfaction with the rigidification of the *Annales* school. (Le Goff, by far the most interesting scholar of the contemporary *Annales* school, expresses his skepticism against the project of the history and memory school termed also *mnenohistory*.)[1] Yet the understanding of history initiated by the *Les Lieux de Memoire* volume (prefaced by Pierre Nora) introduced a very fertile approach also in the deciphering of the Holocaust trauma, and much else.

Yerushalmi, who was perhaps the first to reintroduce Freud's Moses into the contemporary discourse, wrote one of the most representative works of this school, *Zakhor*.[2] He discusses here how

Jewish historical consciousness is entirely based on memory, rather than history writing. (The injunction "remember!" appears in the Holy Writ one hundred and seventy times.) Other major figures of mnenohistory, among them Jan and Aleida Assmann (but mainly the first), focus their research on similar topics. Jan Assmann wrote a book on Moses the Egyptian[3] in which he too analyzes in detail the Freudian concepts of trauma and the latency period. He also covers Halbwachs's theory of collective memory as well as Yeru-shalmi's *Zakhor* in his study *"Erinnern um dazuzugehören."*[4] Here, Assmann analyzes the mnemotechnical function of the command-ments given to Israel at Mount Sinai, among other aspects of mne-motechnics as well as their historical consequences. He speaks of an essential conception in both Freud and Nietzsche: the intrinsic connection of memory to pain and suffering, with the difference being that in Nietzsche pain and suffering are experienced as conscious.

Postmetaphysical philosophy too rediscovers a fairly complex tra-dition from Heidegger through Gadamer to Derrida. Not only in the conceptual content of the significant works listed among that tradition, but also in the hidden dimensions—the reverse side of the overt content, encapsulated in the lost or forgotten meanings of the words (Greek, German) or in the connotations of metaphors. The deconstruction of traditional concepts is a search for hidden, or alternative, and frequently subversive meanings, of which per-haps even the philosophers themselves were entirely unaware, although this we cannot know for sure. In his book *Dissemination*, Derrida discusses Plato's criticism of writing and his preference for the spoken word. Plato's reference to the Egyptian myth can also be perceived as a trump card in the first "history and memory" debate. Even the idea of a latency period is far from an alien concept when one considers Plato's theory of *anamnesis*. At any rate, Derrida's interest in the Freudian suggestion of the archive has something to do with the history/memory debate.

But is this connection not too far fetched? Freud suggests, after all, that in his book on Moses he will strictly follow the method of an objective, positivist, fact-based, scientific inquiry. As I've men-tioned already, Freud is a convinced atheist. For him, religion is an illusion, or if there is truth in it, this is a truth *malgé elle,* to be deciphered by science alone. Thus Freud reads the religious narrative from the perspective of the scientific narrative, without denying that we are confronted with two fictions, since both are fictions. This explains the reference to the "historical novel." But, to repeat the point already mentioned, one of the fictions (the scientific) can solve the riddle of the other fiction (the religious) yet not vice versa. But could this relationship be reversed? No according to Freud, but yes according to Yerushalmi, an adherent of the history and memory school. Is it so shocking to suggest that we read the psychoanalytical interpretation of the story of Moses and monotheism as a fiction (a scientific–historical fiction) and to read this fiction from the perspective and with the help of the biblical story that contains the higher (religious) truth? Could one not follow Freud's method in the reverse and search for the hidden and forgotten meaning, the repressed experience behind the overt psychoanalytical narrative? If one takes as the starting point the biblical story, one can read Freud's story as the historical truth—*mémoire,* the repressed motivational force that needs to be unearthed in order to understand the biblical story's message. Yerushalmi reads Freud essentially in this (reversed) way. He reads Freud's story as the manifestation of a trauma similar to Freud, but not of the trauma of Jews who murdered the man Moses, but as the trauma of the man Freud. This is, to my mind, not an untenable venture. Still, I will not take sides in the Yerushalmi–Bernstein debate that centers also around this point. I would rather say that if one takes two or three heterogeneous aspects of the same thing (here the truth of the fictions), it depends chiefly on the regard, the intellectual interest, the conviction and the perspective of the reader, the analyst, as to which fiction will be the one deciphered, and which will serve as the method of deciphering; which will be the keyhole, and which the key. The relation between key and keyhole is here the relation between different kinds of truth. Freud's Moses offers its readers an opportunity to ruminate on the meaning of historical truth and scientific truth, and on their relationship to each other.

I am still speaking of the intellectual and spiritual interests responsible for the renewed popularity of Freud's odd Moses book.

There is however one yet to be mentioned: the historical question concerning German Jews. Who is a Jew?—asks Freud—Why do I identify myself as Jew? He is a disbeliever, and his language and culture are essentially German. He does not even know Hebrew (a statement Yerushalmi will decode as false). Freud begins to follow the footsteps of Moses in order to find an answer to his question: What makes a Jew a Jew if he is none? What is in the archive that is perhaps responsible for this unidentifiable identity? How can an archive as such be inherited nongenetically? Do I still have something to do with a God I do not believe in?

And here yet remains the question of Christian anti-Judaism and anti-Semitism. Is anti-Semitism really rooted in a neurosis? What is feeding it? An overtly inherited system of beliefs, or a hidden volcano, or both? In our times—when the Pope repents in the name of the Catholic Church, for having entertained for millennia prejudices against the Jews that gave vent to collective hatred and revenge, and when the French Catholic Church asks the victims of the Holocaust for forgiveness—one could reread Freud's book on Moses also from this perspective.

In what follows, I briefly introduce from the current debate on Freud's Moses three representative books that refer and reply to each other: Yerushalmi's *Freud's Moses: Judaism Terminable and Interminable*,[5] Jacques Derrida's *Mal d'Archive* (in English, *Archive Fever: A Freudian Impression*)[6] and Richard Bernstein's *Freud and the Legacy of Moses*.[7] All three participants of the debate understand Freud's book (and each other) against the backdrop of their own tradition and spiritual interest. Yerushalmi is passionately interested in Judaism; Derrida in the question of unconscious traces; and Bernstein in Freud, the author and his work itself.

Yerushalmi proceeds roughly as follows: I am reading a fiction. The psychoanalytical fiction about Moses was invented by Sigmund Freud. Freud—in his own words—has interpreted the Holy Writ as he would a dream. He thus presents his fiction as the correct interpretation of that dream. Let us ponder the astonishing fact that the old and dying Freud developed a fixation on this dream. What unconscious drives pushed him in this direction? What kind of debt had he paid in and through his fiction and to whom? In the last part of his book (the monologue conducted with Freud) Yerushalmi intimates that the older Freud returned to the Bible, the very Bible of his childhood that he received for the second time from his father with a Hebrew dedication on his thirty-fifth birthday. Yet—so Yerushalmi makes us believe—Freud returns to the Bible in not returning to it: he replaces the Bible with psychoanalysis, the Jewish science. According to Freud, argues Yerushalmi, Jewishness does not live anymore in traditional Judaism, but in psychoanalysis. As I mentioned, wittingly or unwittingly Yerushalmi reverses the priority of the two fictions: for him the biblical fiction is the primary historical truth. That is, for Yerushalmi, the Bible proves that the Jews have not murdered Moses, for if they had, the deed would have been not only recorded but also worked out in the Holy Writ. The Holy Writ encompasses the factual truth.

Yet Yerushalmi also employs the Freudian approach, at least partially. He rejects the psychoanalytical reading of the Holy Writ, but has no objection against the psychoanalytical reading of a psychoanalytical text. We are confronted with a fiction: the fiction of Freud. Freud believes that his fiction is the scientific truth. But let us read it as a fiction: let us unearth the trauma that has been covered, repressed, and reinforced by Freud's fiction that he has presented as the truth. Yerushalmi presents us with a Freud who has repressed his essential Jewish heritage, his commitment to the Bible of his father—his own Jewishness and Jewish consciousness. He has completely forgotten that he could read Hebrew; he has completely forgotten that he received the Bible of his childhood on his thirty-fifth birthday from his father with a Hebrew dedication. These repressed contents return in his story of Moses. Behind the fiction lurks the repressed factual truth: Freud's confused relationship to his own Jewishness, the trauma of an atheistic and secular Jew. It is because of this trauma and repression that Freud—according to Yerushalmi—cannot answer the question about his Jewishness other than with a secondary fiction. He uses a scientifically refuted concept, that of neo-Lamarckism, to offer himself at least some solution to the insoluble riddle. Both the theory of the return of the repressed and the explanation of Jewish heritage by neo-

Lamarckism express a spirit of hopelessness. A spirit that—according to Yerushalmi—is essentially un-Jewish.

Despite their great respect for Yerushalmi's work, neither Derrida nor Bernstein can accept the essence of his position. Freud's alleged neo-Lamarckism is based on a misunderstanding: Yerushalmi believes that psychical heritage is genetically coded. Yet the problem of the unconscious memory traces and their heritage still remains a basic issue. Derrida concentrates on the question of the archive, and points his finger at different traces: traces that are not the silent witnesses of a traumatic past experience, but rather signs of a future: he means the messianistic (not the messianic) traces. Bernstein concludes his book on a similar chord, that Yerushalmi's accusation of Freud's hopelessness is poorly founded. Bernstein writes: "Insofar as 'Der Fortschritt der Geistigkeit' defines the character of the Jewish people, there is the promise that they will continue to survive.... This is not 'hopelessness' ... In the spirit of the prophetic tradition that Freud so admired, it is an expression of profound hope."[8]

At this point I would like to add to the three contemporary readings of Freud's Moses my own interpretation.

My story will be brief and a little improvised. I will proceed up to a degree with Yerushalmi: I will read the psychoanalytical story as the fiction that needs to be deciphered, and not as the key to be inserted into the keyhole of the old story of the birth of monotheism, to decipher it. Yet I will not use the biblical story as the key (or one of the keys) to open the Freudian fiction—as Yerushalmi does when he insists that Moses was not murdered, because the Bible always says the truth about the Jewish people—for I do not regard the Torah as the bearer of the "material truth." To my mind neither the concept of "historical truth," nor the concept of factual or scientific truth applies to the Holy Writ, for revealed truth differs substantially from both. This approach does not deny the relevance of reading the Holy Writ as a historical sourcebook; but if one reads it thus, it ceases to be a Holy Writ. To my mind, what Freud wanted to understand through his psychoanalytical stories (the murder of the father, the repression, the return of the repressed)—namely the fascination of religions, their force, their secret—cannot be explained with the help of "scientific" narratives. This Freudian experiment seems naive to me. Freud reminds me of a little boy who wants to find out whether the water in the kettle boils, takes the kettle off the fireplace, and carrys it into his parent's room so that they could tell him whether it is really boiling. What is boiling in a religion, or in a religious text, we will never know whenever we take the text off the fireplace, that is, whenever we create a situation where it does not boil. I can seek historical truth in a holy text, but it then ceases to be a holy text (it stops boiling). The case of Freud's own text is entirely different. The Freudian interpretation of the Holy Writ can be taken off the fireplace, because it is not a religious text at all. It never boiled. Although one can invest faith in psychoanalysis, and this faith can closely resemble religious commitment, the point is to be able to interpret and understand a psychoanalytical text even without having invested one's faith in it. The text should not lose the force of its arguments without faith. Moreover, the text, the fiction of Freud, as with all scientific texts and fictions, opens itself up to falsification. No one was more aware of this than Freud himself.

I will speak of Freud's reading of the myths, rites, and of the Bible, only in connection with the story of the primordial father and the murder of Moses, the trauma and the return of the repressed in the history of monotheistic religion. I am not interested in the question of whether Moses was murdered by the Jews or not. I am ready to accept Derrida's and Bernstein's point that if one searches the archive it makes no difference whether the Jews in fact murdered Moses or only desired or tried to murder him (the attempt or the desire of the attempt is recorded in the Bible), because the experience is traumatic in both cases, and the feeling of guilt coded regardless in the collective archive. In my story only one thing is important: that the murder of Moses is discussed by Freud as a hidden historical fact, and that he sets himself to work in order to decipher this material (scientific) truth and its consequences.

We can repeat the tale, as myths repeat themselves. The primordial father was murdered, but he returned in the image of mighty God(s). The Jews murdered Moses, he who mediated God's

heavy and strict commandments for them and whom they identify
with this God. In a parallel way, Jews, adorers of Jahwe, of this
half-pagan volcano deity, have returned—after a lengthy period of
latency—to the God of Moses, the sole, spiritual, sublime God. The
repressed returns. God will be murdered again, everything begins
anew, yet the primordial deed has not been repeated and will not
repeat itself in exactly the same way.

I have chosen another text as the key to open the door of Freud's
fiction, a text of Nietzsche's. In the *Gay Science*, Nietzsche repeats
his summary of the spiritual result of the nineteenth century, "God
is dead," yet here goes even further. The madman cries out: "We
have murdered him!" Freud, although he does not refer directly to
Nietzsche, must have known about the madman's tale at least from
Lou Salome (with whom he had a very interesting correspondence
about the Moses book). Yet no personal mediation is now needed,
because since the thirties of the last century, every single well-read
European intellectual knows these sentences of Nietzsche and has
ruminated on their meaning.[9] What does it mean that we murdered
God? Who is this "we"? The "we" stands for modern man, the man
of modern positivist science. And who among modern men takes
on himself the odium of having murdered God, the father? The
modern atheist, the disbeliever. Freud identifies himself, with special emphasis, as "*ein gottloser Jude*," a godless Jew. God is dead.
Freud is fatherless. The courageous modern scientist unmasks religion as a neurosis. He murders God. Freud calls himself a godless
Jew. Nietzsche has murdered the Christian God; he has murdered
the Jewish God. More precisely, he is the very man who has murdered the Jewish God. He has murdered its sourcebook, the Holy
Writ, the source of faith: the Torah. He has murdered the alleged
author of this book: he has murdered Moses.

Freud's text says the following: God is dead. I murdered God/
I murdered Moses for the second time. Yet this does not look like
the return of the repressed trauma after a lengthy period of latency. Freud declares himself openly godless. Still, one can detect
a repressed trauma. After all, one cannot murder someone who
never existed. God (in Freud's scenario) is an invention that stands
for the murdered father. He could not have killed God, but the

illusion of God. Thus he takes the kettle off the fireplace and declares: it does not boil, it never boiled. Yet Freud was the one who took the kettle off the fireplace. The term "godless" is, after all, a negation. Aristotle would have said, *steresis.*

Freud repeatedly and openly confesses that he experienced some kind of neurotic compulsion in his relation to the Moses book. For example he writes that once he decided to put the book aside, the topic began to torture him as would a haunting spirit. Later on he adds that as soon as he arrived in England, he was carried away by an irresistible temptation to disclose to the world his still concealed secret. These and similar sentences express the scholar's desire to make his great discovery public, and also the desire of an old man to make use of the little time left for him on earth. But expressions like "being tortured" or "haunting ghost" and particularly *"unheimlich"* (uncanny) also point at something else, viz. at a drive fed by unconscious resources.

Freud is driven to write his book on Moses about a man (a demi-God) who was killed by the Jews. The man who has murdered the Jewish God, the Torah and his author Moses, *ein gottloser Jude,* feels an irresistible drive to offer a psychoanalytical interpretation of the story of Moses, of the giving of the Law, of monotheism, and does all this in his very old age, at the last minute before death. Why not earlier? Why is this old godless Jew tortured by this theme? Why is he driven to it?

In the story told by Freud the primordial father is killed (this murder is the universal human trauma); then the deed is repeated. Moses will be murdered—Moses, who is identified by the Jews with God—and this is the first Jewish story. Jews will never admit this murder. Then, the Son will be murdered, and the Jewish Paul will be the one to tell us that the crucified Son has taken upon himself all the son's guilt, that he redeemed us, all the murderers. (This is the Jewish/Christian story.) Only the Jews will continue to live with the sense of guilt, not because they murdered the Son (which they did not do, a murder that already belongs to the trauma behind anti-Judaism and anti-Semitism). Rather, they will live with the sense of guilt because—and this cannot be emphasized enough— they never admitted the murder of the father/God/Moses.

God is dead. I have murdered the Jewish God, says the godless Jew. If one follows Freud's story, then his deed (the killing of the Jewish father with psychoanalytical science) is to be understood as the return of the repressed, as the repetition of the already much-repeated story. Yet for the first time in Jewish history, one murders the father without denying it: Freud openly admits that he has murdered God. Psychoanalysis murders God in general, for its ambition is to decipher the neurosis called religion as a neurosis, and to explain scientifically not just the content of the religion, but also, first and foremost, its driving force and power. Psychoanalysis has murdered in particular the Jewish God. And Freud as a Jew invented it. But until his old age Freud has never tried to speak of the significance of the new (scientific) murder of God for the Jews. Until this time he has never spoken of the increase in spirituality as the result of the return of the repressed in Jewish history.

Here one may turn back to Yerushalmi's suggestion, that for Freud psychoanalysis was a Jewish science. But to my mind, Bernstein is right: Freud was a universalistic modern scholar who did not believe in Jewish or Christian or Austrian or French science, only in science *as such*, and he would never have called psychoanalysis a Jewish science.[10] Yet even if psychoanalysis was never meant to be a Jewish science, it can still remain a fact that at first it was mainly Jews who discovered and became committed to it. And this has, after all, significance for Freud. Because the Jews have a pioneering task in murdering God, they must also play a significant part in launching the psychoanalytical movement.

On the one hand Freud kills the teaching of Moses (the old Law) in murdering God, but he is also the new Moses, who carries new tablets, the tablets of modern science to the whole of mankind. This is the Moses who breaks the illusion itself; a prophet of the increase in spirituality. Who, had he been younger and less famous, would have been murdered by the people whose language he spoke, whose culture he shared.

If the story were to be terminated at this point, it would be easy to bring this text into harmony with an earlier opus of the master: *The Future of an Illusion*. Since, if the Jews confess to the killing of God by declaring themselves godless Jews as their new Moses did, moreover, if they do it consciously, and do not deny having done exactly this, then there will be no more repression, no trauma, and the repressed will never return. The godless Jew will not be neurotic; he will get rid of the sense of guilt accumulated in the collective archive. And then, perhaps, the illusion, religion itself, will lose its fuel, its driving force.

But, is Freud's story really about this? Perhaps, but not about this alone. For if the book were to be deciphered as such, one could hardly regard it as a gesture of Freud identifying himself with his people—as he says—in one of the most tragic moments of Jewish history, but rather as a confession of love to modern science. But one need not leave the former track altogether in order to proceed.

At the time Freud writes his book, the Jewish people are threatened in their existence. They are threatened by Nazism. And Nazism is—Freud never ceases to emphasize this point—pagan through and through. The Nazis have also killed God in order to put a new God, a man, Hitler, in his place. I have already mentioned briefly Freud's analysis of Nazi hatred of the Jews: The Nazis hate the Jews because they hate Christianity in the image of the Jews. They have killed the Jewish God, the father, yet they have also killed the Son. And when the murdered God returns, it returns in the shape of a God/Satan. If this is so, the main question cannot be reduced to the formal aspect (whether the repressed returns or does not), it becomes the matter of content: what exactly is that which returns and how does it return? *The repressed can return as the advance in spirituality, yet it can also return as the advance in barbarism.* For Freud, both Nazism and Bolshevism are kinds of barbarism. And both the Bolsheviks and the Nazis have murdered God.

In a subchapter of the Moses book titled "The Advance of Spirituality," Freud remarks that the more the people of Israel were mistreated by their God, the more they clung to this God. After having said this, he adds: I cannot yet explain this, I must leave the question open, for this miracle we cannot decipher, there is no psychoanalytical answer. At least not for the time being. Thus he leaves the kettle boiling on the fire. But how long will this "time being" last?

Freud sees now the historical significance of the Jewish people as being that in their history the repressed has returned as an advance in spirituality. Can one kill the Jewish God without also killing spirituality? Or is this spirituality preserved deep down in the archive to the extent that no godlessness can do it harm? Freud has no ready answers to these questions and he says so. Times are tragic. They keep killing God, and the repressed returns. It can return in the shape of neo-barbarism, and also in the shape of a sublime spirituality. Yet we cannot know ahead *in which of these two major forms the repressed is going to return.*

Freud tells the reader that in the eyes of a godless man such as himself, the believers are enviable, for they are well convinced by the existence of a supreme being. What a pity, he adds, that certain life experiences and observation of the world make it impossible for us to accept such a thing.

I do not think that the older Freud returned unconsciously to the Bible he received twice from his father, as Yerushalmi wants us to believe. Nor do I think that he was happy, self-indulgent, and self-satisfied in having killed God; or with the thought that the repressed had returned in the form of psychoanalysis. Freud did not say, after all, that just because we (scientists) have killed God, religion is now a thing of the past, nor did he say that religion will remain with us always. After all he did not prophesy, nor did he extrapolate.

What Freud wanted to achieve first and foremost was, perhaps, *to know himself better.* Yet, in this book, Freud seeks not the part of himself that could have been identified as the source of his neuroses; nor his relationship to his mother (for, I repeat, the mother plays no role in the Moses story at all). Rather, he seeks *the segment of himself which encapsulates the sources of his spirituality.* In this story, as in many other stories told by Freud, spirituality and the sense of guilt are intrinsically related, even in his own being. Freud says without saying: "as a godless Jew I have murdered the Jewish god, I take full responsibility for this symbolic act of murder, I resist the temptation for remaining silent, for I am duty bound to tell you what I believe to be true. I am committed to spirituality yet I am also the bringer of troublesome news: that instinct, violence, and

Agnes Heller

barbarism are the roots of every culture. That violence, barbarism, and force can be sublimated into spirituality, yet, unfortunately, they not always are. That our history is long, our archives are hidden, and that—finally—in the end, not even the most brutal world is entirely without hope."

This is not the final conclusion of the book, for the book is lacking in a final conclusion. Yet this is the way I might read Freud's Moses.

In this book, Freud writes about us, human beings, the following: that "we usually believe in things, which—irrespective of truth—answer our desires." This happens also if we are respecting truth. Indeed, this has happened among all the participants of this debate.

Notes

1. Jacques Le Goff, *Geschichte und Gedächtnis Vorwort zur französischen Ausgabe* (Frankfurt am Main, 1992).

2. Yosef Hayim Yerushalmi, *Zakhor: Jewish History and Jewish Memory* (Seattle, Wash.: University of Washington Press, 1982).

3. Jan Assmann, *Moses the Egyptian: The Memory of Egypt in Western Monotheism* (Cambridge, Mass.: Harvard University Press, 1997).

4. In *Generation und Gedächtnis*, ed. Mihran Dabag and Kristin Platt (Opladen: Leske+Budrich, 1995), pp. 51–75. English translation, "Remembering in Order to Belong: Cultural Memory, the Structure of Belonging, and the Normative Past."

5. Yosef Hayim Yerushalmi, *Freud's Moses: Judaism Terminable and Interminable* (New Haven, Conn.: Yale University Press, 1991).

6. Jacques Derrida, *Archive Fever: A Freudian Impression*, trans. Eric Prenowitz (Chicago, Ill.: University of Chicago Press, 1996).

7. Richard Bernstein, *Freud and the Legacy of Moses* (Cambridge: Cambridge University Press, 1998).

8. Bernstein, *Freud*, p. 116.

9. We know that Freud had not read the collected works of Nietzsche he'd received as a birthday present from Otto Rank, and moreover, that he put these volumes on the highest bookshelf, the one he could not reach. What has Freud repressed in this case?

10. We know how eager he had been in gathering non-Jews into the inner circle of the psychoanalytic movement.

11

Omnipotence and Radical Evil: On a Possible Rapprochement between Hannah Arendt and Psychoanalysis

Joel Whitebook

Now that the "awful" twentieth century, as she called it, has drawn to its violent close, there is little doubt that Hannah Arendt is emerging as one of its foremost political thinkers. During her life, her work was valued by a small and devoted group of admirers, but it never received anything approaching the prestige it is getting today. This is not only because it takes a certain amount of time to absorb and evaluate the work of such a complex thinker; it is also the result of the collapse of communism, and, with it, the decline of a certain form of ideological thinking on both the left and the right. Arendt's thinking was too complicated and independent to be located on the rigid ideological grid that existed prior to 1989. She has variously been described as an ultra-leftist and a cold warrior, a liberal modernist and a backwards-looking classicist, an arrogant elitist and a radical democrat. As opposed to the ideological cataloguers of various stripes, she appropriately referred to herself as a "*Selbstdenker*"—someone who thinks for herself. The current interest in Arendt results from the fact that, with the end of the cold war, there is a hunger for a thinker who, although postideological, can still help us formulate a comprehensive analysis of our situation. And in this regard, Arendt fits the bill.

There is, however, a question that has troubled me about Hannah Arendt for years. How could her brilliance as a political thinker be reconciled with her deep and abiding enmity not only toward psychoanalysis, but also toward psychology and the inner world in general? This is the question I want to examine here.

Before turning to that question, however, I would like to make one point. The paradigm crisis in American psychoanalysis has made the field itself much more sensitive to and interested in political questions than it was during the '50s and '60s. It has often been observed that the old school of ego psychology was militantly apolitical. Sociopolitical reality was, for example, simply subsumed under Hartmann's "average expectable environment" and that was that. It has also been pointed out that American psychoanalysis wasn't as value-free as Hartmann—who had actually studied with Max Weber—claimed. In the '50s and '60s, it more or less tacitly operated with a specific set of values, namely, those of postwar, middle-class American culture. The reasons why the émigré analysts were culturally conservative and wary of politics have often been discussed. Among other things, what they witnessed with the Nazis in Europe and with the McCarthy Committee here made them eager to "adapt." (We should also add that Hartmann and his protégés came from elite *haute bourgeois* backgrounds that made it possible for them to stay above the fray.) And although this attitude is perhaps understandable, it simply wouldn't wash in post-'60s America. The denial of sociopolitical reality is one of the many factors that have led to the crisis in ego psychology.

Having said this, however, I immediately want to warn against a particular danger. Too often well-intentioned critics believe that the way to make psychoanalysis socially and politically responsible is to drastically soften or drop the notion of unconscious psychic reality altogether, with its unsettling antisocial implications. This is simply to move from one one-sided position to its opposite equally one-sided position. I would argue that, rather than softening the notion of psychic reality, psychoanalysis examine the relationship between a robust notion of psychic reality, with all its disturbing implications, and social reality. This is a major task for its theoretical agenda.

There is plenty of biographical material to explain Arendt's antipathy to psychic life. Her early life was rife with losses—including the long and agonizing death of her father from syphilis when she was seven, the death of her beloved grandfather shortly thereafter and the flight from her childhood home in Königsberg because of

World War I. She might have dealt with her suffering by turning her inner life into the object of systematic investigation—a path that has led many people into psychoanalysis. Arendt, however, took a different route. As Elisabeth Young-Bruehl reports in her biography, she made a more or less conscious decision to reject the inner realm. Throughout her life—which seems to have been marked by considerable melancholy—she turned to the sentimental German poetry of her youth as a form of self-therapy. It is, however, beyond the scope of this paper to examine the relation between the facts of Arendt's biography and the details of her theory. This is a fascinating project that still waits to be undertaken. What I want to do, rather, is examine her arguments and see if, despite her repudiation of the intrapsychic, there is a way to build a theoretical bridge between her thinking and psychoanalysis.

Like many *Gymnasium*-educated German intellectuals of her generation, Arendt turned to the "treasure horde" of classical Greece in an attempt to elucidate the nature of the crisis of modernity —which had culminated with Hitler and Stalin—and of modern political thought. This procedure, she thought, would not only illuminate the specific structures of the modern world by contrasting them to the ancient, but would also show what had been lost in the move from the practical philosophy of the Greeks to the political science of the moderns. As might be expected, the results of this approach were double-edged. On the one hand, it did indeed allow her to dramatize the eclipse of political action—which had involved an active citizenry—and its replacement by technocratic planning and a privatized population. On the other hand, however, because she used the categories of Greek political thought to understand the modern world, she missed some of its main features and, more significantly, distorted some of its true advances.

Arendt's main purpose was to repoliticize contemporary public life by demonstrating the deficiencies of the modern technocratic approach to politics—in both its liberal and Marxist forms— compared to an idealized picture of the Greek polis. In the polis, she argued, free and equal citizens—who admittedly were exclusively male aristocrats—attended to the affairs of the city through open debate in the light of day. In the modern state, in contrast, apart from periodic voting in public elections, the citizenry is depoliticized and passive, and public affairs are conducted by a small technocratic elite operating behind closed doors. The Greeks valorized public life in the polis because they saw it as the truly human form of activity, which is to say, it lay beyond the necessities of nature. On the other hand, they viewed the tasks of economic production and biological reproduction—including care for the young—with a degree of contempt because they were concerned with "mere nature." They believed, therefore, that women and slaves should attend to these matters in the private realm of the household, that is, out of public view. This arrangement was, of course, a centerpiece of Greek misogyny.

The shortsightedness and latent classicism of Arendt's account of modernity can best be brought into relief by contrasting it with Hegel's. Whereas Hegel saw modernity as a *thoroughly ambivalent* phenomenon, Arendt tended to view it as a *product of degeneration.* Hegel considered the recognition of "the right of subjective freedom"—that is, the right of individuals to determine their own conception of the good and pursue their own life-projects independently of traditionally binding normative prescriptions so long as they remained within the bounds of legality—as "the pivot and center of the difference between antiquity and modern times." The ancients, in contrast, had attempted to keep subjective freedom suppressed because of the disintegrating effects it would have had on a form of ethical life *constructed on determinacy and limit*—that is, on *finite forms.*

An essential feature of the Greek worldview was an abhorrence of the "unlimited." As opposed to things that are limited, distinct and determinate, the "unlimited" is repugnant for the Greeks because, lacking in form it is unintelligible. Let us not forget that they saw *hubris*—excess—as perhaps the major danger to individual and collective existence and believed that the task of one of their major cultural institutions, tragedy, was to educate the populace about its dangers. (We will compare *hubris* to omnipotence later.) And the hostility toward, indeed the horror at, the "unlimited" permeated every aspect of Greek culture.

This led the Greeks to try to structure their economic life in such a way as to keep market activities in check. For the Greeks, the function of economic activity should not be moneymaking with its "irresistible tendency to grow," as Arendt put it, but the provision of the necessities for the good life. And because those necessities were intrinsically limited, economic activity was limited as well. Like most premodern societies, the Greeks recognized that if the market were emancipated and the accumulation of wealth became an end-in-itself—as it has in modern capitalist societies—a potentially unlimited dynamic would be introduced into the world. Such a dynamic would, in the long run, swamp all other essential elements of an ethical life predicated on limit. Aristotle noted, for example, that when the doctor pursues his art for the sake of moneymaking rather than for the sake of health, medicine loses its virtue. Similarly, the medieval Catholic Church, which was based on a Christianized version of Aristotelianism, put the philosopher Giodorno Bruno—who represented the emerging modern view—to the stake when he claimed not only that an actual infinite was possible, but that it glorified God's existence. In both cases, the possibility that infinity could exist undermined a worldview constructed on a closed intelligible cosmos. The abhorrence of the "unlimited" also contributed to the Greeks' suspicion of subjectivity. For the Greeks, the good life had to be grounded in "worldliness"—that is, the existence of a shared world consisting in institutions that transcended the individual's existence, publicly articulated values, and a consensually validated reality. Indeed, the loss of such a world—"worldlessness" as Arendt called it—was, she argued, at the center of the crisis of modernity.

As opposed to the ancients, Hegel applauded the recognition of subjective freedom as an unequivocal advance. At the same time, however, he acknowledged the enormous destructiveness, which Greek philosophers like Plato and Aristotle had anticipated, that the unleashing of subjective freedom would inflict on the fabric and cohesiveness of traditional society. Indeed, the boldness of Hegel's approach is that he faced the conflict—and therewith the ambivalence of modernity—directly: that is to say, he unequivocally affirmed the right of subjective freedom without denying its destructive consequences. The central question for his political philosophy therefore became: how can that destructiveness be contained in a new form of modern ethical life after the emancipation of subjective freedom? And, of course, his failure to answer this question—which is still very much with us—marked the point of entrée for Marx's critique.

At the level of institutional analysis, Hegel came to realize that the classical institutional scheme, which Arendt would later retain—consisting only in *oikos* and *polis*, private and public—was insufficient for conceptualizing the novel developments of modernity. He therefore introduced his own expanded tripartite scheme, consisting in the family, civil society, and the state, in part, because the classical scheme did not accommodate—indeed, was designed to suppress—the right of subjective freedom. And as most commentators observe, the distinctively new feature in Hegel's scheme was civil society. In contrast to Arendt's view of the social, he did not see civil society simply as the result of the decay of the public realm owing to the penetration of the metabolic processes, that had formerly been contained in the private realm, into it. Rather, Hegel praised the creation of civil society as an achievement in its own right: namely, as the institutionalization of a realm where subjective freedom, primarily in the economic sense, is granted "free play." And under the title of "the system of needs," which was his term for the market, Hegel—as opposed to the ancients who abhorred the unlimited—was willing to allow, indeed affirmed, the introduction of a potentially infinite telos into the world.

What I would like to emphasize in this context is the following. In connection with the introduction of the concept of civil society and his notion of modern ethical life, Hegel also introduced a distinction between the premodern household and the modern family—a distinction that Arendt never makes in a systematic fashion. *Instead, she tends to lump both under the concept of the private.* And again, for Hegel, the introduction of the distinction also has to do with the right of subjective freedom in modernity. With the premodern household, the interests of the community took precedence over the desires of the individual: marriages, for example, were arranged according to tribal, political, or economic considerations rather than according to the subjective inclinations of the individuals involved. In modernity, in contrast, individuals are in principle free to pursue their emotional, sexual, and even economic desires as they determine them, through marriage. Moreover, when economic activities moved from the household to civil society and the family became divested of its economic function, it also became free to be transformed into what Lawrence Stone has called an "affectionate unit."[1] *Hegel considered the experience of intimacy, affectivity, and inwardness in the modern family an essential ingredient in the formation of the subjectivity of the modern individual.* And, once again, he also identified the ambivalence involved with these distinctively modern developments. While he praises modernity for emancipating inwardness and self-reflection and granting them their due, he warns—against the moral and aesthetic romantics—that if they are not reintegrated into the objective structures of ethical life, "the law of the heart" will degenerate into the bad infinity of a groundless and empty subjectivism. To use Arendt's vocabulary, the price of unrestricted subjectivity would be "worldlessness."

Although Arendt does not present a specific analysis of the emergence of the modern family, she does, as I have already indicated, understand the fate of the private sphere in modernity in the same terms she understood the fate of the public realm, namely, in terms of a process of mutual degeneration. As she puts it: "Mass society not only destroys the public realm but the private as well, deprives men not only of their place in the world but of their private homes...."[2] At first glance, her position invites comparison with Horkheimer's and Adorno's. Being good Hegelians in these matters, the Frankfurt school had accepted the connection between the modern family as an affectionate unit and the existence of the modern individual. Therefore, when they perceived a deterioration of the family—owing precisely to the breakdown of its insulated status and penetration by the forces of "mass society"—they argued a decline in the subject must be entailed as well. In other words their theses of the direct socialization of the psyche and the end of the individual went together.

There is a major difference, however, for Arendt was never as keen about the intimacy of the affectionate unit nor about the modern subject as either Hegel or the Frankfurt school. To be sure, she acknowledged that "the intimacy of a fully developed private life, such as had never been known before the rise of the modern age and the concomitant decline of the public realm, will always intensify and enrich the whole scale of subjective emotions and private feelings."[3] But the weight of her entire analysis tends to view the goods to be had in private sphere as inadequate recompense for "the decline of the public realm." She derides the French for their preoccupation with "*le petit bonheur*... after the decay of their once great and glorious public realm."[4] Try as she might to be evenhanded, Arendt's classicist preference for the goods of the public realm continually breaks through in her analysis. Indeed, the quandary created by the fact that most people in the modern age prefer the satisfactions of the private sphere to "the joys of public happiness" and her unwillingness to accept a technocratic approach to politics led her to a rather desperate suggestion at the end of *On Revolution*, namely, that groups of self-chosen political elites be formed as a solution to this predicament.

Arendt, in the final analysis, was not concerned about the decline of the private realm for its own sake, but for the sake of the public. She maintained that a sound public realm requires an intact private realm as its necessary complement. On the more philosophical level, she argued that "a life spent entirely in public ... becomes, as we would say, shallow," for "while it retains its visibility, it loses the quality of rising into sight from some darker ground."[5] The private realm must, therefore, be preserved as a sphere shielded from the light of day in order to provide "the darker ground" from which excellent achievements can rise up and show themselves. It must be preserved, in other words, as the necessary backdrop to the public.

On the more concrete level, Arendt provided an economic analysis of the significance of the decline of the private sphere. She does not locate the "non-privative traits of privacy," which is to say, the positive traits of the private sphere in the novel features of the modern family, namely, affectivity, inwardness, and intimacy. Rather, she locates it in the private property of the household that she very clearly distinguishes from wealth as being "of an entirely different nature." Because it "meant no more or less than to have one's location in a particular part of the world," the significance of the private property—which was held to be sacred by all premodern civilizations—was two-fold. Insofar as it survived the individual members of the family who were born into and passed out of it, the family property contributed to the durability and hence the worldliness of the world. And insofar as one was the head of a household in a particular locale, one became a member of the public realm, which is to say, the community of the heads of the households of that locale. We know, moreover, that, according to the classical scheme, possession of sufficient private wealth was a necessary condition for the participation in public life. It freed a man from the material necessities of life so that he could participate as an active citizen in the *polis* and provided him with the means of acquiring the weaponry to defend it in warfare. In contrast to private property, which consists in the ownership of a specific piece of land, wealth—with which it is often confused—consists in an individual's "share in the annual income of a society as a whole." And, for Arendt, the two are opposed. For the constant expansion of wealth in modernity, which began with the expropriation of the peasant's property, tends to consume all forms of private property that stand in its way. *For Arendt, then, what is objectionable about capitalism's dissolution of the private is not that it destroys the preconditions for modern subjectivity and individuality, but the property conditions for a classical conception of politics.*

It is easier, of course, to observe Arendt's aversion to the unlimited—which constitutes one important and perhaps prereflective element of her Hellenic antimodernism—in her analysis of the rise of the social than in her discussion of the private. As I've noted, the Greek attitude toward economic activity, articulated most notably by Aristotle, was one of apprehension. They realized that, owing to "the growth element inherent in all organic life," economic activities possessed a potentially unlimited dynamic, which, left unchecked, would destroy the conditions of traditional ethical life. They therefore sought to keep economic activity restricted to the private realm in order to keep that dynamic in check. And, with the rise of the social, what the Greeks feared in fact came to pass: economic activity was "emancipated" from the private realm and an "irresistible tendency to grow" was "let loose" on the world to "devour" all the stable structures of the premodern world.

The Greeks also feared the rise of subjective freedom in its other aspect, that is, the rise of the inwardness of the individual. Indeed, many commentators have viewed Socrates' reliance on his inner voice, his *daimon*, to determine his course of action as both a symptom of the decline of the "objective reason" of the polis and a contributor to its decay. And though not as obvious, a similar apprehension concerning subjectivity can also be discerned in Arendt's less than enthusiastic treatment of the rise of inwardness and introspection in modernity and her obvious preference for worldliness, common sense, and the realm of appearance. (The connection between a suspicion of subjectivity and inwardness and a tendency to turn to the ancients is something she shares with Foucault.) Although this apprehension informs her analyses of world alienation and introspection in *The Human Condition*, it becomes particularly clear in a letter to Mary McCarthy. There, Arendt objects to introspection and the quest for personal identity because they—like "the unnatural growth of the natural"—raise the specter of an "infinite regress" and, with it, regression to indeterminacy. With the "inner turmoil" and "kaleidoscopic change" that accompany the odyssey of introspection, "all identities dissolve" and there is "nothing any more to hold on to."[6] The only way to avoid or arrest that regress, for Arendt, is to reject the realm of introspection in favor of the solidity of the shared perspective of the external world. Hegel too, as we noted, recognized that one-sided subjectivism can lead to "measureless excess" and a "false infinite" and therefore had to be brought back to the universal. But, unlike Arendt, he was unwilling to sacrifice the distinctively modern advances in subjective freedom in order to avoid those dangers. To be modern is to accept the fact that—for good and for ill—all closed, finite forms of socialization in the forming of personality have been shattered. Whatever solution to the crisis of modernity is to be found, it must be thought through on the basis of this fact.

Given her skepticism about intimacy and the subjective realm, Arendt's hostility toward psychoanalysis should come as no surprise.

There is, however, another strand in her thinking,—having to do with her more historical and political analyses—that, if followed through, will allow us to build some theoretical links with analysis.

When Arendt first heard about Auschwitz in 1943, she thought, "*This ought not to have happened.* . . . Something happened here to which we cannot reconcile ourselves. . . . This was something completely different." Arendt realized that a fundamental constraint in human history had been breached, which essentially altered the human condition. After that breach, she wrote, "everything was possible."[7] And in one way or another, she devoted the rest of her intellectual career to understanding the nature of that massive schism. At that same time, she also predicted that "the problem of evil will be the fundamental question of postwar intellectual life in Europe"[8]—assuming that everyone else was as disturbed by this development as she. While *prima facie* this was certainly a reasonable prediction, it did not come to pass. Instead, Europe busied itself with recovery and reconstruction, and, with a few notable exceptions, its intellectuals—who are no less prone to denial than anyone else—turned to Marxian sociopolitical analysis, existentialism, or social-scientifically oriented liberalism to try to comprehend their situation. Indeed, it seems to have required something like a latency period of twenty-five years before either Jews or Germans could address the question of the Holocaust in a focused and concerted way.

Recently, however, with the new horrors of Rwanda, Chechnya, and, most particularly, of Bosnia and Kosovo, Western intellectuals have begun to turn their attention to the question of "radical evil"—a term, originating in Kant, that Arendt used immediately after the war, but later dropped. In addition to the obvious need to understand the reappearance of these sorts of atrocities fifty years after the Second World War, I believe there is another reason for this renewed focus on the subject of evil. The collapse of the socialist project and the loss of faith in the liberal notion of progress have caused intellectuals to turn to this quasi-theological concept in an effort to understand the contemporary world. Although I applaud the attempt to face these dark issues directly, I believe that the turn to a quasi-theological concept is in fact misguided and represents an act of intellectual despair. Here, psychoanalysis may be of some assistance.

Whatever its theological connotations, Arendt used the term "radical evil" to mark an essential distinction. She contrasted it with what might be called "average expectable evil," which has been part of human life from time in memoriam. As an example of the later, she cited a typical case where a man "sets out to murder his old aunt." However gruesome, this deed doesn't destabilize our picture of what it is to be human; indeed, it is part of the accepted panorama of human experience. However, with the SS, the situation is different: "The old spontaneous bestiality," she wrote, "gave way to an absolutely cold and systematic destruction of human bodies, calculated to destroy human dignity; death was avoided or postponed indefinitely." I am reminded here of the contrast in Claude Lanzmann's film *Shoah* between the Polish peasants—who are downright Shakespearean in their greed and malice—and the Eichmann-like German officer. Although it was grotesque, I found the peasants' "traditional" envy of the wealthier Jews and desire to get rid of them and grab their property far less disturbing than the unperturbed officer's technocratic lecture about the workings of the death camps—replete with flowcharts and a pointer.

And when Arendt tries to determine the nature of "radical evil" it begins to sound remarkably like the psychoanalytic concept of "omnipotence"—especially as psychoanalytically oriented political theorists like Chasseguet-Smirgel and Cornelius Castoriadis have used it in this same context. Arendt even uses the very term. She tells her old friend and former mentor Karl Jaspers that radical evil is not simply the product of "the lust for power," but arises from "the delusion of omnipotence." Indeed, for Arendt the historical breach, which shouldn't have happened and which now makes everything permissible, consists *in introducing a dynamic of unconstrained omnipotence into the world.*

And like the psychoanalytic theorists, Arendt sees omnipotence as deriving from the drive toward unification and the destruction of plurality—or of difference, to use Chasseguet-Smirgel's terminology. In a response to a letter from Jaspers, asking, "Hasn't Jahwe faded too far out of sight?" Arendt answers that "modern crimes are not provided for in the Ten Commandments." They no longer have anything to do, she writes, with "sinful motives" as they have traditionally been understood.[9] Or to put it differently, they no longer pertain to the domain of the "forbidden," as Joyce Mc-Dougall calls it, but to the realm of the "impossible,"[10] that is, to the attack on reality itself. Arendt tells Jaspers she doesn't know what the "*radical evil*" embodied in these crimes "*really is*," but she feels it "*somehow has to do with ... making human beings as human beings superfluous.*" Superfluity here doesn't only refer to the political phenomenon, analyzed in *The Origins of Totalitarianism*, where modernity creates millions of "stateless people." It also refers to the psycho-philosophical dimension, where the omnipotent drive toward unity seeks to destroy the plurality of the human condition and thereby renders individuals qua individuals superfluous. Arendt argues that more mundane forms of power, seeking to exploit and dominate human beings, use them as means rather than ends, and thereby deprive them of their dignity. But at least it "*leaves their essence as humans untouched.*" The concentration camps, on the other hand, "are laboratories where changes in human nature are tested." The experiments conducted there "succeed not in changing man but in destroying him."[11]

The most extreme attempts to destroy human reality as we know it occurred with the medical experiments, which attempted to defy the limits of our physical constitution and remake the human body—thereby putting the experimenter in the place of an omnipotent God. But in addition to that, there was the social experiment of the camp itself that sought to eliminate central features of the human condition, as Arendt understood them, namely, spontaneity and plurality. The idea that human beings are agents who can spontaneously "*create something new out of [their] resources*" is central to Arendt's theory of action. (It is also the reason why humans cannot be understood "scientifically," for science cannot grasp spontaneity in this sense.) But the "total domination" of the camps—which is essential to totalitarian societies in general—seeks to create "a world of conditioned reflexes, of marionettes without the slightest trace of spontaneity." The sadistically prolonged living death of the camps—to which actual death was often preferable—was a state of existence where all human agency, and hence all human individuality, had been eliminated. And, ultimately, this destruction of spontaneity, Arendt writes, culminated in "the processions of human beings going like dummies to their death."

Arendt saw the plurality of a differentiated social world as an essential feature of the human condition and as a precondition for spontaneity. In eliminating all individuality and plurality, radical evil seeks to reduce its victims to fungible units—"that can be exchanged at random for one another"—in order to dominate and control them. Again, the destruction of plurality culminates in the death camps, where humans are treated as raw material to be scientifically processed through its lethal factories. Arendt argues, further, that the destruction of plurality and the creation of fungible automatons isn't only a tactical strategy on the part of power. On a deeper level, the concept of omnipotence almost logically implies the elimination of a differentiated world. Behind the desire for omnipotence, she detects the wish for self-sufficiency—for monadic autarchy—so familiar to psychoanalysts, where the individual would need no one (or no thing) beyond himself or herself. If, she argues, "an individual man qua man were omnipotent," he would be self-sufficient, and "there is in fact no reason why men in the plural should exist at all." Like the God of monotheism, the omnipotent man would be "one."[12]

With this last observation, Arendt comes close to raising a strictly psychological question, namely, "What is the nature of the wish for omnipotence?" But she doesn't go any further. *She assumes the concept of ominipotence in her discussion of radical evil, but doen't attempt to analyze it.* This is where the psychoanalyst can step in. Analysts within the mainstream Freudian tradition have tended to characterize what Freud called "the original psychical situation" as a self-enclosed, self-contained monad. The differences between the ways it has been conceptualized—as a state of primary narcissism, a dual unity, an undifferentiated field—need not concern us here. (Furthermore, limitations of space prevent me from responding to the criticisms of this conceptualization that have been made by the relational school.) Suffice it to say that Chasseguet-Smirgel, Castoriadis, and others within the Freudian mainstream have taken up the problem of omnipotence in terms of this earliest stage of development. Freud believed that once this original stage—which consists in a state of omnipotent perfection, containing no privation, difference, or otherness—is dissolved, individuals strive "to recover" its unity throughout their lives. This striving, it must be stressed, is as such neither psychologically nor morally good nor bad, but *thoroughly ambivalent*. When it is mediated and sublimated and recreates that unity at a higher more differentiated level, it can lead to the highest achievements of the human spirit: philosophy, music, and religion, for example. But when it is pursued directly, without mediation, this "monster of unifying madness,"[13] as Castoriadis has called it—which seeks to eradicate all difference and recapture the state of primary oneness directly—can lead to the severest forms of individual and social pathology, from clinical psychosis to political totalitarianism.

Chasseguet-Smirgel argues that the fantasy of breaking down the differentiated nature of things in order to regain the undifferentiated perfection of primary narcissism underlies both the individual and collective forms of this narcissistic pathology. The connection between omnipotence and dedifferentiation can, for example, be observed both in the Sadean orgy—which inevitably culminates in dismemberment—and in the experiments of the Nazi doctors. Both represent God-like attempts to break down the differentiated form of the human body and rearrange it according to their own will. Furthermore, despite the militaristic and technological symbolism, Chasseguet-Smirgel locates a maternal fantasy underlying Nazi ideology. She argues the mythology of blood and soil and the attempt to eradicate all difference through genocide represent a wish to return to a state of oneness with the archaic mother. In this context, the ashes of the incinerated victims can be viewed as undifferentiated matter in its purist form.

Having said all this, however, one question remains to be answered. If we assume that the wish for omnipotence is a transhistorical feature of human existence, that is to say, a psychological constant, we have to ask why it became unleashed in the twentieth century. Here I believe the strictly psychological account has to be supplemented with a political and historical analysis. I can only make a few suggestions in this direction. First, there is the obvious fact that the massive advances of our technological power have not only made the pursuit of omnipotence increasingly possible but infinitely more destructive as well. But there is also a deeper factor at work here. As Karl Polanyi has argued, not only the Greeks, but also almost all premodern societies were wary of the unlimited, for it always threatened to undermine the finite and contained forms of their social organizations. Modern European society was the first in history not only to allow the introduction of a potentially infinite dynamic into the world, but also to celebrate it. That is why it represents such a significant rupture in human history. The unprecedented marriage of the endlessly expanding capitalist economy with modern science and technology has introduced a metastatic dynamic into the world that methodically destroys the traditional normative and social constraints, which have historically kept human omnipotence in check. When "all that is solid melts into air," everything becomes permissible. And so far we are having difficulty finding posttraditional constraints to replace the old ones.

Notes

1. Lawrence Stone, *The Family, Sex, and Marriage in England, 1500–1800* (New York: Harper and Row, 1977).

2. Hannah Arendt, *The Human Condition* (Chicago: University of Chicago Press, 1998), p. 59.

3. Ibid., p. 50.

4. Ibid., p. 52.

5. Ibid., p. 71.

6. Hannah Arendt and Mary McCarthy, *Between Friends: The Correspondence of Hannah Arendt and Mary McCarthy, 1949–1975*, ed. Carol Brightman (New York: Harcourt Brace, 1995), p. 242.

7. Hannah Arendt, "What Remains? The Language Remains," in *Essays in Understanding*, ed. Jerome Kohn (New York: Harcourt Brace, 1994), p. 14.

8. Hannah Arendt, "Nightmare and Flight," in *Essays in Understanding*, p. 134.

9. Hannah Arendt and Karl Jaspers, *Correspondence: 1926–1969*, trans. Robert and Rita Kimber, ed. Lotte Kohler and Hans Saner (New York: Harcourt Brace, 1992), p. 166.

10. Joyce McDougall, *Theaters of the Mind: Illusion and Truth on the Psychoanalytic Stage* (New York: Basic Books, 1985).

11. Arendt and Jaspers, *Correspondence*, p. 166.

12. Ibid.

13. Cornelius Castoriadis, *The Imaginary Institution of Society*, trans. Kathleen Blamey (Cambridge, Mass.: The MIT Press, 1987), pp. 294–300.

Reflecting on Judgment: Common Sense and a Common World

Jerome Kohn

. . . und durch diese Entsprechungen wird dichterisch die Einheit der Welt gestiftet.
—H. Arendt

This essay is written for Richard Bernstein for one overriding reason, which is that he, as a scrupulous interpreter of Hannah Arendt's thought, finds a profound problem in what she has to say about, and expects from, the faculty of judgment. In the penultimate chapter of his book *Hannah Arendt and the Jewish Question,* Bernstein focuses "on the relation between thinking, judging, and evil" and finds that Arendt never "gave a fully satisfactory answer to the questions she raised about the relation of thinking and evil," nor "to the precise relation between thinking and judging."[1] It is important to note what is in question here, for Bernstein clearly recognizes Arendt's need, indeed the need of reason itself, for an independent faculty to judge particular cases of right and wrong *in their particularity.* That need arises from the ideological prejudgment that, as the "substitute for a principle of action" in totalitarianism,[2] wreaked havoc on the world by *subsuming* particular cases under suprahuman laws. What Bernstein does not find in Arendt is a convincing demonstration that the activity of thinking, the harmonious inner dialogue of the two-in-one, *liberates* (as she claims it does) the faculty of judgment. True, Eichmann did not think and committed evil deeds, but Heidegger did think and at the "very least … in 1933–4 … failed completely to *judge* accurately what was happening" (*HAJQ*, p. 174).

As Bernstein presents his case I find myself in agreement with much of it, especially when at the conclusion of his chapter he retells, beautifully, the story of Anton Schmidt (actually Schmid) that Arendt tells in *Eichmann in Jerusalem*, the story of "a sergeant in the German army who helped Jewish partisans by supplying them with forged papers and military trucks until he was arrested and executed by the Germans." "Why is it," Bernstein asks, "that there are so few stories to be told about people like Anton Schmidt who, under conditions of totalitarian terror, did not lose their ability to judge what is right and wrong, and to act in accord with their judging?" "In the end … the question that [Arendt] does not answer—which, indeed, may be unanswerable—is how we can account for the differences between Adolf Eichmann and Anton Schmidt" (*HAJQ*, pp. 176–177). I agree completely that there is no answer to *that* question in Arendt or anywhere else. She says only that "the lesson of such stories is simple and within everybody's grasp. Politically speaking, it is that under conditions of terror most people will comply but *some people will not,* just as the lesson of the countries to which the Final Solution was proposed is that 'it could happen' in most places but *it did not happen everywhere*" (quoted in *HAJQ*, p. 178). But when Anton Schmid's story was told in the courtroom, it was greeted with a silence described by Arendt as "a sudden burst of light" in which "a single thought stood out clearly, irrefutably, beyond question—how utterly different everything would be today in this courtroom, in Israel, in Germany, in all of Europe, and perhaps *in all the countries of the world*, if only more such stories could have been told" (quoted in *HAJQ*, p. 176, emphasis added).

The question that Bernstein's criticism of Arendt on the relation of evil, thinking, and judging brings to mind is: What then was Arendt really about in her own reflections on Kant's notion of reflective aesthetic judgment? One of her essential concerns in *The Human Condition*, most explicitly stated in the final part, is worldloss or worldlessness, the gradual alienation of men and women from both the world and the earth since the seventeenth century. She offers no direct suggestion there of how a commonly shared world might be regained.[3] I believe, and hope to indicate in what follows, that Arendt's concern with Kantian reflective aesthetic judgment, with common sense and the *exemplary* validity of particular judgments, was about both the possibility and the difficulty of establishing a common world today. If I am right, then what she was doing in reflecting on the faculty of judgment was not the "aestheticization" of the political, as has often been alleged (not by Bernstein), but on the contrary, the *politicization* of aesthetic judgment, a matter that she believed was inherent in Kant's own work. Worldloss has dire consequences for action and therefore politics, as Arendt made clear in her many analyses of totalitarianism. Could regaining a common world today be the condition through which a new politics, "a politics of natality" (as Jonathan Schell has called it), might be born, a politics in which the totalitarian outrages to humanity that first appeared in the twentieth century might at last be forsworn?

It is only a speculation that Arendt, in her unwritten work on *Judging*, would have dealt with the conditions of the possibility of a common modern world, but a speculation that can be supported by many things she said. To delve into them here would, unfortunately, take me too far afield from the task I have set myself.[4] What follows is divided into four parts: the first deals with the French Resistance, in a way that recalls but is different from Arendt's treatment of it in the preface to *Between Past and Future*. The second part recapitulates what I take to be Arendt's understanding of Kantian aesthetic judgment. The third part gives several examples of my own understanding of aesthetic judgment. The fourth and final part deals with the contemporary world, briefly with what preceded it in Hegel's hugely ambitious and failed account of world history, and with Walter Benjamin's criticism of historicism that, I believe, partly led Arendt to her interpretation of Kant. I am not concerned in this paper to defend Arendt's interpretation of Kant or anyone else, because that would be irrelevant to what she was about: she thought with and against others in order to form her own convictions and come to her own conclusions. Moreover, I will hardly even mention Arendt in what follows. I am wary, frankly, of appearing to attribute to her what is only my speculation. Although

I use many of her own quotations, especially from Kant and to a
lesser extent from René Char and Walter Benjamin, I will not identify them in her writings, since my argument is not explicitly hers.

I want to emphasize, again, that I am not suggesting that Arendt's
book on *Judging* would have been anything like an aesthetics, although in it I believe she might well have considered Merleau–
Ponty's uncompleted philosophy of art. Merleau–Ponty is a thinker
she never paid much attention to until she wrote *Thinking*, the
first volume of her posthumously published *The Life of the Mind*.
There she shows interest in his notion of *chiasme*, the intertwining
or overlapping of mind and body. And many remarks in his very
late and dense essay, *L'Oeil et l'esprit*—for instance that "vision is
a mirror or concentration of the universe ... that ... by virtue of
vision ... the *idios kosmos* opens ... upon a *koinos kosmos*"; or that a
"painting ... [is able] to show ... how the world becomes world";
or that "[t]he world is in accordance with my perspective *in order*
to be independent of me, is for me *in order* to be without me, and
to be the world;" or, quoting Giacometti, "'What interests me in all
paintings is resemblance [which in what follows I shall call "correspondence"]—that is, what resemblance is for me: that which
makes me discover more of the world'"[5]—are entirely apropos to
what I believe would have been Arendt's concerns in her unwritten
volume. In a late note in her *Denktagebuch* (1970) she wrote: "The
sixth sense: judgment—discovered in judging art," where the oper-
ative word is *discovered*.

I

Let me begin, then, with the *evanescence* of a public or common
world as it appeared briefly and unexpectedly in the middle of the
twentieth century, and with the possibility of apprehending that
world today. The poet René Char condensed his experience fighting with the French Resistance during World War II into a long series of aphorisms, written furtively in the heat of combat between
1943 and 1944. There he speaks of images in the common language
of the *maquisards*, unintelligible to outsiders, which, in contrast to
"merely picturesque *argot*" came forth from "the sense of wonder

communicated by the beings and things (*les êtres et les choses*) we live with in continual intimacy."[6] The next aphorism (*FH*, p. 62) reads: *Notre héritage n'est précédé d'aucun testament* ("Our inheritance was left to us by no testament"). Which is to say that what these men experienced and invented new names for emerged from the past but was not handed down (*traditio*) to them: it *appeared* and astonished them—much as the appearance of the immortal gods astonished Homer's heroes—in circumstances of "life and death" in which, Char realizes, "Word, storm, ice, and blood will form, in the end, a common frost" (*FH*, pp. 38, 58).

It is possible to read at least some of Char's aphorisms literally, as if they defined (*aphoridzein*) quotidian existence by revealing a world beyond its limits (*apo-horidzein*). My point is not, however, that there were two different worlds existing simultaneously then or ever, but that the world shared by these Resistance fighters opened up to them within their familiar world, and, further, that if that world can be apprehended today it is because it has been carried over (*metapherein*) into our world by the enduring correspondences of human art. It may be noted that the cares and aspirations of ordinary life in the Third Republic prior to the war held little interest for Char, a profoundly introspective poet, and only with the collapse of France, in the face of the Nazi invasion, did he find the "treasure" (*FH*, p. 195) that all the while had been waiting to be discovered. Hidden in the contingencies of action, the treasure of freedom related Char to his fellowmen in a way he had never known before:

I love those so much enamoured of what their hearts imagine freedom to be, that they sacrifice themselves to keep the little freedom there is from dying. Wonderful, the virtue of common people! (Free will may not exist. Maybe man is to be defined in terms of his cells, his heredity, the brief or prolonged course of his destiny.... Yet, between *all that* and Man there is an enclave of metamorphoses and unpredictables; its entrance must be guarded, it must be maintained.) (*FH*, p. 155)

Hardly even aware of what was happening to them, these comrades-in-arms encountered one another directly, not in the roles they had previously played, sometimes even as outcasts, in the strata of French society, nor in the "prejudices" or "conventional ideas" of what they had come to see as a "shipwrecked civilization" (*FH*, p. 38). Social roles and distinctions as such, "the mediocre turntable of their lives" (*FH*, p. 150), had become irrelevant, and even their personal lives and self-love—Char's "notes owe nothing to self-love" (*FH*, p. 87)—lacked substance when weighed against their newfound equality.

Because they knew each other as peers in the midst of their mutually engaged struggle, Char writes of a

man with no schooling, but grown great under difficulties, as kind as fine weather, [whose] diagnoses were infallible. His conduct was informed with stirring boldness.... He carried his forty-five years vertically, like a tree of freedom. I loved him without show, without undue stress. Unshakeably. (*FH*, p. 157)

The aphorist is

grateful for the good luck that brought the outlaws of Provence to fight on our side. The instinct for the woods in these primitives, their canny foresight, their keen flare in every kind of weather—I would be surprised at any failure from them. I shall see to it that they have shoes like the gods! (*FH*, p. 79)

He becomes aware that his comrades lack any "trace of the stages so often gone through by their fathers," that "the vise of our descent is losing its hold" (*FH*, p. 123). His "heart is glad ... to have a meal with the Bardouins, to shake hands with Marius the printer.... This rock-hold of fine people is a citadel of friendship" (*FH*, p. 17). The equality of the *maquisards* meant not that they were interchangeable, but that as singular individuals they had come to depend on and, more important, to trust each other. "Keep with others what you have promised yourself alone. That is your contract" (*FH*, p. 161). For the first time a man who "joined the Resistance *found* himself" and was no longer a mere "carping, suspicious actor of his life, poisoned with insincerity.... Now he is in *love*, he spends himself, he is *engagé*, he goes naked, he challenges" (*FH*, p. 30). Hypnos, that is, Char himself, awoke and "became fire" (*FH*, p. 87): "Between the world of reality and me today there is no more sad opaqueness (*épaisseur triste*)" (*FH*, p. 188). "The rare moments of freedom," he writes, "are these during which the unconscious becomes conscious" (*FH*, p. 170). "Within our darkness there is not one place for Beauty. The entire place is for Beauty" (*FH*, p. 237).

A strange aspect of their common world was that upon discovering its hidden treasure the *maquisards* were themselves forced to hide. In this respect their experience differed from that of the millions of regular soldiers who were mobilized and organized with the sole intention of destroying the enemy. Precisely not as representatives of an officially recognized government, or party, or even an army, but in the dark of hiding the world that lay between them, binding them together to fight not just against but *for* something, was constituted. While calculating "the arithmetic of situations" their hideout became sacred to them (*Homodépôt sacré, FH*, p. 87), and only there, with "no contact outside the network," their freedom became actual and with it their capacity to transcend their own interests for the real interest of France. "France-in-Caves" reads one of Char's aphorisms in its entirety (*FH*, p. 124).

But at the same time the darkness of their hidden world was illuminated from within by a light much older than itself. Char writes that, pinned to the wall of his hideout, a color reproduction of Georges de la Tour's *Prisonnier* (fig. 12.1)

seems with time to reflect its meaning on our situation. It chokes the heart, but how it quenches thirst! For two years, not a single partisan has come through that door without his eyes being burnt by the meaning of this candle. The woman is explaining, the prisoner listening. The words falling from this terrestrial silhouette of a red angel are essential words, they help at once. Deep in the dungeon, the tallow minutes of light trace and dissolve the features of the sitting man. Skinny as a dry nettle, he has no memory to shake him. The bowl is a ruin. But the swollen gown suddenly fills the whole dungeon. The Word of the woman gives birth to the unhoped-for, better than any dawn.

Char gives thanks to Georges de la Tour for having "overpowered the Hitlerian night with a dialogue between human beings" (*FH*, p. 178).

A still stranger aspect of the world of the *maquisards* is Char's realization that those of them who survive the cessation of hostilities will have to "break with the aroma of these essential years, silently reject" their "treasure," not merely "repress" (*refouler*) it (*FH*,

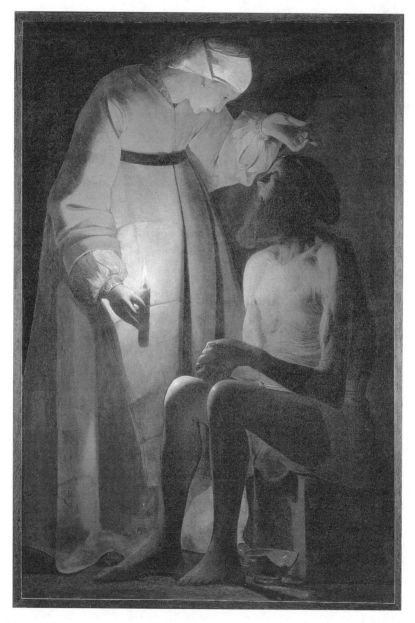

Figure 12.1
Georges de La Tour, *Prisonnier*. Musee Departemental des Vosges, Epinal, France.
Photo by Erich Lessing/Art Resource, New York.

p. 195). He knows that he himself will "go back to the beginning of my most destitute ... quest of myself, without confidence, in naked unsatisfaction." But this sounds paradoxical, for why should the liberation of France, for which these "executors of justice" (*FH*, pp. 211, 217) had struggled, become the condition of their loss of freedom? Had not the men of the Resistance acted together in order to liberate France from both traitors and invaders, from "that army of cowards, with their appetite for dictatorship" (*FH*, p. 20) as well as the Nazis? Why should the overriding purpose of the life they shared, which was to awaken the "drifting wreckage" of France from "her siesta" (*FH*, p. 24), whether successful or not, end in oblivion of what it had meant to them? Char expects that the "coqs of the Void will crow in our ears, once the liberation has come" (*FH*, p. 65), but he also foresees

that our comfortable unanimity, our rabid hunger for justice will be short-lived when the tie is gone that has bound us in combat. . . . We will be quick to forget. We will quit throwing out rubbish, cutting away and healing. (*FH*, p. 220)

He sees not only that the hidden world in which the men of the Resistance found the treasure of freedom in action will disappear at the moment of liberation, which after all is obvious, but that the sense of its *reality* will vanish from their lives as if it had never existed.

The most mysterious aspect of that lost world is the possibility that it can be retrieved today by contemplating the image of its meaning in la Tour's three-hundred-and-seventy-year-old painting and hearkening to the correspondence of that image in what Char wrote of it, which is not a commentary on the painting but his recognition of "the enigma of the flame itself."[7] That possibility is not due to anything like empathy, as if we could feel what the *maquisards* felt, for, as Char puts it in perhaps the most trenchant of his aphorisms, the freedom that these men experienced in action "has worth only for the dead, completion only in the minds that inherit and question it" (*FH*, p. 187). If we can *apprehend* the reality of their experience it is because "the enigma of the flame," revealed in the painting and centuries later disclosed in the poet's words, is preserved in the vast structure of human memory, inert until it is quickened by the faculty of imagination.

II

In the eighteenth century the philosopher Immanuel Kant, convinced that he lived in "an age of enlightenment,"[8] found shocking the implication of the old saying *De gustibus non disputandum est,* that is, that aesthetic judgments are severed from reason and left to the arbitrariness of subjective taste. Earlier, during the precritical period of his thought, in his *Observations on the Feeling of the Beautiful and Sublime* (1764), Kant had subscribed to a version of the then current opinion that aesthetic judgments are not "objective" as they would be if they were wholly determined by their object. But in his *Critique of Judgment,* written some twenty-five years later and regarded by him as the culmination of his critical philosophy, Kant reconsidered the entire question of taste in his examination of the human faculty of judgment (*Urteilskraft*), a project he had left more or less hanging in the first two *Critiques.* In the first part of the *Critique of Judgment,* he found that aesthetic judgments revealed the truly extraordinary power of the human mind to judge particulars in their contingent particularity, without subsuming them under any concept, and yet without making them subjectively arbitrary either. It is the phenomenal reality of a particular rose that we judge when we agree that it is beautiful.

To Kant what we generally think of as practical common sense was a sixth sense that unites the sensations of the five other senses and thereby orientates living creatures in the world. What he discovered was that only in human beings the possibility of their specific common sense, *their* orientation in the world, depends on a distinct mental capacity, a different common sense that he distinguished by calling it in Latin *sensus communis,* and that it, rather than what is subjectively felt, is the ground from which aesthetic judgments arise. By *sensus communis* he meant a sense that all human beings, human beings as such, have in common; it is the source of human *communication,* that is, speech, the *communicability* of subjective feelings, and thus of human *community. Judgments* of taste are not of everything sensuously experienced (*aisthēsis*), but of what the *sensus communis*, through the faculty of imagination, represents and discriminates as fit or unfit to appear in a common world, a world that a community of judges would be pleased to share with one another. Aesthetic judgments are thus reflective, and when exercised what they reflect is other subjects, not only those who are present but also those who are no longer or not yet present. In this sense aesthetic reflective judgment is limited only by the earth and bound only by the past and future dimensions of historical time.

What such judgment requires is an "enlarged mentality" (*eine erweiterte Denkungsart*), an act of the imagination that considers not only actual but also possible points of view,[9] that is, ways taken and ways not (or not yet) taken. When Kant inquired into the realm of aesthetics he found that the judge, the contemplative preserver of works of art, is never alone; or, to put the same thing differently, that aesthetic reflective judgments are *inter-subjective*. By the same token aesthetic judgment epitomizes human reason, the nature of which, as Kant wrote in his reflections on anthropology when the question "What is man?" was uppermost in his mind, is not "to isolate itself but to get into community with others."[10] Today Kant's understanding of aesthetic judgment is important in at least five related respects. It is autonomous in that it does not subsume what it judges under traditional or canonical categories, nor under a universal concept of beauty; it claims, or, as Kant says "courts" or "woos" general agreement, since its validity is not apodictic but exemplary; it pleases in the sheer act of judging the appearances of the world, past or present, natural or man-made; it purports to be the basis of a community that is capable of indefinite expansion in the future; and, crucially, it cannot be taught but only practiced.

Kant formally defined what we mean by beauty as "the form of the purposiveness of an object, so far as this is perceived in it without any representation of a purpose"; and what we judge to be beautiful as "that which without any concept is cognized as the object of a necessary satisfaction."[11] These definitions incorporate what has already been said, and also add to it. Taking the second definition first, to cognize an object as a necessary satisfaction without any concept means that when I judge something in nature or art to be beautiful, I am saying something like "Ah, this in fact delights me, but I cannot yet tell you why it delights me." The implication of the perception of the form of purposiveness in an object that does not represent any specific purpose is that the *appearance* of beauty in the world is meaningful in itself, immediately, before understanding what it may mean or what it may be good for. The difficulty in grasping these definitions is that Kant is referring to the *activity* of judging aesthetically. Afterwards we may start talking about a non-utilitarian purpose, as I am doing here; or when we dispute each other's judgments of taste, as we constantly do, in that contestation we will have to employ concepts, a fact Kant notes when he writes of the "antinomy" of aesthetic judgment.[12] But such purposes and concepts arise from further reflection and are not the basis of the autonomous activity itself. In this sense, and in keeping with Kant's insistence on the role of reason in aesthetic judgments, we might say that artworks are "thought things," not meaning thereby that they are first thought out and then fashioned into objects, which is certainly not always if ever the case, but that in them *mental activity itself is reified.* Cézanne, who knew a lot about this matter, once said that the painter "thinks in painting."[13] How this happens remains ultimately, even for Kant, a mystery of the faculty of imagination, "an art concealed in the depths of the human soul,"[14] but *that* it happens is beyond question.

The autonomous activity of judging aesthetically *depends* on the presence of others, whether they are members of an extant community or, which is at least as important, of a community housed in memory, a *re-membered* community that is no longer present to the senses but *re-presented* by the imagination. Moreover, since no two standpoints, that is, the contingent conditions of a human being's existence in the world, are ever the same, the activity of judging aesthetically expresses—literally presses out from within—the uniqueness of the judge. And since, as we have seen, communicability is the essence of the *sensus communis*, that uniqueness appears in the world as the common quality of a community of judges. Of all the world's appearances beautiful works of art shine forth most, and, if anything, shine forth more distinctly with the passage of time. In aesthetic judgment the past is present to the judge and articulate, not in the sense of responding to specific questions, but by replying, folding back, and resonating through the course of his life. The contemplation of works of art, in addition, arrests the speed of time, a well-known phenomenon, usually and not wrongly thought of as being "taken out of oneself." In aesthetic judgment the world takes precedence over the exigencies, the needs and necessities, of the processes of life, and in that sense the act of judgment is experienced as *being free.*

Of all human artifacts artworks are also the most durable, for they cannot be altered or destroyed. This does not mean that artworks cannot be lost or defaced, or used in a nonaesthetic sense (a painting can be used to hide a hole in a wall), but that aesthetic judgment comprehends its object as a promise made to the world and, moreover, a promise that has already been kept. The community of judges, to whom the notion that artworks are hermetically sealed aesthetic objects existing in a "world" of their own is a contradiction in terms, erases the arbitrariness of subjective taste. That community, striving to agree on what is beautiful and fit to appear in the world, also comprises the creator of enduring works of art. In Kant's felicitous phrase, taste, that is, judgment, "clips the wings" of genius,[15] for the communicability of the beautiful image *is* its reality in the only world there is.

The enduring reality of works of art gives depth to the world, a depth that can and has been explained in many different ways. What matters here is its experience as an immediate pleasure, not the fleeting satisfaction of desire but the "harmonious" operation of our mental faculties "in their freedom."[16] This pleasure is experienced, for example, in the discovery of a particular correspondence that at once preserves the past, deepens the present, and by being pleasant affords reconciliation to the world in which we live, whatever it may be. Kant calls this pleasure "disinterested joy" (*uninteressiertes Wohlgefallen*), a joy experienced when desire, appetite, and considerations of self-interest in general are laid aside or "distanced." To share a common world means to be conscious of being both *in* and *of* a world, the memory of which is anterior to its

Jerome Kohn

existence. Such a world would be a human artifice, made and *judged*
fit for human habitation, a world that in memory, revived by the
imagination, is always already there, prior to its experience in the
present and its potential experience in the future. The nature of
a common world is to grow, to enlarge, to encompass succeeding
generations through the accumulation of its realized correspondences. These correspondences not only provide the present world
with its dimension of depth but also, looked at from the standpoint
of those who have not yet appeared in it, with the sense of its continuity. Or so it seemed to Kant, the greatest thinker of the Age of
Enlightenment, which for him was also an "age of criticism."[17]

III

As an example of Kantian aesthetic judgment let us consider Piero
della Francesca's *Resurrezione* (fig. 12.2). Of course what we see here
is a reproduction, only a reminder of the remarkably well-preserved
original fresco now housed in the Pinacoteca Comunale in San
Sepolcro, the small town in the center of the Italian peninsula
where Piero was born in the fifteenth century. Aldous Huxley called
the *Resurrezione* the "best" and "greatest" painting in the world,[18]
and so it has often seemed to me, though not primarily for the art
historical reasons he offers, however subtle and accurate they may
be. Huxley sees this painting as the consummation of Renaissance
art, surpassing in beauty the classical ideal of the human figure
to which, he believes, it corresponds: "It is the resurrection of the
classical ideal, incredibly much grander and more beautiful than
the classical reality, from the tomb where it had lain so many hundred years."[19] Piero's *Resurrezione* (circa 1463) is unlike any other
depiction of the Resurrection I have seen, most of which portray
the risen Christ overwhelming the soldiers guarding the tomb with
a spiritual, transcendent power immeasurably greater than their
temporal force.[20]

In Piero's fresco the soldiers in the foreground, lying before and
in part obscuring the tomb, are not in flight but asleep, lost in the
soundest sleep imaginable. This might suggest that they inhabit a

Figure 12.2
Piero della Francesca, *Resurrezione*. Pinacoteca Comunale, Sansepolcro, Italy. Photo by Alinari/Art Resource, New York.

different world from that of the massive Christ behind and above them, except that one of them, the only one both of whose closed eyes are shown, is thought to be a self-portrait of the painter. It is as if Piero intended his viewers to contemplate less the depiction of a supernatural event than his dream of what it meant to him. Here the power of the Christ is divorced from any relationship to force. His left leg is raised and the foot planted firmly atop the tomb, as though Piero painted the actual rising, yet there is no suggestion of motion. Of the trees in the background the ones on the left, facing the painting, are barren, while those on the right are green with life, symbolizing death and rebirth, but without any indication of passing time or changing season. The soldiers below and the trees behind direct attention to the Christ who faces full forward, in the direct center of the painting, his open eyes staring into those of the viewer. If the contemplative viewer does not refuse that regard and stares back, he will become transfixed, seized by an unalterable vision. It then may happen that the meaning of that vision will be communicated as an injunction to *wake up*. In contemplation, that is, with his mental faculties operating harmoniously, the viewer then may *think* that he himself has been asleep and *enter* the painting in fellowship with the soldier mentioned above, presumably Piero himself. If the viewer remains in contemplation, before but also in the world of the painting, he then may slowly begin to slough off sleep. I cannot doubt that this was Piero's intention, for over and over this inner awakening, even in recollection, has provided an intense experience of joy, not of the senses alone but of the senses interwoven with the mind.

What I am now trying to communicate has nothing to do with any religious teaching or metaphysical theory about another world. Far from that, Piero's painting has awakened me to the actual world in which I live. When I first looked at this painting I was prepared to see a beautiful image but not to find within my world the possibility of a nonbarbarous world, a world that literally "interests" me insofar as it is between (*inter esse*) me and my fellowman. Nothing in that world has changed except my *self*-interest. The unsatisfiable desire to satisfy desires has indeed changed and become a will, intermittent but strong, to *realize* the commonality of this world by sharing it with others, the only way that can be done.

But at this point it may well be asked: "Is not this vision of a world discovered in a painting simply a fantasy, itself nothing but a dream?" And it may well be argued: "In reality there is no correspondence of that world with the world that you are actually *in* and *of*, which is an unjust, violent, and fragmented world, the very opposite of a common world." All of us have certainly had occasion to doubt, radically, the communicability of our world, and may at times have wondered if our conception of a "world" is not solipsistic and each one of us a nomad, wandering in a desert, a word derived from the Latin *deserere*, a verb signifying separation, unconnectedness, and abandonment. We live, to be sure, in an economically dependant and technologically shrunken world, but have we become humanly related and neighborly in this imposed closeness? Are we not today in fact less linked to our past, and also less confident of what the future holds in store for us than perhaps ever before?

A more complex example of aesthetic judgment, together with its correspondences, may reply to some of these questions. This reproduction (fig. 12.3) is of a painting that has also often appeared to me as the greatest and most beautiful in the world. Goya painted this dog half-submerged in sunlight or golden phosphorescence in the 1820s. Thus it falls among the "black" paintings he made when the Enlightenment and the proclamation of The Rights of Man at the beginning of the French Revolution had been followed by the Terror and the horrors of the Imperial Wars in Spain, which Goya had already recorded in the series of prints known as *Los desastres de la guerra*. The darkness of the black paintings, for example that of two men cudgeling each other even as they sink into and are swallowed by slime, seems to foresee the darkness that descended on the world in the twentieth century, the darkness of human domination in whose shadow we live today.[21] What endures in the *Perro* is the image of a dog that is more human than the men and women Goya painted in the black paintings. This dog is ineffably faithful, not in the sense of inarticulate canine fidelity or the unspoken

Figure 12.3
Goya y Lucientes, *Perro*. Museo del Prado, Madrid, Spain. Photo by Scala/Art
Resource, New York.

fidelity of lovers, but in the sense of *being true* apart from which human life itself becomes a lie: not an ordinary lie that attempts to convince others of what the liar knows is untrue, but the *self-deception* that, according to Kant, is "wickedness," "the corruption of the human heart," and the root of evil.[22] It is not a question of being loyal to someone or something, for "[n]obody and nothing are aware of the dog's existence."[23] We are shown the dog's head, whose eyes seem to be looking in interminate space for a world that is no longer, or not yet there.

Among the correspondences of this great painting one might mention, first, Goethe's roughly contemporary lines that appear late in the second part of *Faust*, which unlike the more familiar first part is filled with verbs in the subjunctive mood, the mood of aspiration rather than achievement:

Könnt' ich Magie von meinen Pfad entfernen,
Die Zaubersprüche gans und gern verlernen,
Stünd' ich Natur vor Dir, ein Mann allein,
Da wär's der Mühe wert ein Mensch zu sein.[24]
(If I could remove magic from my path,
All charms and spells utterly forget,
If I could stand before nature as only human,
Then it would be worth the pain to be a man.)

By showing a *dog* doing just that Goya illuminates the meaning of those lines, namely, that to stand before nature *only* as a human being and not as a wielder of instruments of force and control lies beyond the reach of Faust and modern men in general. Next, and not dissimilarly, the philosopher Emmanuel Lévinas tells a story of his own experience in the abortive defense of France against the Nazi onslaught at the beginning of World War II. He was taken prisoner and interned in a camp in Germany for Jewish soldiers. It was not a death camp, but nevertheless, since the prisoners were no longer regarded as human beings by their captors, he felt stripped of his humanity. One day a dog strayed into the camp, and returned the following day and on each succeeding day. Everyday it greeted the prisoners returning from their labors with a friendly bark, which made them feel that the dog still recognized their humanity. At least until the guards chased the dog out of the camp, at which point, as Lévinas says, "the last Kantian in Nazi Germany" went on its way.[25]

Goya's painting also has correspondences in two contemporary novels, *The Stone Raft* and *Blindness*, by the Portuguese writer José Saramago. In *The Stone Raft* a seemingly bizarre dog who may, like Cerberus, come from the mouth of hell, has no name and all names. It is called Dog, Constant, Faithful, Ardent, and Pilot; it is protean, changes shape, and at times "glows like a jewel" and seems to be "made of gold." In this fantastic tale of the Iberian Peninsula breaking free and drifting away from Europe, a bittersweet parable of a common Europe, it is the dog that guides the human beings to safety. It is *they* who accompany *it*, and its surefootedness, which they lack, seems too certain to be mere instinct. It can no more be explained, Saramago writes, than "the formation of the universe," and in that sense the dog may be read as a parody of "universal" man. But Saramago's story is much more than a parody, for the seemingly supernatural events recounted in this novel are a metaphor for the contingency of the world, which the human characters' superstitious beliefs—Joaquim Sassa's throwing a stone into the sea, Pedro Orce's making the earth tremble with his feet, Joana Carda's drawing a line that cuts the earth in two, and José Anaiço's following of flocks of starlings—purport to "explain." Yet to *experience* the contingency and unpredictability of what actually happens, which even if it can be understood backward is always lived forward, defies any kind of causal explanation. In other words, *not contingency but necessity* stands opposed to the free act of judgment. The dog, rather than those it leads, judges, and in so doing exemplifies humanity in the present world.[26]

Blindness on the other hand is a terrifying parable, on many levels, of the opaqueness of the shadow of total domination cast on our world. Yet here the loss of the ability to see, for which no physiological or neurological explanation can be found, does not result in darkness: on the contrary, in this blindness night and with it rest have been abolished. The nameless blind (there are no names in this novel) are radically disoriented, but their blindness is *white*, as if they "had plunged with eyes wide open into a sea of milk." At first they are interned, brutally guarded, and segregated in an old and now defunct mental hospital, isolated from their city, their fellowmen, and any semblance of the rule of law. The only rules are those of indignity, murder, and destruction. This blindness, however, though not in any medical sense a contagious disease, cannot be contained. Sooner or later it overtakes everyone, including the guards, and the entire city becomes a place of confinement, without hope, cut off from a world that no longer exists: in short, hell on earth, a sort of "natural" concentration camp.

The only character, the wife of the ophthalmologist, who does not lose her sight *sees* the blindness of the others and realizes the loneliness of not *being seen*, except by "the dog of tears." There is nothing extraordinary about this dog, "an animal of the human type," a natural scavenger though not rapacious, "gruff" and "ill-tempered" unless it is drying someone's tears. Followed and protected by the dog, the doctor's wife serves some of the blind ("the girl with dark glasses, the old man with the black eyepatch, the boy with the squint, the wife of the first blind man, her husband, and the doctor") who except for her would be like the rest of the blind, a pack of nomadic animals wandering through the city, consuming the food they stumble on or sniff out, leaving nothing but their waste behind them as they move on in search of more food, transforming a modern city into a wilderness. At the end of the tale, as the blind suddenly regain their sight and slowly return to the norms and practices of their previous existences, the woman understands that none of them, including herself, has ever known a world in which they are related and distinguished (as Arendt would say) as human beings. What she understands makes her weep, and Saramago writes: "it is not that she no longer loved her husband, it is not that she did not wish them all well, but at that moment her feeling of loneliness was so intense, so unbearable, that it seemed to her that it could be overcome only by the strange thirst with which the dog drank her tears."[27] She is not estranged from her husband or the others, but in her extreme loneliness, in her realization that the world lying between them has been *obscured* by their sense of sight, for which the white blindness is a metaphor, no man or woman but only an ordinary dog can console her.

IV

Since these remarks are about the possibility of establishing a common contemporary world, it may be permitted to ask what precisely is meant by "contemporary." Can cultural and political turning points, which seemingly draw a curtain across the past and form the present by summoning the future, be measured calendrically? In Goya's imagination, ironically, the egalitarian culture that was born with the French Revolution late in the eighteenth century perished only a few years into the nineteenth, due to the unintended results of the Napoleonic Empire. But it was explicitly "not the calendar" that the Russian poet Akhmatova had in mind when she spoke of "the real twentieth century." For better and worse, is not the way human beings live together and interact the ground from which every culture grows, which only after it has ended can be measured, with hindsight, in terms of historical time? If so, to consider the huge changes that occurred in the world with the eruption of World War I, changes that still persist, is to conclude that the world that came into being in 1914 has not yet ended.

The American expatriate novelist Henry James experienced the transition from the nineteenth to "the real twentieth century" and described it vividly in a letter to a friend written at the outbreak of war:

The plunge of civilization into this abyss of blood and darkness ... is a thing that so gives away the whole long age in which we have supposed the world to be ... gradually bettering, that to have to take it all now for what the treacherous years were all the while really making for and meaning is too tragic for any words.

If one considers the consequences of the devastation of total war after 1918, the uprooted, stateless, and unemployed masses of human beings, in short the existence of many millions of unwanted people, followed by the terrifying totalitarian "answer" to the predicaments of those people, then it is hard not to be as baffled today as James was in 1914 about the "meaning" of a world thought to be "gradually bettering" *and* that fell into an "abyss of blood and darkness."

The belief in progress, the gradual betterment of the world, was most fully elaborated more than a generation after Kant in Hegel's philosophy of history, according to which the process of the development of the world is determined by *Geist*, by mind or spirit. For the first time with Hegel *history* became the central concept of a metaphysical system whose truth resides in the course of time rather than in eternal being, a truth that is revealed in the *progression* of successive cultures. Thus Hegel took human affairs in their phenomenality, in their appearance and disappearance, more seriously than any previous philosopher had done, and modern historical consciousness, beginning with the nineteenth century's obsession with historicism, whether or not it expresses itself in the terms that Hegel himself employed, implicitly shares with him the belief that mind or spirit, the very principle of intelligibility, is temporal.

Hegel sees *Geist* not only as moving in time, however, but also as *embedded* in change and growth, in evolution and, what matters most, in progress. History may indeed work itself out behind the backs of human beings, using them in what Hegel calls *die List der Vernunft*, the cunning or trickery of reason, but that means only that our consciousness of *Geist* is normally inadequate and not that *Geist* itself exists somewhere other than the human mind, in a suprahuman mind, for instance, or divine will. On the contrary, *Geist* both transcends and is immanent in the world, and becomes self-conscious, fully aware of itself, *only* in the human mind's capacity to know its own time and culture, which is what Hegel means when he names art, religion, and philosophy as the realms of Absolute Spirit. In the art of a period, as in its religion and philosophy, all seeming contingency is transformed into rational, that is, real necessity by the dialectical process of human thought (or at least of Hegel's thought) that does not merely reflect but is identical to the progress of *Geist* in the world.

Nowhere is Hegel's genius more apparent or his influence greater than in the realm of objective *Geist*, by which he means the history of human cultures. It is the common culture of a people that is concrete, and its individuals that are abstract, or, to put it another way, a given culture is the substance of which its individuals are merely accidents. As such, the plurality of cultures as they develop, decline, and vanish is the subject of historical inquiry, in which a common world or culture is the only true individual, the expression and embodiment of a *Volksgeist* or *Zeitgeist*. The spirit of a people or a time works itself out in a *pattern*, which in their needs and passions, and whether or not they are aware of it, the men and women of that culture develop. Which is to say that it has become the task of the backward looking historian not only to know what in fact has happened, but also to discern and disclose its historical significance. According to Hegel, human passion is the efficient cause that moves a *Volksgeist* and the significance of its pattern is the formal cause of that same movement. Hegel calls the latter "the warp, the other the woof, of the vast arras-web of universal history."[28] He himself is conscious, moreover, of a single thread running throughout history, which he calls the *Weltgeist*, the mind or spirit of the history of the entire world. In historical change the *Weltgeist* necessarily progresses in a line drawn through the spiral of dialectical thought: it can only progress because once a *Volksgeist* or *Zeitgeist* has expressed itself in its art, religion, and philosophy, "it has reached its goal" and "its fulfillment is also its passing away." But that passing away, according to Hegel, is itself "progress": "The fruit becomes seed once more, but the seed of another culture that it must ripen." To the philosopher of history, apart from the *Weltgeist* that binds the totality of cultures together in the march of human progress, all past cultures would be destined to "fall into random dustheaps."[29] Hegel's vision may be limited to what he calls "Germanic" or, roughly, European culture, and it is true that he speaks of other cultures in the past tense. But his point is that such cultures are *aufgehoben*—raised up, preserved, as well as negated—in the one culture or common world that he saw as the self-realization and self-fulfillment of humanity.

Yet when we turn to what is most significant in "the real twentieth century" we find that it is the *irrationality* of totalitarian movements, their quest for total power that in the end, in defiance of common sense, turned out to be nothing but an unprecedented potentiality for world destruction. That potentiality was not realized, and perhaps never could have been, but what I want to emphasize, because it is too easily forgotten, is the *success* of totalitarian experiments, conducted in the "laboratories" of concentration camps, both Nazi extermination camps and Stalin's slave labor camps, in robbing human beings of their status even as accidents of the substance of anything like a common or human world. In the camps men and women were made *superfluous*, their sole experience was of not belonging to the world at all, of having no place whatever in the world. All that the extermination and slave labor camps produced were corpses, *dead* men, women, and children on a massive scale, but what tends to be forgotten is that the number of victims and even their suffering, horrifying as they were, are not as unprecedented as the fact that Hitler and Stalin's "experiments" demonstrated that the nature of human beings—to be bearers of rights, ethical persons, and creative individuals, as Hegel believed—can be nullified. That is the meaning of the *total domination of man* and although it cannot be rationally understood, it happened, and is now an irrevocable fact of our world.

The "plunge" of the nineteenth century's belief in progress into the central events of "the real twentieth century" throws into radical doubt the notion of a *Weltgeist* that guides the course of history. Is it possible to understand the total domination of man as the necessary, progressive development of a principle of intelligibility? Does not the evidence refute the idea that mankind as a whole is inevitably progressing toward freedom, not only political freedom but also Hegel's notion of the mind's freedom to understand the rational necessity of whatever happens? When we consider ongoing acts of terrorism, with which we have become all too familiar; the growing numbers of uprooted and unwanted people throughout the world; the possibility of humanity's self-destruction, either quickly by nuclear or other weapons of mass destruction, or slowly by the reckless spoliation of the earth's natural resources; and, perhaps most ominous of all, the interference with human diversity that accompanies the advancing specter of genetic engineering, who of us has not wondered if anything makes sense anymore, or, which is much the same, if "the real twentieth century" is only now coming into its own?

What then can be said of the "commonality" of the world in which we live today? As only a few others have done, the poet Paul Celan tried over and over to imagine the living truth of the catastrophe that befell humanity under totalitarianism in its present correspondences. In a late poem, composed not long before his suicide, he asks:

*Wo bin ich
heut?*

(Where am I
today?)[30]

Perhaps no one has ever known *who* he is, but there have been times—one thinks of ancient Athens, for example, or René Char's short-lived experience in the Resistance—when individual uniqueness appeared in a common world and was recognized by others who shared that world.[31] But Celan's question does not ask *who* but *where* he is. In its lack of any decisive answer to that question the poem more than suggests, it *says* that life today is lived in exile from the world, in an *entwinkelten Stadt* (a "disangled town") ... *an Kommend-Entkommendem deutelnd* ("niggling at the coming-escaping," i.e., at death). No longer secure in the belief of an immutable human nature, we have been too long away and are too *alienated* from our natural home on earth to think that any possible destination in "the vast arras-web of universal history" can ever cover our separation from each other and from the world. Yet insofar as Celan's question corresponds to our experience we owe him thanks, much as Char gave thanks to Georges de la Tour, for attempting to make speech, not mere talk but *human communication*, live again. Paul Celan's art was an oasis in a world he recognized to be a desert and, although ultimately that oasis could not sustain his life, until the end he fashioned difficult images that befit the unprecedented horrors of "the real twentieth century." Even as he drowned himself Celan held those images out, not as guideposts, but as emblems that somehow lighten the obscurity that beclouds our minds when we wonder where we are today.

It may be of some help, finally, to consider Walter Benjamin, who was neither a poet or a philosopher but called himself a literary critic. Yet he was not that either in any conventional sense of the term, which is readily seen in the same passage referred to earlier, the beginning of his essay on Goethe's *Elective Affinities*, published in 1924 when Benjamin was in his early thirties. He writes there of "critical judgment," a term redolent of Kant, and says that its "criterion" lies in the answer to "the basic question of all criticism": whether an artwork's "shining truth content is due to its subject matter or whether the survival of the subject matter is due to the truth content." As already noted, he likened the critic to an "alchemist" whose sole concern is to transmute the "subject matter" of an enduring work of art into "the living flame" of its truth.[32] Thus from the beginning it was clear that the tradition of historicism, which to Benjamin's critical eye meant tracing the continuity or continuous development of the "subject matter" of works of art, was essentially misguided.

There is another aspect of Benjamin's thought that is pertinent to these considerations: he was profoundly, if strangely, influenced by Karl Marx's vision of revolution, and aligned himself with "historical materialism." What that meant to Benjamin is nowhere more apparent than in his last datable work, completed in 1940, the year he took his own life when he was stopped from crossing the border from France into Spain while attempting to escape the Nazi persecution of Jews. That work, *Theses on the Philosophy of History*, is not a tract, as its title might suggest, but a series of highly idiosyncratic paragraphs. In one of them Benjamin writes: "The class struggle, which is always present to a historian influenced by Marx, is a fight for the crude and material things without which no refined and spiritual things could exist."[33] That sounds like pretty straightforward Marxism—the "substructure" as the ground of the "superstructure"—except that Benjamin goes on to say in the following paragraphs that "[t]he true picture of the past flits by. The past can be seized only as an image which flashes up at the instant when it can be recognized and is never seen again." In other words, "every image of the past that is not recognized by the present as one of its own concerns threatens to disappear irretrievably." There is no question here of knowing the past "as it really was," an abstraction, as the intact body of a dead moth is "abstracted" from its life;

the point is rather to seize and hold onto "a memory as it flashes up in a moment of danger." To Benjamin the task of the historical materialist is "to brush history against the grain," which in a sense again recalls Marx, except that for Benjamin human progress is anything but "irresistible" and in fact is only conceivable as a "progression through a homogeneous empty time" (*Theses*, V, VI, VII, XIII), merely a travelogue. One can only wonder what Marx would have made of that.

My last example will make clear, I hope, that Benjamin's view of history unites his understanding of criticism and revolution. Paul Klee's *Angelus Novus* (fig. 12.4) at one time belonged to Benjamin, who in the ninth of his *Theses on the Philosophy of History* interpreted it as follows:

A Klee painting named *Angelus Novus* shows an angel looking as though he is about to move away from something he is fixedly contemplating. His eyes are staring, his mouth is open, his wings are spread. This is how one pictures the angel of history. His face is turned toward the past. Where we perceive a chain of events, he sees one single catastrophe which keeps piling wreckage upon wreckage and hurls it in front of his feet. The angel would like to stay, awaken the dead, and make whole what has been smashed. But a storm is blowing from Paradise; it has got caught in his wings with such violence that the angel can no longer close them. This storm irresistibly propels him into the future to which his back is turned, while the pile of ruins before him grows skyward. This storm is what we call progress.

Klee's new angel, as Benjamin contemplates him, stares not at the viewer (as does Piero's risen Christ) but at the accumulation of historical events, which he perceives as a "single catastrophe." The angel is a sort of *flâneur*, as Benjamin himself was, an observer of the past in its passing, and although the angel would like to remain where he is, in the present, in order to make more than chronological sense of what has passed, he cannot. A storm "from Paradise," which "*we* call progress," gets "caught in his wings" and blows him backward "into the future," while the "pile of ruins" before him grows higher and higher. What this amounts to is no less than the direct opposite of a dialectical understanding of the course of history.

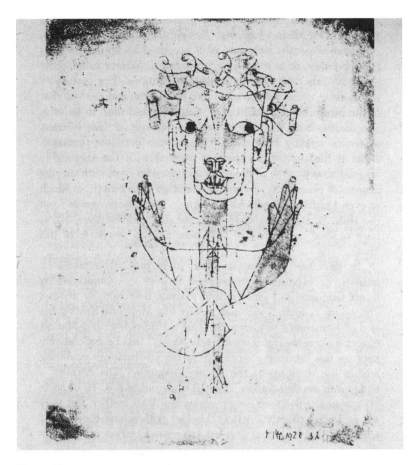

Figure 12.4
Paul Klee, *Angelus Novus.* The Israel Museum, Jerusalem, Israel. © 2003 Artists
Rights Society (ARS), New York/VG Bild-Kunst, Bonn.

For Benjamin, as he envisioned and practiced them, the tasks of the "historical materialist" and literary critic are similar. In neither case is the task "additive," neither seeks to "muster a mass of data to fill homogeneous empty time" (*Theses*, XVII) and both endeavor to "charge" time with "the presence of the *now* (*Jetztzeit*)," a "now ... blasted out of the continuum of history" (*Theses*, XIV). In other words the "historical materialist cannot do without the notion of a present which is not a transition, but in which time stands still and has come to a stop" (*Theses*, XVI). This *poetic* experience of time is, in a nutshell, how Benjamin understood revolution, both the French Revolution of the past, and the revolution that "every second of time" holds "in store;" "the straight gate through which the Messiah might enter" (*Theses*, B). As a critic of literature his task was likewise to disclose a *new past*, and to that end he collected not only events that stop time but also quotations that "are like robbers by the roadside who make an armed attack and relieve an idler [the *flâneur*] of his convictions."[34] Hence Benjamin's peculiar way of *preserving* the past by exploding its continuity is at once a way of *destroying* the present as heir of a tradition and of extricating it from the "wreckage upon wreckage" as seen by the angel of history. At any juncture of historical time, the apprehension of "new beauty in what is vanishing"[35] transmits a past that in its correspondences (Benjamin's "concerns") brings depth to the present. The revolutionary and the critic usher beautiful, that is, "useless" things into the world. These things, actions and quotations ripped from their context, are the "material" in Benjamin's notion of historical materialism and, so he believed, are capable of *transfiguring* the world and of redeeming mankind (cf. *Theses*, I, III, A, B).

Again, it is not the "subject matter" but the originality of thought (Kant's *Selbstdenken*) engendered by the work, that counts:

The genuine picture may be old, but the genuine thought is new. It is of the present. This present may be meager, granted. But no matter what it is like, one must firmly take it by the horns to be able to consult the past. It is the bull whose blood must fill the pit if the shades of the departed are to appear at its edge. (*Schriften* 2, p. 314)

This odd "historical materialist" thus retrieves, as the angel of history whose wings are caught in the storm of progress cannot, *fragments* from the ruins of the past. These fragments "awaken the dead" *without* making "whole what has been smashed." Having violated their original context, the "historical materialist" fits them into a surreal montage of correspondences whose "subject matter" may be neither decipherable nor communicable. "Art," says Benjamin, "posits man's physical and spiritual existence, but in none of its works is it concerned with his response. No poem is intended for the reader, no picture for the beholder, no symphony for the listener."[36] A genuine work of art, as a genuine action, is *for the world* and is its own enduring truth. The difficult and rare pleasure of keeping that truth alive in the modern, everyday flux of "curiosity and contrivance"[37] is what the critic would communicate if he could.

Be that as it may, can reflective aesthetic judgment point the way to the revival of a common world, a world in which nothing judged worth remembering is forgotten, a world not born from but nurtured by memory, Mnemosyne, the mother of the muses? That is the question I have tried to raise, and I suppose the answer must be that it is not likely; and that if our mental faculties do not operate harmoniously, if we fail to move freely among the appearances of our specifically human common sense, and if we cannot imagine *as its own end* the world that willy-nilly we build and rebuild between ourselves, listening in the great plurality of finite human stories for the turning points of its own unending story, hearkening to its *from*s and *toward*s, it will not be possible at all. This, I believe, is the root of the anxiety that Hannah Arendt always felt for the destiny, not of the modern age, but of the world in which we live today.[38]

Notes

1. Richard Bernstein, *Hannah Arendt and the Jewish Question* (Cambridge: Polity Press, 1996), pp. 171–172. This work will be cited hereafter in the text as *HAJQ.*

2. Hannah Arendt, *The Origins of Totalitarianism* (New York: Harcourt Brace Jovanovich, 1973), p. 468.

3. This may seem odd in view of the fact that Arendt had originally thought of calling her book *Amor Mundi*. As early as 1955, however, an entry in her *Denktagebuch* (Piper, 2002) asks: "*Amor Mundi—warum ist es so schwer, die Welt zu lieben?*" Arendt was neither a pessimist nor an optimist—she knew better than *ever* to predict the future—yet *The Human Condition* can hardly be said to reconcile its readers to the world in which they live. True, almost at the end of the book she writes of "the genuine experience of and love for the world," but she relegates this "worldliness" less to the modern actor than to the modern artist.

4. Among the most relevant of Arendt's texts are chapter 7, "The Public Realm: The Common," and chapter 23, "The Permanence of the World and the Work of Art," in *The Human Condition*. Also, when she quotes Kant as saying "The fact that man is affected by the sheer beauty of nature proves that he is made for and fits into this world"; or says herself in regard to Kant, "The *Critique of Judgment* is the only one of his great writings where his point of departure is the World and the senses and capabilities which make men in the plural fit to be inhabitants of it. This is perhaps not yet political philosophy, but it certainly is its condition *sine qua non*. If it could be found that in the capacities and regulative traffic and intercourse between men who are bound to each other by the common possession of a world there exists an *a priori* principle, then it would be proved that man is essentially a political being"—such remarks and many others are immensely suggestive.

5. *L'Oeil et l'esprit*, translated by C. Dallery as "Eye and Mind" in M. Merleau–Ponty, *The Primacy of Perception*, ed. J. M. Edie (Evanston, Ill.: Northwestern, 1964), pp. 165, 166, 181, 187. The translation has been slightly altered.

6. René Char, *Hypnos Waking*, trans. Jackson Mathews (New York: Random House, 1956). In part 4, "Leaves of Hypnos" (*Feuillets d'Hypnos*, dedicated to Albert Camus), from which all the quotations from Char are taken, these words occur in aphorism number 61. Hereafter the quotations will be identified in the text by *FH* followed by the number of the aphorism or page number. Occasionally the translations have been slightly altered.

7. In these words Walter Benjamin, at the beginning of his early essay on Goethe's *Elective Affinities*, metaphorically describes the task of the critic as distinct from that of the commentator. Likening the commentator to a chemist and the critic to an alchemist, he writes: "*Wo jenem Holz und Asche allein die Gegenstände seiner Analyse bleiben, bewahrt für diesen nur die Flamme selbst ein Rätsel: das des Lebendigen. So fragt der Kritiker nach der Wahrheit, deren lebendige Flamme fortbrennt über den schweren Scheitern des Gewesenen und der leichten Asche des Erlebten.*"

8. In his essay "An Answer to the Question: 'What is Enlightenment?'" Kant distinguishes between "an enlightened age" and an "age of enlightenment."

9. Immanuel Kant, *Critique of Judgment*, §40.

10. Immanuel Kant, *Reflexionen zur Anthropologie*, number 897, in *Gesammelte Schriften*, Hrsg. königlich preussischen Akademie der Wissenschaften (Berlin: Reimer, 1900), Bd. 15.

11. I. Kant, *Critique of Judgment*, §17, §22.

12. Ibid., §56.

13. Quoted by Merleau–Ponty, "Eye and Mind," p. 178.

14. I. Kant, *Critique of Pure Reason*, B180–181.

15. I. Kant, *Critique of Judgment*, §50.

16. Ibid., §39.

17. I. Kant, *Critique of Pure Reason*, Axi, note.

18. Aldous Huxley, *Along the Road* (London: Chatto and Windus, 1925), p. 178.

19. Ibid., p. 183.

20. Two exceptions come to mind. In the Frick Museum in New York there is a Resurrection by Francesco Botticini, painted a few years after Piero's and in some ways recalling it, except that Botticini's Christ hardly touches the sepulcher and is represented almost as if he were dancing on top of it. There is also Albrecht Dürer's famous engraving of the Resurrection from his series of *The Passion*, made half a century after Piero's fresco, an engraving of which Dürer might have seen in Venice. But Dürer's Christ, unlike Piero's, is surrounded by a nimbus or otherwordly radiance. Both these works represent what is said in Matthew (28:4): "the keepers [of the tomb] became as dead men." The fact is noteworthy that, essential as it is to their narratives, the Gospels do not describe the Resurrection.

21. Looking at this painting, *Riña a garatazos*, hung adjacent to the *Perro* in the Prado in Madrid, I find it impossible not to think of Hitler and Stalin.

22. Immanuel Kant, *Religion Within the Limits of Reason Alone*, book 1, trans. Theodore M. Greene and Hoyt H. Hudson (New York: Harper Torchbooks, 1960).

23. As Fred Licht says in his finely nuanced study, *Goya* (New York: Abbeville Press, 1979), p. 179.

24. These lines were to have been one of Arendt's epigraphs for her unwritten work on *Judging*.

25. Emmanuel Lévinas, *Difficile liberté* (Paris: A. Michel, 1976), p. 201. I am grateful to Judith Friedlander for first bringing this story to my attention.

26. José Saramago, *The Stone Raft* (New York: Harcourt Brace Jovanovich, 1995), *passim*.

27. José Saramago, *Blindness* (New York: Harcourt Brace Jovanovich, 1997), p. 323.

28. G. W. F. Hegel, *Introduction to the Lectures on the History of Philosophy*, trans. T. M. Knox and A. V. Miller (Oxford: Clarendon, 1985).

29. E. H. Gombrich, *In Search of Cultural History* (Oxford: Clarendon, 1969). I am grateful to Rochelle Gurstein for this quotation, which shows the tenacity among historically minded modernists (and so-called postmodernists, too) of the Hegelian assumption that the significance of the past lies in our dialectical understanding rather than in our judgment of the fruits of its self-awareness.

30. Thus begins an untitled poem first published in *Fadensonnen* in 1968. Celan died in 1970. The translation is by Pierre Joris, *Threadsuns* (Los Angeles, Calif.: Sun and Moon Press, 2000), p. 75.

31. The conditions of the common world of Athens are nowhere more clearly set forth than in Aristotle's *Nicomachean Ethics*, perhaps most clearly in his exquisite analyses of friendship in books 8 and 9. And Sophocles' *Oedipous Tyrannos* remains, in its choral odes, the classic example of the recognition of an individual who did not know who he was.

32. On a far lower level Benjamin's meaning becomes transparent in the almost invariable banality of adaptations of artworks—of novels into plays, plays into movies, etc.—that may seek to preserve the "truth" but succeed only in replicating the "subject matter" of the original.

33. *Theses on the Philosophy of History*, IV, in Walter Benjamin, *Illuminations* (New York: Schocken, 1973), p. 254. Hereafter quotations from the *Theses* will be identified in the text by Roman numeral or letter.

34. Walter Benjamin, *Schriften* 1 (Frankfurt am Main: Suhrkamp, 1955), p. 571, hereafter cited in the text as *Schriften* followed by volume and page number.

35. W. Benjamin, *Illuminations*, p. 87.

36. Ibid., p. 69.

37. M. Oakeshott, *The Voice of Poetry in the Conversation of Mankind* (London: Bowes and Bowes, 1959), p. 63 and passim.

38. Some years after her arrival in America, Arendt discovered a *potential* common world, which she discussed at length and qualified in her book *On Revolution* and many subsequent essays. But nowhere does she so clearly reveal the conditions of her discovery and love of that potential world as in the thick language of a poem she wrote in 1954 (the meaning of which runs parallel to Goethe's lines cited above): "*Ich lieb die Erde / so wie auf der Reise / den fremden Ort / und anders nicht.*"

13

Semprun and the Experience of Radical Evil

Carol L. Bernstein

In two epigraphs to *Literature or Life*, Jorge Semprun adopts a compressed and problematic perspective toward absolute forgetting and absolute evil. The first, more metaphysical quotation, comes from Maurice Blanchot: "Whoever wishes to remember must trust to oblivion, to the risk entailed in forgetting absolutely, and to this wonderful accident that memory now becomes." The second, from André Malraux, states: "I seek the crucial region of the soul where absolute Evil and fraternity clash." As gateways to narrative, the epigraphs seem to contradict one another. That is, whereas Blanchot makes memory's narrative potential dependent upon contingency, Malraux names the opponents in an ongoing epic battle, even though the *mise-en-scène* of the battle is not visible. His implied narrative scenario points either to the quest to arrive at the scene of the clash or the attempt to comprehend the battle itself: either way, absolute forgetting would not seem to allow even partial determinacy. Conceptually speaking, moreover, both citations belong to the domain of absolute antithesis, in which one must confront the opposite or impossible other of one's desire in order to arrive at what one values, here memory and fraternity. In the first, oblivion is the prior condition necessary for experiencing memory as a "wonderful accident." The archetype is a familiar one: lose everything—one's soul, life, memory—in order to regain everything. And here, the terms are as terrifying as any other dyad embraced by the archetype: insofar as memory is constitutive of one's being or identity, one must risk oblivion, perhaps more than once, and give oneself to the accidental in the hope that it will evoke some form of recollection. There is no comment from Semprun on whether accident will serve a re-collective or re-constitutive memory: the difference, as posttrauma studies affirm, entails no less than recovering one's former self or assuming a new one.[1]

If in the first instance, one must embrace risk and trust to what one cannot control, in the second one must identify and endure the "icy mystery"—Semprun's term—of radical evil in order to achieve fraternity.[2] Where the first calls for the erasure of memory, the second casts absolute evil as one agonist in the soul: it is not so very far from the Kantian conception of radical evil as an innate propensity, fostered by self-absorption or narcissism and thus the cause of evil actions.[3] While Kant focuses on the subjective in radical evil, however, Malraux makes the soul a battlefield in which "fraternity" appears as the external or social antagonist to an innate tendency. It is still possible, in this scenario, to look inward and uncover a propensity to evil as part of the human condition, balanced by a hybrid fraternity that is emotionally and conceptually innate but instantiated within a worldly horizon. What Malraux seems to be evoking verges on allegory, which, to be sure, is on fraternal terms with the apparent—and thus not necessarily obvious. But not oblivious either: to map such a narrative is not to trust in accidents. As condensed narrative or *psychomachia*, the aphorism still makes less than full sense for Semprun, for it isn't *propensities* that concern him so much as *experience*. "'What's essential ... is the experience of Evil.... You don't need concentration camps to know Evil. But here [in Buchenwald], this experience will turn out to have been crucial, and massive, invading everywhere, devouring everything.... It's the experience of radical Evil.'" Outer details and activities may form a catalogue of horrors, but they are, nevertheless, subordinate to the "experience" itself (*LL*, p. 88).

I name the paradoxes in these epigraphs not only to register their conceptual difficulties but also to introduce some of the narrative complexities of *Literature or Life*. Semprun's book is neither his first effort nor his last to draw on his experience at Buchenwald. Child of a Spanish diplomatic family that was exiled after the Spanish Civil War, Semprun was a student at the Lycée Henri–IV, preparing to study philosophy at the École Normale when World War II began. He joined the French resistance and was eventually captured and sent to Buchenwald, where he was imprisoned for eighteen months. His first novel, *Le grand voyage* (1963), treats the journey to Buchenwald, and the most recent, *Le mort qu'il faut* (2000), returns to the scene. The concentration camp becomes both the primal scene of evil and its accomplice death, and the scene of writing from which many of Semprun's subsequent works emerge.

More obviously than his other novels, *Literature or Life* seems to balance on the edge between memoir and novel: if the side of memoir is protected by the candid tones in which Semprun points out his fictional inventions (thus guarding the preserve of memory), the side of fiction is served by the intricate, labyrinthine structure of each chapter, which appears to advance by forms of association—what one might call calculated contingency—but nevertheless coils elegantly around itself. Each chapter ending, fully *in*formed by the preceding chain of representations, marks a return to the self that emerged at its beginning. How then, can Semprun entrust himself to oblivion—or embark on a quest in a literary work whose structure is if anything overdetermined? He seems to arrive too soon, in possession of a structural assurance that will underwrite his dangerous journey.

Writing in the present tense, Semprun makes April 1945 the focal point for times prior to and after the day of liberation. It is a point of simultaneous experience and reflection, so that Semprun proceeds with the double consciousness of survivor and memoirist. His experience at Buchenwald was, he claims, not "undescribable" but "unbearable." The challenge to him, as writer, is one of "recreation," for the "truth of ... testimony" requires artifice (p. 13). Is it artifice, then, that creates a space by collapsing time, creating links and associations, turning the unbearable into the imaginable?

Let us assume, however, that Semprun's apparent self-assurance and control over his narrative is not merely the result of a temporal distance from that primal scene in Buchenwald, imaged in the central square in which inmates gathered daily for roll call. When the recently liberated Semprun returns to Paris in 1945, his relations with literature, like his relations with women, seem doomed to frustration. We learn that he spends the next ten or fifteen years with the Spanish Communist resistance to Franco: the period is one in which action—or life—dominates. Only as he becomes disillusioned with Communism does the literary impulse reassert itself.

Suppose, however, we entertain the possibility that the alternatives are not as stark as the title implies, that there is something he isn't revealing, even to himself: that there is something missing. Suppose that the student of philosophy and nascent poet has been cloaking himself in political pursuits, and that both his wounded memory and his early inability to write seem to conspire against full self-realization. Suppose too that the opposition of the book's title—literature versus life—or art and ideas versus action—calls for an examination or resolution that will be deferred. Semprun's impassioned reflections and dialogues on philosophies of death and evil become a mode of holding experience at pen's length. Under these circumstances, the narrative refers less to choice than to overcoming or working through trauma. As trauma theorists note, trauma *happens* but is not *experienced.* Only when it does become available to consciousness, often after it is evoked by some related but nontraumatic event, does the initial event become an experience open to cognition and understanding. Properly speaking, Cathy Caruth claims, trauma is the *relation* between two temporally distanced events, the first suffered but not cognized, the second cognized but not immediately experienced.[4] In such an experiential framework, characterized by delays, inversions, and even latent contradictions, Semprun's epigraphs provide a cover story for another crisis, represented in the recurring challenges to philosophers and their accounts of experience and death, and by linguistic problems relating to their terms. Under these circumstances, the resistance fighter who is captured while carrying a new translation of Kant's *Religion within the Limits of Reason Alone* in his knapsack is not simply the soldier as intellectual, for Kant too must undergo the trials of Buchenwald.

I

In April 1945, newly liberated in Buchenwald, the narrator of *Literature or Life* encounters three allied officers: "They stand amazed

before me, and suddenly, in that terror-stricken gaze, I see myself
—in their horror" (p. 3). The triple emphasis in the sentence
(amazed, terror-stricken, horror), in the words that open the book,
grounds not only an experience common among Allied soldiers
as they liberated Nazi concentration camps, but also an encounter
with an individual who will serve as a conduit to the horrible sights
of massed bodies, dead or alive. How can one speak or write—as
the one who sees *or* the one who is seen—after that moment? As a
survivor, Semprun begins a narrative by speaking for himself: "For
two years, I had lived without a face. No mirrors, in Buchenwald. I
saw my body, its increasing emaciation, once a week, in the shower.
Faceless, that absurd body."

With this opening, Semprun sets forth lines of thought that will
constitute a major problematic in the book. First, the sensory register, here the horrified gaze, will never disappear: "But these men
aren't startled or intrigued. What I read in their eyes is fear" (p. 4).
Reading and looking, however, cannot be understood in their
everyday senses: "It must be my gaze, I conclude, that they find so
riveting. It's the horror of my gaze that I see reflected in their own.
And if their eyes are a mirror, then mine must look like those of a
madman." Semprun, for his part, identifies a perceptual distortion,
in which visuality has no connection to cognitive frameworks. His
response to the stare is a non sequitur: are the soldiers surprised at
the quiet of the woods? "'They say the smoke from the crematory
drove [the birds] away'" (p. 5). A strange mingling of sight, sound,
and smell: In this place, all sensory factors, stimuli, and responses
have changed radically. The senses swing wildly between deprivation and excess: there's no normality here. The sensorium itself,
locus of the capacity of the mind to respond to stimuli, is in radical disarray. For decades after, Semprun avers, the "strange and
haunting smell" of the crematory ovens, one that belonged to that
"primal event" and "foreign homeland" of Buchenwald requires
only "a single instant of distraction from oneself" to return: "The
strange smell would immediately invade the reality of memory. I
would be reborn there; I would die if returned to life there" (p. 7).
This smoke is unimaginable to all who did not experience it, for it
is not the smoke of "household gods" (p. 10). Semprun writes in

paradoxes: in the years to come, memory will be occupied by trifles, attention directed to "the shimmering opacity of life's offerings" (p. 6). If the smell were to return, he would "embrace and inhale" that odor (p. 7). Paradox, then, invades and persists in the realm of the senses.

But if the crematory smoke drives birds away, its cessation allows them to return. This is what Semprun exclaims over when he joins an American lieutenant for a drive to Goethe's home in Weimar, so close to Buchenwald. He is, he tells Lieutenant Rosenfeld, a philosophy student: a term he hasn't used since the man registering him upon imprisonment told him that that was not a profession: to be a student is not a way to survive. The lieutenant thinks that's a good opening to an account of the experience in the camp. Semprun thinks that's "anecdotal"; he wants to begin with the "essential part.... to go beyond the clear facts of this horror to get at the root of radical Evil, *das radikal Böse*":

Because the horror itself was not this Evil—not its essence, at least. The horror was only its raiment, its ornament, its ceremonial display. Its semblance, in a word. One could have spent hours testifying to the daily horror of the camp without touching upon the essence of this experience.... One could recount the story of any day at all ... the fatiguing labor, the constant hunger, the chronic lack of sleep, the persecution by the *Kapos*, the latrine duty, the floggings from the SS, the assembly-line work in munitions factories, the crematory smoke, the public executions, the endless roll calls in the winter snow, the exhaustion, the death of friends—yet never manage to deal with the essential thing, or reveal the icy mystery of this experience, its dark, shining truth: *la ténèbre qui nous était échue en partage*. The darkness that had fallen to our lot, throughout all eternity. Or rather, throughout all history. (*LL*, pp. 87–88)

It's not just evil, he adds: it's radical evil: *Das radikal Böse!* But then Semprun glosses Kant skeptically: for this evil is more than one of the designs "'of the freedom essential to the humanity of man'" (p. 88). What's essential about *this* [my emphasis] is "'that it will turn out to have been lived as the experience of death.... Because death is not something that we brushed up against.... We lived it.... We are not survivors, but ghosts, revenants.... it's not believable.... since death is, for rational thought, the only event that we can never experience individually.... That cannot be grasped except in the form of anguish, of foreboding or fatal longing.... In the future perfect tense, therefore.... And yet, we shall have lived the experience of death as a collective, and even fraternal experience, the foundation of our being-together.... Like a *Mit-sein-sum-Tode*'" (p. 89). Semprun's gloss upon radical evil as one sign of human freedom leads not only to the qualification of a collective experience of death, but to a Heideggerian perspective.

Semprun, then, has lived death—in the past tense: for example, the death of Maurice Halbwachs, who first used the term "collective memory," in the Little Camp (where Jews were imprisoned at Buchenwald, and where the Catholic sociologist was sent after protesting the deportation of his Jewish son-in-law); or the deaths of others, comrades and strangers, in the camp. When Semprun turns later to Wittgenstein, who claims that no one can experience his own death, he has his own experience to contradict the philosopher.

For Semprun, reflection on his experience means turning to Kant, Heidegger, and Wittgenstein as models for citation and dissent, thus constructing his own radical ground, rewriting the history of the philosophy of evil and death. Freed from the immediate scene of the camp, about to reassume his identity as a student of philosophy, he begins by reinvoking the familiar figures. But how can Kant, whose conception of radical evil within the limits of reason names but does not describe Semprun's experience, speak to his recent past? ("'Evil is what is inhuman in man,'" he tells Lieutenant Rosenfeld: it is one possible result of human freedom.) Or Wittgenstein, who states that no one can experience his own death? Or Heidegger, for whom Semprun's recent past is an ellipsis, a silence? Perhaps these inadequacies relate to the terror Semprun feels on hearing his name over the loudspeaker soon after liberation. During the Nazi period, such a command was a call to report ("*Sofort zum Tör!*"): a summons to be taken to one's death. Now all he has to do is return some overdue books to the camp library: Hegel's *Logic*, Nietzsche's *Will to Power*, Schelling's essay on liberty. They are needed to reeducate former Nazis, the librarian tells him. At that time, however, the former student for whom philosophy is not a *Beruf* but a *Berufung* (p. 85), needs these philosophers, along with others, to explain among other things why he is not a survivor but one of a company of "ghosts, revenants." A ghost, he might have said later with Jacques Derrida, is not nothing. But ghosts do not seem to belong to the landscape under Kant's rational purview, or to the lexicon found in Wittgenstein. Just as the descriptive catalogue of Buchenwald *cannot* speak to the essence of radical evil, so the aphoristic claim of Wittgenstein—no one can speak of his own death—does not address his experience: for here he *can* speak of it, and does. If the *revenant* has been beyond experience, no longer in life, Semprun, as *revenant,* is en route to a new engagement with life, to a "not yet." In this respect he exemplifies Derrida's remark, "Given that a *revenant* is always called upon to come and to come back, the thinking of the specter, contrary to what good sense leads us to believe, signals toward the future. It is a thinking of the past, a legacy that can come only from that which has not yet arrived— from the *arrivant* itself."[5] Can we say that *Literature or Life* plays out this dual temporal identity in which the *revenant* looks ahead to his future where, as *arrivant,* he will look back upon his past? The labyrinthine chapters project something like this uncanny structure, in a movement of anticipation, a stance toward his arrival, that is possible only in the *revenant's* orientation toward his future. The future depends in some way on such an uncanny anticipation, or on a structure of reversal in which Semprun, or his persona, looks ahead to the time in which he will look back. In 1945, Semprun is a Marxist specter—although two decades later he will be neither Marxist nor specter.

Such a reversal may have been what Walter Benjamin has in mind when he suggests that the term *déjà-vu* is not well chosen. The process, he writes, is more like a future auditory shock:

One ought to speak of events that reach us like an echo awakened by a call, a sound that seems to have been heard somewhere in the darkness of past life. Accordingly, the shock with which moments enter consciousness as if already lived usually strikes us in the form of a sound.... But has the counterpart of this temporal removal ever been investigated, the shock with which we come across a gesture or a word as we suddenly find in our house a forgotten glove or reticule? And just as they cause us to surmise a stranger who has been there, there are words or gestures from which we infer that invisible stranger, the future, who left them in our keeping.[6]

If we think of this as not only a temporal matter, but as a property of a certain literary form, here a form that oscillates between memoir and fiction, literature past and future, then Semprun's self-doubling makes uncanny sense. Semprun's encounters with philosophers, underscored by Lieutenant Rosenfeld's exclamation on hearing the allusion to Heidegger, constitute one motif, one form of contest in Semprun's future books. The argument proceeds at times by anecdotal shocks, or shocking anecdotes, experiential mediations whose full meaning is both anticipated and deferred.

II

Having "crossed this immense land streaming with absence," having survived his passage over the river Styx, Semprun is convinced that the only thing that could subsequently happen to him is "life." The experience of evil, on the contrary, is "'the experience of death'" (*LL*, p. 89). Not surprisingly, Semprun takes issue with a philosopher on this very question: the certainty with which Wittgenstein declares, "*Der Tod ist kein Ereignis des Lebens. Den Tod erlebt man nicht*" [in French: "*La mort n'est pas un événement de la vie. La mort ne peut être vécue*"; in English: "Death is not an event in life. Death cannot be lived"] (pp. 170–171). In a short novel published in 1967, *L'évanouissement*, Semprun had translated the second sentence as "*La mort n'est pas une experience vécue*" ["Death is not a lived experience"], asserting that French has no proper words for the German *erleben* or *Erlebnis*. Spanish, to the contrary, is a much richer and subtler language: translation into Spanish would have been no problem (*LL*, pp. 171; *L'évanouissement*, p. 67).[7] Semprun rephrases Wittgenstein using the possessive ("*Meinen Tod erlebe ich nicht*") and quotes, in both texts, his notebook comment that the claim is true but meager. Yet his linguistic commentary is secondary to his memory of Halbwachs, the sociologist whose dying he experiences in the Little Camp at Buchenwald. Indeed, Halbwachs's death is the only certain event in his own life—and the event is shared by his friends. The *experience* of death precedes by several chapters Semprun's skepticism about Wittgenstein's statement.

The shared experience of the camp looks more like *Mit-Sein-zum-Tode*, Semprun claims. But no sooner does he convey this to the philosophic lieutenant with whom he has already discussed Kant, than the American informs him of Heidegger's Nazi connections. As in the case of Wittgenstein, the experience precedes the reflection by some time in the *narrative*, although much of the student's reading has preceded the narrative. In *Literature or Life*, it is not until 1992, when he returns to Buchenwald for the first time, that Semprun faces Heidegger's ambiguous past. He returns with three books: the correspondence of Heidegger and Jaspers, Celan's poetry, and Mann's *Charlotte à Weimar*. From the correspondence he learns of Heidegger's silence about German guilt, in the face of Jaspers's polite inquiries. From Celan's "Todtnauberg" he learns of the poet's vain hope for a word from the philosopher:

einer Hoffnung, heute,
auf eines Denkenden
kommendes
Wort
im Herzen . . .

Silence is what Semprun must accept, not because of Heidegger's inadequate replies but because of Celan's vain hope for clarification. Celan, the Jewish poet, writes in German, the language of "barked SS commands" but also of Kafka, Husserl, Freud, Benjamin, Celan himself: "of so many other Jewish intellectuals who created the grandeur and richness of German culture during the 1930s. Language of subversion, therefore: language of the universal affirmation of critical reason" (p. 290).

Working through philosophy and arriving at poetry, Semprun dissolves the grand antithesis between literature and life. Visiting Buchenwald in 1992 with his small arsenal of books—Mann, Goethe, and Celan instead of Schelling, Hegel, and Nietzsche, Semprun learns of an act that falls outside the fraternal experience of death: he sees the card registering his arrival at the camp in 1943, where a sympathetic communist prisoner had listed him as a *Stukkateur* (stucco worker) rather than a student: a listing that made him available for material labor and thus saved his life. This time he doesn't have to assert the fraternity, as if saying it made it happen. It comes to him in 1992, as it had come in 1943. That night, snow falls—the residue of a recurring dream—on his sleep. He is back in 1945, leaving the infirmary compound, where he has just learned of Auschwitz from a surviving *Sonderkommando*. Looking up, he sees the beauty of the night, and "tongues of orange flame [protruding] from the mouth of the squat crematory chimney" (pp. 309–310). He is not beyond repetition, but he is beyond silence. What was compulsion now serves art, even an aesthetic of the sublime. The dream seems to come as a marvelous accident, fraternity as the gift of life. Antithesis and oxymoron still serve his art, the beautiful in the midst of horror, closure in the midst of a persisting image of evil. But that sensory wildness of 1945 has disappeared even within the contradictory closing image. The questioning and the bravado of his quarrel with his "ancients"—philosophers and communists—are silenced within the solvent of his memory.

Notes

1. See, for example, Saul Friedländer, "Trauma, Memory, and Transference," in *Holocaust Remembrance: The Shapes of Memory*, ed. Geoffrey Hartman (Cambridge, Mass.: Blackwell, 1994), pp. 252–263, and Susan J. Brison, "Trauma Narratives and the Remaking of the Self," in *Acts of Memory: Cultural Recall in the Present*, ed. Mieke Bal, Jonathan Crewe, and Leo Spitzer (Hanover, N.H.: University Press of New England, 1999), pp. 39–54.

2. Jorge Semprun, *Literature or Life*, trans. Linda Coverdale (New York: Viking Penguin, 1997), p. 88. (Hereafter referred to as *LL*.) The original French edition, *L'écriture ou la vie*, was published in Paris in 1994, two years after Semprun's return to Buchenwald.

3. See Immanuel Kant, *Religion within the Limits of Reason Alone*, trans. Theodore M. Greene and Hoyt H. Hudson (Chicago, Ill.: Open Court, 1934).

4. See Cathy Caruth, *Unclaimed Experience* (Baltimore, Md.: Johns Hopkins University Press, 1996), pp. 1–9.

5. Jacques Derrida, *Specters of Marx*, trans. Peggy Kamuf (New York and London: Routledge, 1994), p. 196, n. 39.

6. Walter Benjamin, "A Berlin Chronicle," in *Reflections*, trans. Edmund Jephcott, ed. Peter Demetz (New York: Harcourt Brace Jovanovich, 1978), p. 59.

7. Jorge Semprun, *L'évanouissement* (Paris: Gallimard, 1967).

14

The Seventh Demon: Reflections on Absolute Evil and the Holocaust

Shoshana Yovel

Amos is an unmarried professor in his early forties. Together with his closest friend and cousin, Daniel, and Daniel's wife Yael and their children, every Friday they attend the family dinner at the house of Ella and Marcus, Daniel's parents. The following scenes take place on several such occasions.

For some time now, Daniel has been aware that Amos' intense reflections on the past are drawing him more and more toward the big questions. He seems to be suffering. Reading his grandfather's diary, the terror produced by the thought, what if they had failed to escape in time?—phrases saturated with apocalyptic mood, everything excites his nerves. His mind whirls around the inability to understand or explain, the inability to find the missing link; for he believes that, just as science cannot grasp how inanimate matter is transformed into a living cell or cannot locate the exact point of metamorphosis, so it is impossible to pin-point the transition from ordinary evil to absolute evil.

After dinner, they move over to the living room. Yes, Amos answers hesitantly, responding to Daniel's inquisitive look, I'm staying, I would like to talk. They clear the table and drink coffee, then drift into their respective preoccupations, not suspecting where he is about to drag them. Yael leafs through the Robert Capa album that had been lying on the low side-table ever since Amos brought it for Passover; Marcus, yawning, browses through the newspaper;

Excerpt from Shoshana Yovel's novel, *The Seventh Demon* (in Hebrew), Sifriat Poalim, 1999. © Shoshana Yovel.

Ella is still in the kitchen; and Daniel watches Amos with worried curiosity.

And Amos begins without any overture: I've been thinking. In a civilized society we count on a general agreement concerning the basic definitions of good and evil, at least the gist of the social contract. But then came this century's events, and more than anything that happened before, they slapped us in the face, scolded us, demanded that we open our eyes, and finally acknowledge the moral plasticity of human nature. As if someone had a tremendous idea, to find out the true essence of who we are, not through a small group of subjects in a university experiment who press buttons and send out electrical currents, but by turning the whole world into a laboratory. Imagine, the entire world becomes a huge laboratory to test what sort of creature God had created.

— If he made him in his image, just less powerful, imagine the monster who's sitting up there, said Marcus suddenly, dropping the newspaper to the floor.

— Yesterday night I couldn't fall asleep, continued Amos. I thought, how can I present this dilemma so as to express the inexplicable? I told myself a kind of a story ... I mean ...

Yael sat down by Daniel's side. Amos, his face tense, his eyes concentrated, spoke in his own way, his personal style, as if thinking aloud: Consider, for example, the following scenario. Two good friends in Vienna, Doctor Fraenkel, a pediatrician, and Otto Schmidt, a physicist. For years they meet at their regular cafe over a cup of coffee with whipped cream, and passionately discuss Freud or Nietzsche or Karl Kraus. Until lately it hardly mattered that one of them was a Jew and the other not. But bit-by-bit, although they continued to get together, a cloud of uncertainty darkened their friendship. Things got even more complicated after Hitler rose to power, for Otto Schmidt felt a certain attraction to Nazism and secretly yearned for the unification of Austria and Germany. They continued to meet, but with much less ease.

And then one day, Doctor Fraenkel—who, by the way, is still his friend Otto Schmidt's children's physician—says, O.K., let's put down our cards. You think Hitler is a great man, so imagine the following. Here we are all cozy in this cafe, chatting, we brought

along Ernst and Lotchen who are both the same age and by now are
all smeared with chocolate and whipped cream. With your broad
smile, you take out a white handkerchief to wipe their faces when,
just at that moment, a car stops nearby and four men get out of it
and fall on Lotchen and me, kicking us and tearing at Lotchen's
hair, and by the time you come to your senses they have already
dragged us away, bruised and bloody, and you see the expression of
horror on my face—look, you're already pale, in a minute you'll
faint—and I manage to cry out, Otto, this is just the beginning,
don't say I didn't warn you, help Anna and Karl!—What will you
do? Overcome with terror, you will deny me immediately: I don't
know that man, we just happened to be seated at the same table,
leave me alone. You will tremble all over as the frightened waiter
arranges the upset chairs, mumbles something as he picks up the
handkerchief soiled with chocolate and cream and hands it to you,
and you will whisper in Ernst's ear as he gazes at you in disbelief,
that he must forget what happened here today and never admit that
he knew either Lotchen or me. You needn't worry about Ernst, he'll
learn fast enough. Just make sure he doesn't snitch on you and on
Dorothea, because in school they quote Herr Hitler saying that for
the good of the *Vaterland* one must even turn in family members.
Actually, you needn't worry, you support them. Me? They've already
cast me into some cellar, or a concentration camp, separated me
from Lotchen, I don't know what happened to her, what happened
to Anna and Karl, you withdrew from them like from a plague, because now you are finally one Nation, you and the Germans. What
a relief, after years of unnatural association with Hungarians and
Slovaks and Czechs, you finally join your brethren, and the war has
already begun. There was no choice, you say proudly, it's impossible
not to be proud of victories, nothing competes with a victory, and
the army of your Führer advances through Europe like locusts,
leaving destruction and abomination everywhere it passes. Tsk tsk,
let's not exaggerate, you comment, war is a bloody business, what
can one do? How bloody? Well, really, yes ... for you don't grasp
that your success is intoxicating. And what about the invasion of
England? All in good time, you believe, we'll see then the bleeding-
heart English, squirming with regret for having turned down our

Führer's peaceful, extended hand, offering them a share in world domination. And you are advancing into another country, and another, and don't forget Hitler's plan, especially regarding the Poles, and the barbarian Russians who adopted the Jewish virus of Marxism, all these inferior peoples he will turn into Germanic Europe's slaves, what a sublime vision, for since the Germans have appointed themselves the chosen people, they anticipate with a quiver of pride the final moment of consummation. But for Hitler that's not enough, there's a sty in the Führer's eye, he blinks, the Jews, what can be done, for God's sake, with the Jews, all the bullets in the world will not eliminate them, didn't he pledge himself from the very beginning not to give that up?

So they sit in their comfortable armchairs in the sealed room, leaning backwards and raising their eyes, loyal and concerned, to Adolf Hitler, who fixes them with a penetrating gaze and says simply but firmly:

— *Meine Herren*, gentlemen, the time has come!

They continue to watch him, listening attentively, and he says:

— The time has come to cleanse the world of the Jews. Once and for all. Surely you realize, it's not enough, the guns and machine-guns, this way we'll never move forward. A thousand here, two thousand there, even tens of thousands of Jews, but what about the millions?

And when none of them replies, he lets a moment go by and asks:

— What's the final solution to the Jewish problem, gentlemen?

And they already see the muscles in his cheeks twist, and his eyebrows contract. And someone nevertheless mumbles something about the war effort, and other countries and the whole world, for no one has ever attempted such a thing—and the Führer explodes!

Of course nobody ever did such a thing! He screams, of course nobody has ever thought of systematically killing a whole nation, he isn't some shabby mimic, already in *Mein Kampf* he wrote of the necessity to get rid of the Jews! What do they take him for, some clown who doesn't mean what he says? And they remain silent, and he gazes at them with his dark look, and sees them ill at ease, and the silence is prolonged, and he continues to look at them, until he composes himself. Trust me, he says quietly and in a conciliatory tone, trust me, Germany can do it! We can and we shall! The Turks annihilated over a million Armenians, and the world was silent! Who even remembers that today? So the Jews? Again his voice rises to a pitch, we shall kill the Jews to the very last and leave no progeny! And after it's done the world will be grateful. And don't forget, that we're more gifted than the Turks, we'll invent a method for the total and absolute annihilation of the Jews, quick and efficient, Heidrich, where's Heidrich, tell them, isn't it feasible? Mein Führer, mein Führer, they rushed to get him water, he was almost suffocated by the emotion, perhaps the yelling and screaming too, they calm him, mein Führer, don't worry, if that's what you want, we'll give you the Jews. Ten million? Don't worry, we'll find a way. After that he went speechless for three days, lost his voice—

What am I talking about? Otto, you're so certain that these are decent, upright folks. But if you want to become a Nazi, you must understand all it implies. I know it may sound absurd, but imagine Anna, and Lotchen, and little Karl whose godfather you are, how they squeeze us all into a cattle car, and drive us to some God forsaken place, through valleys and dales, without food or water, and even before we realize what's happening, I mean those still alive, we arrive at some strange place, in Poland, why Poland? Perhaps because they have so many Jews the Poles, we're guests there, but no matter, there is room for everybody, if you will only squeeze a little, a bit more, there, good riddance! Not yet? Oh yes, the bodies still need burning, what a messy job. Actually, we should have spared you the bother and died on our own, disappearing quietly, learn from you, such clean folks, orderly, obedient, why can't we just be like you and die without making such a fuss ...

And who knows, you may yet surprise yourself, Otto, the years pass and people get used to things, perhaps you too will stand there on the landing in the camp and yell, and shove, and hit, because someone needs to do these things, and most of those who do are decent people, like you, and perhaps they'll assign you to open the gas valve, for the valve, too, doesn't open by itself, and you'll stand there erect as a soldier and listen, and hear the voices from the inside until all will go quiet, and every once in a while they'll order you to peek through a tiny window and check if we're dead already, for crying out loud, another train is due any minute now—and you look and see little Karl, he can't see you, anymore.

You won't do that? Do you recall the son of Herr Gertner from Hamburg, in whose pension you used to stay when on trips to scientific conventions—Fritz, that's it, Fritz—nice fellow, would bring you the morning paper. He got married in the meantime and already has two kids, the pension closed down. The war worries old Herr Gertner and his wife, but they trust the Führer, decent folks, and Fritz Gertner, wearing an innocent face, pets the cat, meow, meow, what a cute little thing you are, scratching under its chin. Hey Fritz, enough with that cat, see that woman, yeah, that one with the baby and the little girl clinging to her, and the old man leaning hard on his stick because his legs tremble so? Well, at the beginning you still notice such details, but I promise you it will pass quickly, in a month, perhaps two, you won't think about it anymore. It's the resemblance to your Helga that brought about the nightmares that first night, you're a normal person after all, but do you see I was right? Fact is that one evening, by the light of a small lamp, you write home, dear Helga, I miss you very much, I'm doing not bad, it's a bit cold, we're getting double and triple rations of schnapps and cigarettes and there's even plenty of food. I'll try to send you a parcel in the next days. Tell Mutti and Pappi that they can be proud of their son, and that I'm loyal to our fatherland and do what needs to be done, soon I'll probably get transferred somewhere else, Auschwitz or something like that, as soon as I'll get there I'll let you know, I kiss and hug you, yours Fritz.

And Fritz didn't even have time to write home again about the reassignment, it was all done so fast. They need reinforcements there. And so it came to pass that he was standing on the landing, shoving Margaret who stumbled at the end of her strength, fell down, the bitch, just to annoy him, and little Leon in her arms banged his head, he hasn't the time to mess with them, two bullets, he nods to the guards to remove them, quickly, quickly, he shouts, off of the train, everybody off, clear the landing, a fresh transport is due any minute now, quickly quickly, and tell the crematorium operators to hurry up, man, what are they thinking about over at dispatch, how much can a fellow work without a break, they must realize that these Jews for some strange reason insist on dying slowly. Taking their time, the little shits. For a time, after he recovered from some kind of infection he feared reassignment to the east, but to his great relief he was sent as a guard to the factory of huge ovens. What a laugh, they keep complaining that the ovens aren't efficient enough, but you have to remember that the Jews are nothing but skin and bones, ha ha ... true, they cut down on cigarettes and schnapps, but the job is pretty easy. But let's leave Fritz and get back to you, my friend Otto, do you keep up the routine of going to the cafe? Well, no whipped cream now, ha ha ... I heard they arrested Walther, your daughter Mina's husband, you actually liked him and the caricatures he used to draw, you always joked that his big mouth would eventually get him into trouble, but did you really mean it? Perhaps you did, for you truly believe that something grand is happening to you; I heard they all signed on to some declaration there, did they sign on to the gas chambers too, or that you just don't talk about? O.K., O.K., that was before the war, writers, poets, journalists, musicians, you all signed a declaration of loyalty to the regime, to the Führer, to all that this entails, don't forget, *all*! I'm not talking about the cowards, what can one do, people are closest to themselves, that's obvious, and others, politics schmolitics, what do they care, the main thing is the fine orchestra they've got, although the string section suffers, for you had to get rid of all the Jews, of course, but after a few months of hard work the orchestra really did improve. Really, one shouldn't exaggerate. I heard that your friend became head of his department at the hospital instead of Herr Professor Doctor Karl Oster, who was his mentor, sure, a disagreeable business, but what of it—Resign? What will that achieve? Someone else will take over, and one must admit, it's very nice, at his young age ... yes, and Heidegger signed a form prohibiting all Jewish professors from entering the university, including his dear old teacher, old Professor Husserl—just a signature, big deal! They didn't actually mean each and every thing written there. Sure, they burnt some books, and that's never attractive, and the students who participated in the frenzy, shame, but they're young, and the celebration was great, and I heard they went enthusiastically through libraries and publication houses and stores, and hauled away all the books named in the lists that were dispersed. And one must recall that some of the excitement was due to the fact that they would now have much less to be examined on. These nasty Jews, and the liberals, and the communists, it's unbelievable how much they've written. What with Heinrich Heine, hey, who has the list, do we burn Heine or not?—Not Goethe, are you mad?

And do you remember the day when they entered Vienna, your beloved Vienna, that day you looked forward to, when they were met with smiles and kisses. And what if they did close down a few shows? That's a logical concession after all, you say, what's wrong with Johann Strauss, why should he count less than Offenbach? Johann Strauss a Jew? You're kidding me, for a moment you had me worried, all those nice waltzes, what a shame if we had to give them up too. Such luck. Franz Werfel? Yes, we heard he made it to America, had to cross the Pyrenees on foot. Maybe, finally, he lost some weight. And Alma Mahler, the jokes they tell about her over here, that she made some thin American carry her on his back while cursing the wretched Jews and moronic Americans and proudly prophesying that the world stands no chance confronting Herr Hitler. Walter Benjamin? I'm really very sorry, but who's to blame for his impatience? Suicide was his decision, his problem. And what about all the rest? We already know what will happen to all the rest. Poland is full of Jews. How did they get there in the first place, and why did they let them stay? A thousand years? You exaggerate, eight hundred perhaps, so why didn't they become Poles? They *did* become Poles? But they kept on being Jews, all the same! For that's precisely their problem, they must remain Jews, that's what's so annoying about them, and in Prague I saw tombstones of Jews over a thousand years old, I guess from before there were Czechs there, maybe the Jews are the true Czechs, ha ha ... let them tell it to Eichmann ... actually, what are they doing here, those millions, how did they collect themselves there without us noticing, it's about time they realize that the world doesn't want them.

Truth be said, the world hates refugees no less than the Nazis do. And especially, as disagreeable it is to admit it, Jewish refugees. A few thousands can be tolerated, but millions? What can happen to those millions, you're all getting too morbid, a bit of proportion gentlemen, we can't be held responsible for everything that's going on in those terrible countries, is it our fault that the Germans went mad and blindly follow that lunatic Hitler? Now there's a problem. Wasting bombers and bombs on Auschwitz? Risk pilots in order to bomb the train tracks? Really, this Jewish egocentricity, about time they realize that there's a war going on, and there are more important things than saving a few Jews. They're always so persecuted, always complain, when will they learn to restrain themselves, not to be so pushy, so conspicuous, then perhaps they'll be forgotten and left alone. But don't count on it, don't count on the French policeman who cursed the Germans and the war, don't count on him, for if you don't make it out of Paris I'm not sure he won't turn you in to the Gestapo. For Hitler warned the French not to mess with him, and promised that, as long as they cooperate, they'll work it out together. Especially with Marshal Pétain, savior of the motherland, the heart beats with pride, even Hitler respects him. He never did like Jews, either, and somebody whispered in his ear that the detestable de Gaulle has some Jewish blood, ahaa, that explains his large nose ... true, we also have racial laws and we turn the Jews in, for who smeared the French army's honor if not Dreyfus? Hitler realizes this, well, yes, his own family is not exactly *comme il faut* but in some situations one must not be petty.

And when Hitler gives the sign, Franz Buchbinder, third year student in the faculty of law, gladly accepts his supremacy over all Jews. His having failed two exams, and Bruno Opfermann having been denied honors just for being a Jew, further prove the Aryan supremacy. Just for the nerve of thinking they're as good as others they deserve to be punished. And the Oppenheimer family, too? A bit of a problem, there, he knows them since he was a kid and for a while was Walther's playmate. But the problem is solved when he is told that they committed suicide, except for Walther who was smuggled to relatives in England. Sly, these Jews. Professor Huppert? Well that's a shame actually, for some reason Hupert liked him and gave him a passing grade. And what's with old Frau Rothenstein, who during *Kristallnacht* was thrown with her wheelchair into the street, where someone smashed her head? He hesitates, his mother is at a loss, too, old frau Rothenstein, that was so terrible, but after Hitler's last speech on the radio, they say to themselves, we guess that's how it has to be. We shouldn't be bothered by things that are none of our business. We must concentrate on the essential. In a short time, there will be war, and the Germans bear the sacred duty of vanquishing the whole world. So Franz Buchbinder, student, volunteers to join the SS, as his proud mother tells all her friends, who gaze at him respectfully, because as a kid, truth be told, he wasn't that bright. In the last lecture it was put to them, that beginning from today, ordinary people who never raised their hand against anyone, will have to take part in the killing of ordinary people just like them, like their parents, their wives, their children—and it proved not to be such a problem, and there was no need to stress the point with long explanations, not even about the babies; they just had to begin. What luck that most people are used to obeying orders, that they adapt so quickly to situations, and as we do not talk here of sadists, or psychopaths, or common criminals, it's true that at the beginning it was assumed that some special education would be necessary, and that only certain types would do, but to everyone's surprise—

Amos stopped abruptly the stream of words that erupted from him, saw them looking at him astounded, he himself was amazed at what he had uttered, took a deep breath and continued like one possessed: I say to you that this is a greater mystery than the big bang. What did they see when they watched little Hans clutching Nelli's hand, out of which someone snatched, with a burst of laughter, the teddy bear she held, promising her that, anyhow, where she's going it could not protect her. How did it become, so simple, so normal, to shove these two kids into a chamber full of gas, stand outside, have a quick smoke, tell jokes, and wait impatiently for them to die. And then when all, thank God, was over, Ludwig Bergner was tired. They had a satisfactory output today, for in one strenuous effort they managed to finish off all the children in the camp. He stretches, and at long last goes home, where little Friedl and Kurt greet him joyfully as he grasps them in his arms one after the other. Guess what I brought home for you? Here, a teddy bear . . .

Marcus, Daniel and Yael sat silently, and Ella, who joined them in the middle of it all, remained in the doorway, her eyes wide open, her palm over her mouth.

And silence prevailed.

Daniel got up hesitantly and turned on the radio.

Murry Perahia was playing Chopin preludes on the Music Channel.

During the next week Amos meditates, painfully. He lets go of his grandfather's letters and tries to write. Had he found a new way to speak of those things, a new angle? On the Friday following the great outburst, he shows up at his aunt's as usual, alone, although Daniel already called in the morning and complained: mom nags me that you should bring someone along. Our son Eitan can't come, he acts as if he needs to prepare for his exams but actually he's got a new girl and takes advantage of our absence from home on Friday evenings. Since Yotam went away, mom feels that there are too few of us ... how about inviting Ziva, she's been here once ...

— When is Yotam coming back?

— Do I know? He decided to continue on from South America to India.

After dinner they move, as is their custom, to the living room.

Ella, in the kitchen, is still shocked by Amos' monologue of last week. For a few days she walked around gloomily, and now Marcus secretly hopes that the evening will pass quietly. He knows that Ella fears the continuation, maybe that's why she wanted additional guests and looked disappointed when Amos showed up on his own. Marcus peeks at Amos, who seems lost in thought:

— When will we get a chance to meet your girlfriend?

— I don't have a girlfriend.

Marcus raises his eyebrows, as if knowing differently. No girlfriend? How come?

Amos declines to respond, and Marcus sinks back to his newspaper. Daniel goes into the kitchen and emerges with a small dish of butter cookies that melt on the tongue.

Amos gazes at Yael, who leafs absentmindedly through Marcus' newspaper, and says, I intend to write an essay about absolute evil. When I have a draft ready I'll show it to you. They sat quietly, sipping coffee, munching on the cookies, and Amos gets up, murmuring softly, if you don't mind, I want to go home.

From Amos' Journal:

I have stumbled across a play by Lessing's about Faust, of which only one passage remains. Lessing depicts Faust wandering through hell looking for the fastest demon in the world. He runs into seven demons who, when asked who's the fastest, each reply, "me."

— It's a wonder indeed, Faust mocks them, that of seven demons only six are liars ... let's have it, then—he turns to the first—how fast are you?

— I pass through fire unscorched!

— And you? He turns to the second.

— Mine is the speed of the plague!

— And you?

— I am swift as the wings of the wind! says the third.

— And I am swift as the rays of light! says the fourth.

— Oh you miserable creatures, Faust waves them away, whose speed is limited to finite quantities ...

— These are Satan's agents in the world of material bodies, the fifth barges in, and we, his agents in the world of spirits, are far faster!

— You? Asks Faust. Pray then, what's your speed?

— I am quick as the thought of man!

— Ah, answers Faust, but man's thoughts are not always so quick, especially when truth and morals are involved! ... And he turns to the sixth demon, say, how fast are you?

— Me? I am swift as vengeance.

— Vengeance? Whose vengeance?

— The most terrible vengeance of them all, that of the antagonist who keeps his vengeance to himself because it brings him pleasure.

— You call that vengeance? And I who am still alive, and continue to sin?

— Satan lets you sin, and that is his vengeance!

— And that I must learn from a demon, Faust grumbles, get going, you're not nearly as fast as his vengeance ... And you, he turns to the seventh skeptically, what do you have to say for yourself, how fast are you?

— Oh insistent mortal, if I too am not fast enough for you ...

— Well, Faust urges him, how fast are you?

— As fast as the passage from good to evil!

— Ah! Says Faust. Yes, you are my demon! As fast as the passage from good to evil! Yes, none is faster than you!

— Now clear off, he waves the other demons away! Yes, the passage from good to evil! This I have known myself, I know just how fast that is!

Thoughts and points:

"Man after Auschwitz is different." "In Auschwitz, man lost his innocence for the second time." Clichés? Slogans? A curtain of mist . . .

To grasp absolute evil as a phenomenon, not a concept. I, as a historian and not a philosopher, anchor these questions in a concrete social context rather than in metaphysics or theology. The problem, however, is attempting to figure out something we stipulated that cannot be explained. For how can you understand that millions of people, including people who all their lives were considered more-or-less decent, who belonged to all of society's strata, ordinary people who have never hurt anybody, workers, merchants, bourgeois, and intellectuals too—scientists, poets, philosophers, musicians, who epitomized in their achievements man's superiority over the beasts, were capable, almost without exception, of succumbing to a hallucination, based entirely on the idea of creating a glorious new world by a total destruction of all the sacred principles of civilization, by turning the hatred of the other into a postulate, and through the mobilization of absolute evil, evil with no bounds?

Because, even if we assume that man's nature is bad at its core, all that could be imagined until now was bounded by the conceivable. In Auschwitz a mutation occurred. The gene of absolute evil dominated the human race. Can we restore it to the category of a hypothetical contingency? Today we know that human evil, too, is infinite. And the fact that it has materialized through ordinary people, people who, had they never been presented with the political opportunity, would never have lost their ethical personalities—this does not transform their deeds, or the plan that they served, into something ordinary or banal. At the outset of the process of corruption they can still be average, gray, banal people, but absolute evil can never be ordinary or simple. That is why whoever carries out an absolutely evil policy becomes absolutely evil himself. The power of evil envelops him, penetrates him, generates a transformation, a metamorphosis, and he is no longer an ordinary person. Just like arbitrary political power, the tyrant, evil's godfather, the axis around whom everything revolves, cannot be simple or commonplace.

Absolute evil arbitrarily disintegrates the basic universal solidarity by erasing the other's humanity. That's the nucleus of it all. From there the venom spreads. When suddenly the "you" must justify his right to exist, which only the "I" can then approve. And if "I" won't, because I despise him, condemn him, hate him, and think that without him the world would be a better place, "I" use my political power and obliterate him. And so the "I" alone remains and the "you" vanishes. But what kind of "I" can there be without a "you"? When the "I" obliterates the "you," he erases himself. There can be no "I" without "you." And after it has happened once, it is impossible to go on living as if it hadn't. So although the collective consciousness of the whole world cannot digest what happened here and labors to forget, there is no way of overlooking the simple fact that *it was done* and that the whole world has changed as a result. Our understanding of human kind has changed. And as a by-product, the threshold, ground zero, has been raised by a few notches: the threshold of moral blindness, of cruelty, of intolerance, and of hatred. Not that history till now was innocent, but there was a justified hope that civilization would refine the principles of the jungle, ban them and their applications. Our terrible disappointment stems, among other things, from the realization that exactly at the moment when culture seemed to have reached its height, among a nation that had come to symbolize it, humanity collapsed and found itself in the arid land of civilizational loss.

How do these two things fit together?

I don't know if it's possible—the wild competition between reality and imagination, the heedless visceral sweep that carried humankind to a new moral phase. The lips refuse to say it but, in my view, Hitler was more significant than Einstein in the process of reaching unlimited possibility. The total and obsessive manhunt, ideological, scientific, organized, documented, the systematic turning of the other into a non-human, and especially the immense number of the murdered, in the gas chambers, in the crematoriums—changed the human profile far more than the breakthrough into the mysteries of the universe, more than space travel and the first step on the moon.

And another question, actually practical: how to erect a buffer between absolute evil and its agent? How to distinguish between the overall vision of absolute evil and its personal executor? Hanna Arendt observed Eichmann in the glass chamber, thin lips, a bureaucrat with organizational skills, calculates the numbers of the slaughtered like an accountant, merely follows orders—and *that* must stand as a metaphor for the devil? Where is the groundbreaking imagination, where is evil's grandeur, its heroism? No, Arendt didn't want to credit evil with grandeur or depth; she believed that precisely by emphasizing its simplicity, the horror acquires it's earthly-human dimension, that only in this way we shall realize the compelling need for norms and rules to guard us from the ever-lurking danger. But for all her theoretical sophistication, she lost something along the way. Eichmann was a capable executive, he made sure that the trains arrived on time, that the human numbers are consistent with the gas-chamber quotas, that his murderers not let any Jew, be it in caves in the Macedonian mountains, on the shores of Provence, or in attics in Holland, escape. Don't worry: we'll get to the Jews of England, Algeria, we'll reach *every* child, *every* old man hiding in the depths of the cellars and convents, fear not, we'll drag them out one after the other, the Paul Celans, the Max Jacobs, the Primo Levis, because even the Italians capitulated and helped us gather them under the Pope's nose. Don't worry, none will escape, we'll get as far as America. Imagine the tremendous excitement, all those American Jews! A whole armada will cover the seas, Europe will be filled with concentration camps, the industry of death will energize the German nation, a new generation will grow who will long for it. And when all the world's Jews are obliterated, who will stand next in line?—for who can tell where it will all stop? *Banality?* Evil is simple? The same skills that are required for marketing Coca-Cola? Indifference to the quality of "the merchandise"? No, the idea in whose name Eichmann, his masters, and his associates acted had nothing simple about it, and its agents had nothing simple or banal about them. Absolute evil is always extreme, even when there is no greatness. For the idea of absolute evil shatters the limits of the basic social contract and sanctions another option for controlling the jungle: the option of pushing moral concerns out of the human sphere altogether or, more exactly, out of a given history. (Stalin didn't go so far. He had to justify personal persecution by attributing specific guilt to his victims, entirely false, but still there to show the world.)[1] Hitler erased the moral code of human behavior by getting rid of the need to justify his big idea in relation to the individual. Individuals don't count. People don't count. That's how the legal system collapsed: the state committed murders, not executions. No legal action was brought against the millions, not even a make-believe one, because it was unnecessary. Normal behavior, concepts like good and evil, became irrelevant. As if it was agreed that at a certain moment in history, moral considerations ceased to exist if they hindered the application of the ruling ideology. One does not ask himself how to reconcile killing little children with normal behavior, because the answer is: you don't *have* to reconcile it! The Führer had commanded, and an entire nation followed him by obeying orders and not asking questions. Probably this is how it happened: in the kingdom of absolute evil people do what they are told to do and wave away any hesitations about the old virtues—and lo and behold, they start to behave not as if this is right—because this question is pushed aside—but as if there is no moral code of conduct anymore. There are only orders. Does this explain the immense success of the process of adaptation—of inventing human conduct without human virtues?

Amos stopped writing. He was not sure what exactly he was doing. Does the "clinical" description explain anything about how it could possibly have happened in reality? How did it happen that Charlotte Solomon, such a gifted artist, so young, so beautiful, how was she dragged from her home not by a psychopathic rapist but by Helmut, a thoroughly nice guy? In fact, without knowing it, they went to the same high school, some years apart, before Charlotte fled to the south of France. How did he drag her from her hiding place and push her into the cattle train? And after surviving the journey, how was she shoved, shaven, naked, into the gas chamber and later into the crematorium, by Fritz, another nice guy?

Amos paused.

Where is this leading him? And most importantly, what about the *future?* There is no question, he resumed his writing, that our redemption lies only in the overwhelming necessity to separate completely the idea from its realization. For the awareness of absolute evil already exists, even if it is veiled in theoretical sophistry. No way avoiding or escaping that. Its presence is proven beyond doubt. As is its ominous applicability. Nowadays, I say, now that we know, we must safeguard, by all means, the separation of concept and consummation, idea and application. It is the only way to re-establish a civilized society. For we cannot disregard man's capability for self-delusion, his talent for ignoring realities that may shake his comfortable peace of mind. Maybe it is a component of our power to survive, otherwise the human race would have perished long ago, maybe it is a legitimate defense mechanism like proteins, vitamins, nerves. We must, however, remain ever vigilant as to possible breaches of the ethical boundaries, especially breaches so forceful that the fascination or delusion become part of a process of self-destruction; we must constantly check for mutations, for cells that begin to multiply in mad frenzy, for a mode of protection transformed into poison, destroying its carrier.

Amos read what he had written so impulsively, and didn't touch it anymore. I get vertigo from dealing with this, he said to himself—

and also from its connection to the family history. Daniel is right, there is an obsession here. And when Daniel asked him, well, what's with the article?, Amos's expression turned cloudy and he said, I think I'll let it go. The more I deal with it, the less I understand. I can't grasp how abstract hatred gets translated into systematic mass madness, which then develops into a well-oiled industry of slaughter, with its police, spies, collaborators, and dogs, all mobilized to the tremendous effort of not letting any Jew escape. Consider one simple scene: jeeps, yelling, men in uniform, a hundred terrified kids, monks, priests—and all that to drag out one little boy, Pierre. That's the name they've given him, poor bastard, thinking they could trick us, chuckles Hans Birman, the SS officer. For long he's suspected those hypocritical Franciscans of hiding someone, this alias Pierre who's really a Moishale, a few slaps and he'll speak. Worthwhile teaching them a lesson, too, he'll take along the chubby monk ogling him imprudently, doesn't matter, in a few days they'll both flow through the chimney, and he inspects his white gloves for a speck. I write this, but I do not understand what I write.

Like the Thessaloniki Jews, for instance, up in Northern Greece. I don't know exactly why their case most profoundly demonstrates, to me, the mad absurdity of the Nazi death illusion. The Jews of Thessaloniki speak Ladino and Greek. A different world. In the central square, Gestapo agents yell in a German that no one understands. They hear the yelling, see the bulging eyes, the foaming lips, feel the pushing and the shoving, the saliva dripping from the barking dogs' mouths, the locals hidden behind locked grates not daring to interfere, now these Jews are hauled onto trucks, where are they taking them, why do they bother so? Some barely know where Germany is, what do the Germans want with them of all people, *schnell, schnell, herrein,* what are they saying? What do they want? Doesn't matter, the rifles, the mad yelling, have their own internal grammar, the locals look on, not surmising that from this journey few will ever return, days and nights, now they're shoved onto trains, can't see a thing, day and night intermingle, no water, no food, the babies cry, the children sob, the grown-ups stop whispering, where? why? They who in their lifetimes rarely left their villages, the cold intensifies, through the cracks they see white flakes—snow—where are they taking them across such vast distances, to the edge of the world? Auschwitz. A mixture of languages. They understand none. Poland? The kids strain their minds. Where's Poland? Where is it on the world map? Doesn't matter, as in forty-eight hours most of the transport will go up in the crematoriums' smoke. A mirage?...

Postscript

Shoshana Yovel's novel, *The Seventh Demon*, follows the saga of one family over four generations and three continents. After the death of his mother, Paula, Amos Levin browses through old family letters and diaries in an attempt to decipher her enigmatic and cold personality and thus to liberate himself from her shadow. Paula turns out to have been an unloved and rejected child, who became a talented and aspiring artist, but rejected herself when her ambition to achieve greatness failed to be realized. The voyage into the past, the consciousness of the search, mellows Amos's distant approach to life.

IV

Life and Work

15

A Philosopher from New York

Judith Friedlander

I have always believed that, no matter how abstract our theories may sound or how consistent our arguments may appear, there are incidents and stories behind them which, at least for ourselves, contain as in a nutshell the full meaning of whatever we have to say. Thought itself ... arises out of the actuality of incidents, and incidents of living experience must remain its guide-posts by which it takes its bearings if it is not to lose itself in the heights to which thinking soars, or in the depths to which it must descend.
—*Hannah Arendt, cited by Richard J. Bernstein*[1]

In the preface to *Hannah Arendt and the Jewish Question*, Richard Bernstein tells a personal story to explain why he wrote this book. It seemed "appropriate," he says, because "Hannah Arendt loved to tell stories and storytelling is woven into the fabric of her thinking."[2] But that is not the only reason. Dick enjoys telling stories himself and often chooses to write about other philosophers who rely on "incidents of living experience as guideposts" in their own work.

Passionately involved with the world around him, I doubt that Dick would ever look at himself as the subject of philosophical reflection. When asked, however, to tell his own story, he describes his life as a series of contingencies, singling out certain incidents and experiences as having profoundly influenced him as a philosopher. For example: the accidental encounter he had in graduate school with the work of John Dewey inspired him to think critically about what it meant to respond to the unexpected, to "the inescapability of chance and contingency."

At a time when it was not fashionable to take Dewey and the other pragmatists seriously, Dick insisted on doing so, proclaiming in their name that, "We live in an 'open universe' which is always at once threatening and a source of tragedy and opportunity. This is why the pragmatists placed so much emphasis on how we are to respond to contingencies—on developing the complex of dispositions and critical habits that Dewey called 'reflective intelligence.'"[3]

Given Dick's interest in exploring the ways people choose to respond to contingencies, I wanted to hear him describe certain "incidents and stories" from his own life that clearly had a lasting impact on him. Much of what follows comes from an interview I did with Dick for a book I am writing on the New School for Social Research, where he has been teaching since 1989. Dick is important to that project for two reasons: because he has written extensively on John Dewey and Hannah Arendt, both of whom helped, in different periods and ways, to frame the intellectual mission of the New School; and because Dick himself has played a critical role there in recent years in ensuring the future of Philosophy at the institution. In the end, the book on the New School has given me a wonderful excuse to listen to Dick talk about different periods of his life and reflect "on how contingent things make a difference."

The story I tell needs little explanation, beyond acknowledging the problem of bias. Although I faithfully relate what Dick shared with me, often quoting his own words from the interview I taped and from some of his published and unpublished writings, the portrait I draw reflects my concerns. I chose to stress, for example, that Dick grew up during World War II in an American Jewish family of modest means. I felt justified in doing so, for Dick himself embraces his heritage openly, much in the spirit of Hannah Arendt's "conscious pariah." Paraphrasing Arendt, Dick defines the pariah with what I suspect is a certain degree of self-identifying pleasure: "The pariah is a rebel and an independent thinker who rejects the type of assimilation that requires him to lose his identity and to become indistinguishable from other 'abstract individuals.' The Jew as a pariah knows that it is only within the framework of a people that one can live a fully human life. So for all the freedom and independence of the pariah, his identity is bound up with being a member of his people—the Jewish people."[4]

Richard Bernstein was born on May 14, 1932. The youngest of three children, two boys and a girl, he grew up in Borough Park, a primarily lower-middle-class section of Brooklyn. Most of his friends came from second-generation families like his own, with immigrant grandparents from Poland and Russia who landed in New York in the late nineteenth century, impoverished and uneducated. Upwardly mobile, Dick's parents left Borough Park after the Second World War and moved to Long Island, as did many of their friends, vacating apartments that would soon become home to Hasidic Jews.

There was "nothing particularly academic or intellectual" about Dick's family. His father, a furniture salesman, never finished high school. His mother had more education than that, but no professional training or any real exposure to the world of ideas. Dividing her time between raising the family and doing volunteer work, Dick's mother played an active role in the community, demonstrating an "amazing talent for organizing things," a talent she passed down to her son.

The Bernsteins considered themselves Reform Jews, but in the American sense of the term. This means, Dick explained, that although they accepted certain changes in ritual, they also held on to a number of customs associated more often with Orthodox Judaism than with the German Reform movement. In synagogue, for example, men and women sat together to pray, breaking a very old tradition, but at home the Bernsteins continued to observe the dietary laws of *kashrut*, a practice Dick quickly abandoned when he went to college.

Dick has happy memories of his childhood, growing up in a large extended family. Things changed dramatically, however, just before he reached adolescence. Over a period of a couple of years Dick lost a grandfather and three uncles. Then in 1945 his brother Robert was killed "under particularly unfortunate circumstances," while serving as a navigator in the U.S. Air Force in Europe. Dick was twelve at the time and Robert was twenty-two.

Having successfully completed twenty-five missions, Dick's brother was eligible for a furlough and scheduled to come home. Before leaving Europe, however, he volunteered to fly one final mission and this time he did not make it. His B-17 was shot down in Austria over Linz.

For months nobody knew for sure what had happened to Robert. "I remember vividly that I was Bar Mitzvah'd while he was still missing in action." After looking for him for an entire year, the U.S. Army declared Robert dead, but Dick's father refused to accept it. Although a funeral took place, he continued to hope that his son would turn out to be one of those soldiers they kept hearing about who bailed out of their planes onto enemy territory and became prisoners of war. Three members of Robert's crew had had that kind of luck. When the war ended, they visited Dick's family and reported that they never found out what had happened to the others on their plane. All they could do was recite Air Force regulations that instructed the navigator, copilot and pilot to abandon the aircraft last. The matter was settled eighteen months later when Dick's parents received a letter from the Department of Defense, announcing that Robert's body had been identified. For the sake of Dick's father, the family then held a second funeral. "My brother was a very extraordinary individual, very bright, very intelligent, very talented, the kind of person who was also loved, so this was a great family tragedy."

Dick first discovered he had intellectual interests at Midwood High School in Brooklyn, a public school with an excellent reputation. Not having come from "one of those Jewish families that was highly cultured," he had little background to draw on. "I always claimed that the first book I ever read in my life from cover to cover was at the age of fourteen—I didn't read books as a child. It was *Das Kapital*. In English, the Modern Library Edition, condensed."

Dick was not, he insists, an outstanding student, in the conventional sense of the term. As he remembers those years, he was rather rebellious—politically and in other ways. Still, he clearly did well by some set of standards, for he skipped a grade and graduated early in 1949 at the age of seventeen. After high school

Dick went on to the University of Chicago, "almost by a series of contingencies."

Dick studied at Chicago during the Hutchins era. It was, he recalls, a fantastic time to be part of that university: "I sometimes think that *all* my education happened there. It was all going on in Chicago. This is where Nichols and May began, in the University Theater ... George Steiner ... Susan Sontag ... she was in my class. Philip Roth was there. And there was a kind of attitude that if you were a serious intellectual you wouldn't dare go to a place like Harvard or Yale."

Dick received his Bachelor of Arts degree, with honors in Philosophy in 1951, at the age of nineteen, completing the four year program in two years plus a summer. The problem, however, was what to do with a Chicago BA that many American institutions refused to recognize. Oxford and Cambridge did accept the degree, but Dick was not ready to move so far away. He wanted to return to New York and be close to his family. To their credit his parents had not clung on to him after Robert died. They encouraged him to be free and independent, but Dick had a need to go home, at least for a while.

This he did, using the time to take courses at Columbia University's School of General Studies, where he could earn the credentials he needed to be eligible for an American graduate school program. In addition to having to "compensate" for a Chicago degree, he was too young at nineteen to enter graduate school.

Dick enjoyed the School of General Studies a great deal, taking courses in programs across the university: "I did everything from bookbinding, to Greek, to comparative literature, to taking what was the equivalent to a year of graduate philosophy." Two years later, in the spring of 1953, he graduated *summa cum laude*. The following fall he went to Yale in the Department of Philosophy.

Before leaving Chicago, Dick had already decided that he wanted to study philosophy at Yale. So had many others, including his good friend Richard Rorty. "Yale was one of the few philosophy departments that was really 'non-analytic' and open. It was a very exciting place. I made up my mind that that was really where I wanted to go."

Since Dick had been studying philosophy seriously for several years, he advanced through the program at Yale rather quickly. By

1954 he was eligible to teach undergraduates as a part-time instructor, a privilege that came with a heavy course load—the equivalent of four courses per year, or two-thirds the number of classes taught by a full-time member of the faculty.

The stories about Dick's teaching are legion. Dick was only twenty-two at the time he started, about the same age as his students. Assigned to a special program called "Directed Studies," he worked closely with undergraduates, and they adored him. In the early days, his students included, among others, Robert Rifkind, the son of a distinguished judge, who went on to become a lawyer himself and, in the 1990s, President of the American Jewish Committee. Dick also served as faculty advisor for the John Dewey Society, a precursor of SDS (Students for a Democratic Society), supporting projects organized by Yale's student activists like André Schiffrin, one of the group's outspoken leaders. The son of a famous refugee publisher, Schiffrin became an editor, first at Pantheon Books, where he defied the mainstream by publishing works of significant scholarship that took politically controversial positions; then at the New Press, a small house that he founded in the early 1990s to carry on the struggle.

While teaching undergraduates, Dick finished his own course work and participated in a small study group, organized by a young assistant professor, John E. Smith, to read John Dewey's *Experience and Nature*—"which shows you how the contingent things make a difference." Having gone to Chicago, where the very name was an anathema, Dick had no exposure to John Dewey or to the school of American pragmatism. Things were hardly much better at Yale. But Dick found Dewey interesting and, out of a kind of "perverseness," decided to write his thesis on this philosopher, whom others ignored.

The chairman of the department at Yale in the mid-1950s was Charles Hendel. "A remarkable man, Hendel embodied the Yale spirit." When Dick chose to write on Dewey, he asked Hendel to sponsor him and he agreed, even though he could offer very little help. And so Dick proceeded, virtually alone, without the benefit of a thesis director who could provide substantive advice.

In 1955 Dick married Carol Lippit, a Ph.D. student in English literature at Yale, whom he had known since his high school days in Brooklyn. When they first settled down, the young couple lived on little more than $2,000 a year. "Sometimes we worried about whether we would have the extra quarter to buy the Sunday *New York Times*," but otherwise, Dick remembers, they felt basically secure. The real problem he had was finding the time to write his dissertation while teaching a heavy load. Exhausted, he simply had to free himself from his other obligations.

In 1957 Dick finally decided he would resign his teaching position and give himself several months to finish the thesis. To quit like this took a good deal of nerve, for Yale, of course, was very "hierarchical" and graduate students "knew their place." It was with great trepidation that Dick approached Charles Hendel and announced his intentions to resign. "And I never forgot what he said to me. He said, 'Dick, institutions have a way of surviving. If you really think that this is what you need, this is what you should do.' He was wonderful and generous, never angry or annoyed or took the attitude, 'how dare you resign from Yale?'"

Although he needed the time off, Dick also needed money to carry him through the next academic year. But by the time he gave notice in the month of March, he had missed the application deadlines for most of the available fellowships. There was, however, one exception: a new Fulbright program to Israel, the application deadline for which had been postponed due to troubles in the Middle East. Once peace was restored—or what passes for peace in that region of the world—a new deadline was set for April. Encouraged by Paul Weiss, Dick applied and was accepted. Dick finished a draft of his thesis on "John Dewey's Metaphysics of Experience" by the middle of the summer and the young couple departed.

In Israel, Dick divided his time between teaching and research. Based in Jerusalem, at Hebrew University, the only university in the country at the time, he focused his teaching on American philosophy. For his research he worked on some of the problems Israeli education faced, together with a colleague he met in Jerusalem.

Presenting the study to the Israeli Department of Education, Dick noted with pride that this was his first publication ever—*A Study of Some Aspects of Education in Israel* (with Morris Eson).

In 1958 Dick returned to Yale to teach philosophy at the rank of assistant professor. To be a young colleague in the very department where he had just been a student presented some challenges, but he quickly adjusted, becoming close friends with the eminent Paul Weiss. Dick never saw himself as the disciple of Paul Weiss. Still, whenever he speaks about the man, he does so with deep affection and gratitude. Reminiscing about Yale in the late 1950s/early 1960s, Dick remarked that Paul Weiss "probably had the profoundest influence on me at this stage of my life on what it is to be a philosopher."

Paul Weiss asked Dick to work with him on the *Review of Metaphysics*, the journal he had founded in the late 1940s and been editing ever since, in his own idiosyncratic fashion, without an editorial board, or much of a staff. Weiss selected the articles essentially alone, publishing pieces that represented all the major competing tendencies of the postwar period. From the very beginning, the Review was a huge success, intellectually and financially. If you go back and look at the early issues, you will see, Dick remarked, that "even some of the most important analytic articles at the time were being published in the journal."

Working closely with Paul Weiss, Dick learned a great deal about running a scholarly journal, first as manager, then as assistant editor: "He was sharp, crisp, always perceived things. I would make a decision on a manuscript about whether we should publish it and write a letter, then he would read it and rip my letter apart ... that was the kind of friendship." And then one day Dick found a letter on his desk: "Dick, you have learned everything I could possibly teach you, the Review is yours." Dick was delighted, but asked his colleague to wait a few months so that he could finish preparing the book he was editing on the work of John Dewey. When he took over in 1964, Weiss gave him one final bit of advice: "Remain editor only as long as you're learning something and it's fun."

Dick left Yale a year later and the journal left with him. He eventually stepped down as editor in 1971. By that time, he said, there were only two things left: power and prestige and these weren't enough. "I wasn't learning anymore, so I followed Paul's advice."

Reminiscing about Weiss, led Dick to make some general observations about the way Jews were treated at Ivy League institutions in the 1950s and early 1960s:

You have to remember that my generation was the first generation in which Jews were accepted in graduate school without discrimination. Paul Weiss was the first Jewish full professor at Yale in any department in the Liberal Arts. [By the time I got there], if anything you could say that there was almost a kind of Judeophilia. Here was this real WASP institution. Yale was all male ... a high percentage of old Yalies [sons of alumni], mainly Protestant. When I went to Yale you had to wear a tie and jacket to go to the dining room. My students called me, "Sir." I mean it was a world so foreign to me. When I first went to Yale I said, "This is not real." I thought this was a chapter out of F. Scott Fitzgerald.... I thought this was Hollywood. I'm a kid from Brooklyn and New York and Chicago.... I just had no idea that this even really existed. And I think there was a sense that somehow this was a time—I was there, Geoffrey Hartman was there, Harold Bloom— when the Jews were more vital, more alive, more dynamic than the rest of the young people. So I never really experienced any kind of systematic anti-Semitism. I was always outspoken, I mean not on Jewish issues, but on any issue.

Although the fact he was Jewish was not the problem, Dick did not, in the end, get tenure at Yale. Known as the "Bernstein Affair" the negative decision caused a national scandal, creating unwanted publicity for the university, in the newspapers, and on the evening news. To this day people are still talking about it and the affair has gone down in the annals of academe as one of the most contested cases of tenure in the United States. Many claim as well that the outcome was the final nail in the coffin of Yale's Department of Philosophy, whose reputation plummeted soon after and has only recently begun to recover.[5]

Dick came up for tenure in the 1964–1965 academic year.[6] At the time, he was thirty-two years old. Secrecy surrounded the process, but the newspapers surmised that the committee had ruled against the appointment on the basis of Dick's publishing record, something that Dick's supporters on the faculty vigorously disputed. Their young colleague, they complained, was being judged unfairly by a set of criteria more fitting for evaluating the work of a mature scholar, than of someone in the early years of his academic career. When students learned of the decision, they came out en masse to protest, staging huge demonstrations.

On March 3, the *New York Times* ran an article entitled "Students At Yale Picket All Night." They took to the streets to voice strong opposition to the outcome of the vote by a university-wide committee that rejected Philosophy's "unanimous" recommendation to grant tenure to Dick.[7] *Newsweek* counted over 1,000 pickets with slogans demanding that Yale support "creative teaching" and reverse the decision of the committee.[8] The actual number of protesting students came closer to 2,000. An article published in *Time* magazine quoted Paul Weiss as saying that the tenure committee's decision was "stupid, unfair, dismaying." Another colleague, Robert Brumbaugh, added, "We could not have gotten tenure for Aristotle when he was thirty-two, we could not have gotten it for Kant, and on a much homelier level, I could not have gotten it."[9]

In an effort to clarify the university's position, Yale's president, Kingman Brewster, made a statement to students and the press. Breaking the rules of confidentiality, he explained to reporters that the committee on tenure had voted against Dick because the department's recommendation, although technically unanimous, had "not been an unqualified one."[10] President Brewster went on to say that he told the committee to ask the faculty in Philosophy to provide "an unambiguous statement."[11] When the case came back to Philosophy the majority of tenured faculty in the department—the only ones eligible to cast a vote—reversed their earlier position, causing even a louder cry of outrage from the students. Distancing himself from the arguments made against recommending Dick for tenure, Kingman Brewster proclaimed that he had "great personal regard and admiration" for Professor Bernstein, but "this offers no warrant ... for exercising the unusual and largely unused power of presidential appointment."[12] He would not, in other words, overturn the decision of the faculty in Philosophy. Defending his department, Norwood Hanson explained why he had personally changed his vote in an open letter that he sent to the press. The *New York Times* described Professor Hanson as "a 40-year old former fighter pilot whose field is the philosophy and history of science," adding that he "flies a war-surplus P-51 Mustang for recreation."[13] After this provocative introduction, the *Times* reported that Norwood Hanson

regretted making public his criticism of Dr. Bernstein, but was led to because "the matter has reached a stage where protocol and charitable demeanor are out of joint.... Each of us must now search his own heart and speak forth, as one day long hence he may wish he had done." Professor Hanson said he had given "unqualified support" to Dr. Bernstein when the philosophy professors made their original recommendation in November in favor of tenure. He gave two reasons for changing his vote to "a painfully sad (but nonetheless unqualified) negative."

One ... his "recent immersal in Bernsteiniana" had shown it to be "well-structured, clever and urbane," but "uniformly unoriginal, largely expository and exegetic and nowhere bearing the stamp of a 'new departure into unfurrowed conceptual territory.'"

The other reason, he said, was that the "Pavlovian response" of "chanting, protesting, bellicose demonstrators" should not be weighed against the "carefully deliberated verdict of seasoned judges." Otherwise, he said, Yale would become a "banana republic university, drifting aimlessly on the winds of student preference and fashion" and "ultimately a place from which I, for one, will hasten hence."[14]

In describing the scandal, the press generally focused on the concerns of students who believed the academy placed too much emphasis on publishing and not enough on teaching. It offered, however, other explanations as well for why Dick did not get tenure at Yale. The *Times* reported, for example, that, "Some believe that the intense outgoing philosopher, whose manner contrasts with the ironic, detached demeanor of many of his colleagues, has won few friends by his outspoken criticism of some academic procedures at Yale."[15]

The Times also reported on observations made by philosophers from other institutions who suggested that the "specific case of Dr. Bernstein is part of a larger split within the philosophy faculty at Yale—and in American philosophy in general—between the analytical and speculative approaches."[16] They identified Dick and "his mentor Paul Weiss" as being "primarily concerned with metaphysics and the speculative formulation of large systems of thought."

Responding to these remarks, George Schraeder, Chairman of the Department at the time, denied that any such split existed.

Whether they intended to or not, the tone of the statements made to the press announced to the world what everyone at Yale already knew—that the Department of Philosophy was in serious trouble and risked being torn apart by bitter conflict. A few years before Dick came up for tenure, distinguished members of the faculty had retired (Charles Hendel and Brand Blanshard).[17] Their departure shifted the balance of power, causing a great deal of turmoil. Four members of the faculty subsequently resigned and left for the University of Pittsburgh, an astonishing move, given the relative prestige of the two institutions (Wilfrid Sellars, Alan Anderson, Jerome Schneewind, and Nuel Belnap).[18] The defection from Yale turned Philosophy at Pittsburgh into one of the leading departments in the country.

When Dick came up for tenure, he faced a terribly weakened and divided faculty, but one fully aware of his popularity on campus. In reconstructing what happened, it appears that Dick never had the full support of the faculty in the newly configured department. Still, everyone agreed to go through with the motions of recommending him for reappointment. To the committee on tenure, however, they sent another message, implying, in effect, that the university-wide body do the "dirty work" for them. When Kingman Brewster blew the whistle and told the department to make an "unambiguous" recommendation, the majority changed their vote, disgracing themselves, shamefully betraying junior faculty and students who had taken their earlier expression of unanimity at face value.

As the story about Dick spread through the media, inquiries poured in from across the country and abroad. Thirty-six different institutions approached him to explore the possibility of making him an offer. Many departments of philosophy had openings that year—this was the mid-1960s and universities were expanding—and everyone, it seemed, wanted Dick and his journal.

In the end Dick accepted a position at Haverford, in part because it was located near Philadelphia, in an area surrounded by other fine colleges and universities, where his wife Carol too might find a job. A year later she received an offer from the University of Pennsylvania.

Dick arrived at Haverford in 1966, after spending another year in Israel. He remained there until 1989. Together with his colleagues, he created a first-rate department at the college, which became so popular that soon more students were studying philosophy than any other subject. Dick proudly remembers how freshmen and sophomores used to spend all night on line during registration week to get a place in one of the introductory courses that admitted only fifteen students to a section.

During those same years, Dick spoke out regularly against the war in Vietnam and participated as well in local political projects in the Philadelphia metropolitan area. Given his reputation, left-leaning students at Haverford and Bryn Mawr signed up for his classes in considerable numbers.

In the late 1960s and early 1970s, the female students at Bryn Mawr were more active politically than the boys at Haverford. Among the women who enrolled then in one of Dick's classes was,

a young radical who was very far left, much more left than I was, very militant, by the name of Nancy Shapiro.[19] She belonged to something called the Labor Committee, and so anything short of extreme orthodox Marxism was "bourgeois crap." And I was teaching a course, I think it was a course on Western Marxism, with readings by such figures as Habermas and Gramsci. And she got up one day and said that this was a lot of crap. The answer was really in the third volume of *Das Kapital* ... the falling rate of profit. And she and some other students took over the class and reorganized the curriculum. It was actually one of the best courses I've taught, because suddenly students were taking increasing responsibility for what was going on.

It was during this same period that Dick met Hannah Arendt. He remembers her coming to Haverford College to give a lecture on the eve of Passover in 1972. After her talk she joined a group of faculty and students for a communal Seder. Dick was not, he remembers, very interested in Arendt at the time. He was, in fact, "a little hostile," for he was deeply involved with Hegel and Marx and thought her reading of them "was completely outrageous. By the way, I still do."

Expanding on the point, Dick explained why he expected thoroughly to dislike her:

I had written a book called *Praxis in Action*. Many people think that this is my first book, but it's not. I had published others, including one with Yale on Peirce. And when the editor at Yale heard that I had another book, she was a bit indignant that I hadn't shown it to her first and so she asked to see it. I told her I was planning to publish the book with Penn and there were reasons for it. The editor at Penn was a German émigré, Fred Wieck, and I was writing on German thinkers. Even though I didn't want Yale to publish it, the editor took it upon herself to send the manuscript out to a reader. To this day I don't know who that reader was, but there was one thing you could say—the reader was a German émigré because the person was outraged that I would discuss people like Carnap and Dewey in the same book I was discussing Hegel and Marx. At this time in America you could name on one hand who was writing on Hegel and Marx. Why didn't I quote this German source? Why didn't I quote that German source? It was an outrageous kind of review—Why didn't I write the kind of a book I didn't? In my mind I thought that there was only one person in this country who could have had that kind of arrogance. And that must be Hannah Arendt. This was the mind-set.

Hannah Arendt comes in 1972. My book is out. I didn't invite her. Hannah Arendt told my colleague Sara Shumer that "when I come to Haverford, I want to meet Dick Bernstein." I hadn't the slightest idea what it was all about. But she came and we met. I even remember where, it was a place called the Haverford Hotel. And basically why did she want to see me? Fred Wieck, the editor at Penn, the one I liked so much, had sent her my book and she wanted to tell me how much she liked it. You see, in my mind-set, this was the enemy.

Now, it also tells a lot about Hannah. *Praxis and Action* is a book about action and I have in the entire book one little footnote to Hannah Arendt. Instead of having an attitude, as you can imagine, "why didn't you discuss my work, I'm dealing with the same issue," her attitude was: here is somebody trying to work on the same issue I'm interested in.

After their meeting in Haverford, two things happened:

Hannah asked what I was working on. I had gotten an NEH [National Endowment for the Humanities] Fellowship for the coming academic year to write *The Restructuring of Social and Political Theory* and she took it upon herself to give [the proposal] to her editor who was William Jovanovich himself and the next thing I know, I'm invited to the estate of William Jovanovich with Hannah Arendt and Mary McCarthy. We have a lovely lunch and a lovely talk, at the end of which he says, "I want to publish your next book." Because Hannah told him to.

The second thing she did was to invite Dick to come to the New School for an interview with the hope of recruiting him to the Graduate Faculty. In the end Arendt was more successful in placing Dick's book than in persuading her colleagues. The faculty and students split over the idea of making him an appointment and the Dean decided against going forward with the offer. In a letter to Dick expressing her disappointment, Hannah Arendt explained what had happened in the following way:

I don't think that the opposition is due to Byzantine intrigues—if there were intrigues, they certainly weren't Byzantine. The reason as I see it is very simple. I just reread your book [*Praxis and Action*] which I also use for a discussion of Marx in the seminar and I was again struck by the freshness and originality of your thought. The first reaction of the academic milieu to somebody who quite obviously strikes out on his own is always negative, and a number of our doctoral students, though not all, are already quite fixed in their thought habits, and react the same way as the faculty. Glenn Gray was here who as you probably know is a friend and an admirer of yours and very much in favor of this appointment. He told me that he found among the general reaction to your work either great enthusiasm or a certain hostility. I know the situation very well because I was for a very long time the object of similar reactions. And I must say that I find this only natural. One shouldn't get bitter about it and one should not acquire persecution complexes. All academic thinking, whether right, left or middle, is conservative in the extreme. Nobody wants to hear what he hasn't heard before.[20]

By this time, Dick and Hannah Arendt had become very good friends. A few months after his visit to the New School, Dick left for England, where he planned to spend the year with Carol and their four children, writing *The Restructuring of Social and Political Theory*. In the fall, however, he interrupted his stay to attend a conference in Toronto at York University dedicated to the work of Arendt. Sponsored by the Toronto Society for the Study of Social and Political Thought, the occasion gave Dick the first opportunity he ever had to write on Hannah Arendt. Returning to themes he discussed in *Praxis and Action*, he challenged Arendt's reading of Marx and Hegel, and offered his own.

As Elisabeth Young-Bruehl tells it, "The Conference . . . consisted of four papers, two of them by political theorists Arendt knew and respected highly—Richard Bernstein of Haverford College and Ernst Vollrath of Cologne University and the New School—and much discussion, for her interlocutors wanted to know why she, as a political theorist, rejected both the desire to influence others as a teacher and the desire to act."[21]

Hannah Arendt died about three years later. In the intervening months, Dick saw her very infrequently, but every encounter, he said, was intense. "The last conversation I had with Hannah Arendt was probably in the spring before she died (1975). She kept returning to the same theme. She was very disturbed about the New School. She was convinced that they were trying to give philosophy up, and she felt this would be a terrible mistake. I mean I'm not at the New School, I have nothing to do with this, but it was on her mind."

Then Arendt and Gurwitsch died and Jonas retired. By the early 1980s, the Department of Education of the State of New York had rescinded the right of Philosophy to accept new students, placing the same restriction on the Departments of Political Science and Sociology. Responding to the crisis, the trustees of the university appointed Jonathan Fanton president, and he in turn appointed Ira Katznelson as dean. Among his many early initiatives, Ira asked Dick in 1984 to join the "Enabling Committee," a special group of academic advisors, originally created several years earlier to guide the trustees. Expanded and transformed, the committee now met regularly with Ira to help him plan the rebuilding of the Graduate Faculty. "I'm still at Haverford, but I felt it was like fulfilling a testimony: a last testament. It was the last thing [Hannah] had said to me and now I ironically was going to play a role in helping to rebuild this department."

Dick met Ira Katznelson in England in the late 1970s, through the political theorist Steven Lukes. At the time, Dick remembers, Ira was teaching at the University of Chicago, and Dick invited him to attend a seminar he was running in Dubrovnik with Jürgen Habermas on philosophy and social science. The course was part of a program sponsored by the Inter-University Centre for Post-Graduate Studies.

An impressive roster of young intellectuals came to Dubrovnik from Western Europe and the U.S., eager to study with Bernstein and Habermas and to learn more about what was happening politically in the region. There, they met a group of equally impressive dissident intellectuals from Yugoslavia and other countries in Eastern and Central Europe. The Dubrovnik story is long and complicated and has already been told extremely well by Laura Secor.[22] Suffice it to say that the seminar attracted a number of Yugoslav activists who opposed Communism and identified themselves as social democrats. Some of these very same people, however, went on to collaborate with Slobodan Milosevic.[23] To complicate matters further, in 1980 Jürgen Habermas, Dick, and Albrecht Wellmer decided to revive *Praxis*, the dissident journal that the Yugoslav government had shut down a few years before. They would publish an international edition in Western Europe and the United States in cooperation with members of the opposition in the region. Once again they discovered in 1989 that a leading member of their regional editorial board had embraced Milosevic's campaign. Dick served as Editor-in-Chief of *Praxis International* until 1984.

In addition to Ira Katznelson, the seminar in Dubrovnik attracted a number of people who had, or would have, significant ties to the New School. These included Andrew Arato, Seyla Benhabib, Nancy Fraser, Jeffrey Goldfarb, Agnes Heller, Ivan Vejvoda, and Albrecht Wellmer. It was in Dubrovnik, in 1981, that Dick met the dissident Hungarian philosopher Agnes Heller for the first time. Agnes was based in Australia by then, together with her husband Ferenc Feher and their son. A couple of years later they met again at a conference in Frankfurt and Agnes remembers remarking to Ferenc that Dick was a "real dialogical philosopher."[24] He stood out, they agreed, by the way he listened to others and embraced different points of view. As Dick got to know Agnes and Ferenc a little better, he sensed that they might be tempted to leave Melbourne and come to the New School. Dick proposed the idea to the Enabling Committee and the Graduate Faculty recruited them. Ferenc came first and Agnes followed in 1986. While serving on the Enabling

Committee, Dick also recommended that the department bring back Albrecht Wellmer, who had taught there before in the early 1970s as a young assistant professor.

Finally, in 1988 when Agnes was chair, Dick became a candidate as well—for the second time. Once again, he faced opposition, in particular from Reiner Schürmann, who worried that Dick would turn the department into a program specializing in critical theory. In the end, Agnes succeeded in persuading her colleagues to support Dick's candidacy. She had seen him in action, she told them, and knew how receptive he was to the perspectives of others. He would never try to redefine the mission of the department to serve only one school of thought.

As Dick tells the story, "I came [to the New School] very reluctantly, because when Ira first spoke to me, I was very skeptical about whether they were going to put the resources into the department." But he came all the same, took over as chair and quickly won the hearts of Reiner Schürmann and others, including New School president Jonathan Fanton, who had studied at Yale in the mid-1960s and joined the protests on behalf of Dick. Using the department at Haverford as his model, Dick set out to shape a program at the Graduate Faculty of Political and Social Science that was dynamic, pluralistic, and open. Within a few years philosophy became the strongest department in the division.

Despite his initial skepticism and his ongoing struggles to find resources for the department, Dick feels that he made the right decision: "For me it was a very good move. I didn't originally leave Haverford because I was tired or bored. It was not the negative reasons. It was the positive reasons. For me intellectually the whole experience has been very stimulating.... I don't think I would have written faster if I had had less work." Since coming to the New School in 1989, Dick has written four major books, each of which shows in different ways how he embraced and renewed the intellectual traditions of the New School: *The New Constellation: The Ethical-Political Horizons of Modernity/Postmodernity* (1991), *Hannah Arendt and the Jewish Question* (1996), *Freud and the Legacy of Moses* (1998) and *Radical Evil* (2002).

In February 1989, Jonathan Fanton organized a special ceremony and dinner to inaugurate Dick's appointment to the Vera List Chair of Philosophy. For the occasion Dick gave a lecture that he called "Pragmatism, Pluralism, and the Healing of Wounds."[25] The talk, never published, presents a clear picture of what Dick hoped to accomplish in the Department of Philosophy and, by extension, in his own work. He envisioned a program deeply committed to teaching the history of philosophy, as it also explored creating "new constellations," by crossing old ideological divides that had long lost their meaning. In his talk Dick described the current state of the discipline, making reference to a 1904 essay by William James:

One of the most hopeful signs of philosophy in America today is this "unrest in the philosophic atmosphere," this "loosening of old landmarks."[26] The ideological battles of my generation [the Anglo-American/Continental split] are beginning to seem remote and irrelevant. Scars from the wounds of these battles still remain, but there are encouraging signs of the emergence of a new *ethos*—one which bears strong affinities with the *ethos* characteristic of the formative stages of the pragmatic movement. One may discover the ways in which deconstruction shows affinities with pragmatism or with the investigations of the later Wittgenstein. One may realize that Hegel's distinction between *Moralität* and *Sichlichkeit* is relevant for understanding contemporary moral and ethical theory. One may realize that Popper and Foucault are relevant for untangling the complexities of historicism. These interweavings extend to the interplay of disciplines which not so long ago were taken to be quite distinct—philosophy and law, philosophy and literature, philosophy and the social disciplines, philosophy and medicine, etc.[27]

He then went on to describe in greater detail the importance of pragmatism and the New School's historical ties to this American philosophical tradition:

Here I want to remind you of some of the ways in which the history of the New School has been intertwined with the pragmatic *ethos*. One of the founders of the New School was John Dewey. The *esprit* that shaped the New School during its formative years reflected Dewey's deepest educational concerns about what education ought to be in an urban democratic community. Horace Kallen, one of the most sensitive interpreters of the pragmatic tradition was among the first philosophers to teach at the New School.

Perhaps less well known, is the encounter with American philosophy that occurred when the University in Exile was established. Let me single out one strand of this encounter. Some of the first articles published in English by Aron Gurwitsch and Alfred Schutz dealt with William James. Like Husserl they both admired and respected James's pioneering work. They perceived the convergence and overlap between James's investigations and those of phenomenology. They were more than admirers of James. Each was influenced by James's subtle analyses of consciousness and temporality....

One might also mention Hannah Arendt's brilliant interpretation of the American revolutionary experience. Her analysis of political action and the public spaces that it requires bears a strong affinity with Dewey's own understanding of public political activity.

There is a moral—a promise—in these dialogical encounters with American traditions. For the New School philosophers sought to foster a genuine engagement with what is best in American traditions. They were not simply "defenders" of European traditions. Their creative contributions to philosophy are deeply marked by their critical appropriation of American traditions.[28]

In September 1999, the New School recognized Dick for his considerable gifts as a teacher. By this time he had already won four similar awards from other academic institutions. I can think of no better way to finish this portrait than with the words of his current students, many of whom wrote letters about Dick at the time he received the award, echoing the sentiments of earlier generations of student admirers, some of whom go back now nearly fifty years. These letters describe Dick's qualities as a teacher in terms reminiscent of Hannah Arendt's evocation of "vaunted Jewish qualities"—"humanity, humor, disinterested intelligence"—which she attributed to those she placed on her list of "conscious pariahs": Heinrich Heine, Rahel Varnhagen, Sholom Aleichem, Bernard Lazare, Franz Kafka, and Charlie Chaplin.[29] I conclude with selections from two letters:[30]

When I came to the New School, right away I saw that despite the large number of students in the philosophy department, [Professor Bernstein] works hard to make himself available to us, to become familiar with our academic passions on a personal level. Yet it was the first time I sat around a seminar table with him and a small group of students that I knew this professor was going to have a profound impact on me. Spending almost two hours on just one paragraph from Hegel, he challenged us to push ourselves to the limit. "If you want to smell incense, you can go out there on 14th Street, but if you want to do *philosophy*, you'll come in here and *sweat*," he said, as he banged his fist on the table.

A second student added:

Professor Bernstein's ability to teach at a consistently high level is unaffected by the difficult and time-consuming duties of running the philosophy department.... I think that it is a tremendous testament to his unwavering commitment to philosophy that he never appears to think of teaching as one more thing that he has to do. There is no question that he views his philosophical engagement with students to be the most important thing that he does.[31]

Acknowledgments

I would like to thank Richard Bernstein for letting me talk to him about his life in September, 2001, and hope that he will accept my apologies for leading him to believe that I was interviewing him then for the book I am going to write on the history of the New School, a project in which he will indeed figure prominently. I would also like to express my gratitude for the help I received from Seyla Benhabib, Erwin Fleissner, Agnes Heller, Magda Iwanska-Hirsch, Jerome Kohn, Clair Martin, Gustavo Madrigal, Gail Persky, Marta Petrusewicz, and Sonia Salas.

Notes

1. Hannah Arendt, "Action and 'The Pursuit of Happiness,'" in *Politische Ordnung und Menschliche Existenz: Festgabe für Eric Voegelin* (Munich: Beck, 1962), pp. 1–16. Cited in Richard J. Bernstein, *Hannah Arendt and the Jewish Question* (Devon: Polity, 1996), epigraph, p. ix.

2. Bernstein, *Hannah Arendt and the Jewish Question.*

3. Richard Bernstein, *The New Constellation: The Ethical-Political Horizons of Modernity/ Postmodernity* (Cambridge, Mass.: The MIT Press, 1992), p. 329.

4. Bernstein, *Hannah Arendt and the Jewish Question*, p. 45.

5. The *Yale Alumni Magazine* (*YAM*) published an article on the ongoing plight of the department and the university's most recent attempt to address the problem ("Rethinking Philosophy," John Zonderman, November, 1995, pp. 40–43). A few months later, the magazine printed three letters from alumni who had studied

Judith Friedlander

philosophy at Yale in the 1950s and the 1960s. All of the letters had harsh things to say about the department and two of them spoke directly about Dick. Edward Kent (A.B., 1956) described the "ugly and much publicized attack on Richard Bernstein"; while Richard Gaskins (Ph.D. 1971 and J.D. 1975) noted with barbed diplomacy— after speaking first about the "pettiness and bickering that marred our experience as graduate students"—that, "If one needs any other standard for rebuilding the department, one might also look to the recent efforts of a former member of the Yale department, Richard Bernstein, at the New School for Social Research. There's another one that got away" (*YAM*, February 1996, pp. 6–9).

6. Although Dick and I discussed his tenure case at Yale, most of the information reported here comes from accounts published in the press.

7. *New York Times*, March 3, 1965, p. 9.

8. *Newsweek*, March 15, 1965, p. 48.

9. *Time*, March 12, 1965, p. 48.

10. *New York Times*, March 9, 1965, p. 41.

11. Ibid.

12. Ibid.

13. *New York Times*, March 8, 1965, p. 23.

14. Ibid.

15. Ibid.

16. *New York Times*, March 9, 1965, p. 41.

17. Hendel in 1959 and Blanshard in 1961.

18. Sellars, Schneewind, and Belnap in 1963 and Anderson in 1964. Schneewind and Belnap did not have tenure at Yale.

19. Later known as Nancy Fraser.

20. Hannah Arendt, Letter to Richard Bernstein, October 31, 1972, Library of Congress Collection, Washington, D.C., and New School for Social Research, New York.

21. Elisabeth Young-Bruehl, *Hannah Arendt: For the Love of the World* (New Haven: Yale University Press, 1982), pp. 450–451.

22. Laura Secor, "Testaments Betrayed: Yugoslav Intellectuals and the Road to War," *Lingua Franca*, September 1999, pp. 26–42.

23. A political scientist who had to leave Belgrade when Milosevic came to power, Ivan Vejvoda is presently Executive Director of the Fund for an Open Society— Yugoslavia, sponsored by the Soros Foundation. In 1990 he became a member of

the New School's Democracy Seminars, which met annually in East and Central Europe for about ten years.

24. Personal communication, September 2001.

25. Dick took the title for this talk from a paper he had given two months before as his Presidential Address to the Eastern Division Meeting of the American Philosophical Association. See Richard Bernstein, *The New Constellation*, pp. 323–340.

26. William James, "A World of Pure Experience," *Journal of Philosophy, Psychology, and Scientific Methods*, vol. I, 1904, p. 533.

27. Richard Bernstein, "Pragmatism, Pluralism, and the Healing of Wounds," Inaugural Lecture, February 8, 1989 (unpublished manuscript), pp. 15–16.

28. Ibid., p. 17.

29. Hannah Arendt, *The Jew as Pariah*, edited by Ron H. Feldman (New York: Grove, 1978), pp. 65–66.

30. These students wrote to me in the summer of 1999, during my last year as Dean of the Graduate Faculty, with the understanding that their identities would not be revealed, for they had still not finished their degrees.

31. When I wrote this biographical sketch in 2001, Richard Bernstein was still Chairman of the Department of Philosophy. In 2002, he became Dean of the Graduate Faculty, a position he held for two years and served with distinction, providing inspired leadership over a difficult period of transition.

Works by Richard J. Bernstein

Books and Monographs

With M. Eson. *A Study of Some Aspects of Education in Israel.* Jerusalem: Ministry of Education Press, 1958. (Published in Hebrew.)

John Dewey: On Experience, Nature, and Freedom, ed. R. J. Bernstein. New York: Liberal Arts Press, 1960. Reprint: Arno Press.

John Dewey, The Great American Thinkers Series. New York: Washington Square Press, 1966. Reprint: Atascadero, Calif.: Ridgeview, 1981.

Perspectives on Peirce, ed. R. J. Bernstein. New Haven, Conn.: Yale University Press, 1965. Reprinted: Westport, Conn.: Greenwood Press, 1980.
Japanese translation: Bokutaku, 1985.

"The Philosophy of Paul Weiss, Twenty-Fifth Year Supplement," ed. R. J. Bernstein. *Review of Metaphysics* 25 (June 1972).

Praxis and Action. Philadelphia, Penn.: University of Pennsylvania Press, 1971.
British edition: London: Gerald Duckworth, 1972.
German translation: *Praxis und Handlen* (with new introduction). Frankfurt: Suhrkamp Verlag, 1975.
Spanish translation: *Praxis y accion.* Madrid: Alianza Editorial, 1979.
University of Pennsylvania Press edition with a new preface, 1999.

The Restructuring of Social and Political Theory. New York: Harcourt Brace Jovanovich, 1976.
Paperback edition: Philadelphia, Penn.: University of Pennsylvania Press, 1977.
British edition: Oxford: Basil Blackwell, 1976.
British paperback: London: Methuen, 1979.
German translation: *Restrukturierung der Gesellschaftstheorie.* Frankfurt: Suhrkamp Verlag, 1979.
Italian translation: *La Ristrutturazione della Teoria Sociale e Politica.* Rome: Armando Armando, 1980.

Spanish translation: *La Reestructuracion de la Theoria Social y Politica.* Fondo de Cultura Economica, 1983.

Beyond Objectivism and Relativism: Science, Hermeneutics and Praxis. Philadelphia, Penn.: University of Pennsylvania Press, 1983.
British edition: Oxford: Basil Blackwell, 1983.
Swedish translation: *Bortom Objektivism och Relativism: Vetenskap, hermeneutik och praxis.* Götenberg: Röda Bokförlaget, 1987.
Japanese, Korean, Spanish, and Turkish translations.

Habermas and Modernity, ed. with an introduction by R. J. Bernstein. Oxford: Basil Blackwell (Polity Press), 1985.
U.S. edition: Cambridge, Mass.: The MIT Press, 1985.
Spanish translation: *Habermas y la Modernidad.* Catedra: coleccion teorema, 1988.

Philosophical Profiles: Essays in a Pragmatic Mode. Oxford: Basil Blackwell (Polity Press), 1986.
U.S. edition: Philadelphia, Penn.: University of Pennsylvania Press, 1986. (Papers marked with an asterisk are included in this volume.)
Spanish translation: *Perfiles filosoficus.* Siglo vein tiuno editiones is. a. de c.v., 1991.

The New Constellation: The Ethical-Political Horizons of Modernity/Postmodernity. Cambridge: Polity Press, 1991.
U.S. edition: Cambridge, Mass.: The MIT Press, 1992.
Italian translation: *La nuova costellazione: Gli orizzonti etico-politici del moderno/ postmoderno.* Milan: Feltrinelli, 1994.
Bulgarian, Japanese, and Korean translations.

Hannah Arendt and the Jewish Question. Cambridge: Polity Press, 1996.
U.S. edition: Cambridge, Mass.: The MIT Press, 1996.

Freud and the Legacy of Moses. Cambridge: Cambridge University Press, 1998.
(Partial) Hungarian translation included in: *Hagyomány és Freudizmus.* Budapest: Új Vilag Liadó, 1998.
Portuguese translation, 2000.
Spanish translation: *Freud y El Legado de Moisés.* Traduciión de Enrique Mercado. Mexico: Siglo vientiuno editores, 2002.
German translation: Freud und das Vermächtnis des Moses. Philo Press, 2003.

Responsibility of the Philosopher, ed. Obrad Savic, 2000. (Serbian translation of a selection of articles.)

Radical Evil: A Philosophical Interrogation. Cambridge: Polity Press, 2002.

Articles, Reviews, and Miscellaneous

1956
"Decision and Indecision in Contemporary Empiricism." *Ideas* 5/4 (1956).

1958
"Education in Israel." *Ha' aretz,* 16 July 1958 (Tel Aviv, Israel).

Works by Richard J. Bernstein

1959

"Dewey's Naturalism." *Review of Metaphysics* 13/2 (1959): 340–353.

1960

"Knowledge, Value, and Freedom." In *John Dewey and the Experimental Spirit in Philosophy*, ed. Charles Hendel. New York: Liberal Arts Press, 1960.

"Packaged Wisdom." *Commonweal*, 22 April 1960.

1961

"John Dewey's Metaphysics of Experience." *Journal of Philosophy* 57/1 (1961): 5–14.

"The Thought of Stuart Hampshire." A Discussion of *Thought and Action*, by Stuart Hampshire. *Commentary* 31/3 (March 1961): 262–264.

"Charles Sanders Peirce and the *Nation*." *Antioch Review* 21/2 (spring 1961): 15–25. Reprinted in *Nation*, 22 March 1965. Reprinted in *Charles Sanders Peirce: Contributions to the Nation*, part 1, 1869–1893. Compiled and ed. K. L. Ketner and J. E. Cook. Lubbock, Tex.: Graduate Studies of Texas Technical University, 1975.

"Natural Law and a National Consensus." Review of *We Hold These Truths*, by John Courtney Murray. *New Leader*, 22 May 1961.

"A Double-Edged Logic." Review of *The Quest for Being*, by Sidney Hook. *Saturday Review*, 22 July 1961.

"Fromm's Concept of Marx." Review of *Marx's Concept of Man*, by Erich Fromm. *New Leader*, 2 October 1961.

"Wittgenstein's Three Languages." *Review of Metaphysics* 15/2 (1961): 278–298. Reprinted in *Wittgenstein's Tractatus*, ed. I. Copi and R. Beard. New York: Macmillan, 1966.

1962

Review of *American Pragmatism*, by Edward C. Moore. *Journal of Philosophy* 59/10 (1962): 272–274.

1963

"Undergraduate Education Today: Philosophy." *Yale Alumni Magazine* (January 1963).

Review of *The Predicament of Democratic Man*, by Edmond Cahn. *Yale Law Journal* 72/6 (1963).

"Post-Wittgensteinian Dilemmas." Review of *Reason and Conduct*, by Henry Aiken. *Commentary* 35/6 (June 1963): 547–550.

"The Marxist Revival." *Occasional Stiles* 2 (September 1962): 106–115. (Published by Ezra Stiles College, Yale University.)

1964

"Professor Hart on Rules of Obligation." *Mind* 73/292 (October 1964): 563–566.

"Peirce's Theory of Perception." In *Studies in the Philosophy of Charles Sanders Peirce, Second Series*, ed. E. C. Moore and R. Robin. Amherst, Mass.: University of Massachusetts Press, 1964.

"Action, Conduct, and Self-Control." In *Perspectives on Peirce.*

"Myths About the Mississippi Summer Project." *Nation*, 28 December 1964.

Review of *John Dewey and Self-Realization*, by Robert J. Roth. *International Philosophical Quarterly* 4 (fall 1964): 485–487.

1966

"Sellars' Vision of Man-in-the-World, Part I." *Review of Metaphysics* 20/1 (1966): 113–143.

Works by Richard J. Bernstein

"Sellars' Vision of Man-in-the-World, Part II." *Review of Metaphysics* 20/2 (1966): 290–316.

"John Dewey." In *Encyclopedia of Philosophy*, ed. Paul Edwards. New York: Macmillan and the Free Press: 1966.

"The Challenge of Scientific Materialism" (Hebrew version). *Iyyun* 18/1–2 (1966).

1967

"Buchler's Metaphysics." *Journal of Philosophy* 64/22 (1967): 751–770. Reprinted in *Nature's Perspectives: Prospects for Ordinal Metaphysics*, ed. A. Marsoobian, K. Wallace, R. S. Corrington. Albany, N.Y.: State University of New York Press, 1991.

Review of *Lectures in the Philosophy of Education*, by John Dewey. *Social Studies* 58/6 (November 1967): 284–286.

1968

"The Challenge of Scientific Materialism" (English version). *International Philosophical Quarterly* 8/2 (1966): 252–275. Reprinted in *Materialism and the Mind-Body Problem*, ed. David M. Rosenthal. Englewood Cliffs, N.J.: Prentice Hall, 1971.

1969

Review Symposium of *Essays in Sociological Explanation*, by Neil J. Smelser, with a response by Smelser. *Sociological Inquiry* 39/2 (spring 1969): 201–217.

1970

"In Defense of American Philosophy." In *Contemporary American Philosophy, Second Series*, ed. J. E. Smith. New York: Humanities Press, 1970.

"An Interview by Richard Bernstein: Paul Weiss' Recollections of Editing the Peirce Papers."
Transactions of the Charles S. Peirce Society 6/3–4 (summer–fall 1970).

From 1960 through 1970 numerous short reviews of books published in the *Review of Metaphysics*.

1971

Introduction to paperback edition of William James, *Essays in Radical Empiricism* and *A Pluralistic Universe*. New York: E. P. Dutton, 1971.

"Herbert Marcuse: An Immanent Critique." *Social Theory and Practice* 1/4 (fall 1971): 97–111.

1972

Critical review of *The Coming Crisis of Western Sociology*, by Alvin Gouldner. *Sociological Inquiry* 42/1 (1972): 65–72.

"Introductory Remarks" to "The Philosophy of Paul Weiss, Twenty-Fifth Year Supplement," ed. R. J. Bernstein. *Review of Metaphysics* 25 (June 1972): 4–7.

1973

"The Frankfurt School." Critical review of *The Dialectical Imagination*, by Martin Jay. *Midstream* (August–September 1973): 55–66.

1974

"Author's Response," Symposium on *Praxis and Action*. *Philosophy Forum* 14/2 (1974): 171–194.

1975

Review of *Hegel's Theory of the Modern State*, by Shlomo Avineri; and *Hegel*, by Raymond Plant. *Political Theory* 3/3 (August 1975): 344–352.

Review of *The Legacy of Hegel: Proceedings of the Marquette Hegel Symposium,* 1970. *The Owl of Minerva: Quarterly Publication of the Hegel Society of America* (1975).

1977

Introduction to William James, *A Pluralistic Universe: The Works of William James,* ed. Frederick Burkhardt. Cambridge, Mass.: Harvard University Press, 1977.

"Hannah Arendt: The Ambiguities of Theory and Practice." In *Political Theory and Praxis: New Perspectives,* ed. Terrence Ball. Minneapolis, Minn.: University of Minnesota Press, 1977.

Review of *The Life of the Mind,* by Hannah Arendt. Sunday Book Review Section, *New York Times,* 28 May 1977.

Review of *The Moon and the Ghetto: An Essay on Public Policy Analysis,* by Richard R. Nelson. *Chronicle of Higher Education,* 5 July 1977.

"Why Hegel Now?" Critical Study of *Hegel,* by Charles Taylor. *Review of Metaphysics* 31/1 (1977): 29–60.

1979

"Thinking Through Critical Theory." Review of *The Critical Theory of Jürgen Habermas,* by Thomas McCarthy. *Review of Politics* 41/2 (1979): 298–301.

"Kant, Hegel, and Ayer vs. Abraham." Review of *Encounters between Judaism and Modern Philosophy,* by Emil Fackenheim. *Midstream* 25/10 (December 1979): 62–64.

1980

"Comment on the Relationship of Habermas's Views to Hegel." In *Hegel's Social and Political Thought,* ed. D. P. Verene. New York: Humanities Press, 1980.

"Philosophy and the Conversation of Mankind." Critical Study of *Philosophy and the Mirror of Nature,* by Richard Rorty. *Review of Metaphysics* 33/4 (1980): 745–775. Reprinted in *Hermeneutics and Praxis,* ed. Robert Hollinger. Notre Dame: University of Notre Dame Press, 1986.

Review of *Main Currents of Marxism: Its Rise, Growth, and Dissolution,* by L. Kolakowski. *Review of Metaphysics* 33/3 (1980): 635–637.

Review of *Transformation of Philosophy,* by Karl-Otto Apel. *Political Theory* 9/3 (1980): 434–437.

Introduction to English translation of Karl-Otto Apel, *Charles S. Peirce: From Pragmatism to Pragmaticism.* Amherst, Mass.: University of Massachusetts Press, 1980.

1981

"Towards a More Rational Community." In *Graduate Studies Texas Technical University,* ed. Kenneth L. Ketner. Lubbock, Tex.: Texas Technical University Press, 1981.

"Herbert Marcuse—Negativity: Theme and Variations." *Praxis International* 1/1 (1981): 87–100.

1982

"From Hermeneutics to Praxis." *Review of Metaphysics* 35/4 (June 1982): 823–845. Reprinted in *Hermeneutics and Modern Philosophy,* ed. Bruce R. Wachterhauser. Albany, N.Y.: State University of New York Press, 1986. Reprinted in *Hermeneutics and Praxis,* ed. Robert Hollinger. Notre Dame, Ind.: University of Notre Dame Press, 1986.

"Hannah Arendt: Judging—The Actor and the Spectator." In *Proceedings of History, Ethics, Politics: A Conference Based on the Work of Hannah Arendt,* ed. R. Boyers. Saratoga Springs, N.Y.: Empire State College, 1982. Reprinted in *The Realm of Humanitas: Responses to the Writings of Hannah Arendt.* New York: Peter Lang, 1990.

"Human Beings: Plurality and Togetherness." Critical Study of *You, I, and the Others*, by Paul Weiss. *Review of Metaphysics* 35/4 (June 1982): 349–366. Reprinted in *Creativity and Common Sense*, ed. Thomas Krettek. Albany, N.Y.: State University of New York Press, 1987.
"What Is the Difference That Makes a Difference? Gadamer, Habermas, Rorty." *Proceedings of the Philosophy Science Association* 2, ed. P. D. Asquith and T. Nickles (1983). Reprinted in *Hermeneutics and Modern Philosophy*, ed. Robert Hollinger. Notre Dame, Ind.: University of Notre Dame Press, 1986. Hebrew translation: In *Between Theory and Practice*, ed. Y. Yovel and P. Mendes-Flohr. Jerusalem: Magnus Press, 1984.

1984
"Nietzsche or Aristotle?" Reflections on *After Virtue*, by Alasdair MacIntyre, with a reply by MacIntyre. *Soundings* 67/1 (1984): 6–20 (MacIntyre's reply: 30–41).

1985
"Heidegger on Humanism." *Praxis International* 5 (July 1985): 95–114. Reprinted in *Pragmatism Considers Phenomenology*, ed. Robert S. Corrington, Carl Hausmann, Thomas Seebohm. Washington, D.C.: Center for Advanced Research in Phenomenology and University Press of America, 1987.
"Dewey, Democracy: The Task Ahead of Us." In *Post-Analytic Philosophy*, ed. John Rajchman and Cornel West. New York: Columbia University Press, 1985.

1986
"The Question of Moral and Social Development." In *Value Presuppositions in Theories of Human Development*, ed. L. Cirillo and S. Wapner. Hillside, N.J.: Lawrence Erlbaum, 1986.
"Rethinking the Social and the Political." *Graduate Faculty Philosophy Journal* 11/1 (1986): pp. 111–130.
"Structuration as Critical Theory." *Praxis International* 6/2 (1986): 235–249.
"The Rage Against Reason." *Philosophy and Literature* 10/2 (October 1986): 186–210. Reprinted in *Construction and Constraint*, ed. Ernan McMullin. Notre Dame, Ind.: University of Notre Dame Press, 1988.
"The Meaning of Public Life." In *Religion and American Public Life*, ed. Robin W. Lovin. New York: Paulist Press, 1986.

1987
"Philosophy: A Historical Discipline?" In *At the Nexus of Philosophy History*, ed. Bernard P. Davenhauer. Athens, Ga.: University of Georgia Press, 1987. Serbo-Croatian translation: "Filozofija: Istorijska Disciplina?" In *Filozofija i Društvo*, ed. Mihailu Markovicu. Beograd: Center za filozofiju: društvenu teoriju, 1987.
"Agnes Heller: Philosophy, Rational Utopia and Praxis." *Thesis Eleven* 16 (1987): 22–39. Reprinted in *The Social Philosophy of Agnes Heller*, ed. John Burnheim. Atlanta: Rodophi Press, 1994.
"Serious Play: The Ethical-Political Horizon of Jacques Derrida." *Journal of Speculative Philosophy* 1/2 (1987): 93–117. Reprinted in *The New Constellation: The Ethical-Political Horizons of Modernity/Postmodernity*. Cambridge, Mass.: The MIT Press, 1992. Serbo-Croation translation: "Ozbiljna lgra: Eticko-Politicka Horizont Zak Derrida." *Gledista* 5–6.
"One Step Forward, Two Steps Backward: Rorty on Liberal Democracy and Philosophy." *Political Theory* 15/4 (November 1987): 538–563. French translation: "Un pas en avant, deux pas en arrvre: la democratie librale wt la philosophie selon Richard Rorty." *Futor antrieur* (1992).

Works by Richard J. Bernstein

"The Varieties of Pluralism." *American Journal of Education* 95/4 (August 1987): 509–525.

1988

"Interpretation and Its Discontents: The Choreography of Critique"; "Making a Difference: A Plea for Differences—A Reply to Adolf Grunbaum." Both articles in *Hermeneutics and Psychological Theory*, ed. S. Messer, L. Sass, and R. Woolfolk. New Brunswick, N.J.: Rutgers University Press, 1988.

Review of *Whose Justice? Which Rationality?* by Alasdair MacIntyre. *Commonweal*, 20 May 1988.

"Critical Inquiry, Civic Friendship and the Pursuit of Community." *Texas Journal* 10 (spring–summer 1988).

"Metaphysics, Critique, and Utopia," Presidential Address to Metaphysical Society of America. *Review of Metaphysics* 42/2 (December 1988): 255–274.

"Fred Dallmayr's Critique of Habermas." *Political Theory* 16/4 (November 1988): 580–593.

"Hermeneutics and Its Anxieties." In *Hermenuetics and the Tradition*, ed. Daniel O. Dahlstrom, *Proceedings of the American Catholic Philosophical Association* 62 (1988): 58–70.

1989

"Radical Plurality, Fearful Ambiguity, and Engaged Hope." Review of *Plurality and Ambiguity*, by David Tracy. *Journal of Religion* 69 (January 1989): 85–91.

"Foucault: Critique as a Philosophic Ethos." In *Zwischenbetrachtungen Im Prozess der Aufklärung*, ed. A. Honneth, T. McCarthy, C. Offe, and A. Wellmer. Frankfurt: Suhrkamp Verlag, 1989. Reprinted in *Philosophical Interventions in the Unfinished Project of Enlightenment*. Ed. Honneth and Axel. Cambridge, Mass.: The MIT Press, 1992. Reprinted in *Critique and Power*. Ed. Michael Kelly. Cambridge, Mass.: The MIT Press, 1994.

"Pragmatism, Pluralism, and the Healing of Wounds," Presidential Address, APA Eastern Division. *Proceedings and Addresses of the American Philosophical Association* 63/3 (1989): 5–18. Reprinted in *The New Constellation: The Ethical-Political Horizons of Modernity/Postmodernity*. Cambridge: Polity Press, 1991.

"Interpretation and Solidarity: An Interview with Richard Bernstein by Dunja Melcic." *Praxis International* 9 (October 1989): 201–219.

1990

"Social Theory as Critique." In *Social Theory of Modern Societies: Anthony Giddens and His Critics*, ed. D. Held and J. B. Thompson. Cambridge: Cambridge University Press, 1990.

"Rorty's Liberal Utopia." *Social Research* 57 (spring 1990): 31–72. Reprinted in *The New Constellation: The Ethical-Political Horizons of Modernity/Postmodernity*. Cambridge: Polity Press, 1991.

1991

"The Lure of the Ideal." In *Peirce and Law*, ed. Roberta Kavelson. New York: Peter Lang, 1991. Portuguese translation: "A seducdo ideal." *Revista de Semitica e Communico* 3/2: 195–206.

"Does Philosophy Matter?" *The New School Commentator* 2/6 (March 1991): 1–4. Reprinted in *Thinking: A Journal of Philosophy of Children* 9/4 (1991).

"Una revis'on de las conexiones entre incommensurabilidad y ortredad." *Isegor'a, Revista de Filosof'a Moral y Politica* 3 (April 1991): 5–25. (Spanish translation of "Incommensurability and Otherness Revisited.")

"John Dewey: Philosopher of Democracy." Critical study of *John Dewey and American Democracy*, by Robert Westbrook. *Intellectual History Newsletter* 13 (September 1991): 48–55.

1992

"Reconciliation and Rupture: The Challenge and Threat of Otherness." In *Discourse and Practice*, ed. Frank Reynolds and David Tracy. Albany: State University of New York Press, 1992. Reprinted in *The New Constellation: The Ethical-Political Horizons of Modernity/Postmodernity*. Cambridge: Polity Press, 1991.
"The Resurgence of American Pragmatism." *Social Research* 59 (winter 1992): 813–840. Spanish translation: "El Resurgir del Pragmatismo." In *El Giro Posmoderno*, edicion a cargo de José Rubio Carracedo. Malagra: Philosophica Malacitena, 1993.
Review of *The Critique of Power*, by Axel Honneth. *Political Theory* 20 (August 1992): 523–527.

1993

"An Allegory of Modernity/Postmodernity: Habermas and Derrida." Reprinted in *Working Through Derrida*, ed. Gary B. Madison. Evanston, Ill.: Northwestern University Press, 1993. Reprinted in *The New Constellation: The Ethical-Political Horizons of Modernity/Postmodernity*. Cambridge: Polity Press, 1991.
"The 'modern/postmodern' debate." In *Development and Modernity*, ed. Lars Gule and Oddver Storebø. Bergen, Norway: Ariadne, 1993.
"Postmodernism, Dialogue and Democracy: Questions to Richard J. Bernstein." In *Postmodern Contentions: Epochs, Politics, Space*, ed. J. P. Jones, W. Walter, and T. Schatzki. New York: Guilford Publications, 1992.

1994

"Hans Jonas: Rethinking Responsibility." *Social Research* 61/4 (winter 1994): 833–852. Reprinted in the *Hastings Journal*.
"Linguistischer Idealismus bei Fraser und Gordon." In *Auf der Suche nach der Gerechten Gesellschaft*, Herausgegeben von Gunter Frankenberg. Frankfurt: Fischer Taschenbuch Verlag, 1994.

1995

"American Pragmatism: The Conflict of Narratives." In *Rorty and Pragmatism*, ed. Herman J. Saatkamp, Jr. Nashville, Tenn.: Vanderbilt University Press, 1995.
"Whatever Happened to Naturalism?" *Proceedings and Addresses of the American Philosophical Association* 69/2 (November 1995): 57–76.
"Are We Beyond the Enlightenment Horizon?" In *Knowledge and Belief in America*, ed. William M. Shea and Peter A. Huff. New York: Cambridge University Press (Woodrow Wilson Center), 1995.
"Rethinking Responsibility." *Hastings Center Report* 25/7 (1995): 13–20.

1996

"The 'Banality of Evil' Reconsidered." In *Hannah Arendt and the Meaning of Politics*, ed. Craig Calhoun and John McGowan. Minneapolis, Minn.: University of Minnesota Press, 1996.
"Did Hannah Arendt Change Her Mind? From Radical Evil to the Banality of Evil." In *Hannah Arendt: 20 Years Later*, ed. Jerome Kohn and Larry May. Cambridge, Mass.: The MIT Press, 1996.
"The Retrieval of the Democratic Ethos." *Cardoza Law Review* 17/4–5 (March 1996): 1127–1146. Reprinted in *Review of Japanese Culture and Society* 7 (December 1995): 1–12. Reprinted in *Habermas on Law and Democracy: Critical Exchanges*, ed.

Works by Richard J. Bernstein

Michel Rosenfeld and Andrew Arato. Berkeley, Calif.: University of California Press, 1998.

"The Hermeneutics of Cross-Cultural Understanding." In *Cross-Cultural Conversation (Initiation)*, ed. Anindita Niyoga Balslev. Atlanta, Ga.: Scholars Press, 1996.

1997
"Hans Jonas's *Mortality and Morality*." *Graduate Faculty Philosophy Journal* 19/20 (2/1) (1997): 315–321.

"Provocation and Appropriation: Hannah Arendt's Response to Martin Heidegger." *Constellations* 4/2 (October 1997): 153–171.

"Demokratie als moralische Lebensweise." *Frankfurter Rundschau*, April 1, 1997.

1998
"Community in the Pragmatic Tradition." In *The Revival of Pragmatism: New Essays on Social Thought, Law, and Culture*, ed. Morris Dickstein. Chapel Hill, N.C.: Duke University Press, 1998.

"Faire la part de ce qui sépare Rorty et Habermas et se situer dans l'entre-deux." In *De Rorty à Jürgen Habermas: La Modernité en Question*, ed. Françoise Gaillard, Jacques Poulain, and Richard Schusterman. France: Centre culturel international de Cerisy-la-Salle, 1998.

1999
"Responsibility, Judging and Evil." *Revue Internationale de Philosophie* 53/208 (1999): 155–172.

"Faith and Reason: Response to Pope John Paul II's encyclical letter, *Fides et Ratio*." *Books and Culture: A Christian Review*, July/August, 1999.

"Provocazione e appropriazone: la reposta a Martin Heidegger," Italian Translation of "Provocation and Appropriation: Hannah Arendt's Response to Martin Heidegger." In *Hannah Arendt: Intoduzione e cura di Simona Forti*, Milano: Edizion, Bruno Mundaduri, 1999.

Review of "Alexander Nehamas, *The Art of Living*." *Bryn Mawr Review of Comparative Literature* 1/1 (1999), http://www.brynmawr.edu/bmrcl.

"Jan Assmann's *Moses the Egyptian*: The Memory of Egypt in Western Monotheism" *Graduate Faculty Philosophy Journal* 21/2 (1999): 233–253.

New preface for 1999 edition of *Praxis and Action*. Philadelphia, Penn.: University of Pennsylvania Press.

2000
"Gadamer: Tiefe Affinität zum Pragmatismus." *Frankfurter Rundschau*, February 2000.

"Arendt on Thinking." In *The Cambridge Companion to Hannah Arendt*, ed. Dana Villa. Cambridge: Cambridge University Press, 2000.

"La identidad hispano/latino." *Revista Internacional de Filosofia Politica*, no. 16, December 2000: 181–183.

"Creative Democracy—The Task Still Before Us." *American Journal of Theology and Philosophy*, 21/3, September (2000): 215–228.

"Verantwortlichkeit, Urteilen und das Böse." In *Hannah Arendt Revisited: "Eichmann in Jerusalem" und die Folgen*, ed. Gary Smith. Frankfurt: Suhrkamp, 2000.

2001
"Comment on Hispanic/Latino Identity." *Philosophy and Social Criticism* 27/2 (2001): 44–50.

Works by Richard J. Bernstein

"Religion and Public Life: Engaged Pluralism." *Modern Schoolman*, January/March 78 (2–3) (2001): 189–198.

"Arendt's Zionism." In *Arendt in Jerusalem*, ed. Steven Ascheim. Berkeley, Calif.: University of California Press, 2001.

"Kant at War with Himself." In *Rethinking Evil*, ed. Maria Pia Lara. Berkeley, Calif.: University of California Press, 2001.

2002

"Reflections on Radical Evil: Arendt and Kant." In *Culture and Enlightenment; Essays for György Markus*, ed. John Grumley, et al. Burlington, Vt.: Ashgate, 2002.

"Reflessioni sul male radicale: Arendt e Kant." *La Società Degli Individui* 5, no. 13, 2002.

"Putnams Stellung in der pragmatistischen Tradition." In *Hilary Putnam und die Tradition des Pragmatismus*, ed. Marie-Luise Raters und Marcus Willaschek. Frankfurt: Suhrkamp, 2002.

"The Constellation of Hermeneutics, Critical Theory, and Deconstruction." In *The Cambridge Companion to Gadamer*, ed. Robert J. Dostal. Cambridge: Cambridge University Press, 2002.

Forward to *Richard Rorty: An Annotated Bibliography of Secondary Literature* by Richard Ruma. A volume in Studies in Pragmatism and Values (SPV), ed. John R. Shook. New York: Rodopi Press, 2002.

"Evil and the Temptation of Theodicy." In *The Cambridge Companion to Levinas*, ed. Simon Critchley and Robert Bernasconi. Cambridge: Cambridge University Press, 2002.

"McDowell's Domesticated Hegelianism." In *Reading McDowell: On Mind and World*, ed. Nicholas H. Smith. London: Routledge, 2002.

"The Origins of Totalitarianism: Not History but Politics" *Social Research* 69: 2 (summer 2002): 381–401.

Contributors

Seyla Benhabib is the Eugene Meyer Professor of Political Science and Philosophy and Director of the Program in Ethics, Politics, and Economics at Yale University. Her publications include *Critique, Norm, and Utopia* (1986); *Situating the Self* (1992); *The Reluctant Modernism of Hannah Arendt* (1996); *Transformations of Citizenship: Dilemmas of the Nation—State in the Global Era* (2000); *The Claims of Culture: Equality and Diversity in the Global Era* (2002), and *The Rights of Others: Aliens, Residents, and Citizens* (2004).

Carol L. Bernstein is Mary E. Garrett Alumnae Professor of English and Comparative Literature at Bryn Mawr College. Her books include *Precarious Enchantment: A Reading of George Meredith* and *The Celebration of Scandal: Toward the Sublime in Victorian Urban Fiction.* She is currently working on cultural memory and the ethics of narrative, as well as on Walter Benjamin and the trajectory of the sublime.

Jacques Derrida is Directeur d'Etudes at the Ecole des Hautes Etudes en Sciences Sociales and cofounder of the Collège Internationale de Philosophie, as well as visiting professor at the University of California at Irvine, New York University, and the New School for Social Research. Among his many books are *Writing and Difference; Voice and Phenomenon; Of Grammatology; Dissemination; The Postcard; Glas; Specters of Marx; Politics of Friendship;* and *Adieu to Emmanuel Levinas.*

Nancy Fraser is the Henry and Louise A. Loeb Professor of Politics and Philosophy at the Graduate Faculty of the New School for Social Research and coeditor of *Constellations: An International Journal of Critical and Democratic Theory.* In 2004 she holds the Spinoza Chair in Philosophy at the University of Amsterdam. Her books include *Redistribution or Recognition? A Political-philosophical Exchange* (2003), with Axel Honneth; *Justice Interruptus: Critical*

Reflections on the "Postsocialist" Condition (1997); *Feminist Contentions: A Philosophical Exchange* (1994), with Seyla Benhabib, Judith Butler, and Drucilla Cornell; and *Unruly Practices: Power, Discourse, and Gender in Contemporary Social Theory* (1989). Her current research is on postnational democratic justice.

Judith Friedlander was Dean of the Graduate Faculty of Political and Social Science and Eberstadt Professor of Anthropology at the New School for Social Research from 1993–2000. She is currently serving as Acting Dean of Arts and Sciences at Hunter College (City University of New York). Her work focuses on questions of ethnicity, nationalism, and identity politics in Mexico, France, and the U.S. Among her published works, she is author of *Vilna on the Seine: Jewish Intellectuals in France Since 1968.* At the present time she is writing a book about the New School for Social Research.

Jürgen Habermas is Professor Emeritus at the University of Frankfurt and Professor of Philosophy at Northwestern University. He has written extensively in the areas of critical theory, moral-philosophical theory, and the pragmatic theory of language. His recent works include *Between Facts and Norms; The Inclusion of the Other; On the Pragmatics of Communication; Wahrheit und Rechtfertigung;* and *The Future of Human Nature.*

Geoffrey Hartman is Sterling Professor of English and Comparative Literature (Emeritus) at Yale University; Project Director, Fortunoff Video Archive for Holocaust Testimonies; and Visiting Distinguished Professor of the Humanities at New School University. His recent publications include *The Longest Shadow: In the Aftermath of the Holocaust; A Critic's Journey: Literary Essays;* and *Scars of the Spirit: The Struggle Against Inauthenticity.*

Agnes Heller is Hannah Arendt Professor of Philosophy at the New School for Social Research in New York. She is the author of numerous books, among them *The Time Is Out of Joint: Shakespeare as Philosopher of History; A Theory of Modernity; An Ethics of Personality; Biopolitics;* and *A Philosophy of History in Fragments.*

Jerome Kohn is Trustee of the Hannah Arendt Bluecher Literary Trust and Director of the Hannah Arendt Center at New School University. He has written on a variety of aspects of Arendt's thought and edited many of her previously unpublished and uncollected writings. The most recent volume of those writings, *Responsibility and Judgment*, was published by Schocken Books in 2003.

Thomas McCarthy is Professor of Philosophy and John Shaffer Professor in the Humanities at Northwestern University. His publications include *The Critical Theory of Jürgen Habermas; Ideals and Illusions;* and *Critical Theory.* He is the editor of the MIT Press series *Studies in Contemporary German Social Thought.* His current research concerns the roles of race and development in modern and contemporary social and political theory.

Contributors

Richard Rorty has taught philosophy at Wellesley College, Princeton University, and the University of Virginia, and is now Professor of Comparative Literature at Stanford University. His books include *Consequences of Pragmatism; Contingency, Irony, and Solidarity; Achieving Our Country;* and *Philosophy and Social Hope.*

Charles Taylor is Professor Emeritus of Philosophy at McGill University and author of many books, including *Sources of the Self* and *The Ethics of Authenticity.*

Joel Whitebook is a philosopher and practicing psychoanalyst in New York City, and Assistant Professor of Psychology at Columbia University College of Physicians and Surgeons. He is the author of *Perversion and Utopia: A Study in Psychoanalysis and Critical Theory* and *Fighting Freud: Michel Foucault's Struggle against Psychoanalysis* (forthcoming). His research interests include the theory of the subject, the limits of the linguistic turn, and the "hermeneutics of suspicion."

Shoshana Yovel is a novelist. She is the author of *Simply Amos* (Hebrew).

Yirmiyahu Yovel is Hans Jonas Professor of Philosophy at the New School for Social Research. His books include *Dark Riddle: Hegel, Nietzsche, and the Jews; Commentary to Hegel's Preface to the Phenomenology of Spirit* (in Hebrew); *Spinoza and Other Heretics; Kant and the Philosophy of History;* and *Kant and the Renewal of Metaphysics* (in Hebrew).

Index